Java Deployment

Mauro Marinilli

201 West 103rd St., Indianapolis, Indiana, 46290 USA

International Standard Book Number: 0-672-32182-3

Library of Congress Catalog Card Number: 2001089629

Printed in the United States of America

First Printing: September 2001

04   03   02   01   4   3   2   1

Trademarks

Warning and Disclaimer

ASSOCIATE PUBLISHER
Michael Stephens

ACQUISITIONS EDITOR
Carol Ackerman

DEVELOPMENT EDITOR
Bryan Morgan

MANAGING EDITOR
Matt Purcell

PROJECT EDITOR
George E. Nedeff

COPY EDITOR
Nancy E. Sixsmith

INDEXER
Kelly Castell
Erika Millen

PROOFREADER
Melissa Lynch

TECHNICAL EDITOR
Bryan Morgan

TEAM COORDINATOR
Lynne Williams

MEDIA DEVELOPER
Dan Scherf

INTERIOR DESIGNER
Anne Jones

COVER DESIGNER
Aren Howell

PAGE LAYOUT
Michelle Mitchell

Overview

Table of Contents

About the Author

Mauro Marinilli got his first computer (a pioneering Commodore VIC20) when he was 12. He began publishing computer technical articles for an Italian specialized magazine some years later, where he remained a popular columnist until the 8-bit, listings-driven era was finished. In 1999, some months before graduating as a Computer Engineer from the University of Rome's "La Sapienza," he started to work full-time as a Java developer. During that period, he presented at many conferences worldwide (the last so far was at Trento AH 2000, with Mona Laroussi). After several projects, both in the industry and for research, he joined a mid-sized Italian software firm, Datamat, as the chief Java developer responsible for the GUI team developing the new meteorological software system used by the Italian Air Force. At the beginning of 2001, he transformed his long-standing hobby into full-time work as a freelance author specializing in Java programming.

He collaborates with the University of Rome 3 and other research organizations. His research interests are Intelligent Information Filtering, Information Retrieval, Human-Computer Interaction, and Adaptive Hypermedia, with papers published on conference proceedings and specialized reviews. He is the author of several Java articles at Gamelan.com and contributes to several open-source projects.

Marinilli grew up and currently lives by the sea (he couldn't live anywhere else), where he enjoys all seaside sports, sailing, scuba-diving, canoeing, and simply beach jogging; and when away from a desktop, he enjoys the warmth of his friends.

Dedication

To my parents, in spite of all, for bringing me into this world.

Acknowledgments

I want to thank the many people who have contributed to this book, and especially all the professionals at Sams Publishing who taught me the many details of writing a technical book. I'd like to thank Michael Stephens, the Associate Publisher, for his courage in embracing this project in a quite adventurous way. Without his insight, this book wouldn't exist.

Thanks to Carol Ackerman, the Acquisition Editor, who constantly and discreetly prodded and helped me to keep on-track. Development Editor Bryan Morgan, who was almost a co-author, refined my raw (very raw) manuscripts first. Thanks also to Project Editor George Nedeff and Copy Editors Nancy Sixsmith, Cynthia Fields, and Vipul Minocha. Last, but not least, thanks to formatter Katie Robinson. This book was written in an unusually short period of time, and it would not have been possible without the commitment of those I mention here and others I am not even aware of.

I am also grateful to the many friends that supported me in this delicate moment. Vilfrido, Willy, and Jose, for encouragement and those memorable dinners. Enrico, a companion of many adventures and a precious true friend, for his invaluable presence. Francesco, and my ex-colleagues and friends at Datamat (Emilio, Sandro, Mario, Roberto, Andrea, Stefano, and Antonio, among others) for their warm support during these months; and many others who would take too long to mention, even those who took other paths in their lives. Thanks to my sister Claudia and my parents for their patience with me and my legendary untidiness.

Finally, heartfelt thanks to all the people who contributed to this technology, perhaps with the genuine intent of helping to improve other people's lives: From the engineers at Sun to developers in the newsgroups, open-source community volunteers, and the many other individuals that indirectly contributed to this book.

Tell Us What You Think!

As the reader of this book, *you* are our most important critic and commentator. We value your opinion and want to know what we're doing right, what we could do better, what areas you'd like to see us publish in, and any other words of wisdom you're willing to pass our way.

As an Associate Publisher for Sams Publishing, I welcome your comments. You can fax, e-mail, or write me directly to let me know what you did or didn't like about this book—as well as what we can do to make our books stronger.

Please note that I cannot help you with technical problems related to the topic of this book, and that due to the high volume of mail I receive, I might not be able to reply to every message.

When you write, please be sure to include this book's title and author as well as your name and phone or fax number. I will carefully review your comments and share them with the author and editors who worked on the book.

Fax: 317-581-4770

E-mail: feedback@samspublishing.com

Mail: Michael Stephens
              Associate Publisher
              Sams Publishing
              201 West 103rd Street
              Indianapolis, IN 46290 USA

Introduction

I was a teenager when I published my first article about the programming techniques used in a videogame I wrote. "Killer Satellites" was an extravaganza of squared, flashy monochromatic sprites for the MSX home computer, as they called those little 8-bit toys running at 3.57MHz with 64KB RAM. Unbelievably, it was a success, and I was called in to supply anything I could imagine, in any language, provided that it was reproducible in a printed listing. Now I am here to write the introduction of my first book. I don't know if this time it will turn out in another unexpected result. You, the reader, will say.

This book is intended to provide a complete picture of the deployment options currently available for the Java platform (including Java 1.x), counting theoretical, design-oriented advice and practical source code. It is a vast and complex subject because of the variety of different situations involved, the different options available to the developer, and the intrinsic complexity of the deployment issue itself.

Whenever possible, examples were chosen in order to cover popular needs among developers and to propose a solution to less-common, complex strategic engineering issues. The trade-off between these two facets was one of the most critical aspects in planning this book.

This book is arranged so that readers can read it selectively, depending on their needs. The following section illustrates the organization of the book's content.

Structure of This Book

This book is divided into four parts. The first part introduces software deployment for Java, both theoretically (Chapters 1 and 2) and practically (Chapter 3).

Part II describes the deployment issue for the Java platform, beginning with a discussion of the software design involved (Chapter 4). The remaining chapters discuss deployment for different situations. Wireless and other J2ME-compliant devices are covered in Chapter 5, together with a brief mention of J2EE deployment. Chapters 6 and 7 discuss some practical solutions to the deployment of legacy Java code and the difficult task of building customized deployment solutions, respectively.

Part III covers the JNLP technology; it can be read with no prior knowledge of the preceding parts. Readers that want to learn more about this technology could begin reading this book directly from Part III.

Part IV, the Appendixes, covers a variety of material. Appendix A provides an alternative guide to the material contained in this book. Among other things there is a useful catalog of all the code examples and a little UML documentation guide provided for reference. Appendices B and D cover JNLP technology, illustrating a summary of the JNLP 1.0 specification and a general JNLP utility library, respectively. Appendix C mentions some deployment technologies not covered in the book.

I developed the code in this book using J2SE JDK 1.3.1 on a Windows 98 machine powered by a Pentium II. I used a variety of development environments and tools, depending on circumstances. Among the others, I employed JBuilder 4 Foundation and NetBeans as IDEs when not using Sun's JDK directly, Tomcat 3.2.1 as Servlet container and Apache 1.3.17 as Web server. I used a variety of development kits as well. For JavaCard development, I employed the JavaCard Kit 1.2.1 from Sun, J2ME Wireless Toolkit 1.0.1 from Sun, and the iDen developer suite from Motorola for MIDLet support and so on.

Some of the code instructions in this book's listings are highlighted in bold only for emphasis. Sources are available for download from www.samspublishing.com. When you reach that page, click the "Product Support" link and enter this book's ISBN code (0672321823) to access the page containing the code. Some useful resources are also available at my personal Web site, www.marinilii.com, following the link "Books".

The following is an overview of what is covered in each chapter.

Part I: Introduction

Chapter 1: "Deploying Java"

This chapter introduces the software deployment issue.

Chapter 2: "An Abstract Model for Deployment"

In this chapter, a general, abstract reference model is proposed. This model will be the basis for the whole book.

Chapter 3: "Existing Solutions"

Chapter 3 reports some real-world solutions to the deployment problem for Java software. The solutions discussed in this chapter are representative of what is available concretely to developers.

Part II: Deployment Engineering

Chapter 4: "Designing for Deployment"

This chapter focuses on the software design and the overall development organization for an effective software deployment.

Chapter 5: "Deployment Options for Non-J2SE Clients"

Chapter 5 discusses the deployment options available on the J2EE and J2ME platforms with practical examples.

Chapter 6: "Deploying Existing Software"

In Chapter 6, the issue of rethinking the deployment strategy of already written Java code is debated providing practical solutions.

Chapter 7: "Building Your Own Deployment Solution"

This chapter discusses the problems faced by developers who need to design and build a new, ad-hoc deployment solution. Several common examples are added, included a complete deployment solution suitable for advanced intranet deployment.

Part III: JNLP

Chapter 8: "A JNLP Quick Launch"

In Chapter 8, the JNLP technology is introduced by concrete, reusable examples.

Chapter 9: "The JNLP Protocol"

This chapter presents JNLP from a top-down, conceptual viewpoint. The basic JNLP concepts and its file structure are discussed as well.

Chapter 10: "Defining the Client Environment"

Chapter 10 digs into the details of the JNLP specification, providing practical examples.

Chapter 11: "Runtime Client Services"

This chapter discusses the runtime services provided by a JNLP Client to deployed applications. Several utility classes are provided.

Chapter 12: "Server-Side Deployment Support"

This chapter discusses the server-side support for JNLP, including the discussion of a servlet-based implementation of a JNLP server.

Chapter 13: "A Complete Example"

Chapter 13 presents a complete example of a non-trivial application deployed with JNLP and provides some general advice on using such technology for applications deployment.

Part IV: Appendixes

Appendix A: "A Little Handbook for Java Deployment"

Appendix A summarizes some design advice contained in Chapter 4, provides a full catalog of all the examples presented in this book, and discusses other important details regarding software deployment for Java.

Appendix B: "The JNLP Specification"

This appendix reports the JNLP specification as of version 1.0 of the Sun's Java Specification Request (JSR).

Appendix C: "Other Deployment Technologies"

Appendix C presents examples of other deployment technologies.

Appendix D: "A JNLP Utility Library"

Appendix D discusses the implementation of an utility library for JNLP-deployed applications used in some of the examples of Part III.

Introduction

IN THIS PART

Deploying Java

IN THIS CHAPTER

This introductory chapter presents the deployment of Java software with a discussion of the current pervasive state of this computing technology. At the end, some general concepts are introduced that will form the base of the remaining book.

The Java Runtime Environment

What is software deployment all about, and how does it apply to Java?

Generally speaking, the software deployment process is a sequence of steps as detailed in Figure 1.1. This is a deceptive diagram because, as we will see, things are not so simple.

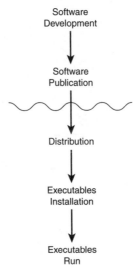

FIGURE 1.1

The software deployment lifecycle.

It could help to think of our latest favorite application that we downloaded from some Web site and installed on our computer. Someone developed and then published it for use.

However, the scenario could be slightly different; we could have downloaded the latest videogame to a handheld device using another form of the Internet (for example wireless protocols rather than HTTP). The installation in that case could have taken place automatically, given the simplicity of our client device.

With the main subject of this book, the Java platform, suddenly the two previous cases get blurred into one, because both previous cases could have been implemented in Java. Figure 1.2 illustrates this.

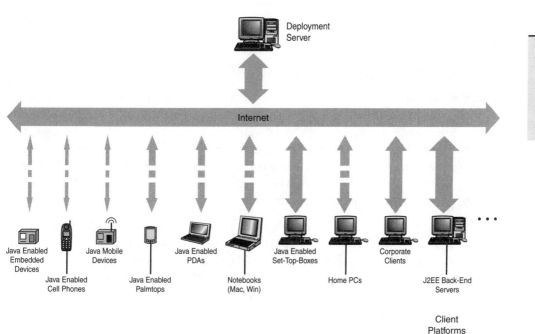

FIGURE 1.2

The Java Internet-enabled deployment scenario.

Figure 1.2 depicts many of the platforms Java can run on, together with the typical connection bandwidths (a dotted arrow indicates there is not a permanent connection to a network).

Inexpensive computational power in the form of consumer devices pervading our daily lives, together with the Internet revolution, promise an unprecedented development both within the computer industry and in our society. We do not know how the world will look on the other side of this change, but we can say that Java will play an important role. Likewise, techniques aimed at distributing and maintaining Java code will also play an important role.

When it comes to deploying Java code, we must consider not only the executables and their related resources, but also a unique-to-Java piece, the Virtual Machine, in its different flavors and its runtime support (core libraries, support utilities like the RMI registry, and so forth). Because the Virtual Machine is required to run the Java code, this is like saying that if you want to listen to the music contained in some disks, you must buy and bring home the special disk player as well. Therefore, deploying Java software, at least presently, is more complicated than deploying native executables. This is because the client platforms so far do not come with pre-installed, up-to-date Java Runtime Environments (JREs). The JRE to be installed depends on the specific platform, as do the size and the communication mechanism, and many other parameters. This completely changes the situation, and makes the deployment of Java software different from all other software.

The Desktop Front

Depending on your perspective, the battle for allowing Java on the PC desktop can be thought of as a WWII scene where allies try to conquer a position by bravely parachuting light infantry. From another vantage point, the Windows OS can be viewed as the last paradise to be guarded against clumsy Java weapons and fanatic marketers. Indeed, Sun has tried hard to gain some ground on the desktop. Technological attempts included first Java applets, and then the Plug-in, followed by JIT technology or Hotspot. The latest attempt, the Java Native Launching Protocol (JNLP), will be the subject of Part III of this book.

Java executables on the desktop (such as PCs, Macs, and Linux machines) suffer from a serious deficiency. In order to be run, they need to download an installation of a bulky piece of software that weighs in at around 5 megabytes. Of course, there are alternative solutions, like taking advantage of your Web browser's JVM or using JREs pre-installed on some OSes, but these usually turn out to be closer to compromises than proper solutions. This is a severe hurdle. Even worse, the size of the J2SE JRE has been constantly increasing (see Figure 1.3). Fortunately, J2SE size seems to be stabilizing.

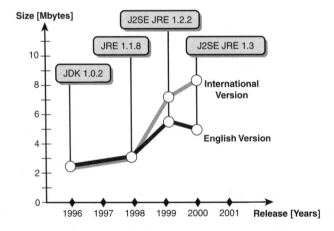

FIGURE **1.3**

The size of the JRE for desktop platforms has been constantly increasing.

NOTE

In Figure 1.3, the size (y-axis) refers to the download dimension of the JRE installation package, and the 1996-figure (JDK 1.0.2) refers to a development kit, which includes a compiler and other tools. The x axis lists the release year for each version. This data refers to Win32 versions.

More importantly, the Internet connections are improving relentlessly, so that paradoxically, it is now quicker to download the 5MB bundle for the J2SE JRE for Windows than it was to download the smaller JDK 1.0.2 package in 1997. As we will see, this plays an important role in favoring new software deployment techniques.

If Java wants a bigger role on the desktop scene, it needs to land soundly, that is, to gain the capability to run full-fledged applications with the latest JREs, on that ground. This can be compared to the ancient epic story of the Troy siege, where Greeks resort to a gigantic wooden horse to fool Trojans and penetrate the city. Probably Sun engineers do not need to be as astute as Ulysses, but they won't progress very far if they don't find the correct solution. We will address a proposal in Part III, "JNLP."

Virgin Lands

Apart from the fiercely fought battle for Web-enabled desktops, there is much more promising and (apparently) easy ground to be won on handheld, wireless devices and other specialized hardware. These devices are addressed by the J2ME edition, the Java Card, and the Java Embedded Server technologies. Also, Jini Technology will play an important role in this market.

NOTE

Embedded devices are all devices based on simple microprocessor architectures—simple because they are designed to run only very specialized programs, unlike PCs, where hardware is designed to run different kinds of programs. For example, a coffee machine cannot run a spreadsheet program because its hardware is specialized for certain operations only. The same is true for a PDA (Personal Digital Assistant) or a cell phone. Because of their focused nature, embedded devices can vary greatly from one another. Differences are captured in the APIs that each device supports. Sun has defined special configurations and profiles to address this problem. When two devices are said to belong to the same configuration they share a common, minimum set of APIs. Differences are described using profiles. An example of a profile is the J2ME Mobile Information Device profile, or MIDP.

Given the nature of client machines in this market, deploying Java code could become rather easy or quite difficult. It could be easily compared to desktop applications because executables for the consumer and embedded markets are generally much smaller and simpler. Nevertheless, deploying such Java programs could be difficult if cross-device software editions are enforced. An example of a difficult deployment is a word processor that is available on Java-enabled cell phones, high-end digital assistants , and other Java platforms. This example requires a careful software design and smart deployment techniques. The risk is to write many different versions of the same application, each one specialized for a given device, which diminishes the advantage of the Java language. The bytecode format with which they are written is the only thing these versions would have in common.

The Server Side

The deployment of J2EE software is quite easy when compared to deploying today's J2SE or J2ME applications. The reason stems from the high-level nature of the Enterprise Edition specification. J2EE programs run in a well-defined, standard environment and this helps the deployment procedures. Ironically, these kinds of applications require less sophisticated deployment techniques. J2EE programs are less mobile than other Java edition programs. Furthermore, they typically reside on a limited number of servers, managed by expert employees who are often developers themselves.

Deployment: A Neglected Topic

Java has been designed for the Internet age; however, deploying Java executables is not so easy. In fact, it is becoming even harder because Java is expanding into new environments such as cell phones, smart cards, and car dashboards. The deployment issue has historically been a neglected one. In the past, a floppy disk sufficed. Then, as the hardware grew, so did the software, and a couple of floppies (followed by a CD-ROM) would have done the trick. Now we are in the Internet age, and an average connection can support much more than a stack of CDs. Simply because it is interactive, it can enable more sophisticated deployment features which were not even thinkable before the Internet advent. In addition, consider the fact that we are still in the infancy of this phenomenon.

All this power is still poorly used as well as poorly understood. The Internet is a relatively new media. We constantly hear about all its wonders, but its real potential is still far from being fully grasped by us.

Historically, deployment has been partly regarded as a usability problem, related to Graphical User Interfaces (GUIs). GUIs came into play with special installation software intended for the average customer.

With these graphical installation programs came the complexity, both perceived and real. The very idea of an additional "helper" application that supports our application software on the client machine sounds dangerously complex. In some ways, it is, especially when you consider the extra code that must be written just to handle the deployment issue. Also, these applications force us to address distributed software issues in the whole life cycle of our application, from the very first design.

The problem is that all this complexity is rarely ever really needed. Cool deployment technology has always been perceived as an extra, with a very low priority level. There was the user, after all, who could always stand some additional dialogs for choosing proxy settings, current OS builds, version numbers, and the like. As we will see, this perspective has radically changed with the advent of the Internet.

Another kind of cost is related to what we described earlier. Placing a form of application helper on all the client platforms, even the more diverse, could be expensive. Given the platform-neutral nature of Java this becomes even more difficult, if not impossible. As we will see, the concept of an application helper will be an important part of our deployment abstract model, detailed in Chapter 2, "An Abstract Model For Deployment."

Some Benefits of Deployment

Deployment techniques were intended to support the installation of software, in a once-and-for-all fashion. Now things are changing, because devices are increasingly connecting to each other, and deployment is becoming a kind of established service, where software is released more often, maintained, customized, and even billed over the network. We will see how deployment can be used as a marketing instrument, or as a means to lower development costs, or again to add value and services to the software being deployed.

Old Solutions

This section introduces some topics that will be fully expanded upon in Chapter 3. Here the aim is to offer an intuitive introduction to concepts that will be described later using the abstract model in Chapter 2.

How has the problem of deploying Java software been attacked so far? We will introduce some simple scenarios that will be detailed in the following chapters.

Good Old Applets

In the early days of Java, applets were all the rage. An incredible amount of literature was written about them, and developers were told about the incredibly easy Java development for the browser platform. To determine whether they were successful, select ten popular Web sites of your choice, and see whether they have an applet on their index page. Probably not.

What's gone wrong with applets? Many things. The applet model is not all bad and, in some situations, it is quite useful. The problems arose when developers and Web designers asked too much from applets, and, conversely, browser implementers didn't answer their queries (or at least they didn't answer very quickly).

Here are some of the weak links in the implementation of the Java Applet construct:

- The Applet lifecycle model is too simple. It is good for a "Hello World" exercise, but quite impractical for more complex tasks.

- Applets arrived in the middle of the "browser war", between Microsoft's Internet Explorer and Netscape Navigator and they suffered for this. Slightly different implementations, difficulties in expanding to newer JREs/libraries, and so on prevented applets from seeing widespread success.

- Loading an elaborate Web page could be boring at times, but loading an applet larger than one hundred KB could prove to be even more tiring. Even worse, some libraries like `javax.swing` must be bundled together with the code to be deployed, which forces the amount of bytes to be downloaded to be even larger.

- The sandbox security model is often too limiting for developers, and implementing the signing for different browsers could become a complete nightmare.

- On the user interface side, the ugly warning signal that appeared in any applet window made applets the very last choice for Web designers. Overall, the current applet implementation within the two main browsers tends to provide the user with an unpleasant experience. Those gray boxes left on the Web page for ages, the lengthy pauses browsers stumble into while launching them, and so on are all hallmarks of the poor applet user interface.

However, the idea of applets is still very valuable and useful. Applets have zero installation and successive update costs. Their installation is completely automated within the browser. In Part III, "JNLP" we will see the Java Network Launching Protocol at work, and how Sun, other companies, and committed individuals worked to solve the shortcomings associated with Java applets.

Sun's Plug-In

As mentioned, one problem with applets is the forced limitation of using only the browser's own JVM. Both Microsoft and Netscape browsers currently support 1.1.x versions of the Java platform, so this limitation is quite serious. This and other problems are solved through the use of Sun's Java Plug-in software. The <OBJECT> tag that replaces the <applet> one in Web pages enables browsers to launch the plug-in utility with the given applet as an argument, bypassing the browser's internal JVM.

The Java Plug-In is intended for intranet users because of the size of the software itself that ships with a JVM (Java 2 Standard Edition, the latest version) included. Indeed, the Plug-in is included in Sun's J2SE JRE for Windows and is optional in J2SE SDK distributions for Windows. Although the Java Plug-in solves most incompatibility problems between the two main browsers, other issues still remain. The two major browsers have different extension architectures, and therefore the Plug-in download experience for the enduser is different depending on the browser used.

Apart from these minor deficiencies, the Plug-In enables applets to take advantage of all J2SE features such as code signing applets and native methods but it does not solve the problem of organizing different JREs on the same client platform. In fact, another limitation is the inability of different versions of the JRE contained in the Plug-in to coexist on the same computer at the same time.

The Sun Plug-in deserves a closer look because it represents a typical scenario in Java deployment techniques. Figure 1.4 shows in detail what happens with an illustration of the download and execution of an object from a Web browser given the related application/MIME type. It is a sequence diagram with some extra details. Optional steps are depicted with dashed arrows (the download and installation of the Plug-In) while the processes involved with the applet execution on the client side are shown.

The Plug-In solution is typical for Java deployment because it makes use of an application-helper (that is, a piece of software that helps the application to be launched). This helper takes charge of installing and managing a JRE on its own. Given the problem with the deployment of Java executables (the lacking of an up-to-date, standard and shared JRE already installed on the client platform) this is currently the only way to go. The user must first install an application helper that will then manage the download and execution of Java code locally.

Seen in this light, the release of the JNLP protocol should come as no surprise. It is the natural evolution of the Plug-in initiative, and before that, as the extension of the applet idea by means of a local application helper.

Installer Software

If asked how software was distributed before the Net, your reply would probably describe the typical installer utility as a piece of code that handled all the installation while running on your machine. In other words, a substitute for a human operator specialized in the installation of software on client machines.

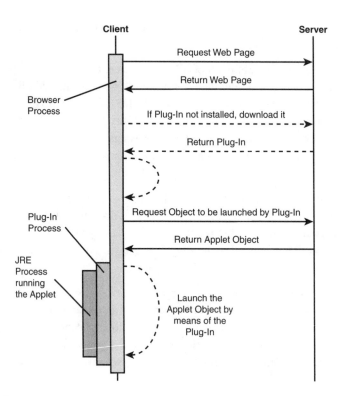

FIGURE 1.4

Sequence of actions when launching an applet from the Sun Plug-In.

Installer software can connect to the Net to complete the installation or it can include all the data needed within the same executable file as itself. In the second case there is a waste of downloaded resources, because users often prefer to install only the "typically" needed pieces, instead of cumbersome extensions.

Regarding the size of the entire installer plus the data to be installed, the Java situation becomes worse than other platforms. Typically, developers tend to create multi-platform installers, so they are, in effect, forcing endusers to download chunks of data they don't need. In fact, although the executable to be deployed is written in Java with little platform-dependent code, the process of installing software is inherently platform-specific.

Another potential danger that Java software deployed by means of installer utilities is exposed to is how to handle the JRE issue. A conservative policy would be to install the executable first, and then check whether a suitable JRE is already installed on the client platform. Then, either download it from the Web or simply launch the newly installed software. Another approach could be to blindly bundle the JRE together with the installer utility and the executable to be installed first, thus requiring endusers to download from 5 to 8 MB of potentially useless data on their computers (see Figure 1.3). As we will see in Part III, solutions like the JNLP protocol can be used to simplify installer utilities as well.

A problem with installer software is that the resolution phase is performed after the installer download locally on the client machine. As we will see, the resolution phase is when the client or the server, or both —depending on the particular software design— has realized what resources need to be installed on that machine. Knowing this before the download can save bandwidth, but places the burden of the resolution phase on possibly over-busy servers. Furthermore, some installers comprise management data useful only to the installer utility itself that eats up bandwidth. Examples of this are messages for a dozen or so supported languages. Bandwidth problems aren't to be overlooked by optimistic scenarios, because bottlenecks arise from contingent causes as well. When installing software at the office, for example, the particular hour of the day can hinder the swift download of the required software, if not block it completely.

Another observation on installer utilities is that they don't cover the stages in the application lifecycle such as the update. These stages are left to other helper utilities or to the whim of the developer.

When examining the impact this kind of deployment software has on organizations, it is important to note that installer utilities per se don't completely exclude the role of the deployment system administrator. This is in contrast to the applet case and partially the Plug-in solution (in this case, the Plug-in installation could be performed by specialized workforce as well).

Application Management Tools

We have discussed all the main deployment techniques available for Java developers. Now it is time for something quite unpopular to the Java platform. Traditionally, deployment was a service that was part of the system administrator's responsibility. It is now natural to see software application management solutions providing deployment services and vice versa.

Multiplatform application management solutions implemented in Java are something we will not see in the near future for several reasons. Java is such a general platform that it has not yet developed some centralized administration facilities, at least restricted to some platform editions. On the other hand, it is worth mentioning them to better grasp the weak points of Java in this area. First, given the very nature of the Java platform, it is difficult to reach the nuts and bolts of operating systems to the level of detail needed by application management solutions. Because Java is a somewhat anarchic platform on the client side, lacking of centralized support for basic services such as a persistent registry or standard equivalents, administrative features such as the remote management of client installations is quite difficult to achieve. Appendix C, "Other Deployment Technologies" provides material on this class of management tools.

A Perspective Change

This section discusses the additional evolution of today's deployment techniques. These topics are neither science fiction nor ready-to-use advice, but nevertheless are concepts worth reviewing.

Sun proposed the Sun One initiative at the beginning of 2001 as a counter-offensive to the competitor .NET platform from Microsoft. Of course, deployment of Java software can be seen as a Web service itself, and we will see in Chapter 2 how an abstract model can assist in this aspect. Of course, the net-centric perspective of the Java platform could be easily exploited when deploying software to remote clients. Only time will tell how deployment will fit into this new perspective, but the growing support for the JNLP protocol is promising.

Abstracting the Software Experience

The entire deployment issue has enormous potential to shift the current idea of software to a new level.

An effective deployment can improve overall software quality. In scenarios where executables are downloaded, installed, and managed seamlessly from the Net without requiring the average user to ever be aware of the physical files currently involved, the perceived feeling of the software experience itself changes.

When continuous upgrades are possible and painless (thanks to wider distribution channels and more effective deployment technologies) the software itself is seen as more of an abstract service rather than a bundle of files currently running on your local device. This process of abstraction is common across all the technologies as they evolve over time. This trend will affect software as well. Consumer applications will possibly become more abstract and more dynamic, with logos, splash screens, and GUIs naturally evolving over time, much like the wrapper of our favorite snack. The brand- and the user-perceived experience will become more important. This, among other things, will increase the advantage of first-comers into new and old markets. When software could be easily updateable, the difference will be the brand, or other factors. This is something that will have a large impact on marketing, other than the way software will be designed and produced. Today's software marketers try to lure users in rather rough ways such as bothering them with pop-up dialogs with big "Register Now" buttons, whereas very few realize the power that deployment techniques can have on the diffusion of their software.

A General Definition of Software Deployment

The lifecycle proposed in Figure 1.1 is not realistic when it comes to the details of today's software deployment technology. We will now introduce a useful abstraction, general to all kinds of software deployment that comprise Figure 1.1. We will get into the practical details in the next few chapters. Here we focus on a general, wide perspective about software deployment.

In Figure 1.5 is a representation of the *Deployment Circuit*. It is the starting point of our journey into the software deployment world.

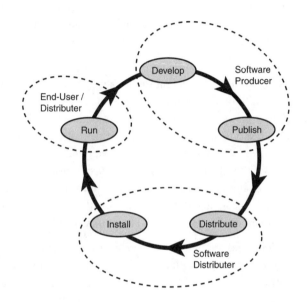

FIGURE 1.5
The deployment circuit.

NOTE

Modeling the deployment cycle is a complex issue, beyond the scope of this book. The model proposed herein has been designed to be the more general but useful model for real-world Java developers. More extensive, detailed, and theoretically comprehensive models for those who are interested can be found in the up-to-date material available at my personal Web site.

In Figure 1.5, the journey of a set of resources bundled together as a software executable is defined in the following five stages:

- **Development**—The software developer develops the software, planning its deployment since the beginning.

- **Publication**—The software developer releases the software.

- **Distribution**—The distributor organization releases the software to endusers.
- **Installation**—All the needed pieces are properly placed on the client platform, left ready to be launched by endusers.
- **Running**—Finally, the installed software is launched on the client platform.

The word *circuit* is not chosen casually. The concept of a deployment circuit is similar to the steps of delivering a milk bottle to a house. After the production and the packaging, bottles are transported to consumer homes, happily emptied by customers, and left outside the door to find their way back to the factory. A whole organization with its costs and benefits is behind this service.

Another implicit concept is the *cycle-ness* inherent to the fact that updates will follow installations and so on, just as empty milk bottles are followed by filled ones. Therefore, a Deployment Circuit must be set up by means of Web servers and such, and maintained. The period of these cycles has been shortened with the advent of new distribution channels, in other words, the Net in all its forms, and the evolution of the software industry, is heading toward integrated, up-to-date services rather than standalone, once-for-all installed applications. In addition, competition presses to shorten these cycles. If software vendors can rely on more effective deployment circuits, they can afford more releases with shorter time-to-market, and so on. We will discuss the potential benefits of deployment circuits shortly.

The *interactivity* between clients and distribution servers is also required, in its roughest form, in milk deliveries too. For example, when the family components vary in number there's the need to adjust the number of delivered bottles. With software, appliances are much more critical, because we must know exactly what is already installed on client machines, together with other data like the identity of each enduser, the hardware platform they are using, and so on.

Previous definitions and approaches to the software deployment issue in literature were less aware of the real overall processes taking place in the software industry with the advent of the Internet, in all its forms. As a result, we saw cycle-ness, interactivity, and the establishment and maintenance of the whole circuit related to the software deployment as a sophisticated service, offered by a *distributor* entity to both a software *producer* and an *enduser*.

Deployment Circuit Issues

Let's examine in detail what this approach entails.

Related Costs

A deployment circuit has a series of costs associated with it. These costs are as follows:

- **The cost of setting up the circuit**. Buying distribution servers, connecting them to the Net, or hiring skilled personnel to take care of installing the software on your organization's computers are major costs. Likewise, buying the needed wireless bandwidth for assuring the weekly update of the software running on your agents' handhelds across the country is another sunken cost.

- **The cost of running the circuit**. If you deploy your software by using mailed CDs, you must bear the costs of preparing, packaging, and sending these CDs. If you have specialized personnel in addition to system administrators, the costs include the hours they spend while paying a visit to all your employees, plus the time the latter remain idle while the installer staff is performing the physical installation and finetuning the endusers' computers.

- **The cost of ensuring the reliability of the circuit**. This depends on the quality that is needed for the given circuit. If we were deploying software on space satellites, we cannot afford any errors.

- **The cost for software producers of outsourcing this service to external organizations**. This is nothing new in companies specialized in distributing software. For example, just think of the shareware phenomenon on the Web. Currently distributors limit their service at file downloads, often installers. Then they provide additional services such as billing, statistics, and the like. What is possible with the current technology, today, is much greater than this.

Main Benefits of Circuits

Circuits have many benefits, depending on the kind of actors involved.

For software producers, employing a deployment circuit is about gaining a powerful competitive advantage, exploiting the features of sophisticated deployment circuits while possibly outsourcing the complexities and possible risks to a third-party (the *Distributor*).

For endusers, the net effect is an enhanced service, given that the services (implemented by deployed software) are more ubiquitous, less implementation-dependent and much easier to manage, as well as possibly more reliable and personalized.

For distributors, it is possibly the rise of a new profession, something akin to a software broker.

Taking Advantage of the Circuit for Adding New Services

After the deployment circuit has been built, the next step is to add extra services that take advantage of the distribution channel or the application helper installed on the clients. These services could be more diverse, but we will focus on those closest to deployment.

The most common services are debugging, various types of management, the offering of a richer client environment, and customization. Advanced services include the need for particular clients such as enhanced reliability.

Integrating a standard form of debugging into the deployment circuit is almost straightforward, given the capabilities of the Java 2 platform with regard to remote debugging, for example. The step of adding new services to the deployed executables is also made easy by taking advantage of the application helper eventually installed on client platforms. A typical and useful advanced service offered by deployment circuits is the so-called management on-the-run. Take, for instance, a J2EE executable running 24×7 on a back-end server. The capability to update it while running is critical in this case. As we will see, deployment circuit vendors rarely offer these kinds of services.

Here again, a new era is beginning. In the future, we will assist in the creation of a whole new generation of such services, taking advantage of the Internet and of the ubiquity of computing devices, possibly running Java code, naturally.

A Formal Definition of Software Deployment

Finally, we are ready to propose a definition of software deployment closer to the new scenarios prompted by the Internet. We will see the practical consequences of these concepts in the next chapter.

A definition of *software deployment* is a technical facility consisting of the establishment and maintenance of a deployment circuit between a business service provider and a business service client.

In turn, the definition of a *deployment circuit* is a virtual connection supporting the Provider's business services by means of the delivery, assembly, and management of software resources and configurations on a client environment.

Connection policies are defined by the (software) business service provider. We refer to the distributor as the deployment circuit supplier.

In conclusion, our vision of software deployment is network-centric, service-minded, and focused on roles as well. These are all concepts not heavily highlighted before, but nevertheless very important. As we delve into more technical aspects, we will use the Java platform extensively and progressively. The next chapter will explore the details of an abstract deployment lifecycle model, and Part II and Part III will discuss the specifics of Java software deployment and, in particular, the JNLP protocol.

An Abstract Model For Deployment

IN THIS CHAPTER

In this chapter, we will define an abstract model for Java software deployment. We don't have the space for detailing everything, because the scene is quite vast. From handhelds to back-end servers, from smart cards to home PCs, never before has a single technology promised so much to software deployment, and, conversely, posed so many challenges. Are Java developers ready for such a challenge?

An Introduction to the Model

In the last chapter, we saw a general definition of software deployment from a network-aware, service-minded perspective. Now, it is time to bring Java into the scene, getting into the details of the software deployment lifecycle. Our approach will be desktop and application-oriented, but it will be useful for all other Java contexts as well.

The Application Helper

Another useful concept is the *Application Helper (AH)*, a program running locally on client platforms that support the download, physical installation, and subsequent runtime of the applications to be deployed. Java programmers are familiar with the idea of an *Application Container (AC)*, namely another process that takes care of our Java program by possibly providing extra services such as special APIs, system resources access, and so on.

> **CAUTION**
>
> The Application Helper concept is more general than that of the Application Container. For example, the Helper could merely launch the application and then terminate. An AC instead is responsible for providing services to the application while it is running. For example, the Sun Plug-In mechanism described in Chapter 1, "Deploying Java," could be thought of as an AH case. Conversely, the applet model and the JNLP launcher are cases of Application Containers.

We will focus an important part of our model around the AH. As we saw in Chapter 1, for reasons inherent in the nature of the Java technology, the AH-based solution is the most obvious one. On platforms in which Java code is not the native code (the overwhelming majority of devices on the market so far, even on Web-enabled desktops) an extra JVM is needed. Therefore, why don't we add more features to it, given the fact that they come relatively inexpensively (we saw in Figure 1.3 in Chapter 1 that the current download size of a JRE is at least around 5MB) compared to the possible advantages?

This approach will influence our deployment model, possibly losing some generality for concreteness and usefulness. Together with introducing the AH, we will see more details of our deployment model, especially those general to the whole model, and not limited to the AH role.

The Client Environment Concept

The AH could be thought as the interface between the Deployment Server and the *Client Environment*. As we will see in detail later, the Client Environment is the formal description of the current configuration of the client platform: hardware plus software and anything else needed, such as end-user identity and type of connection. We may think of it as an XML file, for example. We're not interested in its implementation, rather the abstract concept that could be found in all kinds of software deployments.

The Deployment Policies Concept

If the Client Environment defines the current client instance, on the server side we have a set of policies that define exactly who must install what. These policies, called *Deployment Policies*, are issued by the Software Owner, who from our point of view often corresponds to the Software Producer. The *Resolution Phase* is the act of deciding what to do, given what we have on the client platform (the Client Environment definition), what we are supposed to deliver (the resources to install), and what we are told to do (the Deployment Policies).

An Example

An example could be the following, expressing in pairs <attribute, value> for describing the Client Environment and in pseudo-code for the Deployment Policies:

```
Client Environment: <platform, Java-Enabled cell phone>, <type of user,
consumer> , <memory resources,512K Ram>, <license, evaluation>
```

Deployment Policies:

- Assertion 1.

  ```
  If (license=="evaluation") INSTALL "timebomb.jar"
  ```

- Assertion 2.

  ```
  If (platform==" Java-Enabled cell phone" and memory resources>256K)
  INSTALL ("core.jar", "sprites_1.1.jar","extensions_2.1.jar")
  ```

This will send four JAR files to the user's cell phone, that, once installed together, will run the wanted version of the video game chosen by the user (in this example, assertions are thought to be in an OR logical relationship).

Figure 2.1 illustrates the basic role of the AH, that of the interface between the client and the Deployment Server. Given this role, it is natural to think of the AH as being charged with the Resolution Phase. This is not always the case. Indeed, often the Resolution Phase is shared between the AH and the Deployment Server. Generally speaking, the amount of responsibility to give to the AH is a typical matter of client-server load balancing, as we will see in Chapter 4, "Designing for Deployment."

FIGURE 2.1
The Application Helper role.

What we will do now is to basically use the AH for defining a whole class of deployment circuits that will be the concrete base for our deployment lifecycle model.

The Model Basics

We will introduce our model incrementally. First of all, we will introduce the main stages that form the essential steps in all software deployments. In turn, we will detail each of these phases, reaching the complete picture.

In Figure 2.2, the deployment process is divided into six major steps. The subject that mainly executes is in charge of that phase is shown on the right side.

Deployment begins from software analysis (for example, to define the Deployment Policies) and design, as you will see in the second part of this book. After the software is developed and released, the next step is to publish it. The outcomes of the Publication stage are all the pieces (and the instructions on how to deploy them) ready for the Distribution Phase. The Distributor takes care of correctly dispensing the right pieces to the right clients in order to build a properly running application. In order to do so, it needs the pieces themselves (JAR and other files) properly described, as well as the required Deployment Policies (the instructions to who and how to dispense the application). In order to do so, the Distributor employs one or more Deployment Servers (DS), in which resources are stored ready to be requested by/pushed to end-users. Independently, the Deployment Server could be configured by the Distributor organization.

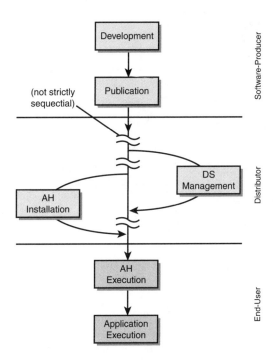

FIGURE 2.2
The basic deployment model.

2

AN ABSTRACT MODEL FOR DEPLOYMENT

NOTE

The Distributor's job is to assure the correct deployment of the application to the client platform. The role of the Distributor can be covered by an organization, a system administrator, or the same Software Producer.

Asynchronously, after the software has been published, End-Users can begin downloading it through the Distributor's channels. Because generally we need an AH installed on the client machine (despite the fact that AH isn't really necessary), we have to download and install it the first time. For simplicity, this is thought to be done by the Distributor. After the AH installation has finished, it is launched, managing the installation of the application and then, in turn, launching it. The AH will then take care of providing other deployment services to the application while the latter is running. Services provided by the AH to the launched application could be, for example, a just-in-time download of some needed resources, reporting logging activity back to the Deployment Server, and so on.

TIP

We are introducing an abstract model, so roles such as Distributor, Producer, and the various phases may sound a bit intangible at first. We will see concrete examples after the complete introduction of the model. Until that moment, you can think about the real-world production scenario that you are more experienced with. For example, in a medium-sized software house, the Producer and the Distributor could be two colleagues working on the same project. You could think of a common installer utility as an example of AH, a Web server that hosts some applet classes as a Deployment Server, and so on.

Before digging into the main phases, let's review them in the following section:

Phase	Description
Development	The software to be deployed is released with the related Deployment Policies for publication
Publication	At the end of this stage, the software is ready for end-user installation
Deployment Server Management	Maintenance and management operations on Deployment Servers
Application Helper Installation	The AH is installed for the first time on the client platform
Application Helper Execution	The AH is launched
Application Execution	Finally, the application is executed

Another important part of the model is the actors it defines. Let's intuitively recap the roles so far. The next section will cover all of them in greater detail:

Role	Description
Distributor	The organization, team, or single employee that is in charge of correctly distributing and installing the software
Producer	The organization or team that develops the software.
Software Owner	The organization that owns the rights for that software and decides, among other things, the Deployment Policies. For simplicity, is intended to be coincident with the Software Producer.
End-User	The single person that will use the software deployed on the client platform.

As in Figure 2.2, the Producer is in charge of the Publication Phase. This is not exact because this stage could be thought of as being split in two substages, in which the Software Producer is responsible for issuing to the Distributor the resources that compose the application to be deployed, together with the instructions on how to compose those pieces during the installation. Another item that the Software Producer releases to the Distributor is the set of policies the owner wants to put into effect for its software. The rest of the Publication Phase is the Distributor's job. The "real" publication is external, allowing resources to be available to the wanted End-Users. In this second publication subphase, only the resources to be assembled on client platforms are available to End-Users, whereas Deployment Policies and resource descriptions are not released publicly.

NOTE

The *Producer-To-Distributor Publication Phase* is a bit more than a usual software release. Together with the resources (JAR files, native libraries, and other material needed for the program correct installation), the Resource Descriptions and the Deployment Policies are released as well. This phase is directed to the Distributor only.

Finally, as published, a given release or a whole software application could be "unpublished" or removed from the Deployment Server. That doesn't mean the application cannot run on clients that have already installed it. It simply means that it will no longer be available for any kind of user for distribution and installation in the future.

Let's refine the AH Execution Phase as well. From the first time the AH is launched, AH has to analyze the client situation so that it (or the deployment server, or both) has decided what action must be taken. This will affect the application itself. Let's see how.

After the AH is launched, generally it can check out the current situation trying to connect back to the Deployment Server. Depending on the response, the AH may switch to one of the following stages:

- It attempts to download and install the wanted application.
- The application has already been installed, so the AH launches it (this is modeled in Figure 2.2).
- Some management is needed, such as updating a JAR that is part of the application, while this one is not running.
- It performs some management or configuration on itself.
- It exits. This case has not been reported on the diagrams because it has little information. However, it is nevertheless needed. Some AH can shut off the launched application as well. This is the case with Application Containers.

We have three new phases that replace the AH Execution one, as shown in Figure 2.3. This figure shows a more refined model as well. Also, in the following diagrams, the arrows back to the AC Check-Out Phase haven't been reported for clearness.

NOTE

We are using the word "application" as a synonym for "Java executable"; that is, a Java program that could be executed by a JVM on a given client platform. We are not limited to Java applications, but we include all sorts of programs—such as servlets, applets, and Java code running on embedded systems.

Another important piece that is still missing is what goes on in the Application Execution Phase. Whenever the AH has to launch the application, it must launch the JVM, passing it the proper parameters (classpath, other parameters, and so on). Even before that, the AH must ensure that the JRE has been correctly set up, required optional packages (formerly known as extensions) have been properly installed, and native libraries have also been correctly set up.

Generally speaking, the AH could be implemented in Java itself, so probably the JRE launch would happen before. However, this is a special case, regarding only the AH, not the application to be launched. So, after a *JRE Preparation Phase* (care of the AH), the application could be finally launched. During the application execution, some library could be needed (this mechanism is similar to the lazy class loading performed by the JVM: Items are loaded when needed, not before), so the AH takes care of downloading and installing them. We have a Resource Installation Phase that is very similar to the other installation phases.

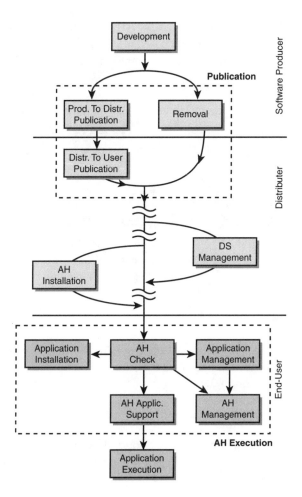

FIGURE 2.3

The lifecycle model in a greater level of detail.

NOTE

Before the advent of deployment solutions such as JNLP clients or commercial tools, developers had to write the code to perform such services from scratch. Downloading just-in-time resources from the Internet, for example, involves the writing of a custom class loader that would download classes and other resources remotely, as needed.

Other important services could be provided by the AH to applications during their execution. The *On-The-Run Management Phase* is composed of debugging, on-the-run updating, and other various services while the application is running, such as remote debugging. The AH Execution Phase is depicted in Figure 2.4.

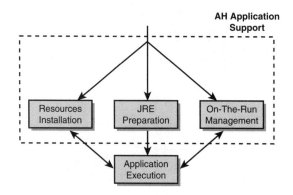

FIGURE 2.4
The AH Execution Phase in detail.

The overall picture is quite complete. After zooming into the major phases, we will illustrate the detailed model with some well-known cases.

NOTE

Note that the knowledge gained so far is enough to browse the rest of this book, eventually returning just below here for clarifying some details when needed.

The Complete Model

The AH Check-Out Phase is generally made up of two main stages: After a preliminary communication between the AH and the Deployment Server (whenever possible) and an eventual user authentication, the Resolution Phase will take place.

The AH-DS Connection Phase represents the optional connection establishment between the AH and the Deployment Server prior to the Resolution Phase.

The Resolution Phase consists of checking the outcome of decisions regarding the whole deployment lifecycle.

The Resolution Phase can be performed on the server or by the AH itself. It is not required to be carried out right after the AH connects back to the server. Nevertheless, for simplicity, we will report this phase right after the AH connection with its Deployment Server. Of course, the AH could even avoid connecting back to the server all the time, or it cannot, because the client platform is currently offline, and so on.

The very idea of a Resolution Phase is quite theoretical. We will see this phase in detail in the next section.

CAUTION

There is an important difference between the "Application Update" and "On-The-Run Application Update" phases, in that the first is a very basic stage provided by all the AHs, basically consisting of file replacement on the local client platform. In the second case, the AH must be able to replace pieces of the application while this one is running, without damaging its operation.

Finally, we are now ready to take a look at the complete deployment model, as shown in Figure 2.5.

Practicing with the Model

It's time to begin to use our model, beginning with some easy and familiar cases. Note that the phases we discussed can also be viewed as *features* a given deployment solution might provide. From this perspective, we can compare different deployment technologies based on the deployment features they provide.

A Well-Known First Example

Let's take a look at a well-known case: the typical installer utility, described through our deployment model. We discussed it before, but we need to be more precise, and can compare it with other deployment technologies. Figure 2.6 illustrates the model instance in this situation.

From Figure 2.6, we can grasp the difference between this deployment means and other more articulated deployment solutions. Note that, for example, the Resolution Phase is very limited, because the AH (the installer utility) can only install the application or run it before exiting.

Also interesting to see is the Distribution-To-User Publication Phase. Here, it consists of packaging the resources into the installer bundle according to the given client platform, and leaving the obtained executable available for downloads or other forms of delivery.

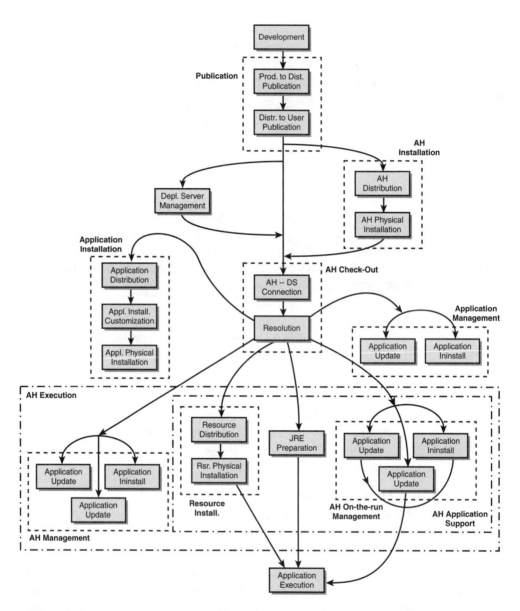

FIGURE 2.5

The full-blown deployment model.

2

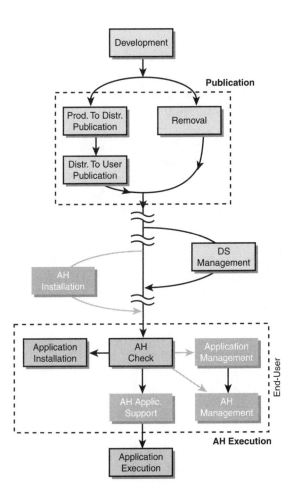

FIGURE 2.6

The installer utility scenario.

In this case, the AH Installation Phase doesn't occur, clearly, because the installer utility is executed only once. In some cases, though, installer utilities register some little programs to be
invoked in case of uninstallation. This case is quite rare in Java because of its platform-neutral
nature. (For the interested reader, however, we will discuss several platform-specific Java
installers in Chapter 3, "Existing Solutions").

> **NOTE**
>
> The installer utility finishes its job after the application is installed. Consequently, the AH Application Support Phase is void in this case because the application, once installed, is totally independent from the installer.

A final remark concerns the client system resources required during the AH Execution Phase (that is, while running itself and installing the application) that for large applications could be demanding. We will take another look at this very popular class of deployment means in Chapter 3, in which we will discuss a commercial product.

Another Example—The Sun Java Plug-In

As a matter of exercise, let's examine the Sun Java Plug-In in order to illustrate the model at work. The Sun Java Plug-In was described in some detail in Chapter 1. It will help us to further clarify the model with an already discussed case. The Plug-In is bundled with any Sun JRE package that can be downloaded, for example at `http://javaweb.eng/plugin/`.

The AH consists of the browser together with the Plug-In utility that launches the application. A normal Web server can work as a Deployment Server because the executables to be deployed are simple Java applets. The AH Installation Phase occurs whenever the browser and then the Sun Plug-In are installed.

Only simple Deployment Policies can be enforced by the Software Producer using this product. The applet model imposes a relaxed control over end-users attempting to download a given page containing that applet. Of course, having a dynamic Web server could allow for more sophisticated control. On the client side, the Application Installation Phase is performed by the Web browser, which saves the applet locally in the browser cache.

Regarding the AH Application Support Phase, it is interesting to note that the On-The-Run Management Phase is not void in this case. The Plug-In provides standard runtime services to the launched applet (that is, the standard applet container).

The following phases are empty in this case:

- *Application Management*   Because the application launched as an applet, the runtime control over it by the AH is very limited.
- *Resources Installation*   The Plug-In does not have the capability to download and install resources on the applet's behalf.

The AH Management Phase, though quite simple, is performed by the Plug-In control panel.

Recapping All the Stages

To summarize what has been said so far, each model step is detailed below. To complete this subsection, all the stages are described later in reference Table 2.1.

Distribution

Given the importance and frequency of this subphase, we will describe its function in some detail.

First of all, this phase depends on the kind of connection established between the client and the Distributor. If this connection is a standard network connection, even one as temporary as that of a home modem, the Distribution Phase will consist basically of a file transfer, using some given protocol. This is almost always the case, so it is safe to refer to this situation. Despite that, the model is abstract enough to handle other types of distribution means. The outcome of this stage doesn't depend on the particular type of connection; at the end of any Distribution step, we will have (mostly by the AH) the given item, freshly delivered from the Deployment Servers. Note that eventually caching mechanisms will be handled explicitly by the AH. Another important feature of this phase is the capability to conserve bandwidth by delivering only the needed items. See the Resources Installation During AH Application Support Phase that follows for details.

The AH Application Support Phase is composed of three steps.

1. Connects back to the Deployment Server, possibly performing some form of authentication, if needed. We can assume that the client will always begin the deployment, even when the AH operates as a background demon process, waking up as instructed by the Deployment Policies and starting a server communication. We will see the rare cases where this is not true when discussing the whole model.

2. Resolves the items to transfer, involving the Deployment Policies and the other inputs in the Resolution Phase described later.

3. The transfer of the requested items takes place.

Development

The Development Phase is an important part of the whole deployment lifecycle, and is the focus of the second part of this book. Its outputs are the software resources to be deployed and the Deployment Policies that define the deployment itself. Both resources and policies are represented in some meta-information format intelligible to the Distributor.

Publication

This stage is composed of the Removal step or, alternatively, the following two successive steps:

1. *Producer to Distributor Publication*   This is an internal publication, for Deployment Servers only. The Deployment Policies and annotated Resources (seen previously in this chapter) are released in this phase.

2. *Distributor to End-User Publication*   This step takes the Deployment Policies and Annotated Resources output of the preceding step as input (they are arranged in rigid sequence in the model). As an output, it produces the resources ready to be deployed by AHs wherever they are installed. Basically, the job of the Distributor in this initial phase is to "understand" the language spoken by the Producer, in order to enforce it with clients.

AH Installation

During this phase, the AH is installed itself. That is, it is registered permanently into the underlying platform environment as an executable. It is composed of two successive steps:

1. *AH Distribution*   The AH is distributed as another resource. For simplicity, the server from where the AH is downloaded is thought to be the Deployment Server for normal application resources.

2. *AH Physical Installation*   After having completely transferred onto the client platform, the AH itself must be installed. In order to do so, this phase is usually carried out by end-users, system administrators, or less-sophisticated installer facilities.

Deployment Server Management

Represents the management of the Deployment Servers made by the Distributor. This can include replication, load balancing, updating, redundancy configuration, and so on. Our model is focused on the client aspects of deployment, so we won't refine this step any further. Indeed, this is an important phase, but it is beyond the scope of this book.

AH Check-Out

This is conceptually an important phase in our model regarding the client side of the deployment process. The decisions taken by the AH are gathered in this phase. In the lifecycle proposed in Figure 2.5, all the phases reached by the AC Check-Out stage must be thought of as being linked with an arc back to this phase in a sort of never-ending execution loop, until the AH exits or it is shut down. Those arcs are not represented graphically for visual cleanness. The objective of this phase is to decide which action the AH has to perform on behalf of the client application and the given Deployment Policies.

This stage is composed of two successive steps:

1. *AH-DS Connection*   A connection with the Deployment Server is established by the AH or, less commonly, vice versa. When this connection cannot be carried out, the AH can decide what to do using other strategies. Basic policies could be hard-wired in the AH

2

code, and some property file could be used, among other things. It is important to point out that this phase could not take place in all cases, and the AH should be able to support off-line mode as well. Then, in some cases, the AH itself could be very thin so that a client-server connection could be established with very little client support. This case is quite common in limited computational environments, such as the downloading of a piece of code into a Java-enabled embedded device.

2. *Resolution*   This is a crucial conceptual phase in the model. It can be thought of as deciding what to do, given the current situation and the given instruction.

Application Installation

This phase is in charge of installing the application to be launched on the client platform for the first time. Usually, the AHs are platform-specific, so they know where to place things, whether to create shortcuts on the desktop if in Windows, or whether to create launching scripts. It is composed of three successive steps:

1. *Application Distribution*   Again, a distribution step; the application is delivered as another resource from the DS to the client platform.

2. Application Installation Customization.

3. Application Physical Installation.

JRE Preparation During AH Application Support

The AH initializes the correct JRE (version and edition are given by the Deployment Policies) with the proper related parameters (for instance, the maximum heap size, the classpath, or the application's parameters). The result of this step is the launch of the proper JRE configured for the Application Execution step.

Application Execution

The application is finally ready to be executed in the prepared JRE environment. When required, the AH could perform one of the two operations (Resource Installation and AH On-The-Run Management) in the AH Application Support Phase.

Resources Installation During AH Application Support

The application is running, and the AH is working to support it. It is composed of two successive steps:

1. *Resources Distribution*   It works like other distribution phases. After a preliminary connection back to the Deployment Server, the resources to be transmitted to the client are resolved. Then, the file transfer begins using the given protocol.

2. *Resources Physical Installation*   Once the resources are actually on the client platform, they are installed automatically by the AH.

This phase is not supported by AH that don't support the Application Container modality. One important parameter here is the so-called *Differencing Granularity Level*. This is the capability of the established deployment circuit to save bandwidth by skipping the distribution of already installed resources. The finer the granularity of the differencing mechanism, the higher the potential bandwidth savings.

> **NOTE**
>
> An example of a differencing mechanism is the JARDiff format used by the JNLP pro-tocol. When given two JAR files, one already downloaded and installed and the other one going to be downloaded, requests only the difference of the two files, with a granularity level of the single Java class. See the Part III, "JNLP," or Appendix B, "The JNLP Specification," for more details.

On-The-Run Application Management During AH Application Support

The On-The-Run Application Management During AH Application Support Phase describes the features of some advanced AHs during the application execution.

This stage is composed of three possible steps:

1. *Debugging*   Whenever an exception reaches the AH, it can perform some form of remote debugging with the Deployment Server (or other servers). It works with versions of the JRE that support remote debugging.

2. *On-The-Run Updating*   While the application is running, some parts of it can be replaced during this phase, possibly without causing the current execution to abort.

3. *Other On-The-Run Management*   Several of these kinds of services are possible. For example, a mechanism of remote logging or updating of some business data could be performed in this phase, taking advantage of the deployment infrastructure.

Application Management

The Application Management Phase comprises operations performed by the AH while administrating the installed applications. Note that the application to be managed is not running. The operations performed in this stage are basic operations offered by most AHs.

This stage is composed of two possible steps:

1. *Application Update*   An application update begins, which can involve some AH-local OS communication or some other special procedures. The installation or removal of related resources is thought to be performed during the Resource Installation Phase. After all necessary resources are managed, some extra operations are possible to conclude the update and are thought to be gathered here.

2. *Application Uninstall*   This process is similar to the update procedure for beginning and finishing extra operations that could be performed in this phase.

AH Management

The AH itself can be administered. The administration process organizes all the functions related to AH management and is performed by the AH itself or other programs. This stage is composed of three possible steps:

1. *AH Update*   When the AH must update itself.

2. *AH and Application Configuration*   A useful step for remotely administering Java applications installed through this AH becomes especially interesting for large organizations. In this step, the AH configuration is performed; as with application configuration, both processes can be run remotely from the DS or locally by the end-user.

3. *Other AH Management*   Other AH administration operations are possible here. Indeed, the AH could be thought of as very useful operating extensions into client platforms for services other than deployment.

Finally, as a reference, the following table catalogs each step in terms of its inputs, outputs, and a brief description.

2

AN ABSTRACT MODEL FOR DEPLOYMENT

TABLE 2.1 Stages in the Deployment Model

Phase Name	Description	Input	Output
Development	Produces the software to be deployed	specifications and requirements	
Publication	The software, opportunely packaged in Annotated Resources is ready to be distributed to clients		
Producer-to-Distributor Publication	Gives out pieces to deploy to Distributor	Development's output	Annotated Resources, Deployment Policies
Distributor-to-End-User Publication	Distributor processes items delivered by Producer in order to be used on its Distribution network	Annotated Resources, Deployment Policies	Resources ready to be delivered and installed on client platforms by the Distributor
AH Installation	Installs the AH on the client in a two-step sequence		
AH Distribution	The AH is delivered	DS request	The AH files are stored locally on the client platform

TABLE 2.1 Continued

Phase Name	Description	Input	Output
AH Physical Installation	AH pieces are assembled together	The AH files transferred in the previous step	The AH correctly installed, ready to run
DS Management	Comprises the various management activities performed by the Distributor to ensure the distribution network working	No specific input needed, apart from Deployment Policies	The correct functioning of the Deployment Server(s)
AH Check-Out	Switches from an AH state to another one		
AH-DS Connection	AH tries to connect to DS	In	Out
AH Resolution	In order to support the Application execution, the AH switches to perform other operations	Deployment Policies, Annotated Resources, and other data requested by the Policies	A plan, composed as a sequence of actions the AH has to perform
AH Management	Administering and managing the AH itself. It's made up of three main, optional steps		

2

AN ABSTRACT MODEL FOR DEPLOYMENT

TABLE 2.1 Continued

Phase Name	Description	Input	Output
AH Update	Updating the AH software	The request to perform the update	The AH is successfully updated to the newer version
AH & Application Configuration	The AH is administrated	The request	The AH settings have been successfully changed
AH Other Management	Other possible management	In	Out
Application Management	The application is administered by the AH executing Deployment Policies or user's commands		
Application Update	Application is updated	The request for updating	The updated application
Application Uninstall	Application is removed from the client platform	The request to remove the installation	The client platform with old application's freed resources

TABLE 2.1 Continued

Phase Name	Description	Input	Output
AH Application Support	Provides support during application runtime to the application itself		
AH Appl. Support-Resource Installation	Supports the application while installing needed resources		
Resources Distribution	Resources are delivered from the DS to the client platform	A request for the given resources	Resources are locally stored
Resources Physical Installation	Resources are properly installed and this installation is communicated to the running application	Resource files delivered before	The various resources correctly installed and ready to be used by the running application
AH Appl. Support -JRE Preparation	Before launching the application, the proper JVM environment is set up	Instructions on how to set up the JVM environment	A JRE process properly launched

TABLE 2.1 Continued

Phase Name	Description	Input	Output
AH Appl. Support -AH On-The-Run Management	Support for on-the-go different management services	Request for a management service	The requested management service correctly executed on the running application
Debugging	The application is debugged, possibly remotely, using Java2 built-in capabilities	An anomalous exception caught by the AH while the debugging option is switched on and supported by the AH itself	The debugging service has been executed
On-The-Run Updating	The application is updated by the AH while the previous is still running	A request for a more up-to-date application is issued	The application is correctly updated while running
On-The-Run Other Management	Management services are provided to the running application	The request for this service	The service accomplished by the AH on the running application

2

AN ABSTRACT MODEL FOR DEPLOYMENT

TABLE 2.1 Continued

Phase Name	Description	Input	Output
Application Execution	The application is finally run	The JVM properly set environment, plus other system-dependent resources correctly installed, like native libraries, devices, etc.	The given business service the application has to produce, for an End-User interacting with it.

The Actors In the Model

An important part of the abstract model is played by the various actors. Because the deployment phenomenon is a complex one, the roles involved with it are not as straight-forward as they may seem at first.

Resolving Things

In order to fully describe these roles, we have to think about what their final outcome produces. As we will see, it is useful to keep your thinking centered in the Resolution Phase.

The Producer's responsibility is to build a software product and prepare it for deployment. The outputs of the Producer-To-Developer Publication Phase are three kinds of items, as we saw before:

- The resources to be deployed.
- A description for each resource so that the Distributor knows exactly what to do with them.
- The Deployment Policies, designed by the marketing staff or somebody else in the Software Owner organization.

The first two items together are known as Annotated Resources. The easiest and standard way to annotate a Java resource when under the form of a JAR file is to put some meta-information in the META-INF standard directory of the JAR file itself.

We will think of resources as being annotated; that is, self-described (here, we are interested in describing the deployment matters only). There could be a variety of different techniques to describe resources, such as Java property files, DB entries, or XML files. The concept here is that the annotation must work as the basis for the Deployment Policies' definition and actuation.

NOTE

It is as if the Deployment Policies were a function, and the Annotated Resources and the Client Environment Definitions were its main input parameters.

Figure 2.7 presents the roles with their responsibilities seen from the Resolution Phase perspective.

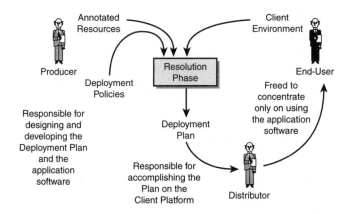

FIGURE 2.7
Roles and responsibilities centered around the Resolution Phase.

2

AN ABSTRACT
MODEL FOR
DEPLOYMENT

The Developer Role

We have seen that a piece of software is produced by an organization that often controls the exploitation rights on it. To keep things simple, we have always referred to the *Software Producer* as the vendor and marketer of the services offered by the software. Of course, this is not always the case, and generally speaking, we have to introduce at least another role, that of the *Software Owner*. Nevertheless, this is a technical software book. We are interested with in the engineering of the deployment event, not with marketing or social issues. So, rarely will we refer to a Software Owner being separate from the Software Producer.

The Software Producer role could be played by an entire organization or just a few individuals—there are many possibilities. What is useful is to separate another specialization from this role: that of the Deployment Engineer. A *Deployment Engineer* is a developer or a team of developers specialized in software deployment. They will work together with their developer colleagues and with the Distributor organization to deploy the software being constructed. We will dedicate the whole second part of this book to this role, so don't worry if we put it aside for a while.

The Distributor Role

In addition to the Producer, there is also the *Distributor*, which is a central role in the overall deployment challenge. It is worth spending some time discussing the role here.

The Distributor role could be played by many different subjects. It has been traditionally covered by Software Producers themselves, struggling to reach their consumers.

We can have administrator staff covering the responsibility of deploying software, especially in large organizations. In this case, Distributors and End-Users belong to the same client organization. Deployment administrators tend to be experienced working with Windows Registry or system files, paternalistically rebuking users when traces of old MP3 exchange programs are found on client computers and the like. They are responsible for the correct deployment and customization of the needed software. The problem with this approach is that it is quite expensive if it is to be performed without automatic tools, such as application managers (for customizing remotely many clients, for example) and utility installers.

Another form of Distributor is the class of organizations that distribute shareware and other similar software products. Despite the fact that they often avoid the responsibility of the full Distributor role, they do take care of making software installers available to users for download and cover a first-help service in case of problems during installation. Depending on the case, the Distributor role could be quite complex. For world-wide delivery, the Distributor organization can employ massive server replication to handle the deployment on a very large scale, efficiently and reliably. Often, we refer to the Deployment Server as the main instrument in the Distributor's hands. This is just an abstraction for coping with these general issues more easily.

The Distributor's task is to correctly enforce the deployment policies on the given annotated resources for the given end-users population. Achieving this usually requires sophisticated distribution technology, together with elaborated auxiliary services such as security, user authentication, and different levels of reliability.

It is the intrinsic complexity of this job that makes economic sense to outsource it from core software development.

The End-User Role

The *End-User* is the happiest of the three roles because all the efforts involved in assuring a better deployment service are ultimately aimed at increasing the user's fruition of the business service offered by the software itself.

After having produced such a huge technology effort through the construction of a powerful and reliable deployment circuit spanning several continents, we risk the destruction of all our efforts without a careful design in the End-User experience portion of the deployment process. Here, we will mention just a few aspects while leaving more design-driven topics for the second part of the book.

> **NOTE**
>
> It is important to realize that for some inexperienced End-Users, it is even hard to tell the difference between the AH and the application itself. More generally, designers and programmers should always keep the typical client-side launching scenario in mind. A common bad design hint is the long sequence of different splash screens (first the AH; then the application start-up; then the application Web connection back to server data) proposed to the end-user by some AH-launched applications. (For an example, see Chapter 7, "Building Your Own Deployment Solution.")

Figure 2.8 illustrates the whole deployment process, as perceived by the End-User. The numbers next to arrows describe the sequence of execution steps from the user's perspective.

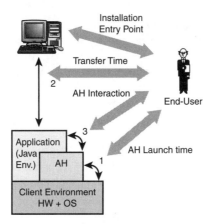

FIGURE 2.8
End-User perceived complexities in the deployment process.

An unskilled End-User is aware only of those parts of the process that are *visible* to her or him. Let's examine the main points of End-User interaction with our deployment model.

1. *Entry Point Complexity*   The complexity of the sequence of actions the End-User has to carry out to launch the whole deployment process. Often automatically deployed applications are somehow hidden from the End-User's access, so this factor is negligible, especially for inexperienced End-Users.

2. *AH Launch Time*   Often can include the transfer time as well.

3. *AH-End-User Interaction Complexity*   The perceived complexity when interacting with the AH. Also for the AH management task, for those AHs that offer such a facility.

4. *Transfer time*   Each resource that has to be installed, eventually including the AH itself.

5. *Awareness of the Involved System Processes*   The layered boxes in Figure 2.8 express this often-overlooked aspect. It's like opening up a Chinese box, only to find another one inside and so on. This is something to be aware of at design time, especially for limited-resource environments such as embedded devices.

Complexity here is intended to be thought of as that viewed by the End-User. Naturally, different users may experience different levels of complexity for the same tasks; or, more importantly, experienced complexity may vary in time or with the working stress load.

> **NOTE**
>
> The sequence and the timing between the various steps is essential to the End-User's own experience of the deployment process. As an example, if not properly addressed by the AH design, the On-The-Run Resources Installation Phase could be confusing for users because of its unexpectedness during normal application execution.

The Overall Picture

We saw the roles involved in the model and the tools used to accomplish their tasks. It's time to put all the pieces together and discuss the resulting scenario. Let's begin from Figure 2.9.

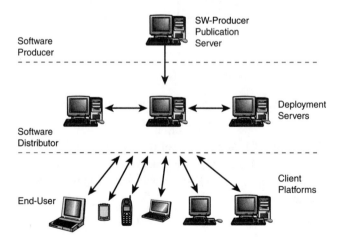

FIGURE 2.9
The deployment model seen from the physical installations involved for each role.

On the left side of the figure are reported the various roles for each involved platform, with the digital information flow linking the various machines. Focusing on the server side of this diagram, we have always mentioned a conceptually unique Deployment Server. Of course, it is an abstraction, both because several groups of servers could deploy a given set of applications only, and because all classic server-side techniques such as load-balancing, data replication, proximity detection, discovery mechanisms and the rest are suitable in this scenario. Nevertheless, given our client-centric approach, we won't cover these issues in detail. However, we will cover them in Chapter 12, "Server-Side Support" (regarding JNLP), and partially in Chapter 7 for more general, home-grown deployment solutions. In both cases, they will be covered only from a developer, high-level viewpoint. Again, Figure 2.9 describes only an aspect of our deployment model. It focuses on the Internet approach, whereas the model can handle other more general cases as well.

Now we are ready for a more in-depth discussion on the proposed deployment model's details.

Discussing the Model

In this section, we will get into the detail of the more important aspects of our deployment model. The rest of the book will concretely show the topics we are going to introduce now.

> **NOTE**
>
> This is a two-fold model. On one side, it describes concrete, real-world deployment solutions; on the other side, it can be used as a design tool to set out the whole Java deployment problem. We will see its usage as a design tool in the second part.

Let's begin by taking a step back to examine deployment lifecycle issues.

Java Deployment Lifecycle Issues

In the following section, we will see some of the details related with the concepts described in the lifecycle of Figure 2.5. We have already discussed the Resolution Phase, leaving out the details of its inputs. It is now time to fill this gap.

Deployment Policies

The Deployment Policies are needed in order to define the intended detailed behavior of the whole deployment process. They can contain the following information:

- *Connection Policies*   As discussed before, connections play an important role in modern software deployment, and the capability to fine-tune their properties is very desirable.

Connection to the Deployment Server is very useful for AH, so that a variety of more sophisticated choices are possible.

For an antivirus application, for example, an extra service (performed in the AH On-The-Run Management Phase in Figure 2.5) could check to see whether the locally installed antivirus has been itself infected and, in this case, could offer some server-related recovery services.

A variety of connection-related policies are possible. For example, we could allow clients to always make an attempt to connect to a server. Or, we could present the client with an option only when a connection is available. Finally, we could specify when to establish the connection (connecting at the end of a session doesn't slow down the application startup. Updates and other changes are effective only from the next session).

- *Distribution Policies* his set of policies pertains to the server side of the deployment process. An example of this group of policies could be the replication policies for Deployment Servers organized in a network. This type of policy is actuated by the Distributor in the DS Management Phase (refer to Figure 2.5).

- *Policies Based on Different Client Properties* This set of policies applies to the client side of the deployment process and may involve, for instance, the specification of the JRE version needed to run the application.

- *Client Updates Policies* The software owner could want to be sure to specify how and when the Application Update Phase is executed. Another important attribute that is often useful is the relation of the Update Policy to the End-User's intervention. So, updates could be performed explicitly or in the background, without even letting the user know what is going on.

  As an example of this group of policies, we can think of scheduled updates—each month, for instance. Another common policy is the definition of whether to ensure that a given release is installed by a given group of users as mandatory. This gives the certainty to Deployment Engineers (see Chapter 4) of the deployed units on client platforms. Finally, the more common policy is to leave updates as a user's preference, specifying whether the AH should prompt for new updates checked at every AH-DS Connection Phase (refer to Figure 2.5), or leave it up to the user's initiative.

- *End-User Policies* Designed together with users' definition and related information, these policies may regard the authorization for some classes of users to perform some operations on AHs, or to be aware of new software releases and of which kind. Typically, a hierarchy of accesses to given software editions is the chosen mechanism for complex user definition scenarios. When developing software for consumers, it is often preferable to make evaluation-type of users aware of new releases that are available only by payment. This is a case of deployment techniques being used as marketing means (refer to Chapter 1, "Deploying Java").

Of course, other data could be employed for defining useful policies for software deployment. We will get back to these issues in the remainder of the book.

Client Environment

Defining the client environment involves a whole branch of Computer Science, the so-called *Software Configuration Management* discipline, and even other specialization fields. We will see what it means throughout the rest of this book, for developers, particularly in relation with the Java techniques already developed. Given the potential vastness of the topic, we will be concise and intuitive.

To be specific, we can view the client environment as being made up of properties. We will see the main (and more common) groups of client properties, but it is clear that they could be even more diverse, and trying to list all the possible groups is of little help now. Another thing to say is that sometimes properties are evident to us as *humans*, but not to our software that must use them. As we will see at the end of this chapter, the type of connection is one-way in a satellite communication with consumer clients. This is apparent to Developers, but must be formally represented by means of a property belonging to the connection group. Formally and exhaustively defining the client environment is not only a theoretical matter, it also becomes useful during analysis when modeling the domain in object-oriented fashion.

- *End-User Data*   Properties related with the user and its role, plus license information and other items. It is often secured.

- *Connection Properties*   Various data about the kind of connections supported by the given client.

- *Installed Java Libraries*   Third-party and "javax.*" libraries already installed on the given platform.

- *Installed Java Extensions*   Eventually installed Java 2 standard extensions.

- *Installed Java Runtime Environments and Other Java-Related Installations*   Naturally, JREs present on the client platform with their exact version and eventually other Java-related material (such as installed JNLP client, and so on) need to be known when resolving resources to download.

- *Installed Application Resources Configuration*   The exact version of each piece that compose the whole application that has been previously installed.

- *Recovery Data*   To ensure various reliability techniques, data about lost connections, abruptly terminated downloads, and the like.

- *AH Management Data*   Needed also for administering and configuring the AH.

- *Installed Application Business Data*   Resolution can depend on business data as well, depending on the particular application domain.

- *Platform-Dependent Data*   Properties in this group are used for platform-dependent AH installations, for example; or in a low-level context, such as with Java-enabled embedded devices.

NOTE

The location where this data is kept is not necessarily on the client-side. Depending on the particular domain, some or all of these properties could be stored on the Deployment Server or somewhere else.

AH Costs

The AH offers deployment services to the launched application, but these come at a cost. With the term *cost*, we mean here both resources and time costs, but mainly the latter, in a user-oriented perspective. The more striking cost, as perceived by the user, is the total launch time, especially for the first execution, when we assume there's nothing yet installed on the client platform (refer to Figure 2.8). In the following count, the JVM installation time is thought of as being part of the AH Installation Time, together with the distribution time.

```
Total Maximum Waiting Time at Application's First Launch =
        AH Installation Time +
        AH Launch and Resolution Time +
        Application Installation Time +
        JVM Launch Time +
        Application Launch Time.
```

Let's discuss this briefly.

- As we know, there are some fixed costs when deploying and generally running Java code. The JVM and the application launch times cannot be shortened by any deployment techniques.

- The total amount of time for the very first installation could be quite high, so there is a real need to cut it down in some way. The technique more commonly used in these cases is to split this sum, separating the processes of AH Installation from Application Installation (refer to Figure 2.5) that are the biggest addenda in this simple formula.

Summing up all the times we run the application, the previous count becomes as follows:

```
Total Maximum Waiting Time at Application's First Launch =
        AH Installation Time +
        Application Installation Time +
```

```
( AH Launch and Resolution Time +
JVM Launch Time +
Application Launch Time ) * Number-of-Runs.
```

Let's discuss this formula, as well.

- Now, as the number of runs increases over time, the initial installation costs get repaid. This justifies the usage of this technology for End-Users who will use the application quite often. In cases where the total number of runs is small, there is no incentive in using it for End-Users. This is, again, similar to what is said in Chapter 1. It is sometimes called the "plug-in syndrome", in which users browsing the Web are unwilling to download a bulky plug-in requested when browsing some trendy site.

- Another common-sense piece of advice comes from thinking about the number of different applications managed and installed by a single AH. When there are more applications installed by the same AH (the second addendum becomes a sum itself together with the last one) the AH installation cost also gets negligible in time, so that it could be thought of as being paid back when compared with other technical solutions. As we will see (also in Chapter 3), this is a strong incentive to promoting a single-AH Java deployment technology for consumer diffusion.

- In limited computational resource client environments, the AH installation time could be negligible, given the size of resources to be distributed and installed, whereas the JVM launch time could be zero on Java native platforms. What can become critical then are the other costs associated with each executable run, especially in consumer applications. An unexpected critical cost could be during the AH Check-Out Phase, represented by the preceding AH Launch Time figure, especially for wireless and other bandwidth-critical AH-DS connections.

The preceding considerations look ideal for a limited, well-controlled environment, in which such "heavy" initial costs could be afforded or imposed, and in which the number of times the installed applications will be executed is predictably high. In this scenario, the adoption of a Java-based sophisticated deployment technology could make economic sense, not only for software producers taking advantage of Java's features, but also for software consumers. This is the typical case of an organization producing its own software to be deployed to its own employees through an intranet or an extranet. Then, the costs of deploying the software on the organization's client platforms will be paid back over time.

We will see some techniques to reduce such costs depending on the situation, when dealing with the developer's side of the Java deployment process, in Part II of this book, "Deployment Engineering."

2

AN ABSTRACT
MODEL FOR
DEPLOYMENT

Twists Of Java Deployment

Deploying Java software is not like deploying other software executables. The large range of capabilities covered by Java executables on so many different platforms makes covering all the possible cases a large task. We conclude this chapter by examining how our deployment model applies to a very particular case.

Figure 2.10 showed a case that is not as rare as one may think at first. A Java-enabled decoder set-top-box supports the viewing of encrypted satellite television. Periodically, not only the encryption keys, but the whole client-side software needs to be replaced in order to keep pirates at bay. At first, this situation seems quite far from the large-sized, Internet-minded deployment model we concentrated on in the previous discussion. We won't talk about security issues here, but instead we will see how the model shown in Figures 2.3 and 2.5 applies to diverse cases of Java deployment.

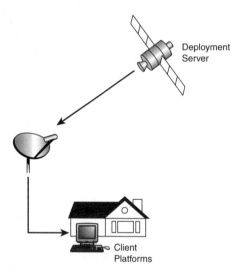

FIGURE 2.10

A particular case of deployment.

First of all, the presence or absence of an AH in our deployment strategy will influence all the involved steps. Let's examine the case in which we don't have an AH at all, so that all the deployment phases must be accomplished with only minimal help from the client-side. Then, we see that this case presents a sever connection hurdle because the client-server connection is unidirectional; that is, from the server satellite toward the sky-dish and no way back. Distribution of new software happens at given server-directed times by simply flooding the client with the software to be installed at a given signal. Let's briefly gather some observations from the application of our abstract model to this case.

- The Publication Phase and the Distribution Phase to the client are in strictly rigid contextual sequence.

- Given that the case is too Spartan to comprise a new AH Installation Phase or any AH Management Phase at all, we can think of these two phases as being empty.

- All the Resolution Phase is actuated on the server-side, and we can always think of the JRE as running, so that the AH Application Support Phase is minimal.

- We can think of our (essential) deployment system as being limited basically to the Application Installation Phase and the Application Management Phase.

- Steps such as Application Installation Customization or Application (Complete) Uninstall are very minimal if not completely absent.

This is an extreme case, one rarely faced by developers. Nevertheless, it is useful to show some of the possible twists of Java software deployment and how the proposed model can describe such cases as well.

We will examine details of other cases (from the developer's perspective) like this one in Chapter 5, "Non-J2SE Clients."

Summary

In this chapter, we have introduced a general, abstract model for Java software deployment that we will use as a reference throughout the book. We concluded by showing how the proposed model can describe a particular case of Java software deployment.

The model can be summarized in the following elements:

- The stages that compose the lifecycle of a general deployment circuit implementation— The basic set of steps is shown in Figure 2.3.

- The four model roles are Software Producer, Software Owner (often coinciding), Distributor and End-User. Figure 2.7 depicts some of the interactions between model roles.

- Other concepts and definitions such as the Application Helper, the Client Environment, and Deployment Policies that formalize some aspects of the deployment phenomenon.

We will often use the graphical representation of the model steps (Figures 2.5 and 2.3, its simpler version) because the model is more concrete and easier to handle, in both adaptation to the given case and for discussing design issues.

In the next chapter, we will conclude our introduction to Java deployment by examining some of the real-world solutions available for developers.

Existing Solutions

IN THIS CHAPTER

This chapter will cover existing ready-to-use solutions aimed at the deployment of Java software for industry-quality programs.

Introduction

Deployment solutions can be thought of as being divided into two main groups: one group is specific only to Java programs; the other is suitable for other technologies as well, including Java. We will focus on Java-specific deployment solutions because they are the only ones that assure the better exploitation of Java's features. There are also many general deployment and application management solutions that are suitable for Java deployment. These include Marimba's Castanet, NetDeploy, and many others that we won't discuss here—to keep us strictly focused on our main topic, deployment.

When choosing a deployment solution, there are many parameters to consider, including technical ones (scalability, deployment lifecycle coverage, and so on) and commercial ones (price, licensing, and so on). In this chapter, we will cover only technical details, for the purpose of illustrating the current commercial state-of-the-art in the field, rather than proposing any particular opinion on products.

We will take advantage of the abstract model described in Chapter 2, "An Abstract Model for Deployment," in order to present all the systems in a coherent and more precise way.

JNLP Implementations

The most important JNLP implementation, and the reference implementation as well, is the Java Web Start from Sun. Other JNLP client implementations are still immature as products, or need to be better known among developers (JavaURL, or OpenJNLP for instance). JNLP server implementations are mentioned as well.

Java Web Start

The idea behind Web Start (see its home page at `http://java.sun.com/products/javawebstart`) and the underlying JNLP protocol is the use of an Application Helper that can interact with the Web browser, but is also usable without it. The Application Helper provides runtime services to the launched application. Web Start supports the deployment of applets as well. In the following discussion, we will refer to Figure 3.1 (in which we omitted the DS Management Phase because we are interested in client issues). For more detailed topics, we refer to Figure 2.5.

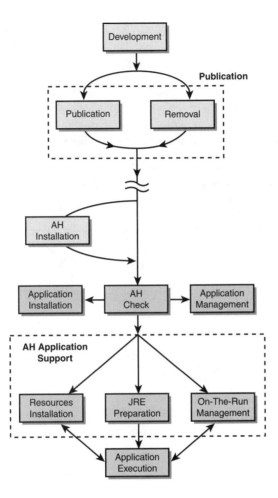

FIGURE 3.1
With JNLP and Java Web Start, the deployment lifecycle coverage is complete.

CAUTION

Figure 3.1 looks quite reassuring because Web Start seems to cover almost all the stages of the deployment process. It should be noted that Web Start is still an immature technology regarding the details of the deployment lifecycle phases covered.

3

EXSISTING
SOLUTIONS

As we know from Chapter 2, these kinds of services belong to the AH Application Support Phase shown in Figure 2.5. That is to say, Web Start works like an Application Container, offering runtime support to applications beyond the automatic download and installation from a Web site and related updates.

We will dedicate an important part of the book to Web Start and the underlying JNLP technology. Here, we will examine the Web Start software product (as of version 1.0) from an End-User perspective, without taking care of the behind-the-scenes mechanisms involved.

In Figure 3.2, a commercial application is launched from a Web page. This begins the installation process. This is one case of the *Installation Entry Point* we mentioned in Figure 2.8, in this case for applications launched with Web Start.

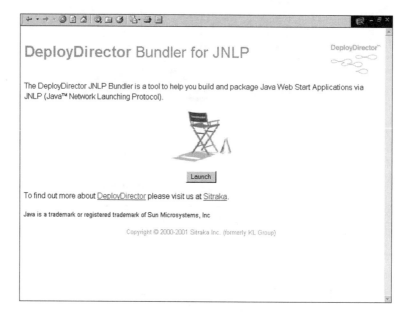

FIGURE 3.2

The installation entry point for an application deployed with Web Start.

Referring again to Figure 2.8, once launched, the download is clearly shown to the user. In Figure 3.3, we see the dialog box showing the download progress during an application installation.

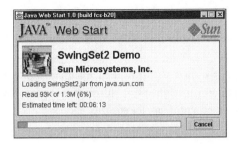

FIGURE 3.3
The Application Installation Progress dialog box.

Web Start is important because of Sun's support (together with other industry leaders) that will allow the JNLP technology to establish itself as the de-facto standard Java deployment technology. This means that the lowest-common-denominator for deploying Java applications using J2SE will be JNLP and, on the client side, Web Start.

There are several reasons why Web Start is promising as the leading client-side JNLP client:

- It is officially supported by Sun and other major vendors that collaborate on the JNLP specification. For additional references, see Appendix B, "The JNLP Specification."
- It centralizes JRE management on the local platform. Different JNLP clients (or AHs in our more precise terminology) would store and manage JREs differently, in a possibly incompatible way.
- A unique client look will help users as well, securing the investment in proposing it also to less-experienced end-users.
- Developers will minimize the cost/barrier in deploying their own custom AH (the client launcher) on clients.
- It will have a substantial head start against other possible JNLP client implementations.
- Developers will use it as a reference scenario when building Web-deployable J2SE applications or applets, taking advantage of lowering development costs when developing to a well-known and documented standard.
- Possibly, as the technology matures and stabilizes in the future, it will be incorporated in the J2SE JRE distribution.

Indeed, one may think of Web Start as the locomotive pulling the JNLP train.

The major features permitted by this technology are the following:

- A Web-centric approach to Java applications
- Native desktop integration of installed applications

3

EXSISTING
SOLUTIONS

- Centralized management of different JRE versions

- Automatic installation of any resource, from JAR files, extensions, native libraries, and JREs

- Security features such as signed JAR files, hence signed applications, and the tuning of permissions with the aim of implementing different levels of restricted execution environment such as that found in the applet security mode

- Applications can be launched independently of Web browsers or an Internet connection

Furthermore, as regards the AH, it presents a friendly Java Swing user interface that is perfectly integrated into the native platform.

There are other limitations as well, such as the restriction to use only Java 2 (1.1.x JREs are not supported), minimalism of some deployment options, or the fact that it is restricted to HTTP connections only. We will examine these problems and others in detail from a developer's perspective in the Part III of this book, "JNLP."

Reliability

Web Start is quite fragile when it comes to dealing with broken connections or user-interrupted downloads. Unfortunately, these are common occurrences in the real world. Currently, in these cases, the user has to restart the download again. See Figure 3.4.

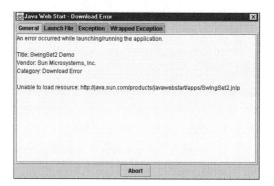

FIGURE 3.4
Java Web Start doesn't support the resumption of interrupted downloads.

AH & Application Configuration

As can be seen in Figure 2.5, the AH & Application Configuration phase is reachable from the menu Edit—Preferences. The End-User can administer Proxy connections (see Figure 3.5), install JREs, and select options for the creation of shortcuts and other launching facilities. Other options are related to security (see Figure 3.6); users can inspect all registered certificates. Also, the cache area is accessible (organized as folders containing the various resources on the local hard disk), together with information about the JVM's standard output (see Figure 3.7).

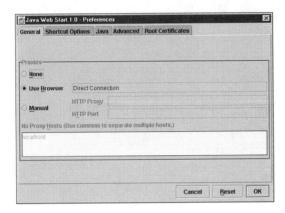

FIGURE 3.5

The Preferences Settings dialog box for proxy settings.

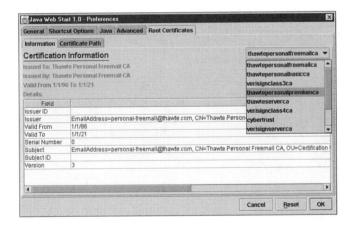

FIGURE 3.6

The Preferences Settings dialog box for security-related details.

3

EXSISTING SOLUTIONS

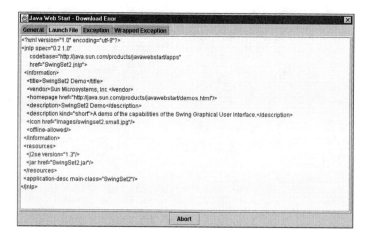

FIGURE 3.7
The Preferences Settings dialog box for advanced settings.

Java Web Start has been designed for developers as well, as one can see from Figure 3.8, where in addition to the user error message, even the JNLP file has been reported for debugging.

```xml
<?xml version="1.0" encoding="utf-8"?>
<jnlp spec="0.2 1.0"
    codebase="http://java.sun.com/products/javawebstart/apps"
    href="SwingSet2.jnlp">
<information>
  <title>SwingSet2 Demo</title>
  <vendor>Sun Microsystems, Inc.</vendor>
  <homepage href="http://java.sun.com/products/javawebstart/demos.html"/>
  <description>SwingSet2 Demo</description>
  <description kind="short">A demo of the capabilities of the Swing Graphical User Interface.</description>
  <icon href="images/swingset2.small.jpg"/>
  <offline-allowed/>
</information>
<resources>
  <j2se version="1.3"/>
  <jar href="SwingSet2.jar"/>
</resources>
<application-desc main-class="SwingSet2"/>
</jnlp>
```

FIGURE 3.8
The Error dialog box reports debugging information as well.

JREs Management

A useful feature of JNLP is its capability to manage multiple JREs (despite the handicap of being limited to specific J2SE editions) as shown in Figure 3.9. In the future, this will be very valuable when many different Java programs will be installed on the same computer, and developers can save bandwidth, packaging their applications without the related JRE.

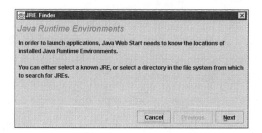

FIGURE 3.9
The JRE Maintenance Facility in Java Web Start.

> **NOTE**
>
> Some detailed features of Web Start are competitive with other more complex commercial products, intended for corporate enterprise scenarios. The versioning specification allowable in JNLP, for example, is more sophisticated than other more powerful deployment solutions such as DeployDirector.

We will see the details of Web Start when we extensively cover its underlying foundation, the JNLP protocol, from the developer's viewpoint in Part III, "JNLP."

Commercial Solutions

Let's take a look at some commercial Java deployment solutions. We will focus on three major representative cases of some real-world Java deployment problems.

Sitraka's DeployDirector

Sitraka's DeployDirector offers full coverage of all the deployment circuit's stages for Java applications, leaving out only the Software Development Phase. (Sitraka was formerly known as KL Group).

Getting into the deployment lifecycle details, it covers almost all the phases in Figure 2.5 except for a few. The AH On-The-Run Management stage is partially covered, apart from a sound logging system, whereas the Publication Phase is unstructured, making it difficult for third-party Distributors to adopt this deployment solution. Despite these limitations, DeployDirector is currently one of the most complete deployment solutions available for Java.

Its architecture is composed by an AH to be installed on the client platform. It consists of a server-side application that implements the Deployment Server together with a repository facility for the resources to be deployed.

The whole system is Web-centric in that the Deployment Server is implemented though servlets operating with standard Web and application servers such as IBM Websphere, Apache (Tomcat and JServ), and Bea WebLogic. On the client side, the AH works together with an applet, and the Web browser is fully integrated.

The DeployDirector software architecture is built around four main components:

- Client Application Manager. The AH being installed on the client platform. JNLP clients are also supported, Web Start included.
- Server Application Manager. The server-side software tool for managing the Deployment Servers.
- The Vault. The repository for resources to be installed on client platforms. It resides at Deployment Servers.
- The Remote Administration Tool. The GUI console is used to set deployment policies, prepare resource descriptions, and manage the other services available to this deployment circuit's implementation.

To the server side, DeployDirector lists many interesting features, including the following:

- Deployment Servers' reliability tuning through server redundancy and replication, using the concept of clusters of Deployment Servers.
- Deployment Server-Application Helper connection optimized through a fine-grained, byte-level differencing mechanism.
- Security. The Deployment Server-Application Helper connection could be secured using SSL. Resources are accessible through a two-step process of authentication and authorization.
- A user-friendly GUI that centralizes the management of all deployment policies, software publications, and management data for the administrator (on Deployment Servers).
- A high level of customization, provided to developers by means of a pluggable class architecture.
- On-The-Run-Management services such as an extensive logging service of client operations on Deployment Servers.

On the client side, other remarkable features are as follows:

- Multiple JRE management. This allows the central organization of JREs, locally managed by the AH.

- There are three different possibilities for Deployment Policies regarding the strategy of updates. Updates can be mandatory at application launch, user-requested, or automatic.
- Highly customizable, both in technical settings (proxy settings, for example) and in user interface.

Also to consider is the very good quality and availability of technical documentation.

Several missing features are as follows:

- As said before, the role of the Distributor is not general enough to be performed by third-party organizations taking advantage of this software. This tool has been provided mainly for in-house deployment; that is, for companies that produce, deploy, and use their own software.
- Little details (as of version 1.3) such as a difficult management of standard JRE distributions, a not-so-finely-grained JRE version definition, and so on.
- Finally, some stages are partially covered, as mentioned before. The only additional service beyond standard deployment services is a logging system that can be used for statistics, properties inspection, and other management operations. Also, publication features are a bit too coarse, especially for complex product lines.

The power of the addressable Deployment Policies comprises update strategies, per-user policies, connection options, and so on. A quite rich set of policies, though with only a few possible values, is available that covers all the more useful cases.

DeployDirector is a complete new-generation deployment solution that addresses the needs of organizations using Java software and necessitating sophisticated control on their own produced Java software.

DeployDirector Bundler for JNLP

A related utility is offered by Sitraka, mimicking its more sophisticated DeployDirector's GUI for visually creating a JNLP file for deploying Java code by means of the Java Network Launching Protocol.

InstallShield Java Edition

Having seen the importance of installer utilities, it is time to cover one of them practically. We mention InstallShield Java Edition here simply because it is an installer utility written in Java. Figure 2.6 demonstrated the particular case of our reference abstract deployment model adapted to installer utilities. It is time to see concretely what this class of products (listing, among others, Denova's JExpress, InstallAnywhere, and so on) offers to Java developers.

First of all, the fact that it is written in Java doesn't necessarily mean it will run on all the Java-supported platforms. Indeed, as of version 3.5, it is restricted to just a few: namely, Windows, Solaris and Linux (Red Hat 6.2). It provides the following features:

- JNLP-compliant, so Web Start can be used for launching the deployed applications.
- Support for native libraries taking advantage of the Java Native Interface (JNI).
- JRE bundling, for installing the JRE when there are no pre-existing JREs locally installed.
- Final format options. The installer can be obtained as a Java class file, Java applet, ".exe" executable on a Windows platform; or as shell scripts for Solaris and Linux installations.

For a general discussion of this kind of technology, see the discussions in the previous chapters.

Java Deployment for Existing Solutions

Java and the Internet took existing software solutions by storm, too. It would be too lengthy even to mention the many Java-extensions available on the market for the various software appliances. Instead, we will focus on what Java implied for the deployment of database products. We will examine Oracle's Forms solution, just to select one, but all the major DB vendors provide similar competitive solutions as well.

The following case is representative of a certain class of "shallow-enabled" client porting of the Java technology that prevailed as one of the main usages of the applet technology in enterprise client applications.

Oracle's Forms Server

Java can be useful as a thin client in order to integrate server-side established technologies such as the Oracle database application. This is done using the Forms Server architecture via applets running in a common Web browser.

This technology includes a browser plug-in (much the same as the Sun's Plug-In technology) called JInitiator, It offers more up-to-date JRE environments on the client platform where the Oracle applets are run.

This is a typical example of a certain use of the Java technology that is very common when server-side established solutions need to be ported to the Web. Despite the fact that JInitiator and the Forms Server technology can be run from the Internet, their most common use is in corporate intranets—to access centralized data stored in Oracle server databases. Here, we are interested in showing the client-side deployment aspects of this and similar technologies.

In this case, anyway, Java technology has been used as a mere thin client; few of the very valuable features of the Java platform have been exploited. Nevertheless, this approach works, allowing Web browser clients to be able to execute quite sophisticated transactions. The AH installation costs, anyway, are the same as the Sun Plug-In discussed in Chapter 2.

When facing concrete deployment of Java software complexity-compatibility trade-offs, engineers have often given up the purity of the Java platform as such, favoring a better compatibility with the underlying platform, as we will discuss in the next section.

Nailing Down Java

When dealing with the deployment of Java executables today, few environments support natively up-to-date JREs. Anyway, there is always the other way around. That is, instead of carrying an interpreter to the place you need to run your classes, you can always package your bytecode in something native. In this way, Java is considered to be an intermediate language, from which you could create platform-dependent executables. Also common is an intermediate solution, consisting only of packaging the Java executables in a platform-dependent way. We will see a case of both these approaches in a moment.

> **NOTE**
>
> Because this technical solution is related to the various platforms, we describe it here in this chapter. It is, of course, not a proper solution, in that you probably lose the best features of the Java platform. Nevertheless, it is a technique for deploying Java code to client platforms, so we will have a look at some related products, just to explore this alternative, too.

There are tools such as these for all the major platforms. We will refer to just two of them: a utility for the Mac and another one for the Windows platform to complete the picture.

Apple's JBindery

JBindery is a packager utility for integrating Java software into the Mac OS. It is a deployment technology in that it enables Java software to be packaged and executed only on a given platform: the Mac OS. Indeed, there are often cases when an application is required to access platform-dependent features or to wrap developed applications in a more system-integrated way so that the end-user will find it more usable. JBindery is able to package Java classes and JAR files in a Mac-like appearance with many possible features, as follows:

- Adding a Mac Virtual File System to the Java application. This typical Mac feature permits the bundling of many different files together into one, such as the bundling of an HTML page together with all its images, applets, and so on into a file shown by the Mac OS as a unique HTML file.

- Specifying all Java-related information, such as the classpath, standard output, main class, execution parameters, and other various properties to be added to the Java environment, and so on.

- Security issues. It is possible, for instance, to modify the -verify/-verifyremote command-line switches for the JVM, or modify OS' settings for the firewall, HTTP proxy, and so on.

JBindery can work as a launcher only— to launch the Java class on the Mac OS without packaging it.

PLC's JOVE

PLC's JOVE is a translator of bytecode that essentially transforms your Java executable into native Wintel code. To do so, it adds a little runtime support to the package, together with the translated program to be executed natively by the runtime support. In the translation and packaging support, the code is optimized to additionally enhance the performance. The outcome is a single platform-dependent executable. This solution is quite different from the other packager utilities, in that it translates the code, too, changing it deeply. The advantage is fast performance, but there are also drawbacks, such as limitations in supporting all Java bytecode instructions. For example, dynamic loading of classes is not supported. Before translating a Java executable this way, you have to run a verifier utility to see if the program can be translated into native code with this technology.

Other Java Deployment Means

In this section, we examine other interesting Java technologies related to deployment.

Mobile Agents

Defining mobile agent software is not simple; there are many slightly different definitions, and the whole topic is still evolving as an experimental technology. To shed some light on this promising Java phenomenon we will introduce it briefly here, and we will mention one product.

Briefly, we can say that a mobile agent is software that is

- goal-driven, or as they like to say, proactive.
- autonomous. It can be left working on its own, reacting to changes and events from outside.
- able to communicate with other agents.
- mobile. It can move from one host computer to another one.
- adaptive. It can adapt its behavior based on its own past experience.

Given these properties, and the fact that mobile agents are designed for the Internet age, it is clear that they deal with the software deployment issue. Particularly, we are interested in the word *mobile*, which is the capability that this kind of technology has to transfer itself and operate on platforms different from the original one.

Given these definitions, it is clear that Java is the perfect implementer's choice. Java is platform-independent, so what could be better suited in moving from one host to another? Next, it can make use of many handy features, such as dynamic class loading, reflection, and so on. But what is more important is its intrinsic security, so that remote hosts can receive mobile agents without fear of malicious behavior.

We will examine the Aglet case, developed by IBM and available from their Web site. As the terms indicate, Aglets are thought of as a mix between the applet concept and that of a mobile agent, as described before. We can think of *Aglets* as *mobile applets* that have a well-defined lifecycle that involves their own deployment to Aglet-enabled hosts spread over the network. Aglets can move themselves from one host to another one, or they can be taken from somebody outside them. Aglets interact through the use of messages, both synchronously and asynchronously. The Aglet model uses the *context* concept. Contexts remain permanently on the host where they were created; aglets travel from one context to another.

The Aglet lifecycle comprises events for each stage that allow developers to plug into their own event-listener classes and to take advantage of the Java class framework implementing the Aglet concept, together with the other classes that loosely resemble the Applet-related classes.

Let's have a closer look at what we are interested in: the Aglet deployment process.

Aglets are transferred from one context to another by means of an Aglet Transfer Protocol (ATP) that conceptually performs the following operations:

1. The Aglet is serialized.
2. The serialized Aglet and its bytecode classes are physically transferred to the destination context.
3. The two byte streams are reconstructed at the destination host site.
4. The Aglet is brought to life again, by launching its bytecode classes and restoring its previous state.

All this is obtained with a single method, belonging to the `Aglet` class:

```
myAglet.dispatch(new URL("atp://marinilli.com/main_context"));
```

Note that here the proposed deployment process has an important property: It preserves the *state* of the *object* being deployed. That is important. We basically deployed classes, in Chapter

2 and throughout this book, with few exceptions. Of course, our model makes provisions for customizing the classes once deployed on the client platform, but it doesn't provide such a feature.

There is currently a lot of work going on with mobile agents totally implemented in Java, and the prospects seem quite promising for real-world, sophisticated applications.

TowerJ

TowerJ technology is an original approach that deserves a brief mention here. It is aimed at back-end, high-performance servers that run Java code (J2EE mostly), in which the powerful computing environment allows for more sophisticated technologies while still running usual Java code when needed, or using specially-compiled native executables that permit high performance on mission-critical servers. The main piece of the architecture, apart from the compiler technology, is its special JRE environment, capable of running Java code in the so-called "mix-mode."

Deployment Engineering

PART
II

IN THIS PART

Designing for Deployment

IN THIS CHAPTER

In this chapter, we will address the deployment design issue. There are so many different situations in real-world scenarios that we are forced to keep our discussion at a rather generic level. The remaining chapters will dig into the practical details of Java deployment.

Introduction

In this section, we will introduce some concepts that will help to address the vast issue of designing a deployment circuit for a Java application. After a short discussion of the role of a deployment engineer and other considerations, we will examine a simple methodology for an effective setting out of the deployment design task.

> **NOTE**
>
> Another practical source of information on this aspect (providing advice on choosing the best deployment option for a given situation) is Appendix A, "A Little Handbook For Java Deployment," in which all the material proposed throughout this book is organized in an alternative, succinct and practical way.

Deployment Engineer Role

In Chapter 2, "An Abstract Model for Deployment" we mentioned the role of the developer(s) specialized in deployment. Such a developer (for simplicity, we refer to just one person) is responsible for the correct and effective deployment of the whole application. When the required deployment services are simple, there are no problems. For a one-shot installation, for example, the deployment engineer would package the application with a software installer utility and publish it on a Web server or on other distribution channels. For these simple kinds of deployment, it makes little sense to talk about a specialized developer; one of the programmers who built the software would be able to effectively package it for deployment, too. This is common practice in smaller software firms.

The problems will appear when more sophisticated deployment services are required, when deployment tools are not so simple to use, and when the deployment options for a given situation are, say, half a dozen at least. What to do then? Which deployment technology should you use? Clearly, in these cases, deployment is not a secondary issue; a wrong choice could spoil the application effectiveness, at least from an end-user perspective. This chapter will provide some advice about the deployment engineer role.

Lifecycle Considerations

Often, deployment is seen as a mere appendix to software development. This could be true in some cases. Generally speaking, the more the deployment services we want to employ, the earlier deployment considerations should be used to influence software design. The best situation is where deployment considerations are taken into account since the design phase of the software lifecycle. This is not wishful thinking, but concrete reality. Let's take an everyday example. Some deployment solutions offer, among others, localization services to cut down the size of the resources to install. If localization data is not planned out and organized accordingly, the localization feature (provided with no additional effort for developers) will be wasted or, even worse, could tamper the whole deployment effectiveness.

The key point here is to realize that deployment is no longer a simple, one-shot service. Thanks to the Internet and to more sophisticated technologies such as Java itself, deployment services are growing into advanced business software support services. Like all new technologies, despite being already technically feasible, non-trivial deployment services are still considered an unnecessary complication and are not widely used. Old habits are hard to change, even among Java developers.

Separating and specializing on a per-function basis, the software services needed by an application is a key for enhancing the overall software quality and cutting down development time all at once. We already discussed such topics in Chapter 1, "Deploying Java." Here, we focus on the evolution of deployment services and their transformation into a powerful software infrastructure provided to business applications that developers are still too hesitant to embrace. In order to gain acceptance, deployment services have to be given a more important role in the software development and in the overall software lifecycle, as discussed in Part I, "Introduction."

Non-J2SE Platforms

The topics discussed in this chapter are focused mainly on the Java desktop environments (JDK 1.x and J2SE). Desktop applications are more difficult to deploy because of the great availability of deployment options. Deciding the deployment strategy for J2ME or J2EE executables is much easier because there are fewer options available to developers. With J2ME, there are essentially two main reasons that prevent a complete exposition of the various J2ME deployment techniques:

- Configurations and profiles are quite different from device to device, and it is of little use to attempt to discuss all the J2ME deployment options together as a whole.

- More importantly, each profile provides its own deployment mechanism and, given the limited nature of the client devices, there is no room for alternative deployment solutions.

4

DESIGNING FOR DEPLOYMENT

Regarding J2EE, this platform provides its own complete standard deployment mechanism. Although there are more options for alternative deployment methods than the J2ME (given the abundance of hardware and software resources on this environment), it makes little sense to discuss alternative deployment options on this platform, for the following reasons:

- Given the server-side nature of J2EE executables, deployment issues are less vital than those on consumer or desktop environments.

- The nature of users (not end-users, but programmers and developers who use J2EE software for their own applications) allows for a simpler deployment mechanism. Often J2EE applications are deployed via CD-ROM or using a Web connection.

For more J2ME and J2SE deployment details, see Chapter 5, "Deployment Options for Non-J2SE Clients".

Planning the Deployment Strategy

Paradoxically, given the great number of options available, choosing how to deploy Java software for J2SE or legacy 1.x platforms is not easy. We will propose a simple approach to solve this puzzle.

Our approach is to solve the Java deployment issue in three steps:

1. Choose the deployment services.
2. Decide how to implement the chosen deployment services and how to solve the first installation problem.
3. Implementing what was thought out in the previous steps.

Both deployment services and means will be introduced in the following sections, in which we will detail the three steps proposed here.

Several criteria should guide our decisions. Depending on the situations, we could shape our design around different factors: end-user priorities, short time-to-market, minimum development costs, and so on.

Basically, there are two main approaches to practical software deployment: the minimal one, in which only the simplest deployment services are needed; and the radical approach, in which more sophisticated services are required.

Deployment Services

We saw in Chapter 2 that one could establish a deployment circuit offering various kinds of services. The purpose of this chapter is to provide advice for designing the proper deployment circuit for our Java software.

We will isolate a set of standard features that will guide us through the specification of our deployment requirements. We will begin from the abstract model for Java software deployment.

In Chapter 2, we devised several phases that can be seen as features that the deployment circuit can provide to its client applications. Particularly, we focus here on the following services (among those discussed in Chapter 2):

- Application Installation
- Application Management
- AH Application Support (excluding On-The-Run Management)
- AH Management
- AH On-The-Run Management

Note that these services are ordered on the basis of their occurrence in real-world deployment circuits. One can think of the Application Installation service as the barest of all the deployment services. Then comes the capability of updating the installed software (Application Management) and so on. Furthermore, commercial deployment solutions tend to offer a coherent set of features. Hence, we can think of such a ordering implying the inclusion of all the preceding services (ranks 1, 2,…, n-1), together with the given one at rank n. That implies, for example, that those deployment circuits offering some AH management services, supposedly offered in various forms, also offer Application Installation, Management, and basic AH Application Support services as well.

Of course this ranking is arbitrary; in some special cases, we could have a deployment circuit featuring application installation and some AH On-The-Run Management services only, without any Application Management. Nevertheless, we are interested in a practical set of standard services applicable in the most common cases.

This list could be useful for guiding us through the design of general-purpose deployment circuits, but it is rather ineffectual in most daily deployment tasks. To follow the line of the practical approach, let's specify better our standard services. Although the previous list of services is quite complete, it is still too abstract. We solidify it in the following (ordered) list of deployment features:

- One-Shot Installation. Corresponds to the basic job done by any installer utility, comprised in the Application Installation Phase. We assume that every deployment circuit provides such a feature.
- Automatic Updates. The most common service in the Application Management Phase is the capability of updating installed applications seamlessly.

- Additional JREs Support. The capability of the deployment circuit of handling the auto-matic installation and subsequent use of different JREs.

- JNLP 1.0 Deployment Services. As a milestone in our standard services list, we use the services provided by JNLP 1.0. We will discuss them as follows.

- Ad-Hoc Deployment Services. In-house developed services—these could be the most different or sophisticated, and are not provided by standard deployment solutions.

Regarding JNLP, we will discuss it thoroughly in Part III, "JNLP." Here, we will consider it to be a black-box; we are interested only in the protocol's features (as of version 1.0) as a refer-ence for defining our services. For more information, see Chapter 9, "The JNLP Protocol" or Appendix B, "The JNLP Specification".

We assume the following main features for JNLP 1.0:

- Security. A secure deployment solution, which means that end-users can trust a reliable JNLP Client because it will not allow any harmful behavior by deployed applications.

- Versioning and incremental updates. Each resource can be tagged with a version id, and managed accordingly. Incremental updates are obtained using the JARDiff format.

- Multiple JRE management, and automatic installation of additional JREs and optional packages.

- Desktop integration. Deployed applications are integrated on the native OS, providing shortcuts, launching scripts, or other platform-dependent mechanisms.

- Offline operation. Deployed applications can work even without a connection with the deployment server. Even if it is a somewhat minimal feature, it is widely used in prac-tice.

- Automatic installation of native code/libraries. Some Java programs may need some plat-form-specific support for running.

- AH Management console. Although not part of the specifications, we assume the JNLP AH provides to end-users a form of graphical configuration console.

Next, we will discuss another important aspect of the deployment design. We saw how the use of formalized services descriptions (although pretty simple for convenience) help us to define what we want from our deployment circuit. We still need to clarify *how* we will implement the desired services.

Deployment Means

There are substantially two methods for implementing the intended deployment circuit. Those "basic" ones use only the JRE (eventually providing self-developed code to implement the needed deployment services) and "specialized" ones that are full deployment solutions to be customized to developers' needs (for example, third-party solutions such as DeployDirector).

Both means are legitimate and equally useful. Often, specialized development solutions don't cover all the possible real situations, and developers are forced to implement an ad-hoc deployment circuit using the JRE or other native resources only. On the other hand, choosing not to rely on the services provided by a specialized tool will force developers to build such a software facility from scratch.

We intend to provide here a practical range of deployment means, those most commonly used in real-world situations. In order to do so, we have to sacrifice some conceptual criteria. In particular, we will blend together third-party deployment solutions with basic Java technology (that is, simple JREs). This is for simplicity and also because a JRE often comes shipped with a deployment technology itself (we are referring to Sun's JRE distribution that comes shipped with the Plug-In technology).

Explicitly mentioning the various JRE versions as deployment means also has the benefit of shedding some light on the often-overlooked issue of re-engineering the deployment of already-deployed Java code. In Chapter 6, "Deploying Existing Software," we will see an example of such potentially intricate situations.

Another deployment "means" we often neglect (but which is still widely used) consists of the use of specialized workforce. Employees that take care of installation and configuration of software systems are a valuable though rather expensive way of effectively deploying software, Java applications included. Despite the fact that it may look quite strange to mix concepts as diverse as a JRE with deployment workforce, for completeness, we will consider those concepts as legitimate deployment "means."

There are, of course, many other deployment technologies that we don't mention here, such as general application management systems (we mention them briefly in Appendix C, "Other Deployment Technologies"). The following proposed list is intended to be flexible, to be expanded on a per-case basis, and to include all the needed situation-specific tools (just like the deployment services list discussed in the previous section).

The deployment "means" we will consider are as follows:

- JDK 1.0.2
- JRE 1.1.x
- J2SE JRE in its various versions
- JNLP Client + JRE
- Third-party deployment solutions
- Specialized personnel—this is assumed to be the most powerful of all the deployment means

The means listed previously imply a Java platform for the deployed software as well. Of course, each of these means can be customized and expanded to handle the given situation in

4

DESIGNING FOR
DEPLOYMENT

different ways at the developers' discretion. Other possible means could be added to the list (such as some native-support or some particular third-party deployment solution, for example).

We will assume that the chosen deployment means is the same as the application to be deployed. One can imagine cases where this is not true; for example, we could use the Plug-In technology (that is, J2SE) for deploying Java 1.x code. Although theoretically possible, it is quite unusual in real cases because it implies the installation of two different Java environments, and only one will be used for the application execution. Anyway, this could be needed when deploying legacy code. (This case is discussed in the Chapter 6.)

Deployment Design Box

Let's introduce a simple graphical instrument that will ease the exposition of deployment design options for our software.

In the diagram shown in Figure 4.1, we have the planned deployment services on the y-axis and the means to obtain them on the x-axis. A point on such a diagram express graphically how many deployment services a Java software employs in relation with the potentiality of the current means employed.

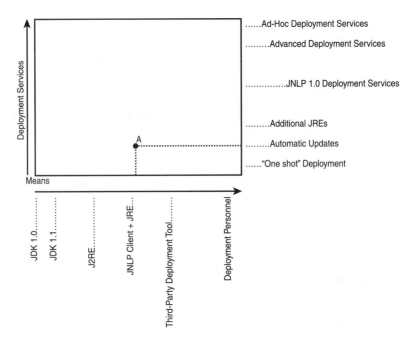

FIGURE 4.1

The Deployment Design Box.

This type of diagram has many limits (for example, it assumes that services are contained in a hierarchical fashion, it is not always true, it is highly imprecise, and so on). It was designed mainly to better introduce and discuss some common situations. Nevertheless, it can be adapted to a great variety of real cases (modifying the values used on the axis) and purposes (as we will see in some examples in the next section).

Another important aspect is the *cost* associated with the points (that are deployment circuits instances) on the diagram. Cost is a generic term, used here to indicate various parameters such as license fees (JNLP is free, but another third-party technology may not be), the complexity posed to the end-user, or other parameters. It depends on the situation and the current economic constraints. Costs are intuitively progressing from bottom-left (simpler means for simpler deployment services, so cheaper) to top-right (more powerful circuits, so more expensive).

In the following section, we will see some uses of the proposed diagram.

Sets of Deployment Circuits

We said that each point in a deployment design diagram represents a particular deployment circuit. Hence, sets of such points represent a collection of deployment circuits, such as area A in Figure 4.2.

The area B indicates the set of all the possible deployment circuits that can be implemented using the standard JNLP 1.0 technology; that is, customizing the technology without adding further services by means of some proprietary code that takes advantage of some JNLP features.

NOTE

As we will see, it is a common practice to extend deployment means with specifically developed code in order to implement more easily a given set of deployment services, as discussed following.

We will examine plenty of such areas in the following section.

Showing the Limits of Each Deployment Technology

Figure 4.3 illustrates a possible use of the Deployment Design Box. A point on the diagram in Figure 4.3 represents a deployment circuit described by the employed Java technologies (horizontally) and the given deployment services provided (vertical axis). The dotted curve describes the level of services available when employing a given Java technology (the "means" horizontal axis).

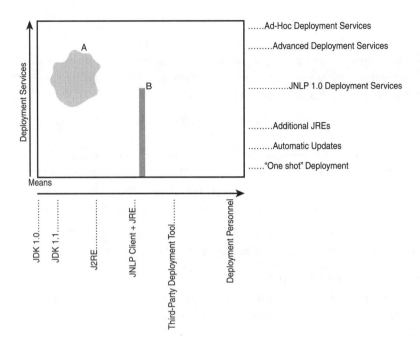

FIGURE 4.2
The Deployment Design Box showing sets of deployment circuits.

In the shaded area above the dotted line, extra coding effort must be provided by developers in order to obtain the related deployment services. For example, it is possible to provide a full-fledged deployment circuit implementing some sophisticated deployment services with a Java 1.0.2 platform (point A in the diagram), but it really makes no practical sense given the amount of work needed. It would be more sensible to switch to a newer Java environment such as Java 2 or, if that is not possible, to consider the purchase of a third-party deployment solution (point B).

Let's suppose we want to achieve the same level of services as A and B using the JNLP technology. Given that JNLP 1.0 doesn't provide such services (point C on the dotted line), we are forced to implement them by ourselves. The work needed for implementing such services is represented by the arrow W. Choosing this option (JNLP deployment technology plus some coding and testing effort) bring us to point D. Which is the better alternative depends on the cost of Java developers compared to the license fees of the chosen third-party technology, plus the cost of devoting some internal staff to the study of the commercial tool.

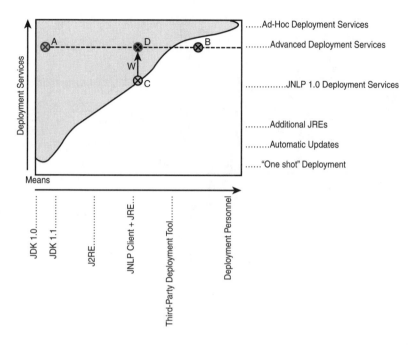

FIGURE 4.3
The Deployment Design Box showing the so-called ad-hoc area.

Comparing Different Java Deployment Means

Let's see another use of these diagrams for comparing different Java deployment technologies.

An installer utility can deploy any Java software, independently of whichever technology it is supposed to run on, but it usually provides no deployment services apart from the one-shot installation. This is represented in Figure 4.4 with the shaded box at the right of the diagram.

By contrast, employing a specialized workforce for software deployment allows for a much more powerful range of deployment services. Theoretically, almost any deployment service could be implemented by skilled employees. This is represented in Figure 4.4 by the vertical box on the right.

The third area in Figure 4.4, by contrast, represents the set of all the deployment circuits that can be established free of charge; that is, affording only the customization effort provided by the deployment engineer. This is possible thanks to the availability of JREs and JNLP Clients with no additional fees.

4

DESIGNING FOR DEPLOYMENT

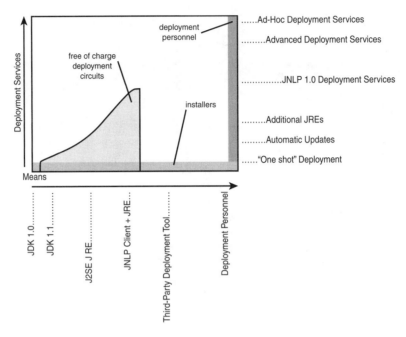

FIGURE 4.4

A diagram comparing different deployment solutions.

Despite the deployment circuits that can be implemented with installer utilities overlap with those that could be created with the free JNLP or the Plug-In technology, other parameters apart from mere feasibility should be taken into account, such as the ease of packaging, the power of deployed application, and so on.

Diagrams such as Figure 4.4 depict only deployment-related information, while giving no details about the constraints the given technology imposes on deployed applications. Thus, Figure 4.4 says nothing about the fact that an applet is somehow limited in some of its functionalities if not properly signed, or that a JNLP-deployed application can take advantage of runtime services not available to normal, stand-alone applications.

Improving an Existing Deployment Circuit

Another use of the deployment box is to graphically represent the options available when we want to upgrade the services provided by our already deployed software (such as any software, deployment circuits are subject to revisions and enhancements too).

Let's take an apparently simple case of an old JDK 1.1.x application deployed using a commercial installer utility (point A in Figure 4.5). It is time now to provide automatic updates to our software because competitors are pressing with new releases. We have different options. Referring to Figure 4.5, we have to choose a point on the line L1.

After a quick market search, we discover that the available third-party tools are too expensive for our budget. Hence, the most obvious choice is to implement in-house the wanted service, without changing the Java edition and saving all other costs but development. This option is represented by point B in Figure 4.5.

Other choices are possible, though. Point C corresponds to using a standard J2SE JRE, implementing our old application as an applet and using the Plug-In facility included into the JRE distribution. This has a cost in porting the existing software to the Java 2 platform and transforming it in an applet, but then there are no other costs for the developers.

The other possible option is to employ the JNLP technology (point D). This way, automatic updates are achieved by the locally installed JNLP client, and only the porting from JDK 1.1.x to J2SE is needed.

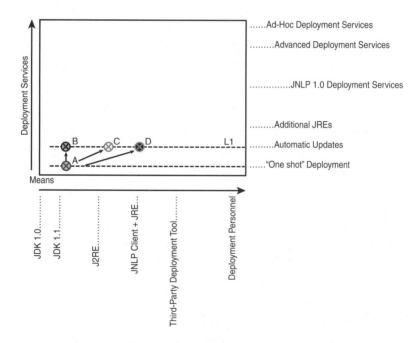

FIGURE 4.5

The Deployment Design Box used for studying alternative deployment solutions.

Each arrival point (that implies a different deployment circuit enhancement strategy) has its own characteristics. Point B implies some coding effort that is absent in the other choices. On the other hand, Points C and D need a code upgrade to J2SE; this could be a problem in some cases.

Concrete examples of adding deployment services to old Java code are discussed in Chapter 6.

4

DESIGNING FOR
DEPLOYMENT

> **NOTE**
>
> We can note another feature of deployment design diagrams. When we move from one point to another *vertically* and the arrival point lies in the gray area of Figure 4.3, we need an in-house coding effort to implement that deployment service. Instead, when we move *horizontally*, we change the deployment means, and this impacts mostly on the client-side, as we will discuss later.

After having introduced the main concepts that will guide us through the planning of our deployment solution, we will use them to discuss the possible alternatives.

A Deployment Method

Having introduced some useful concepts, we are ready to illustrate a methodology for taming the Java deployment issue. It is a simple steps sequence that is intended as a first guideline that can be adapted as needed.

We propose the following procedure for approaching the deployment design:

1. Decide which deployment services you need, among those previously defined or others.

2. Choose the wanted deployment technology. There are mainly two choices: to use a standard, ready-to-use deployment technology or to write yourself the code that implements the wanted deployment circuit, building on top of one of the Java deployment means listed before.

3. After the deployment services and the means to provide them are chosen, the deployment engineer will carry out the implementation of the specifications obtained in the preceding two steps. We will see below how this step can be divided in other substeps.

Let's see some details of the proposed steps.

Choosing Deployment Services

This step is quite delicate because a wrong decision could be disastrous in a later stage. A more powerful deployment circuit than needed could seem an unnecessary waste at first, but it may leave room for future enhancements. On the contrary, underestimating the level of needed deployment services could tamper future application upgrades (if any) or even imply to re-deploy completely the AHs (i.e. the deployment circuits clients) on all the client installations.

Graphically, it amounts to drawing a horizontal line on the Deployment Design Box at the given service level. Figure 4.6 shows the line corresponding to the On-The-Run Debugging service (see the abstract model in Chapter 2) that we considered as an advanced deployment service.

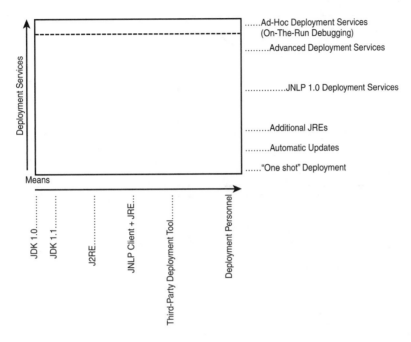

FIGURE 4.6
The Deployment Design Box used for choosing a deployment service.

Note that we have inserted the wanted service name in the vertical axis, above the "Advanced Deployment Services" (that is, those provided by advanced third-party deployment tools). Given that this special service is not provided by any deployment tool on the market, we categorized it as an "Ad-Hoc Deployment Service."

It is important to be aware of the chosen technology effect for clients. In fact, choosing a given technology also has an impact on end users.

Choosing Deployment Means

After we decide which deployment services we want to employ for our application, we choose the deployment technology that will implement those services. Figure 4.7 shows this graphically. We individuate the point A that corresponds to a precise deployment circuit.

Also note that the planned point in Figure 4.7 lies above the curve (introduced in Figure 4.3 and depicted in Figure 4.7, as well), meaning that our chosen deployment circuit must be implemented in-house, specializing the set of deployment services provided by JNLP.

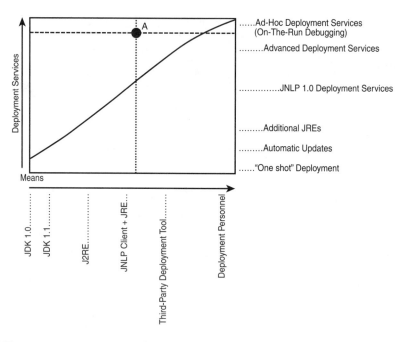

FIGURE 4.7

The Deployment Design Box used for choosing a deployment means.

The chosen deployment circuit (point A in Figure 4.7) is ready to be implemented. We will use the JNLP technology (that is a suitable JNLP Client, like Java Web Start on client computers and a JNLP server utility on the deployment Web server) with some custom code that will implement the wanted extra-services (in this case, a runtime remote debugging facility) for our client applications.

Implementing the Designed Deployment Circuit

Depending on the choice we made in the previous stage, this activity could be as easy as writing down an XML file and some JAR files, or as complex as implementing a whole deployment solution from scratch.

In the following discussion, we will use the term "application resources" for generic files (JRE installation package, Java sources, images, and so on) that compose the application. After the deployment engineer processes them, we obtain a set of *deployment resources*; that is, another set of files that is ready to be published for deployment. Deployment resources are simply the application resources properly packaged.

Adapting a Standard Deployment Solution

In this case, the sequence of activities could be carried out as follows (we will see in detail any of the subsequent items following).

1. Identify all the application resources.

2. Organize the application resources in modules.

3. Implement the modules using the chosen deployment technology, producing all the needed material (JAR and XML files, Web pages, and so on) for the proper deployment.

4. Once deployment resources are ready, they need to be transferred on the deployment server, eventually providing some server tuning, and so on.

It is interesting to see how often developers take for granted the many application resources they employ in their applications, especially if they use an integrated development tool (IDE). There could be many types of such resources; a brief list will make the discussion more concrete:

- A given JRE, needed in order to run the application, is an application resource

- The complete set of classes, icons, properties files and all other application-specific resources

- Proprietary and third-party libraries that the application code relies upon

- Other resources (required optional packages, native libraries, and so on)

The number of such resources could be great; and new releases, modifications and other common accidents in a software lifetime may transform deployment (especially for non-trivial deployment services) into a nightmare. To tackle this source of complexity, deployment engineers can resort to organize application resources in groups, called *modules*. Such groups should comply with a simple rule: Together they have to cover all the application resources, and they should avoid to overlap their contents. This way, modules would form a strict decomposition of the application resources set. Thus, all the needed pieces are transferred to clients without useless repetitions. Modules can be tagged with several data such as platform dependencies, language specialization, version, compatibility list with other modules, and so on. This way, modules will stay more organized, and it will be easy to maintain even the most chaotic set of application resources. Often, deployment engineers make use of concepts borrowed from Software Configuration Management (SCM), a discipline we will discuss in a section at the end of this chapter, in order to organize more effectively the many configurations of items they have to manage.

This issue is not restricted only to the deployment development phase, but also to the entire application lifecycle. Let's consider, for example, an application that makes use of add-on

4

DESIGNING FOR DEPLOYMENT

components downloaded via our deployment circuit. New versions of such add-ons are progressively released, and the end-user population could have a widely diverse assortment of add-ons. For easier client configurations, tracking and debugging the organization of resources in modules is essential in this case. The many possible combinations of installed modules can be tracked easily. Modules could be thought of as linking application and deployment resources.

Once all modules are defined (and even before, their basic structure is thought out), we are ready to map such modules onto the deployment technology constructs in order to begin the implementation of our deployment circuit.

Unfortunately, each deployment solution handles such a concept (grouping of resources) in a different way, and often provides more than one clustering mechanism, thus confusing deployment engineers. We will see in Chapter 13, "A Complete Example," a concrete yet simple example of what is said here, which uses the JNLP technology as the chosen deployment means.

The concrete "creation" of deployment resources organized in modules follows the particular deployment technology chosen. Often, it will involve the packaging of application resources sets into JAR files and the creation of other support files.

Once all the deployment resources are created and the deployment mechanism has been tested, all the pieces are ready to be published on the deployment server, packaged in a CD-ROM, and so on.

Implementing an Ad-Hoc Deployment Solution

When you need a transport means for delivering your lovingly crafted products to your customer, you go to the deployment means salon for picking what your pockets can afford. Depending on the circumstances peculiar to your situation, you may discover that no off-the-shelf deployment product is good for you. You have no choice but to build yourself your own deployment means. Usually, you will not begin completely from scratch; instead, you will assemble some pieces together, adding your own code on top of them (a practical example of this situation is given in Chapter 7, "Building Your Own Deployment Solution," with the *deploylet* package). Of course, before undertaking such a complex activity, you should ask yourself if it is worth building it, and if you don't have any simpler (and cheaper) solutions at hand. Third-party advanced deployment solutions, the JNLP protocols, and the commercially-available installation packager utilities are all sound and valid deployment means that cover a wide range of scenarios and that allow for a rich customization. Unfortunately, there are several cases where their use is not possible.

In these limited cases, some extra activities have to be carried out (in addition to those of the preceding section):

1. Planning the ad-hoc deployment solution

2. Designing the (possibly client-server) architecture

3. Studying how to define and implement client configurations, deployment policies and annotated resources

4. Implementing, testing, and releasing all the planned items

Implementing a complete deployment solution is not a simple task, and involves so many variables that a general discussion would be inevitably either too long or too shallow. We will devote the entire Chapter 7 to this issue by providing practical code.

While traditional client-server systems have been thoroughly studied and many technologies are available to developers, the implementation of a deployment circuit may need to address some peculiar problems that developers are seldom experienced with solving. For instance, malfunctions in application helpers are quite difficult to fix once the product is deployed because AHs are located remotely on a potentially great number of client platforms, and customers rely on them to run their products. Providing a "self-deploying" AH, although a possible solution, makes the engineering task even harder. We will see an example of such a design shortcoming in a concrete example of Chapter 6.

Nevertheless, developers can use the abstract model of Chapter 2 as a concrete design aid, especially in the analysis phase, in which requirements and domain-related concepts have to be quickly and effectively nailed down. This, together with some general advice from client-server and network-oriented technical books, will provide a satisfactorily sound foundation for a professional deployment solution development.

Finally, a last note about the role of the AH. Often, it is not necessary to provide such a facility; depending on the wanted deployment circuits and the particular situation, one can avoid the implementation of such a complex piece of software. In Chapter 7, we will see a complete deployment solution that, by taking advantage of a particular scenario, is able to provide an extremely wide range of deployment services without the implementation of an ad-hoc AH.

First Installation Problem

This issue, particularly important for Java applications, deserves a brief additional discussion.

As we saw in Chapter 1 and mentioned in Chapter 2 as well, the most peculiar aspect of deploying a Java application is the problem of how to install the desired (and up-to-date) JRE on the client platform. While this is not a problem for J2ME and JavaCard-compliant devices (because they come already with a preinstalled, reliable JRE), it turns out to be a sensitive issue for desktop computers. As we said in Chapter 1, maybe the real hurdle for a wide expansion of Java on this class of computing platforms is not the performance issue (that is constantly increasing, thanks to new JVM technologies) but rather the bulky size of the JRE installation package, especially for non-English locales (worsened by eventual optional packages and third-party libraries). If this problem cannot be solved completely, it may be eased by careful deployment planning. Technologies such as JNLP and almost all other third-party deployment tools provide mechanisms to preinstall a JRE on the client platform. Some ad-hoc mechanisms can be devised, too, for answering to more problematic situations (Chapter 7 shows several ad-hoc solutions that provide the JRE installation, too).

Furthermore, another important (and often neglected) aspect is that the strategy to solve the first installation problem has to consider the end-user as well. One of the key factors (so often overlooked by developers) for choosing the best option for solving this issue is to know which kind of user is going to interact with the application. This problem gets less decisive in those environments in which users are somehow required to use certain applications (as in corporate intranet environments) and in which you can assume end-users will undertake a complex (from an inexperienced user viewpoint) installation procedure.

We will touch this issue often in the remaining of this chapter and in other chapters as well. Chapter 13 provides a concrete discussion of these topics for the JNLP technology.

In the following section, we will take another approach—discussing together the most recurring situations.

Common Scenarios

In this section, we will briefly describe the possible options, depending on the type of communication channel between the deployment server and the client platform.

Web-Based Deployment

In this section, we will discuss application deployment via the Internet. This scenario is potentially the most difficult to face for Java developers because of several reasons:

- The first-time installation problem is quite critical, especially when connection bandwidth or reliability is an issue.
- A high degree of control on end-users is required. That is, given the high cost of the first-time installation (from an end-user perspective), Java-deployed applications tend to be disadvantaged compared with other native deployment solutions.
- A greater complexity is needed to accommodate a potentially large set of different client configurations, such as supported platforms (Linux, Mac, Windows, Solaris, AIX, and so on), different locales, or geographical nearness issues.

All these issues can be addressed using a very basic deployment circuit (downloading an installation package, for instance) or using some specialized deployment solution. In the latter case, the JNLP technology is often the most common choice.

Intranet Deployment

Intranet deployment is based on the same technologies as Web-based deployment, but offers several advantages for developers:

- In an intranet environment, developers have a tighter control over the client platforms and the connection with the deployment server. This permits the establishment of more sophisticated deployment circuits. For example, a very common feature is the automatic update of deployed software. This allows developers of in-house software to release their products earlier while taking advantage of the testing done by more experienced users for software debugging. The patched-up application modules will be newly deployed (often in a totally transparent way to end-users) on client platforms. This can shorten dramatically the whole software lifecycle. A concrete example of taking advantage of such an environment is reported in Chapter 7.

- Also, the type of users and their possible platform configurations are more predictable, allowing for a simpler deployment preparation.

In such a "privileged" environment, more sophisticated services are possible, even using less-powerful deployment technologies. Nevertheless, the ease of installation of more sophisticated deployment technologies can favor the use of such technologies for shortening software development time (including its deployment). Figure 4.8 shows an example of such a situation.

In Figure 4.8, JNLP is used for providing automatic updates of an intranet application. Other simpler technologies would have sufficed as well, but using JNLP will save developers time and work. The amount of work developers have been "saved" could be intuitively depicted with the W arrows in Figure 4.8 (it is as if JNLP performed that work on their behalf). Point B is what they could achieve with the JNLP technology, and point A is the level of service they needed in this case. Of course, they are somehow wasting much of the JNLP power. There is nothing wrong with such a "misuse" in this case. The fact is that often such power comes associated with some additional costs (fees or, as in this case, a possibly heavier end-user burden).

We will see several examples of deployment for this scenario (among the others, see the code examples provided in Chapter 7). Like the Web deployment case, JNLP is a safe solution when combined with the Plug-In technology.

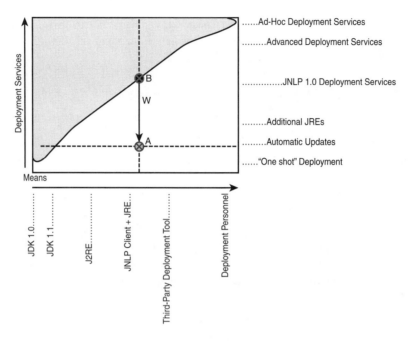

FIGURE 4.8
Using JNLP only for automatic updates.

Deployment via a Physical Support

This deployment option is still quite popular and attractive for developers and marketing staff, given the low costs of such deployment supports and the ability to reach otherwise inaccessible customers. In Chapter 7, we will see a concrete example of such an option. What is interesting to note here is that often such an alternative is used as a way to distribute software rather than a complete deployment means. Once installed, the software usually takes advantage of an existing Web connection for further deployment services. Also, JNLP and other advanced deployment tools can be used for this type of support. This option is quite attractive when deployment via a CD-ROM is part of a more general deployment strategy, as discussed in the next case.

Multiple Deployment

Of course, the deployment strategies previously described can be used together, obtaining the advantages of all the single deployment techniques. A common way to proceed is to package the application for Internet deployment (thus covering both the intranet and Web channels) and then packaging it on a CD-ROM for physical distribution. In this case, the standard general-purpose deployment means such as JNLP and some third-party deployment tools are best suited to handle this kind of deployment because deployment engineers can package their application once and deploy it seamlessly through several different channels. In Chapter 7, we provide an example of ad-hoc deployment using CD-ROMs.

Client Configurations and Software Configuration Management

This section covers some advanced topics generally not needed in simpler cases, but required for a sound resource management in more complex situations. We already mentioned how configuration techniques could be useful for managing modules and the various resources involved in the deployment.

We will focus on the client side of the abstract model exposed in Chapter 2. In doing so, we will slightly change our approach, making it become more practical. We will mention the more important concepts in the software-configuration discipline, whose principles are useful to rigorously set out and successively manage any non-trivial software deployment.

First of all, let's see what configuration management is all about. *Configuration management (CM)* is a discipline for controlling generic items over their whole lifecycle. These items are organized in *configurations*—sets of both hardware or software units treated like a single logical entity. There are four distinctive elements in any configuration management activity:

- Configuration Identification. Identify and document the characteristics of configuration items.
- Configuration Control. It is necessary to control changes to configurations and their related documentation.
- Configuration Status Accounting. Record and report the information needed to manage configuration items.
- Auditing. To verify the conformance of the configuration items to given specifications and contractual requirements. Despite an important part of CM, we won't see it here. We are interested in using the SCM discipline for purposes other than contractual ones.

Software configuration management (SCM) is the application of configuration management to software systems. When applied to software artifacts, the previous first three activities become the following ones.

- Configuration Identification. At any given time, the configuration of the software could be identified. This involves using a consistent versioning notation.
- Configuration Control. Software configuration changes are systematically recorded. Although this is always the case during software development, it may turn out to be useful or even necessary for software deployment.

- Configuration Status Accounting. The *traceability* of the software configuration is maintained throughout the software lifecycle.

We won't get into the details of software configuration management because it is beyond the scope of this book. Here, we are interested in using SCM techniques to rationally organize and manage the deployment process. Naturally, you can avoid using such techniques, but it is like using your credit card without ever controlling your bank account. Though easier at first, it may become dangerous in the future.

Note

Though the best way to proceed is through the use of rigorous SCM techniques, for simple deployment needs some simplified SCM techniques could be used instead—saving time and producing the desired benefit.

A simple and effective way to keep your software deployment under control is to use the client configuration concept.

Client Configurations

A *client configuration* can be defined as the set of all the items that are meaningful for our Java software from a deployment perspective.

For example, a client configuration could be composed of the user identity, a given JRE, and a set of JAR files that compose our application.

Basically, it is a snapshot of what we need to have properly installed on a client computer in order to run our application. Note that the platform type itself is a part of the client configuration. So, if we plan to provide two platform-dependent versions of our software, we need to have at least two different client configurations.

A client configuration is the exact description of what minimally has to be installed on the client platform in order to run the application. One can extend this concept to include in it the user identity or other client-specific data that are meaningful for deployment.

Two Examples

An application is described by the following client configuration.

Parameter	Value
JRE	Sun 1.2.2-004
Optional Packages	JAI 1.0 for Solaris
	Java3D 1.2 for Solaris
Application Resources	file "`my-app-2.0.jar`"
	file "`my-lib-1.3.jar`"
	file "`res-1.1.zip`"
OS	Solaris on Sparc

Another application is described by the following client configuration.

Parameter	Value
JRE	Sun 1.2.2-004
Application Resources	file "`my-app-2.0.jar`"
	file "`my-lib-1.1.jar`"
Available Memory	at least 256 MB
OS	Windows

The formalism used here is only demonstrative; every deployment solution has its own notation for managing resources.

Common Case

Usually a client configuration for a Java application is an instance of the following parameters:

- The JRE that executes the application
- Needed optional packages (if running on a J2SE environment)
- Third-party Java libraries
- Native libraries
- Native resources (platform-dependent executables, and so on)
- Underlying OS, eventually specifying its hardware architecture (for example, Solaris on x86)
- User identity, meaningful for the deployment process
- All application resource files: JAR, ZIP, or any other file that composes the application

Many other parameters could be used when needed, such as initial heap size, locale, and so on when meaningful for the deployment process. In Part III, we will discuss in detail how client configurations are described under the JNLP technology. A very simple example of a deployment server that records all of its client's configurations is given in Chapter 6.

Summary

This chapter covered the design of deployment circuits from a developer's perspective. After illustrating some introductory concepts (deployment services, Deployment Design Boxes, and so on), we proposed a standard general procedure for designing the deployment support for our application. We discussed some of the more interesting aspects connected to deployment design.

With this chapter, we concluded the theoretical discussion of Java deployment. The remaining chapters of this book will all provide example code eventually accompanied with some theoretical advice.

Chapter 5 will cover some examples of deployment for non-J2SE Java platforms.

Deployment Options for
Non-J2SE Clients

IN THIS CHAPTER

In this chapter, we will cover the deployment of Java editions different from J2SE.

This book is mainly devoted to Java programs designed to run on desktop machines, using Java 2 Standard Edition or version 1.x of the Java platform. This is due to the large amount of interest the issue of deployment has in such cases. Despite this, there are two other areas of Java that need our attention: the Java 2 Micro Edition (J2ME) with all its configurations and profiles and the Java 2 Enterprise Edition (J2EE). We don't have the space to fully address the topic of software deployment for such platforms, neither would it be especially useful (for instance, there are already a great number of books published about J2EE deployment).

We will also cover the deployment of Java Card applets. They could be considered a world apart (even from J2ME) given the peculiarity of the hardware they run on, but they are an interesting case of Java code deployment.

Overview

Some platforms where Java programs can run are presented together with their related Java 2 edition in Figure 5.1. This figure doesn't mention all possible platforms (for instance, one can think of network computers, Internet screen phones, card devices, etc.).

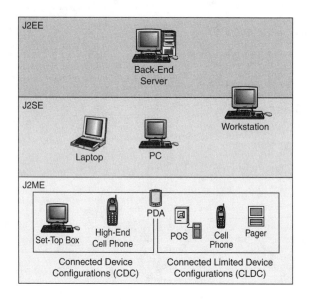

FIGURE 5.1

Java 2-enabled devices.

In Figure 5.1, we can see that J2ME is currently split into two parts, or *configurations*, as briefly explained in Chapter 1, "Deploying Java." We will discuss J2ME deployment options in the next section.

J2ME Deployment

Deploying J2ME code depends on the configuration and the profile in exam. Providing a full exposition of such a broad topic is beyond the scope of this book. Instead, after a minimal introduction to the J2ME platform, we will focus on the MID Profile (MIDP) for mobile devices. This includes support for wireless phones, two-way pagers, and other mobile devices.

An Introduction to J2ME

J2ME is different from other Java 2 editions in that APIs, physical input/output facilities, and available memory vary greatly from one device to another. This could be a problem if the same application were to be deployed on different classes of devices. Fortunately, this is rarely the case.

> **NOTE**
>
> Indeed, the J2ME architecture has been built with the tacit assumption that the case of "cross-development," spanning different profiles on possibly different configurations was a very rare case in common practice.

To harness all this complexity while preserving the advantages of the Java platform (portability, security, and a high-level language widespread among developers), Sun engineers have devised a particular architecture, composed of a few configurations for defining the common features for a class of devices. These configurations comprise the virtual machine, core libraries, and some APIs, while leaving the differences of each device to be described by a so-called profile.

Profiles are thought to gather together not only common devices (such as cell phones) but also common applications.

The two configurations currently provided for the J2ME platform are the following:

- **Connected Limited Device Configuration (CLDC).** Designed for devices with constrained hardware resources (principally CPU and memory). Typically, such devices run on either a 16- or 32-bit CPU with 512 Kbytes or less memory available for client applications and the Java platform itself.

- **Connected Device Configuration (CDC).** Essentially, this configuration is designed for next-generation devices with more robust resources than CLDCs. Typically, these devices run on a 32-bit CPU, and have at least 2MB of RAM totally available for the Java platform and client applications.

One requirement among device manufacturers is the capability to dynamically change the features provided by the device. That is, the software is not hard-coded within the device once and for all, but could be to some extent dynamically loaded. Here, deployment techniques come into play. We discussed in the previous chapter the design issues related with Java deployment that still apply here.

The configurations don't address lifecycle issues (installation, launching, and removal), leaving these and other features to their profiles. Consequently, we are obliged to discuss deployment issues on a profile basis. This would be beyond the scope of this book, so we will see in detail the deployment of only one interesting profile, the Mobile Information Device Profile (MIDP).

Deploying MIDlets

The *Mobile Information Device Profile (MIDP)* is a set of Java APIs that, together with the Connected Limited Device Configuration (CLDC), provides a complete J2ME application environment. It defines issues such as user interface, the application model, networking, and persistence storage for mobile devices such as cellular phones and two-way pagers.

The code proposed here was developed and executed on the J2ME Wireless Toolkit from Sun, available at `http://www.javasoft.com/products/j2mewtoolkit/`.

Application Descriptor Files

An application descriptor file is a text file, encoded with Unicode, with the suffix .JAD. It is made up of text lines composed as follows:

```
[attribute-name]+': '+[value]
```

Such attributes can be read by MIDlets using the static method `MIDlet.getAppProperty`. Listing 5.1 shows an example of a JAD file.

LISTING 5.1 An Example Of a Java Application Descriptor (JAD) File

```
MIDlet-Name: MIDletApplication
MIDlet-Version: 0.0.1
MIDlet-Vendor: myself
MIDlet-Jar-URL: http://www.myself.org/apps/app.jar
MIDlet-Jar-Size: 1234
MIDlet-Data-Size: 256
```

Attributes in a JAD file can be divided into two main groups, depending on whether they are required or not.

Required attributes in every JAD file are the following:

- `MIDlet-Name`. Specifies the name of the application that will be shown to the user.
- `MIDlet-Jar-URL`. The URL from where the JAR file can be downloaded.
- `MIDlet-Version`. The MIDlet version.
- `MIDlet-Vendor`. The MIDlet vendor.
- `MIDlet-Jar-Size`. The size of the JAR file

Optional attributes for JAD files:

- `MIDlet-Data-Size`. The minimum number of bytes of persistent data required by the MIDlet. The device should ensure that this memory is available to the application to be run, while it can optionally provide more.
- `MIDlet-Description`. A brief description for the user.
- `MIDlet-Info-URL`. A link to the application home page.
- `MIDlet-Icon`. An icon that (depending on the particular device) will be associated with the application. The PNG image file format is used.
- Application-specific attributes are used to configure the MIDlet via its JAD file. These are attributes (and values) read only by the MIDlet. For example, the following line in a JAD file would indicate to the MIDlet to be launched the configuration property:

```
prompt-user-at-startup: true
```

NOTE

Attributes beginning with "`MIDLet-`" are thought to be "system" attributes, and are reserved. Application-specific attributes cannot begin with the "`MIDlet-`" prefix.

Other attributes (such as `MicroEdition-Profile` and `MicroEdition-Configuration`), together with some of those presented previously, can be specified in the JAR file itself as an entry in the MANIFEST.MF file.

An Example

We will show an example of a MIDlet application deployment that uses some extra deployment services—in this case, a license utility for registering unlicensed copies of the software. The application is deployed on the client wireless device, thanks to the JAD file shown in Listing 5.2.

LISTING 5.2 The Application Descriptor for Our Application

```
MIDlet-1: amid, /splash.png, com.marinilli.b2.c5.AMIDLet
MIDlet-Jar-Size: 7296
MIDlet-Jar-URL: amid.jar
MIDlet-Name: AMIDLet
MIDlet-Vendor: Maurosystems
MIDlet-Version: 1.0
```

The application class source is shown in Listing 5.3.

LISTING 5.3 The AMIDlet Class.

```
package com.marinilli.b2.c5;

import javax.microedition.midlet.*;
import javax.microedition.lcdui.*;
/**
 * Chapter 5 - A Sample MIDlet
 *
 *
 * @author Mauro Marinilli
 * @version 1.0
 */

public class AMIDLet extends MIDlet implements CommandListener{
  private List mainList;
  private MIDLicenseManager licenseManager;

  /**
   * Constructor
   */
  public AMIDLet() {
    licenseManager = new MIDLicenseManager(this);
  }

  /**
   * Invoked when the MIDlet is paused
   */
  protected void pauseApp() {
  }

  /**
   * for cleaning up resources
   */
  protected void destroyApp(boolean parm1) throws MIDletStateChangeException {
    licenseManager = null;
```

LISTING 5.3 Continued

```java
    mainList = null;
  }

  /**
   * To launch the MIDlet
   */
  protected void startApp() throws MIDletStateChangeException {
    mainList = new List("Select a Number",
                        List.IMPLICIT,
                        new String[] {"Option 1","Option 2","Option 3",
➡"Register"},
                        null);

    Display.getDisplay(this).setCurrent(mainList);
    mainList.setCommandListener(this);
  }

  /**
   * handles user commands
   */
  public void commandAction(Command c, Displayable d) {
    int pos = mainList.getSelectedIndex();
    if (pos==3){
      licenseManager.register();
    }

    try {
      show("Hello!", "OK?");
    }
    catch(Exception err) {
      show("Error", "general exception");
    }
  }

  /**
   * utility method to show modal alerts
   */
  private void show(String title, String txt){
    Alert a = new Alert(title);
    a.setString(txt);
    a.setTimeout(Alert.FOREVER);
    Display.getDisplay(this).setCurrent(a);
  }

}
```

In Listing 5.3 (lines 41–49), the MIDlet is started with the standard startApp method, prompting the user with a list of options (the MIDlet main menu). The commandAction method (lines 54–66), similar to the actionPerformed method, handles user commands from the option list (as it registered for, at line 48). Some methods pertain to the MIDlet lifecycle: pauseApp, destroyApp, startApp.

Only the "register" option triggers a real action (it activates the license registering form in line 57), whereas all other options will show a fake message (line 61). The show method at lines 71–76 simply shows a full-screen message until the user explicitly closes it.

When launched via the Sun MIDlet emulator, our simple program opens up showing an option list, as shown in Figure 5.2.

FIGURE 5.2

The sample application at work.

When the user selects the registration option, the MIDLicenseManager is invoked (line 57 in Listing 5.3) for starting the registration procedure, whose menu is shown in Figure 5.3.

NOTE

The MIDLicenseManager class is general-purpose and not bound to the particular application code used for launching it. See following for a discussion of this class.

FIGURE 5.3
The user requests to register its copy.

As an aside, one of the more characteristic challenges when writing MIDLets is the ability to produce cross-device usable software, especially when it comes to screen management and user interaction. Depending on the kind of device the MIDlet is running on, the screen size and overall user interaction may change very much. Figure 5.4 shows the same communication as Figure 5.3, but with the MIDlet running on a pager device.

FIGURE 5.4
The user types in the license data into a two-way pager.

Getting back to the MIDlet interaction, once the user filled in the registration form, the data is sent (wirelessly or with other device-dependent type of connection) to a Web server, where it is evaluated. If the license id and password are valid, a positive response is returned to the MIDlet, and the message in Figure 5.5 is shown to the user.

FIGURE 5.5
The response of the registration procedure.

In order for this mechanism to work, a servlet is needed for handling the server side. The servlet is presented in this same chapter, in the J2EE section, as an example of J2EE deployment.

The interesting piece here is the MIDLicenseManager class, reported in Listing 5.4.

LISTING 5.4 The MIDLicenseManager Class

```
package com.marinilli.b2.c5;

import javax.microedition.io.*;
import javax.microedition.midlet.*;
import javax.microedition.rms.*;
import javax.microedition.lcdui.*;
import java.io.*;

/**
 * Chapter 5 - A General Purpose, Simple License Manager
 *
 * @author Mauro Marinilli
 * @version 1.0
 */

public class MIDLicenseManager implements CommandListener {
  private RecordStore keyStore;
```

LISTING 5.4 Continued

```java
  private MIDlet midlet;
  private String licenseId = "";
  private String passwd = "";
  private Form form;
  private TextField idTextField;
  private TextField pwdTextField;
  private final static String SERVER_URL = "http://localhost:8080/license/
➥midp?license-id=";
  private boolean successfullyRegistered = false;
  private Displayable returnDisplayable;

  /**
   *
   */
  public MIDLicenseManager(MIDlet m) {
    midlet = m;
    // Create a new record store for keys for this midlet suite
    try {
      keyStore = RecordStore.openRecordStore("keys", true);
      int items = keyStore.getNumRecords();
      System.out.println("items="+items);
      if (items > 0) {
        String roughLicenseId = new String(keyStore.getRecord(1));
        if (roughLicenseId!=null)
          licenseId = unscramble(roughLicenseId);
        String roughPasswd = new String(keyStore.getRecord(2));
        if (roughPasswd!=null)
          passwd = unscramble(roughPasswd);
      } else {
        // the recordstore has to be initialized
        String n = "";
        keyStore.addRecord(n.getBytes(), 0, n.getBytes().length);
        keyStore.addRecord(n.getBytes(), 0, n.getBytes().length);
      }
    } catch (RecordStoreException rse) {
      System.out.println("MIDLicenseManager() "+rse);
    }
  }

  /**
   *
   */
  public boolean isLicensed() {
    return (licenseId != "");
  }
```

LISTING 5.4 Continued

```
/**
 * scrambles a string
 */
public String scramble(String s) {
  return s;
}

/**
 * un-scramble a string
 */
public String unscramble(String s) {
  return s;
}

/**
 * Registering a copy
 */
public void register(){
  returnDisplayable = Display.getDisplay(midlet).getCurrent();
  if (returnDisplayable==null)
    returnDisplayable = new Form("Hello");
  if (isLicensed()) {

    Form f = new Form("Software Already Licensed");
    f.append("Impossible to register an already registered copy.");
    f.append("Please contact support for help");
    Display.getDisplay(midlet).setCurrent(f);
    f.setCommandListener(this);
    f.addCommand(new Command("back",Command.BACK,1));
    return;
  }

  idTextField = new TextField("Insert Licensed User", "", 12,
➥ TextField.ANY);
  pwdTextField = new TextField("Insert License Code", "", 15,
➥ TextField.PASSWORD);
  form = new Form("Registration");
  form.append(idTextField);
  form.append(pwdTextField);
  form.addCommand(new Command("ok",Command.OK,1));
  form.setCommandListener(this);
  Display.getDisplay(midlet).setCurrent(form);
}
```

LISTING 5.4 Continued

```java
/**
 * connect to the license server
 */
public String connect() {
  HttpConnection c = null;
  InputStream is = null;
  OutputStream os = null;
  StringBuffer message = new StringBuffer();

  try {
    c = (HttpConnection)Connector.open(createURL());
    String outcome = c.getHeaderField("outcome");
    //in case of no connection return null
    if (outcome==null) {
      return null;
    }

    if (outcome.equals("true"))
      successfullyRegistered = true;
    // open the InputStream
    is = c.openInputStream();
    // read the servlet output
    int ch;
    while ((ch = is.read()) != -1) {
      message.append((char)ch);
    }
  } catch (Exception exc) {
    System.out.println("connect() "+exc);
  }
  return message.toString();
}

/**
 * process commands
 */
public void commandAction(Command c, Displayable d) {
  if (c.getCommandType()==Command.OK) {
    String s = "";
    Gauge gau = new Gauge("Checking License",false,8,0);
    Form frm = new Form("Please Wait.. ",new Item[] {gau});
    gau.setValue(2);
    Display.getDisplay(midlet).setCurrent(frm);
    licenseId= idTextField.getString();
    passwd = pwdTextField.getString();
```

LISTING 5.4 Continued

```
      gau.setValue(4);
      String msg = connect();
      gau.setValue(6);
      if (msg==null) {
        s = "Connection Unavailable" ;
        msg = "Please try again later.";
        licenseId = "";
        passwd = "";
      } else {
        gau.setValue(8);
        if(successfullyRegistered) {
          save(licenseId, passwd);
          s = "Registration Successful";
        } else {
          licenseId = "";
          passwd = "";
          s = "Invalid License";
        }
      }

      Form f = new Form(s);
      f.append(msg);
      Display.getDisplay(midlet).setCurrent(f);
      f.setCommandListener(this);
      f.addCommand(new Command("back",Command.BACK,1));
    }
    if (c.getCommandType()==Command.BACK) {
      Display.getDisplay(midlet).setCurrent(returnDisplayable);
    }
  }

  /**
   * save data persistently
   */
  private void save(String id, String pwd) {
    try {
      String scrambled = scramble(licenseId);
      keyStore.setRecord(1, scrambled.getBytes(), 0, scrambled.getBytes()
➥.length);

      scrambled = scramble(passwd);
      keyStore.setRecord(2, scrambled.getBytes(), 0,
➥scrambled.getBytes().length);
      //close the recordStore
```

LISTING 5.4 Continued

```
      keyStore.closeRecordStore();
    } catch (RecordStoreException rse) {
      System.out.println("MIDLicenseManager-save() "+rse);
    }
  }

  /**
   * create an URL
   */
  private String createURL(){
    return SERVER_URL + scramble(licenseId) + "&license-pwd="
➥ + scramble(passwd);
  }

}
```

In the constructor (beginning at line 31), the repository where the (encrypted) license data is stored is retrieved from the device's persistent memory. In case it is not yet present, it is created from scratch.

> **TIP**
>
> For development purposes, MIDlet emulators have a command for clearing up the persistent memory. You can use it to test out this example more than one time.

The registration procedure begins with the `register` method (lines 80–103), which prompts the user for the license data. Users would obtain these codes after purchasing the software license from a Web site, by a sales representative, and so on. After filling in the form, when the user activates the "ok" command, the `commandAction` method at line 140 is invoked. A progress bar is shown to the user while trying to connect with the server. The connection is handled by the `connect` method at lines 108–135. Then, accordingly with the connection results, the persistent data are updated (at line 160), and proper explanatory messages are shown to the user.

By means of the `isLicensed` method at lines 58–60, the client MIDlet can query the `MIDLicenseManager` instance, and can dynamically enable more features available only to registered copies.

The server URL (line 24) corresponds to the deployment scheme presented in Listing 5.12 (discussed later in the J2EE section of this chapter, together with the details of the client-server interaction).

The security implementation has been kept minimal—don't lengthen too much of the code. Methods such as `scramble` (lines 66–68) for encrypting sensitive strings and `unscramble` (lines 73–75) to decrypt them are just illustrative. Data is encrypted, both when saved persistently on the client device and when transmitted to the server for validation.

This class uses the persistence service offered by the MIDlet profile. This way, thanks to the persistent data stored in the hosting device, the `MIDLicenseManager` instance is able to recognize an already registered copy and will alert the user, as depicted in Figure 5.6.

FIGURE 5.6
The response of the registration procedure for an already registered copy.

Next, we will see another case of a non-J2SE deployment, also with a concrete example.

Java Card Applet Deployment

In this section, we will give an overview of the deployment issues of the smallest Java computing environment currently commercially used: the Java Card platform. We will begin with a brief presentation, leveraging our knowledge of other Java platforms by describing the differences and then we will see an example of deployment.

The Java Card Environment is a world apart from J2ME devices. The differences are both in the hardware limitations and a completely different lifecycle from the usual interactive applications, both in development and in execution. Another reason for this difference, as we will see, is the required compatibility with the pre-existing ISO 7816 standard for smart cards. We will give an overview of the Java Card platform in the following section.

The Java Card environment is quite interesting because of the hardware limitations and peculiarities of this kind of platform. Let's begin with the hardware. The memory configuration of a smart card could be in the order of 1KB of RAM, 16KB of EEPROM and 24KB of ROM. Of these resources, the Java Card Runtime Environment (JCRE) occupies a good part of the ROM. The remaining types of memories are left to Java Card applications, known as *applets*, because of their ability to be downloaded and executed even after the card has been issued (that is, its ROM memory has been written out).

> **NOTE**
>
> Although ROMs are written once and for all, and RAM is erased when power goes off, EEPROMs (Electrically-Erasable Programmable ROMs) are slower, but able to keep data persistently, independently from power sources.

Given this amount of resources, even the tiniest Java 2 Micro Edition environment wouldn't fit. The solution was to adopt only a subset of the Java technology. Indeed, rather than a subset, it seems like a completely new Java platform, as we will see now. We will introduce only the needed details in order to give an overview of the deployment procedure on this platform.

Supported Java Features	Unsupported Java Features
Three small primitive data types only (`boolean`, `byte`, `short`)	All large primitive data types (`long`, `double`, `float`)
Optional support for integer (`int`) primitive data type	Primitive `char` types and strings (`String` class)
One-dimensional arrays	multidimensional arrays
Single-spaced item	dynamic class loading (the whole `System` class is absent)
Java packages, classes, interfaces, and exceptions	Security Manager
All Object-Oriented features	Garbage Collection
	Serialization
	Object Cloning
	Multiple Threads

Another difference is in the standard libraries supported. Given the peculiarity of the card environment, standard libraries were completely rewritten. The system libraries available for a standard Java Card Runtime Environment (JCRE) are the following.

- `java.lang` package. A tiny subset of its counterpart for the Java 2 platform. Only a few classes are present, and these have been heavily shortened. First of all, the `Object` class provides only the default constructor and the `equals` method. Other classes in this package are `Throwable` and `Exception`; and nine subclasses, including `NullPointerException`.

- `javacard.framework` package. Provides core functionalities for Java Card applets, such as the `JCSystem` class that substitutes the `System` class in other Java platforms. The most-used classes of this package are the `Applet` class, from which all applets must subclass; the `APDU` class, which we will see in a while; and `PIN`, that is an equivalent of the password used to authenticate cardholders (PIN is an acronym for personal identification number).

- `javacard.security` and `javacardx.crypto` packages. These are intended to be used together for providing cryptographic services to card applets. They don't provide concrete implementations; these are left to the JCRE manufacturer, with the help of the underlying card vendor's implementations. Finally, a curiosity: Due to the United States export regulatory requirements, the `javacardx.crypto` package has been defined as an extension package.

Another remarkable difference is in the naming convention for packages and applets because they need to be compliant with the mentioned ISO 7816 standard for smart cards. This naming convention forces applets and packages to be identified by an application identifier (AID) sequence of bytes. Intuitively, these byte strings look similar to IP addresses, in that groups of these addresses are assigned by an external committee and then companies specify the exact address within their assigned namespace. The first five bytes represent the company id, and are assigned by the ISO external authority. Then, a variable number of bytes (from zero to 11) are defined internally by the company to name its products.

Now that we have examined the platform, we are ready to examine the card runtime environment.

The Java Card Runtime Environment

Before getting into the details of the JCRE, it is important to describe the lifecycle of an applet inside a smart card. Figure 5.7 describes it, highlighting the main stages that a Java-enabled smart card passes through.

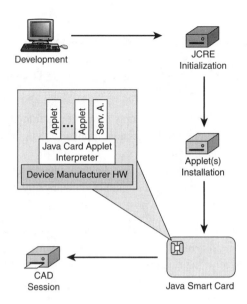

FIGURE 5.7

The lifecycle of a Java Card applet.

First of all, the application is developed with software on a desktop computer, where the developers can take advantage of tools such as Integrated Development Environments (IDE), debuggers, emulators, and so on. Finally, the final CAP files are obtained and the stage of JCRE initialization takes place. The virtual machine is initialized, and all the JCRE support objects are created. This stage is performed only once during the card lifetime.

Another stage is applet installation. When applets are installed, the JCRE creates applet instances, as prescribed in the installed code, along with the other objects to store business data. Such objects are created in the EEPROM memory. This is one of the most interesting features of Java Card applets: the capability to be loaded dynamically. Most of the previous smart card software was hardwired onto ROM at card initialization, once and for all. The applet installation stage can be repeated many times.

In Figure 5.7, the final layering of the different computation environments is shown. It is composed of the pre-existing manufacturer hardware topped by the Java Card interpreter that executes installed client applets together with some other system applets.

Let's examine the card lifecycle in more detail. When we introduce smart cards in ATMs or other devices, cards are activated, and the code they contain is executed. Such devices are called *card acceptance devices (CADs)*. The period of time from the card activation inside such a device to the end of the business transaction and subsequent removal is called a *CAD session*.

At the end of a CAD session, when the power is removed from the card, the JCRE is only sus-pended. Thanks to the persistent storage (EEPROM) the whole computation state is preserved. Only transient objects (created in RAM for security and performance reasons) are permanently deleted. The next time power is switched on, starting a new CAD session, the JCRE interpreter will be reset to the beginning of the main loop.

During a CAD session, the card program emerges from hibernation and starts to run. Usually, its main activity is communicating with the hosting application via the CAD hardware support. This I/O process is known as *application protocol data units (APDUs) I/O*. APDUs are low-level data packets exchanged between applets and the host application. APDUs can contain both data and commands, and are processed by one of the currently installed applets that even-tually will return an APDU response to the host application.

An important feature offered by the interpreter is the atomicity of operations and transactions. Simple operations, such as modifying the fields of a class instance, are ensured to be atomic by the JCRE, (that is, the state after the operation will be either modified to the new value or restored to the previous one—no inconsistent states are possible). Transactions are supported via an API that allows developers to encapsulate several operations in one transaction. In case of failure during the transaction execution, all performed operations are rolled back, which restores the computation state to just before the transaction started.

The Java Card Virtual Machine (JCVM) differs from the usual JVM because it is separated in two pieces: one (the interpreter) on the card, and the other (the converter) is implemented as a software program running on a workstation or PC.

The converter job is to create card executables files from the Java `.class` files. Such exe-cutable files are called *CAP (converted applet)* files. Together with CAP files, the converter produces export files, containing descriptions of the CAP file. The export files are similar to C header files, and are produced only to be used internally by the converter for linking and verifi-cation purposes.

The converter plays an important role: to transform the class files into a compact, optimized format suitable for execution on such a limited environment. Furthermore, is responsible to check for compliance with the Java Card language specification. It would raise an error if, for example, a long variable would be used in one of the input class files.

The CAP file format (the main output of the converter) is itself JAR-compatible (that is, com-pliant with the ZIP standard format), but it is optimized for occupying the minimum size, using compact data structures and limited indirection for the ZIP format. CAP files are conceptually equivalent to what JAR files are on other Java platforms: a standard means of distributing Java programs.

The other piece of the JCRE, the interpreter, is what physically resides on the smart card and enables a normal smart card to support the Java Card platform. It performs the tasks of execution of bytecodes, allocating space for the created Java objects (remember that garbage collection is *not* supported) and ensuring runtime security.

Applet deployment would not be possible without another software module, the installer, which resides with the interpreter on the card. It works together with an off-card installation software, during a CAD session, for downloading and installing the CAP file.

We have seen some details of the Java Card platform. It is now time to make them concrete with an example.

An Example

In order to run the code in this example, it is necessary to have installed the Java Card Development Kit Version 2.1.2 or higher from Sun. The kit is available for downloads at `http://www.javasoft.com/products/javacard/`.

> **NOTE**
>
> The JavaCard SDK can only be run on Windows NT 4.0 with Service Pack 4 or Solaris on SPARC platforms. See the related "readme" file for more details.

Listing 5.5 shows an example of a Java Card applet. It is very simple, but it will serve our purpose of illustrating the deployment of Java Card applets from the Java source code to the final data transfer into the chip card.

For the scripts, we will use simple Windows scripting that could be adapted easily to any Unix-like command-line environment.

To deploy our applet, follow these steps:

1. Write the Java source code, and compile it successfully.
2. Run the converter tool provided with the development kit, obtaining a CAP file.
3. Converting the CAP file in a sequence of low-level APDU commands to install the applet onto the card.

Listing 5.5 shows our `CardTest` applet. It is only a demonstration applet; it does not perform any useful task, neither does it use any standard APDU type in the processing. Nevertheless, it will help us follow all the main steps from the source development to a basic, on-card applet installation.

LISTING 5.5 The CardTest Applet Class

```java
package com.marinilli.b2.c5;

import javacard.framework.*;

/**
 * Chapter 5 - An example Java Card Applet
 * This applet writes back dummy byte sequences. It is meant to show the
 * Java Card applet development process only.
 *
 * @author Mauro Marinilli
 * @version 1.0
 */

public class CardTest extends Applet {

  //standard APDU input offset values
  public final static byte THIS_CLA = (byte)0x90;
  public final static byte  INITIALIZE_TRANSACTION = (byte)0x20;
  public final static byte  COMPLETE_TRANSACTION= (byte)0x22;
  public final static byte  INITIALIZE_UPDATE= (byte)0x24;
  public final static byte  COMPLETE_UPDATE= (byte)0x26;

  // dummy byte sequences returned by this applet
  private final static byte[] INIT_SEQUENCE = { (byte)0x1, (byte)0x2 };
  private final static byte[] COMPLETE_SEQUENCE = { (byte)0x1, (byte)0x3 };
  private final static byte[] INIT_UPDATE_SEQUENCE = { (byte)0x1, (byte)0x2,
➥ (byte)0x3 };
  private final static byte[] COMPLETE_UPDATE_SEQUENCE = { (byte)0x1,
➥ (byte)0x1 };

  /**
   * Constructor.
   * Only this class's install method can create the applet object.
   */
  private CardTest() {
    //perform some initialization here
    // ...
    register();//register this instance
  }

  /**
   * Installs this applet.
   * @param byteArray the array containing installation parameters
   * @param offset the starting offset in byteArray
```

LISTING 5.5 Continued

```
 * @param length the length in bytes of the parameter data in byteArray
 */
public static void install(byte[] byteArray, short offset, byte length) {
  new CardTest();
}


/**
 * Implementation  of the standard method for processing an incoming APDU.
 * @param apdu the incoming APDU
 * @exception ISOException with ISO 7816-4 response bytes
 */
public void process(APDU apdu) {
  byte buffer[] = apdu.getBuffer();

  if (buffer[ISO7816.OFFSET_CLA] == THIS_CLA) {
    switch (buffer[ISO7816.OFFSET_INS])    {
      case INITIALIZE_TRANSACTION:
        writeBack(apdu, INIT_SEQUENCE);
        break;
      case COMPLETE_TRANSACTION:
        writeBack(apdu, COMPLETE_SEQUENCE);
        break;
      case INITIALIZE_UPDATE:
        writeBack(apdu, INIT_UPDATE_SEQUENCE);
        break;
      case COMPLETE_UPDATE:
        writeBack(apdu, COMPLETE_UPDATE_SEQUENCE);
        break;
      default:
        ISOException.throwIt(ISO7816.SW_INS_NOT_SUPPORTED);
    }
  }
}

/**
 * An example method that writes back a given byte array through the apdu.
 */
protected void writeBack(APDU apdu, byte[] bytes) {
  byte buffer[] = apdu.getBuffer();

  // set apdu for data output
  apdu.setOutgoing();
```

LISTING 5.5   Continued

```
    apdu.setOutgoingLength( (short) (3) );

    // output header
    apdu.sendBytes( (short)0, (short) 3);
    // writes data
    apdu.sendBytesLong( bytes, (short) 0, (short) 0 );
  }


}
```

Listing 5.6 shows the commands to compile it. Note the use of the -g option, which is needed because the converter tool determines the local variable types by checking the LocalVariableTable attribute within the .class file. Such an attribute is generated only if the -g option is used.

LISTING 5.6   Compiling the CardTest Applet

```
set JC_HOME=...
javac -g -classpath % JC_HOME%\lib\api21.jar  CardTest.java
```

Then, when the CardTest.class file is produced, we need to transform it in a CAP file. We use the converter utility, together with an optional input file (called CardTest.opt in the example) that declares all input options for the conversion process. Such a file is shown in Listing 5.8.

LISTING 5.7   Compiling the CardTest Applet

```
set _CLASSES=%JC_HOME%\lib\apduio.jar; . . . ;%JC_HOME%\lib\
[ic:ccc]api21.jar;%JC_HOME%\lib\capdump.jar;
xcopy /s %JC_HOME%\api21_export_files\*.* exp\
java -classpath %_CLASSES% com.sun.javacard.converter.Converter
[ic:ccc]-config CardTest.opt
```

At line 1 of Listing 5.7, for brevity, we omitted to mention all the JAR libraries found in the /lib directory of the installed Java Card Development Kit. At line 2 of Listing 5.7, we copy the export files for the standard libraries in a temporary directory, from where we will access them from the -exportpath option in Listing 5.8. We said that EXP files are much like C header files, needed for linking and other utility purposes (in Listing 5.9 is shown an example of such a file converted in plain text).

LISTING 5.8 The Converter Input Options File `Cardtest.opt`.

```
-out EXP JCA CAP
-exportpath exp\
-applet  0x1:0x0:0x0:0x0:0x1:0x3:0x1:0x0:0x1:0x1 com.marinilli.b2.c5.CardTest
com.marinilli.b2.c5
0x1:0x0:0x0:0x0:0x1:0x3:0x1:0x0:0x1 1.0
```

The options file (listed in Listing 5.8) instructs the converter tool to produce EXP, JCA, and CAP files as output of the conversion. JCA files are pseudo-assembly text files, from which CAP files could be created; we will not use them here. The `-exportpath` command-line switch defines where the required EXP files (needed for linking libraries) are located. The `-applet` option defines the applet's AID and its Java class. In this example, the AID is totally invented. Finally, package name, package AID, and major version followed by minor version (separated by a dot) are provided to the converter.

Sun also supplies a tool for viewing the contents of an EXP file. When invoking it as in the following, it will produce the text representation of the EXP file created by the converter from our applet class file:

```
java -classpath %_CLASSES% com.sun.javacard.converter.Exp2Text -classdir com/
➥marinilli/b2/c5
```

Such a file is reported in Listing 5.9.

LISTING 5.9 The Human-Readable Representation of the `CardApplet` EXP File

```
export file { // com/marinilli/b2/c5
  magic 00FACADE // in hex
  minor_version 1
  major_version 2
  constant_pool_count 2
  constant_pool {
    Constant_Utf8_info {
      tag 1
      length 19
      bytes com/marinilli/b2/c5
    }
    CONSTANT_Package_info {
      tag 13
      flags 0
      name_index 0 // com/marinilli/b2/c5
      minor_version 0
      major_version 1
      aid_length 9
```

LISTING 5.9 Continued

```
      aid 0x1:0x0:0x0:0x0:0x1:0x3:0x1:0x0:0x1
    }
  }
  this_package 1
  export_class_count 0
  export_classes {
  }
}
```

We still have to physically transfer the CAP file onto our smart card. Sun's development kit provides a utility for sending APDUs to the smart card. Our last step will be to create the APDUs to be sent to the smart card. The installer itself has been implemented as an applet.

Using the follow command, we launch the script generator (the -nobeginend option will avoid to include the standard "CAP Begin" and "CAP End" APDU commands that we have to customize later).

```
java -classpath %_CLASSES% com.sun.javacard.scriptgen.Main com\marinilli\b2\c5\
➥javacard\c5.cap -nobeginend
```

We obtain the output shown in Listing 5.10, the list of APDU commands (a sequence of bytes) that define our CAP file.

LISTING 5.10 The APDU Script Generator Output

```
Java Card 2.1.2 APDU Script File Builder (version 0.11)
Copyright  2001 Sun Microsystems, Inc. All rights reserved.


// com/marinilli/b2/c5/javacard/Header.cap
0x80 0xB2 0x01 0x00 0x00 0x7F;
0x80 0xB4 0x01 0x00 0x16 0x01 0x00 0x13 0xDE 0xCA 0xFF 0xED 0x01 0x02
➥ 0x04 0x00 0x01 0x09 0x01 0x00 0x00 0x00 0x01 0x03 0x01 0x00 0x01 0x7F;
0x80 0xBC 0x01 0x00 0x00 0x7F;

// com/marinilli/b2/c5/javacard/Directory.cap
0x80 0xB2 0x02 0x00 0x00 0x7F;
0x80 0xB4 0x02 0x00 0x20 0x02 0x00 0x1F 0x00 0x13 0x00 0x1F 0x00 0x0E
➥ 0x00 0x0B 0x00 0x36 0x00 0x0C 0x00 0x67 0x00 0x0A 0x00 0x13 0x00
➥ 0x00 0x00 0x6C 0x00 0x00 0x00 0x00 0x00
➥ 0x00 0x01 0x7F;
0x80 0xB4 0x02 0x00 0x02 0x01 0x00 0x7F;
0x80 0xBC 0x02 0x00 0x00 0x7F;
```

LISTING 5.10 Continued

```
// com/marinilli/b2/c5/javacard/Import.cap
0x80 0xB2 0x04 0x00 0x00 0x7F;
0x80 0xB4 0x04 0x00 0x0E 0x04 0x00 0x0B 0x01 0x00 0x01 0x07 0xA0 0x00
➡ 0x00 0x00 0x62 0x01 0x01 0x7F;
0x80 0xBC 0x04 0x00 0x00 0x7F;


// com/marinilli/b2/c5/javacard/Applet.cap
0x80 0xB2 0x03 0x00 0x00 0x7F;
0x80 0xB4 0x03 0x00 0x11 0x03 0x00 0x0E 0x01 0x0A 0x01 0x00 0x00 0x00
➡ 0x01 0x03 0x01 0x00 0x01 0x01 0x00 0x14 0x7F;
0x80 0xBC 0x03 0x00 0x00 0x7F;


// com/marinilli/b2/c5/javacard/Class.cap
0x80 0xB2 0x06 0x00 0x00 0x7F;
0x80 0xB4 0x06 0x00 0x0F 0x06 0x00 0x0C 0x00 0x80 0x03 0x01 0x00 0x01
➡ 0x07 0x01 0x00 0x00 0x00 0x1F 0x7F;
0x80 0xBC 0x06 0x00 0x00 0x7F;


// com/marinilli/b2/c5/javacard/Method.cap
0x80 0xB2 0x07 0x00 0x00 0x7F;
0x80 0xB4 0x07 0x00 0x20 0x07 0x00 0x67 0x00 0x02 0x10 0x18 0x8C 0x00
➡ 0x01 0x18 0x11 0x01 0x00 0x90 0x0B 0x87 0x00 0x18 0x8B 0x00 0x02
➡ 0x7A 0x02 0x30 0x8F 0x00 0x03 0x3D 0x8C
➡ 0x00 0x04 0x7F;
0x80 0xB4 0x07 0x00 0x20 0x3B 0x7A 0x05 0x23 0x19 0x8B 0x00 0x05 0x2D
➡ 0x19 0x8B 0x00 0x06 0x32 0x03 0x29 0x04 0x70 0x19 0x1A 0x08 0xAD
➡ 0x00 0x16 0x04 0x1F 0x8D 0x00 0x0B 0x3B
➡ 0x16 0x04 0x7F;
0x80 0xB4 0x07 0x00 0x20 0x1F 0x41 0x29 0x04 0x19 0x08 0x8B 0x00 0x0C
➡ 0x32 0x1F 0x64 0xE8 0x19 0x8B 0x00 0x07 0x3B 0x19 0x16 0x04
➡ 0x08 0x41 0x8B 0x00 0x08 0x19 0x03 0x08 0x8B
➡ 0x00 0x09 0x7F;
0x80 0xB4 0x07 0x00 0x0A 0x19 0xAD 0x00 0x03 0x16 0x04 0x8B 0x00 0x0A
➡ 0x7A 0x7F;
0x80 0xBC 0x07 0x00 0x00 0x7F;


// com/marinilli/b2/c5/javacard/StaticField.cap
0x80 0xB2 0x08 0x00 0x00 0x7F;
0x80 0xB4 0x08 0x00 0x0D 0x08 0x00 0x0A 0x00 0x00 0x00 0x00 0x00 0x00 0x00
➡ 0x00 0x00 0x00 0x7F;
0x80 0xBC 0x08 0x00 0x00 0x7F;


// com/marinilli/b2/c5/javacard/ConstantPool.cap
0x80 0xB2 0x05 0x00 0x00 0x7F;
```

Listing 5.10 Continued

```
0x80 0xB4 0x05 0x00 0x20 0x05 0x00 0x36 0x00 0x0D 0x02 0x00 0x00 0x00 0x06
➡ 0x80 0x03 0x00 0x03 0x80 0x03 0x01 0x01 0x00 0x00 0x00 0x06 0x00
➡ 0x00 0x01 0x03 0x80 0x0A 0x01 0x03 0x80
➡ 0x0A 0x7F;
0x80 0xB4 0x05 0x00 0x19 0x06 0x03 0x80 0x0A 0x07 0x03 0x80 0x0A 0x09 0x03
➡ 0x80 0x0A 0x04 0x03 0x80 0x0A 0x05 0x06 0x80 0x10 0x02 0x03 0x80
➡ 0x0A 0x03 0x7F;
0x80 0xBC 0x05 0x00 0x00 0x7F;


// com/marinilli/b2/c5/javacard/RefLocation.cap
0x80 0xB2 0x09 0x00 0x00 0x7F;
0x80 0xB4 0x09 0x00 0x16 0x09 0x00 0x13 0x00 0x03 0x0E 0x25 0x2C 0x00 0x0C
➡0x05 0x0C 0x06 0x04 0x08 0x05 0x10 0x0C 0x08 0x09 0x06 0x09 0x7F;
0x80 0xBC 0x09 0x00 0x00 0x7F;



APDU script file for CAP file download generated.
```

To use the generated output, we need to cut the text header and footer leaving only the APDU commands (comments are skipped by the tool). Then, we add right at the beginning of the text file the following sequence:

```
powerup;
// Select the installer applet
0xA4 0x04 0x00 0x09 0xa0 0x00 0x00 0x00 0x62 0x03 0x01 0x08 0x01 0x7F;
// CAP Begin
0x80 0xB0 0x00 0x00 0x00 0x7F;
```

While appending at the end the above-mentioned sequence:

```
// CAP End
0x80 0xBA 0x00 0x00 0x00 0x7F;
// create CardTest
0x80 0xB8 0x00 0x00 0x0b 0x09 0x1 0x0 0x0 0x0 0x1 0x3 0x1 0x04
0x01 0x00 0x7F;
powerdown;
```

The generated file, given in input at a suitable CAD via the APDUtool will install our applet on the card in a three-step sequence:

1. The standard installer applet (already resident on the card) is instructed to download our applet using an APDU sequence.

2. Data is transferred via APDUs to the installer applet that writes it in memory.

3. Finally, always using the installer applet, we create an instance of our newly downloaded class that is ready for execution.

There are more deployment options for Java Card applets, such as Rom applets. We have covered here a simple, though complete, deployment scenario.

And now, from one end to the other of the Java computational range: the Java 2 Enterprise Edition platform.

J2EE Deployment

Despite the J2EE widespread presence on the server, we will introduce it briefly here, to discuss the deployment scenario for this platform. The interested reader can see *Building Java Enterprise Systems With J2EE*, by Paul Perrone (published by SAMS), which is one of the many books on this subject. Given the abundance of publications on this topic, we will only cover it briefly. J2EE applications are aimed at server-based, rich computational environments, in contrast with the platforms covered earlier in this chapter. Here, hardware constraints and low-level issues are not a problem.

A Brief Introduction

First of all, here is a little overview of the involved roles. The EJB specification partitions the responsibility of development and deployment to up to six well-known roles. These can be individuals, teams, or separated firms, as follows:

- **The bean provider** provides reusable business components adhering to the EJB specification.
- **The container provider** offers the software container needed to run EJB components.
- **The server provider** supplies the application server software.
- **The application assembler** is responsible for the overall application architecture, integrating together existing components or writing them from scratch as needed to produce the final application. The assembler must understand (along with the application workflow) all the settings needed to be specified to successfully customize and deploy the final application.
- **The deployer** is responsible for installing the application components (that is, the output of the application assembler) in the target application servers. The deployer needs to be aware of the differences between the various servers, containers, and beans involved in the deployment. Another important issue is the adaptation of the deployed application to the current security settings and other customer-sensitive data.
- **The system administrator** takes care of the deployed application during its running in an operational environment.

In the following paragraphs, we will describe in detail the job of a J2EE application deployer. A typical J2EE deployment may involve the configuration of the following:

- The root URL where the application is available to end-users
- The username, password and other data for connecting to databases
- Business configuration data that depend on the particular application domain
- The system users that will play the role of system administrators for the application

Let's get into the details of J2EE deployment.

A Java enterprise application is defined as a hierarchy of directories and files in a standard layout. One type of these files, known as *deployment descriptor files*, are essential in J2EE deployment. They are XML files that describe how to package J2EE components into an application. They provide structural and application assembly information.

Deployment descriptors are used in EJB JAR files as well as Web modules (packaged as WAR files), with different syntax conventions. In turn, Web modules and EJB modules are packaged together in application archives (EAR) files. Both EAR and WAR files are special JAR files with a different suffix.

The deployer performs two activities on the assembled application:

- Installing the application that is copying it into the operational J2EE server, generating container-specific classes and interfaces.
- Configuring the installed application. Analysis entities such as security roles defined by the application assembler need to be mapped to user groups and accounts on the operating environment.

  Another task is to ensure that all external dependencies are resolved.

Enterprise Java Bean Files

Enterprise Java Bean files are JAR files containing the following:

- Java class files and their home and remote interfaces
- Java class files for any classes and interfaces the enterprise bean code depends on, that are not included in the EJB file
- The EJB deployment descriptor, usually named `ejb-jar.xml`, in the `META-INF` directory
- The `MANIFEST.MF` standard manifest file in the `META-INF` directory

Web Archive Files

Web Archive (WAR) files contain the following:

- JSP pages and related Java classes
- HTML static pages, image files, and so on
- The `classes` subdirectory in `WEB-INF` that contains any Java class files and needed resources for Servlets and JPSs
- The Web deployment descriptor, usually named `Web.xml` in the `WEB-INF` directory
- The `MANIFEST.MF` standard manifest file in the `META-INF` directory

Enterprise Archive Files

Enterprise Archive (EAR) files contain the following:

- EJB modules
- Web modules
- The `application.xml` file in the `META-INF` directory, containing runtime information for the application
- The `MANIFEST.MF` standard manifest file in the `META-INF` directory

A simple example of Java enterprise software deployment is given in the following section.

A J2EE Example

Here, we will deploy the servlet mentioned in the MIDlet section previously introduced. It is shown in Listing 5.11.

LISTING 5.11 The `LicenseServlet` Servlet

```
package com.marinilli.b2.c5;

import javax.servlet.*;
import javax.servlet.http.*;
import java.io.*;
import java.util.*;

/**
 * Chapter 5 - A Simple Servlet License Manager
 *
 * @author Mauro Marinilli
 * @version 1.0
 */
```

LISTING 5.11 Continued

```java
public class LicenseServlet extends HttpServlet {

  /**
   * Initialize global variables
   */
  public void init(ServletConfig config) throws ServletException {
    super.init(config);
  }

  /**
   * Process the HTTP Get request
   */
  public void doGet(HttpServletRequest request,
                    HttpServletResponse response)
                        throws ServletException, IOException {

    String id = unscramble(request.getParameter("license-id"));
    String pwd = unscramble(request.getParameter("license-pwd"));
    Boolean outcome =  new Boolean(check(id, pwd));
    response.setContentType("text/html");
    response.addHeader("outcome", outcome.toString());
    PrintWriter out = response.getWriter();
    if (outcome.booleanValue()){
      out.println("Congratulations for registering your copy!"+
                  " Thank You for your choice. Please visit our Web site.");
    } else {
      out.println("Sorry. License Not Valid.");
      out.println("Please Try Again.");
    }
  }

  /**
   * Clean up resources
   */
  public void destroy() {
  }

  /**
   * un-scramble a string
   */
  private String unscramble(String s) {
    return s;
  }
```

LISTING 5.11 Continued

```
/**
 * check if this pair is a valid license
 */
private boolean check(String id, String pwd) {
  //
  return (id.charAt(0)==pwd.charAt(0));
}


}
```

Let's comment on Listing 5.11 before getting into its deployment details.

The simple client-server communication protocol requires the client to issue a GET request passing in two parameters: `license-id` and `license-pwd`. The server (that is, our `LicenseServlet`) checks to see if the pair (id, password) is valid, and returns the result back to the client. The resulting Web page is used by the client MIDlet to be shown directly to the user via the wireless device screen (lines 37–43 in Listing 5.11).

The result of the password-id validity check is appended as a header to the HTTP response (namely, "outcome" with values "true" or "false") at line 35. Also, here the `unscramble` method relating the communication security (lines 55–57) has been kept merely idempotent for simplicity. The `check` method returns true when the license id matches the password input by the user (Lines 22–25) simply controlling if the first character is the same. A more realistic implementation would require a key-validation function, accessing a database or some data file, and so on.

Deploying the License Servlet

Normally during development, all the application-related files are left "loose" in the `WEB-INF/classes` directory in the application's document root. This could be a legitimate deployment option, but often, it is preferred to pack all those items in one WAR file for easier distribution.

In Tomcat, for example, all Web applications are gathered in the directory `Webapps` in the Tomcat home directory (from here on `<TOMCAT_HOME>`). Note that with few changes the following procedure is applicable to any other standard servlet containers.

We are assumed to have created the application directory (in our case, `license`). Within it, the directory `WEB-INF` contains the `classes` directory (for all the Java classes; in our case, just one) and the `Web.xml` file shown in Listing 5.12. All other files (HTML, JSP, and so on) may be put in the application directory. In our simple case, we don't have any static content file. Then, one may zip the resulting directory tree—once completed and tested—into a WAR file to be distributed to other servlet containers that will run our License Servlet.

The steps necessary to package the application for deployment are the following:

1. Copy the WAR file under the Web application root of the servlet container.

2. When installing the WAR file, optionally we can add a new context (in order for the servlet container to properly recognize our application) to the `server.xml` file (located at `<TOMCAT_HOME>/conf/server.xml`). This is not necessary if the application is placed in the Webapps directory and uses standard defaults. We will skip this step, assuming the standard situation.

3. Having done so, it is enough to launch the servlet container, and test the servlet using an URL compliant with that described in Listing 5.12.

LISTING 5.12 The `Web.xml` Web Application Deployment Descriptor File

```
<?xml version="1.0" encoding="ISO-8859-1"?>

<!DOCTYPE Web-app
    PUBLIC "-//Sun Microsystems, Inc.//DTD Web Application 2.2//EN"
    "http://java.sun.com/j2ee/dtds/Web-app_2_2.dtd">

<Web-app>
    <servlet>
        <servlet-name>
            license1
        </servlet-name>
        <servlet-class>
            com.marinilli.b2.c5.LicenseServlet
        </servlet-class>
    </servlet>
    <servlet-mapping>
        <servlet-name>
            license1
        </servlet-name>
        <url-pattern>
            /midp/*
        </url-pattern>
    </servlet-mapping>
</Web-app>
```

Refer to Listing 5.4 for details on the corresponding client for this server application.

Summary

In this chapter we have discussed some issues about the deployment of non-J2SE code. In particular, we saw examples of J2ME's MIDlets, JavaCard applets and J2EE servlet deployment.

For the remainder of this book, we will focus mainly on the J2SE platform, the most difficult platform for Java deployment given the great number of available options and different situations.

Deploying Existing Software

IN THIS CHAPTER

In this chapter, we will provide some considerations for adding deployment services to pre-existing Java code. Moreover, rather than discussing the various possibilities abstractly from a theoretical point of view, we will see a simple yet complete example of full rethinking of a pre-existing software. This example will also be useful to illustrate some of the general techniques described in Chapter 4, "Designing for Deployment."

Overview

Adding deployment services to pre-existing Java programs is a more complex issue than one may think at first. Despite the fact that legacy Java code is often no more than few years old, the sheer availability of communication mechanisms (all major high-level protocols, RMI, sockets, CORBA, and so on) often is too confusing for the average developer facing the need of tailored deployment. Likewise, the choice of a standard deployment solution could be quite complex. Developers have to decide which means among many (applets, JNLP, third-party solutions, and so on) is best suited for their current situation.

Unfortunately, following a bad habit in software development, deployment is often neglected and practically ignored until the development phase has finished. As we already discussed, this could be a costly way to proceed, but it is still very common. It is not enough to provide a great number of deployment means (as Java does, together with the Internet) for developers and managers to change their old habits.

In this chapter, we will cover both the issue of adding deployment services to our software (what we described as establishing a deployment circuit) and solving the merest deployment issue: Just let users have the software installed on their computers. The previous approach can be seen as a radical use of deployment services in our software; the latter is a more shallow one, in which we are interested in the first installation only.

Generally speaking, many of the considerations discussed in Chapter 4 still apply here. The reader is encouraged to refer to Chapter 4 to integrate this section's content.

We will focus on the J2SE 1.x versions because they provide the widest freedom of choice. J2ME and J2EE were discussed in the previous chapter.

Main Solutions

The major deployment solutions that developers can use when solving the deployment riddle for their Java software are those already discussed in the first part and in Chapter 4 (and summarized here):

- **JNLP**. For developers, JNLP is a complete bonus. It is free, it saves programmers a lot of effort, and it is rather simple to use. Despite some technical weak points (only J2SE code could be deployed, and only on an HTTP connection, for instance), its main drawback comes from the burden posed to the end-user, especially for the first time launch (refer to Chapter 3, "Existing Solutions"). As it is spreading and its features are evolving, these shortcomings should be smoothed in time.

- **Installers**. Software installers accomplish the minimal, "one-shot" installation, and often provide other simple services such as pointing the user to the product Web site, offering an integrated registration form, and so on. We won't cover them here in detail because their use for application deployment is quite straightforward. Interested readers can visit producers' Web sites (refer to Chapter 3) for thorough documentation.

- **Personnel**. This consists of addressing the whole deployment issue, using skilled staff that performs the installation on users' computers. It is used only for limited user populations, often working in an intranet environment. It may turn out to be the most expensive deployment solution.

- **Third-party deployment solutions**. Software products such as DeployDirector and the others discussed in Chapter 3 belong to this category. Despite being quite powerful, both in terms of overall reliability and deployment features, these products may be expensive—both from a license fee standpoint and for the effort needed to master them for first-time use.

- **Applets**. The applet concept is a great solution for the problem of basic deployment. Unfortunately, the Java Plug-In product is needed for full-fledged applets, and this could be quite expensive for users in many situations (in terms of download time, for example).

- **Ad-hoc deployment solutions**. Apart from employing a skilled workforce, this is generally the most expensive (in terms of development resources) but most powerful solution. We will devote a great part of this chapter to illustrating a practical example of this type of deployment solution.

Table 6.1 shows the main kinds of "off-the-shelf" deployment solutions in relation with some general parameters.

TABLE 6.1. Deployment Solutions

Deployment Solution	Java Edition	Needed Connection	Deployment Features	User Costs	Developer Costs	Needed Server Support	Installed Appl. Richness	Code Adaptation
JNLP	J2SE	HTTP	Basic	High	Low	Low	High	Low-Medium
Installers	Any	Sporadic / None	Installation only	Medium	Low	None	High	Low

TABLE 6.1. Continued

Deployment Solution	Java Edition	Needed Connection	Deployment Features	User Costs	Developer Costs	Needed Server Support	Installed Appl. Richness	Code Adaptation
Personnel	Any	None	High	Low	High	None	High	Low
Third-Party Solutions	Any	Various	High	Low	Medium	Various	High	Low
Applets	Java 1	HTTP	Basic	Low	Low	Low	Low	High
Applets with Plug-In	J2SE	HTTP	Basic	High	Low	Low	Medium	High

In this table, the major choices are compared using imprecise evaluation parameters. The aim is to provide an initial, intuitive overview of the tradeoffs implied in the available deployment solutions.

The parameters considered are as follows:

- **Deployment Solution**. One of the major deployment techniques discussed above. The ad-hoc option has not been considered because of its excessive generality.
- **Java Edition**. It may have two values: Java 1 (intending JDK 1.x) and J2SE. We restricted our discussion to the J2SE only in this chapter.
- **Needed Connection**. The kind of connection required by the chosen deployment solution.
- **Deployment Features**. The level of features supported by the given deployment solution (refer to Chapter 4).
- **User Costs**. The burden posed to the end-user (considered not familiar with computers programs).
- **Developer Costs**. The development (and the subsequent deployment) effort in license fees, workforce wages, and other costs.
- **Needed Server Support**. The minimum server support required. This can be thought of as a part of the overall deployment costs. Low is intended for a basic web server. Third-party solutions vary greatly in this parameter.
- **Installed Application Richness**. How powerful the installed application could be. This column is significant only for applets.
- **Code Adaptation**. The last column shows how that given solution is combined with already written Java code. For example, although installation packagers work well with

any kind of Java software, JNLP clients can deploy only J2SE software, and with some restrictions in their code, too. Transforming a pre-existing program into an applet could reveal an unexpectedly complex problem.

Deployment workforce costs were thought of as being part of development costs for ease of assessment with the other items.

Finally, let's discuss an interesting example that will practically illustrate many of the challenges developers face when they choose to radically modify the existing code to establish a complete deployment circuit. In real-world situations, building ad-hoc solutions often comes together with code rewriting, as this example also shows.

An Example

As an example, we will construct an ad-hoc solution for the deployment of already written code. After having introduced the case, we will see the old code, and finally we will discuss the proposed solution in detail.

The Scenario

A bank uses Java (developed in-house) for transaction recording and other various data processing tasks for its many branches. Connections with the central server are obtained using proprietary lines and a pre-existing, non-standard communication hardware.

Another priority for management is the capability to allow different offices within the bank organization to develop and use their own software for particular tasks.

Given some important changes in the business organization (a merger with another bank, for instance), the management decided to renew its software, with the following goals:

- Expanding the installed software, making it ready for future, not-yet-known features. Leveraging the existing software is a priority, given its relatively recent adoption.

- Making the new software fully backward-compatible with the previous version. Many offices have ported their old programs to Java and they use them daily.

- Keeping a tight central control over all clients, ensuring the highest level of security.

- Minimizing costs. This implies keeping the old, proprietary communication channels, and to use the less-is-possible human personnel for software management and upgrades.

Bank IT engineers were asked to design such software.

From our viewpoint, this could be seen as a case in which establishing a deployment circuit while ensuring full compatibility with already written Java code could solve all the requested constraints.

Standard solutions are difficult to employ here, for both technical reasons (given the peculiarity of hardware connections) and economic reasons (the costs of third-party deployment tools whenever usable in such a particular context).

We will illustrate a solution that will ensure full compatibility with the already-running old Java software, using a well-known technique for dynamic class loading that is widely used in commercial deployment systems. The only cost to pay, apart from development, is for redistributing a J2SE-based new client version to all clients.

The adopted solution will show us several things:

- Typical trades-off when designing a custom deployment solution with the important priority of backward compatibility.

- The custom class loader mechanism at work. This technique is used (among the others) in JNLP client implementations.

- How to ensure full compatibility of existing code while providing advanced deployment features.

The Old System

For simplicity, we think of a basic, simple, pre-existing system, with a classic client-server architecture. All clients communicate with the central server using socket connections on proprietary hardware. This drastically cuts down the choices we have for third-party, inexpensive solutions; and practically leaves us with the ad-hoc approach only.

In Listing 6.1, the client of the previous system is shown:

LISTING 6.1 The `OldBankClient` Class

```
package com.marinilli.b2.c6.bank;

import java.io.*;
import java.net.*;

/**
 * Chapter 6 - The old BankClient
 *
 * @author Mauro Marinilli
 * @version 1.0
 */

public class OldBankClient {
  Socket socket = null;
  DataOutputStream out = null;
```

LISTING 6.1 Continued

```
DataInputStream in = null;
private String thisClientId;

public OldBankClient() {
  thisClientId = "client0";
  try {
    socket = new Socket("localhost", 3333);
    out = new DataOutputStream(socket.getOutputStream());
    in = new DataInputStream(socket.getInputStream());
  } catch (Exception e) {
    System.out.println("BankClient- Couldn't work out the connection: "+e);
    System.exit(1);
  }
  try {
    executeTransaction();

    // dismiss connection
    sendCommand('q');
    out.close();
    in.close();
    socket.close();
  } catch (IOException exce) {
    System.out.println("BankClient- executing transaction: "+exce);
  }
  System.out.println("BankClient- Client Log out.");
}

private void post(String data) throws IOException{
  sendCommand('p');
  out.writeUTF(data);
}

private byte[] get(String serverFilename) throws IOException{
  sendCommand('g');
  out.writeUTF(serverFilename);
  int size = in.readInt();
  byte[] b = new byte[size];
  in.readFully(b);
  return b;
}

private void executeTransaction() throws IOException{
  byte[] b = get("test.txt");
  post("hello everybody");
}
```

LISTING 6.1 Continued

```
private void sendCommand(char c){
  try {
    out.writeChar;
    System.out.println("BankClient: send command "+c);
  } catch (IOException exce) {
    System.out.println("BankClient- "+exce);
  }
}

private void cache(String name, byte[] b) {
  try {
    FileOutputStream fos = new FileOutputStream("cached/"+name);
    fos.write(b);
    fos.close();
  } catch (IOException exce) {
    System.out.println("BankClient- cache("+name+") "+exce);
  }
}

public static void main(String[] args) throws IOException {
  OldBankClient c = new OldBankClient();
}

}
```

> **NOTE**
>
> For simplicity, we have omitted all security and other details in the code, to better
> concentrate on the deployment aspects. One can imagine an SSL (Secure Socket
> Layer) connection, and/or a more elaborate protocol, managing classloader permis-
> sions, and so on.

Essentially, after the connection is established, our application performs some business transaction. When finished, it closes the connection. Branch Offices were allowed to modify the
code to add their special services (mortgages, statistics, and so on) as needed.

Once the socket connection is established with the server, our protocol (a very simple one) permits the following operations:

- Clients can upload textual data on the central server using the GET command.
- The POST command lets clients download files from the central server.
- The QUIT command allows for a graceful session shutdown.

Our application is inherently IO-bounded and, in this version, the server connection was always assumed to be available (refer to Listing 6.1) for the transactions to be successfully accomplished.

We won't show here the server code because it is very similar to the code of the server implementation we will discuss in Listing 6.4.

Our Solution

Given the strict requirements described previously, we are forced to an ad-hoc solution. We will build our own Application Helper (refer to Chapter 2, "An Abstract Model for Deployment") that will take care of all the software deployment, taking advantage of the J2SE class loading mechanism.

This solution has a high first-time activation cost because we need to redeploy the new software to all the clients. This is needed only once, anyway. The following updates will be handled by our application helper in a transparent way.

Some Design Issues

Strictly speaking, the J2SE class loader mechanism adds a new level of indirection to our applications. When specifying our own class loader, we can control how classes are loaded into the JVM and where to find the resources they access. It is much like a Java program being able to load and execute another Java program.

It is not a surprise that customizing the class loader is a commonly used technique for implementing deployment services on the J2SE platform.

Often, when porting existing code to new architectures, developers realize that some new arrangements would be required. When creating deployment facilities for our software, we are just adding a new group of software services to the existing code. Often, making this distinction explicit is the wisest architectural choice.

This is the case in our code, too. Instead of using the existing code for implementing the deployment services (for example, taking advantage of the existing GET command), we will follow the design principle of total separation between deployment services and other business-oriented code. This approach could duplicate code at first, but it pays off in the medium–long run in terms of flexibility and design coherence.

Another code rearrangement, based on feature clustering is operated in business code. Some basic commands (corresponding to protocol ones) are factored out in a class of its own, providing standard communication services to other business classes. This additional rearrangement allows us for showing a simple yet very common case of code reorganization prompted by the adding of deployment services.

> **NOTE**
>
> Reorganizing already written code for deployment is often a good chance for rethinking the whole software architecture, as this example shows.

Following the advice of Chapters 2 and 4 on typical application helpers architectures, we divide our code into two main parts: business and deployment-related classes. After such a first division, we individuate two classes that will implement the application helper layer: one for controlling the overall deployment and another one that implements our custom class loader. Also, business code has been rationalized, creating the class BankClientManager that groups together all basic protocol commands, so that business transactions can use them.

In Figure 6.1, a diagram describes the proposed class architecture.

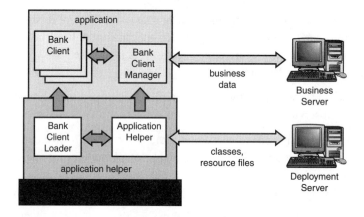

FIGURE 6.1

Software architecture for our ad-hoc deployment solution.

As seen in Figure 6.1, the deployment layer is made of two classes, whereas the business layer is composed of at least two classes (one that provides protocol support, and one or more where the actual business code is implemented).

Deploying Existing Software

CHAPTER 6

151

6

DEPLOYING
EXISTING
SOFTWARE

One can imagine another arrow linking the `BankClientLoader` class with the system class loader into the underlying JRE. We omitted it for clarity, but we will discuss its implications later when talking about our custom class loader code.

The Implementation

Our proposed implementation consists of five classes, organized as described in the previous section.

Of course, this is a basic implementation. Our purpose is to show the basic structure of and ad-hoc deployment solution providing full support for pre-existing code.

Before getting into the code details, let's recap each class role:

- **ApplicationHelper**. Launches the application.
- **BankClientLoader**. It is our custom class loader, created by the ApplicationHelper class.
- **BankClientManager**. This class encapsulates the communication protocol, providing higher-level methods to business classes.
- **BankClient**. An example of a business class (a class that implements the business code).
- **BankServer**. The server that listens for client requests. For simplicity, we implemented both the deployment server and the business server in this class.

When a user launches the client application, the `ApplicationHelper` is invoked, and after having created an instance of itself and of the `BankClientLoader`, it issues a CHECK command on the server.

Such a command is used for deployment only, and only the `ApplicationHelper` is assumed to invoke it. After the CHECK command has been completed, the client cache is ready for application execution, and the method `launch` in the `ApplicationHelper` launches the application appropriately.

The heart of the deployment mechanism is the class loading procedure. Requested classes are first searched into the local cache. By means of overwriting the cache contents, we are able to launch new code transparently to both users and other running applications.

In Listing 6.2, the `ApplicationHelper` class is shown.

LISTING 6.2 The ApplicationHelper Class

```java
package com.marinilli.b2.c6.bank;

import java.lang.reflect.Method;
import java.lang.reflect.Constructor;
import java.io.*;
import java.net.MalformedURLException;
import java.net.Socket;
import java.util.Properties;

/**
 * Chapter 6 - The Application Helper
 *
 * @author Mauro Marinilli
 * @version 1.0
 */

public class ApplicationHelper {
  private BankClientLoader loader;
  private Socket socket;
  private DataOutputStream out;
  private DataInputStream in;
  private String thisClientId;
  private Properties appHelperSettings;
  private final static String PROPS_FILE_NAME = "appHelper.properties";
  public final static String CLIENT_DIR = "clientdir/";
  public final static String CACHE_DIR = CLIENT_DIR + "cached/";
  private final static String DEFAULT_MAIN_CLASS_NAME =
"com.marinilli.b2.c6.bank.BankClient";
  private String OFFLINE_ALLOWED = "offline-allowed";
  private String CLIENT_ID = "id";
  private String launchClassName;
  private boolean offline = false;

  /**
   * Constructor
   */
  public ApplicationHelper() {
    loadProperties();
    thisClientId = appHelperSettings.getProperty(CLIENT_ID, "client0");
    try {
      socket = new Socket("localhost", 3333);
      out = new DataOutputStream(socket.getOutputStream());
      in = new DataInputStream(socket.getInputStream());
    } catch (Exception e) {
```

LISTING 6.2 Continued

```
      System.out.println("ApplicationHelper()- Couldn't work out the
connection: "+e);
      offline = true;
      if
(appHelperSettings.getProperty(OFFLINE_ALLOWED).equalsIgnoreCase("false")){
        System.out.println("ApplicationHelper()- Cannot execute offline.");
        System.exit(-1);
      }
    }
    try {
      if (!offline)
        check();
    } catch (Exception e) {
      System.out.println("ApplicationHelper()- check()"+e);
    }
  }

  /**
   * It implements the check command
   */
  public void check() throws IOException{
    try {
      out.writeChar('c');
      out.writeUTF(thisClientId);
      int newItems = in.readInt();
      if (newItems!=0) {
        //there is a new version in sight
        //we must download it
        byte[] b;
        for (int i = 0; i < newItems; i++) {
          // download a new file in cache
          String fileName = in.readUTF();
          int size = in.readInt();
          b = new byte[size];
          in.readFully(b);
          cache(fileName, b);
        }
        //read the class to be launched
        String launch = in.readUTF();
        if (launch!="")
          launchClassName = launch;
      }//-(newItems!=0)
    } catch (Exception e) {
      System.out.println("ApplicationHelper- check() "+e);
```

LISTING 6.2 Continued

```java
    }
  }

  /**
   * check if a file is in cache
   */
  protected boolean isCached(String item){
    File file = new File(CACHE_DIR);
    if(file.exists() && file.isDirectory()) {
      File[] dirContent = file.listFiles();
      for(int i = 0; i < dirContent.length; i++) {
        if(dirContent[i].getName().equals(item))
          return true;
      }//-for
    }
    return false;
  }

  /**
   * It stores a file in the local cache
   */
  protected void cache(String name, byte[] b) {
    try {
      FileOutputStream fos = new FileOutputStream(CACHE_DIR+name);
      fos.write(b);
      fos.close();
    } catch (IOException exce) {
      System.out.println("ApplicationHelper- cache("+name+") "+exce);
    }
    System.out.println("ApplicationHelper- saved in cache: "+name);
  }

  /**
   * It gets a file from the cache directory
   * @return a File
   */
  public File getCachedFile(String filename){
    File file = null;
    try {
      file = new File(CACHE_DIR, filename);
    } catch (Exception e) {
      System.out.println("ApplicationHelper- getFile(): " + e);
    }
    return file;
  }
```

Deploying Existing Software

CHAPTER 6

155

6

DEPLOYING
EXISTING
SOFTWARE

LISTING 6.2 Continued

```java
/**
 * transform a fully qual. class name in a simpler name
 */
protected String getCacheClassFileName(String className) {
  String result = className;
  if (className.indexOf('.')!=-1)
    result =className.substring(className.lastIndexOf('.')+1);
  return result;
}

/**
 * Loads properties file
 */
private void loadProperties(){
  try {
    appHelperSettings = new Properties();
    FileInputStream in = new FileInputStream(CLIENT_DIR+PROPS_FILE_NAME);
    appHelperSettings.load(in);
    launchClassName = appHelperSettings.getProperty("launchClass",
DEFAULT_MAIN_CLASS_NAME);
    in.close();
  }
  catch (IOException ex) {
    System.out.println("ApplicationHelper- loadProperties(): "+ex);
  }
}

/**
 * this method downloads and caches a file, taking advantage of the GET
command
 *
 */
public File getRemoteFile(String serverFilename, boolean isClass) throws
IOException {
  out.writeChar('g');
  out.writeUTF(serverFilename);
  int size = in.readInt();
  byte[] resBytes = new byte[size];
  in.readFully(resBytes);

  if (resBytes.length!=0) {
    String cacheName = serverFilename;
    if (isClass)
      cacheName += ".class";
```

LISTING 6.2   Continued

```
        cache(cacheName, resBytes);
        return getCachedFile(cacheName);
    }
    // file not found
    throw new FileNotFoundException("File " + serverFilename +
            " not found neither in cache nor in the server.");
}


/**
 * launch the app via main() method
 */
private boolean mainMethodLaunch(Class mainClass){
    boolean launched = true;
    try {
        Class[] types = { Class.forName("[Ljava.lang.String;") };
        Method mainMethod = mainClass.getDeclaredMethod("main", types);
        Object[] p = new Object[0];
        mainMethod.invoke(null, p);
        System.out.println("ApplicationHelper- appl. launched invoking:
"+mainMethod);
    } catch (Exception ex) {
        // ok, no main() method
        launched = false;
    }
    return launched;
}


/**
 * launch the app via constructor(s)
 */
private boolean creationLaunch(Class mainClass){
    boolean launched = true;
    // first, try default constructor
    try {
        Object ob = mainClass.newInstance();
        System.out.println("ApplicationHelper- appl. launched creating:
"+mainClass+"( )");
    }
    catch (Exception ex) {
        // it doesn't support the default constructor
        // just use the first of its constructors
        try {
            Constructor cons = mainClass.getConstructors()[0];
            int paramNumber = cons.getParameterTypes().length;
```

Deploying Existing Software

CHAPTER 6

157

6

DEPLOYING
EXISTING
SOFTWARE

LISTING 6.2   Continued

```java
        Object[] arg = new Object[paramNumber];
        Class[] param = cons.getParameterTypes();
        for (int i = 0; i < paramNumber ; i++) {
          //for each parameter, initializes it using its default constructor
          arg[i] = param[i].newInstance();
        }
        cons.newInstance(arg);
        System.out.println("ApplicationHelper- appl. launched creating:
"+cons);
      } catch (Exception exc){
        launched = false;
      }
    }
    return launched;
  }

  /**
   * This method launches the whole application
   *
   */
  public void launch() {
    boolean successfullyLaunched = false;
    loader = new BankClientLoader(this);
    try {
      Class mainClass =
          loader.loadClass(launchClassName, loader.getClass(launchClassName));

      // first, try to use the main() method
      successfullyLaunched = mainMethodLaunch(mainClass);

      // if not present, try to create an instance
      if (!successfullyLaunched)
        successfullyLaunched = creationLaunch(mainClass);

      if (!successfullyLaunched)
        System.out.println("ApplicationHelper- unable to launch application.");

      // after launched class finished, exit application
      shutDown();

    } catch (Exception e) {
      System.out.println("ApplicationHelper- Launch Failed. "+e);
      e.printStackTrace();
    }
```

LISTING 6.2   Continued

```
  }

  /**
   * This method shuts down the whole application
   *
   */
  private void shutDown() throws IOException {
    System.out.println("ApplicationHelper- closing application.");
    out.writeChar('q');
    out.close();
    in.close();
    socket.close();
    saveProperties();
  }

  /**
   * save deployment properties
   */
  private void saveProperties(){
    try {
      FileOutputStream out = new FileOutputStream(CLIENT_DIR+PROPS_FILE_NAME);
      appHelperSettings.store(out, "— Application Helper Properties file —");
      out.close();
    }
    catch (IOException ex) {
      System.out.println("ApplicationHelper- saveProperties(): "+ex);
    }
  }

  /**
   * Main method that launches the appl. helper and consequently,
   * the whole application
   */
  public static void main(String[] args) {
    ApplicationHelper applicationHelper = new ApplicationHelper();
    applicationHelper.launch();
  }

}
```

In its constructor, the ApplicationHelper instance tries to connect to the server (generally the deployment server is different from the business server, not like this simple case). Depending

Deploying Existing Software

CHAPTER 6

159

6

DEPLOYING
EXISTING
SOFTWARE

on a setting in its property file, it is possible for the application helper to launch the application even if the server connection is not working. The CHECK command (lines 62–87 in Listing 6.2) sends the client id to the server, and eventually receives a list of files to be cached and the name of the application main class. Being able to send files in cache at first is important because in this way the server can control which class (consequently which application) is launched on the client.

The ApplicationHelper class is also the one solely responsible of the deployment cache management, implemented straightforwardly as a directory in which classes and other resources are stored when downloaded from the server.

It is interesting to see how the application is started, using the launch method at lines 235–259 in Listing 6.2. After creating the class loader and using it to load the main class (as discussed later), the launch sequence proceeds as follows:

1. A first try is performed, invoking the mainMethodLaunch method (lines 185–198) to launch the main class via its main method.

2. If the main class doesn't have a main method, the creationLaunch method is invoked. This method (lines 203–229) will try to create an instance of the class. The default constructor is invoked. If this fails (if it does not exist, it is not accessible, and so on), a constructor (the first of the constructor's list returned at line 214) is used, trying to create all the needed parameters using their respective default constructors. If one of the parameter class does not have a default constructor, or if it is a primitive type, this attempt fails. If neither the main method nor the constructors succeeded, the application launch fails.

3. After the application ended, the shutDown method (at lines 265–273) is invoked for exiting the application helper. Note that if the business code will invoke System.exit, the shutDown method of the application helper won't be invoked.

Note that the whole launch sequence makes an heavy use of the Java reflection features.

The other piece of our simple application helper is the custom class loader, shown in Listing 6.3.

LISTING 6.3   The BankClientLoader Class

```
package com.marinilli.b2.c6.bank;

import java.util.*;
import java.net.*;
import java.io.*;
import java.util.zip.*;

/**
```

LISTING 6.3   Continued

```
 * Chapter 6 - The Custom Classloader
 *
 * @author Mauro Marinilli
 * @version 1.0
 */

public class BankClientLoader extends ClassLoader {
  private ApplicationHelper helper;

  /**
   * Constructor
   */
  public BankClientLoader(ApplicationHelper h) {
    helper = h;
  }

  /**
   * Gets a resource from the currently available resources
   * the order is the following: <br>
   *   - cached files <br>
   *   - super.classloader's resources <br>
   *   - server resources <br>
   */
  public URL getResource(String name) {
    URL resource = null;
    try {
      if (helper.isCached(name))
        return helper.getCachedFile(name).toURL();

      resource = super.getResource(name);
      // check the obtained resource
      try {
        System.out.println("BCL- resource="+resource.getContent());
        resource.getContent();
      } catch (Exception e) {
        // the url is empty or null
        System.out.println("BankClientLoader- getResource( "+name+" ) EMPTY:
"+e);
        resource = helper.getRemoteFile(name, false).toURL();
      }
    } catch (IOException e) {
      System.out.println("BankClientLoader- getResource( "+name+" ): "+e);
    }
    return resource;
  }
```

LISTING 6.3 Continued

```
/**
 * see superclasss
 */
public InputStream getResourceAsStream(String name) {
  URL url = getResource(name);
  InputStream is = null;
  if (url != null) {
    try {
      is = url.openStream();
    } catch (IOException e) {
      System.out.println("BankClientLoader- getResourceAsStream( "+name+" ):
"+e);
    }
  }
  return is;
}

/**
 * see superclasss
 */
public Class loadClass(String name) throws ClassNotFoundException {
  // This is the actions sequence:
  //
  // 1. check if the class is in local cache,
  //    if it is the case, load the class in cache
  //
  // 2. if it's not in local cache, try with the super classloader
  //
  // 3. if it is not in cache and not loaded by the ancestor classloader
  //    then ask it directly to the remote server
  //
  // 4. if not found otherwise, quit throwing an exception

  Class neededClass = null;

  // 1. check if it is cached
  if (helper.isCached(helper.getCacheClassFileName(name)+".class")) {
    System.out.println("BankClientLoader- class: "+name+" loaded from local
cache");
    neededClass = loadClass(helper.getCacheClassFileName(name),
getClass(name));
  }
```

LISTING 6.3 Continued

```
    // 2. if not found, see if super-classloader has class
    if (neededClass == null) {
      try {
        neededClass = super.findSystemClass(name);
        if (neededClass != null) {
          System.out.println("BankClientLoader- class: "+name+" loaded from
super classloader");
          return neededClass;
        }
      } catch (ClassNotFoundException e) {
        // ignore this error
//        System.out.println("BankClientLoader- class not found in super
classloader, name="+name);
      }
    }

    // 3. if still not found, look for it on the server, using a standard GET
    if (neededClass==null) {
      try {
        File f =  helper.getRemoteFile(name, true);

        if (f.exists()) {
          neededClass = loadClass(helper.getCacheClassFileName(name),
getClass(name));
        }
        else
        System.out.println("BankClientLoader- - class: "+name+" not found on
server.");
      } catch (Exception ex) {
        System.out.println("BankClientLoader- loadClass() while GET: "+ex);
      }
    }

    // 4. finally, throw an exception
    if (neededClass == null) {
      System.out.println("BankClassLoader- couldn't find class: "+ name +"
anywhere.");
      throw new ClassNotFoundException("BankClassLoader- couldn't find class:
"+ name);
    }
    return neededClass;
  }

  /**
```

LISTING 6.3 Continued

```
 * see superclasss
 */
public Class loadClass(String className, byte[] b){
  return defineClass(className, b, 0, b.length );
}


/**
 * This method returns a cached class
 * @return a cached class as a byte array
 */
protected byte[] getClass(String className){
  // flatten up package information
  String fileName = helper.getCacheClassFileName(className);
  byte[] b = null;
  int size = 0;
  try {
    File f = helper.getCachedFile(fileName+".class");
    size = (int)f.length();
    b = new byte[size];
    DataInputStream dis =
        new DataInputStream(f.toURL().openConnection().getInputStream());
    dis.readFully(b);
  } catch (Exception e){
    System.out.println("BankClientLoader- getClass("+className+"): "+e);
  }
  return b;
}


}
```

The most important thing to note in Listing 6.3 is the class loading mechanism implemented in the loadClass method (lines 73–129). The class loading procedure is the following:

1. Look for the requested class in the local cache.

2. Ask for the class to the super classloader.

3. Request the class directly to the server.

This mechanism allows for replacing already installed classes with newer versions that need only to have the same class name and be saved in the client cache. The third step is important, too, because it allows for direct server download of classes that are neither in cache nor in the classpath. In this way, completely new applications can be installed in the local cache just by specifying the main class only. Thus, once the new main class is executed, all the other classes it needs are downloaded just in time from the server if not present locally (this happens only the first time, anyway). In fact, thanks to the classloader mechanism of the J2SE platform, the needed classes are loaded by the same classloader that loaded the invoking class, if not otherwise explicitly specified (as it is done at line 240 of Listing 6.2). Hence, all classes used by the main class are loaded by our custom class loader as the classes needed by those classes, and so forth.

Another important part of our architecture is the server class, shown in Listing 6.4. It is a simple, multithreaded, socket-based server. For simplicity, we kept the deployment server (essentially the method implementing the CHECK command and the management of the downloadPolicy properties) and the so-called business server (the other protocol commands) together in one class. That is to say, there are always two server threads for each client process. One server instance works conceptually as a deployment server, providing classes and other files to the client application helper, whereas the other server thread assists the business application independently from the other instance.

LISTING 6.4 The BankServer Class

```
package com.marinilli.b2.c6.bank;

import java.net.*;
import java.io.*;
import java.util.*;

/**
 * Chapter 6 - The Bank Server
 *
 * @author Mauro Marinilli
 * @version 1.0
 */

public class BankServer implements Runnable {
  public final static char QUIT_COMMAND = 'q';
  public final static char GET_COMMAND = 'g';
  public final static char POST_COMMAND = 'p';
  public final static char CHECK_COMMAND = 'c';
  public final static String SERVER_DIR = "serverdir/";

  private DataOutputStream out;
  private DataInputStream in;
  private Properties downloadPolicy;
  private String header;
  private Socket clientSocket;
  private final static String PROPS_FILE_NAME = "downloadPolicy.properties";
```

LISTING 6.4 Continued

```java
private final static String NEWEST_POLICY = "newest";
private final static String NO_DOWNLOADS_POLICY = "none";
private final static String DEFAULT_POLICY = NEWEST_POLICY;

/**
 * Constructor
 */
public BankServer(Socket s) {
  clientSocket = s;
  loadProperties();
}

/**
 * The Thread's run
 */
public void run() {
  header = "BankServer["+Thread.currentThread().getName()+"] - ";
  System.out.println( header + "Connection Accepted.");

  try {
    out = new DataOutputStream(clientSocket.getOutputStream());
    in = new DataInputStream(clientSocket.getInputStream());
  } catch (IOException e) {
    System.out.println( header + "creating streams "+e);
    System.exit(-1);
  }
  char command = ' ';
  try {
    while ((command = in.readChar())!=-1) {
      // process incoming command
      if (command==QUIT_COMMAND) {
        System.out.println( header + "Command: QUIT.");
        System.out.println( header + "Client closed session.");
        break;
      }
      if (command==CHECK_COMMAND) {
        executeCheck();
      }
      if (command==GET_COMMAND) {
        //read the incoming string because it is the path to the requested
file
        String path = in.readUTF();
        File f = new File(SERVER_DIR+path);
        int size = (int)f.length();
```

LISTING 6.4   Continued

```
              out.writeInt(size);
              System.out.println( header + "Command: GET "+path+" size:"+size );
              if (f.exists()) {
                FileInputStream fis = new FileInputStream;
                sendToClient(new DataInputStream(fis), path);
              } else {
                // resource not found,
                // send back an empty msg
                sendToClient(new DataInputStream(new ByteArrayInputStream(new
byte[0])), path+"(not found)");
              }
            }
            if (command==POST_COMMAND) {
              //read the incoming array because it is the posted data
              String data = in.readUTF();
              System.out.println( header + "Command: POST (data=\""+data+"\")");
            }
          }//-while
          System.out.println( header + "shutting down client connection");
          out.close();
          in.close();
          clientSocket.close();
          // to avoid troubles in a multi-threaded environment
//        saveProperties();
        } catch (IOException e) {
          System.out.println( header + "Main while: "+e);
          System.exit(-1);
        }
      }

      /**
       * implements the check Command, server-side
       */
      private void executeCheck() {
        // change name
        String tName = Thread.currentThread().getName();
        Thread.currentThread().setName("Deployment-"+tName);
        header = "BankServer["+Thread.currentThread().getName()+"] - ";
        try {
          String clientId = in.readUTF();
          String[] clientRecord = read(clientId);
          if (clientRecord==null) {
            write(clientId, DEFAULT_POLICY, "1.0", null, null);
            clientRecord = read(clientId);
```

LISTING 6.4 Continued

```
      }
      String policy = clientRecord[0];
      String installedVersion = clientRecord[1];
      String replaceItems = clientRecord[2];
      String launchClass = clientRecord[3];
      if (launchClass==null)
        launchClass = "";// for protocol's sake

      System.out.println( header + "CHECK: for client: "+
                              clientId+",\n\t policy: "+
                              policy+",\n\t installedVersion: "+
                              installedVersion+",\n\t replaceItems="+
                              replaceItems+",\n\t
launchClass="+launchClass);

      if (policy.equals(NEWEST_POLICY)) {
        // the client is required to download the new version
        String[] items = getItems(replaceItems);
        out.writeInt(items.length);
        File f;
        for (int i = 0; i < items.length; i++) {
          f = new File(SERVER_DIR + items[i]);
          out.writeUTF(items[i]);
          int size = (int)f.length();
          out.writeInt(size);
          FileInputStream fis = new FileInputStream;
          sendToClient(new DataInputStream(fis), items[i]);
        }
      } else if (policy.equals(NO_DOWNLOADS_POLICY)) {
        out.writeInt(0);
      }
      //last, notify to the client the new main class, if any
      out.writeUTF(launchClass);

    } catch (IOException e) {
      System.out.println( header + "executeCheck: "+e);
      System.exit(1);
    }
  }

  /**
   * It obtains tokens from a string
   */
  private String[] getItems(String s){
```

Listing 6.4   Continued

```
    ArrayList result = new ArrayList();
    StringTokenizer st = new StringTokenizer(s,";:");
    while (st.hasMoreTokens()) {
      String w = st.nextToken();
      result.add(w);
    }
    String[] a = new String[result.size()];
    result.toArray(a);
    return a;
}

/**
 * It sends data to the client
 */
private void sendToClient(DataInputStream dis, String name){
  System.out.println( header + "sendToClient. " + name);
  byte[] buffer = new byte[1024];
  try {
    int read =0;
    while ((read = dis.read(buffer)) != -1) {
      out.write(buffer, 0, read);
    }
  } catch (IOException e) {
    System.out.println( header + "send data back to client: "+e);
  }
}


/**
 * Loads properties file
 */
private void loadProperties(){
  try {
    downloadPolicy = new Properties();
    FileInputStream in = new FileInputStream(SERVER_DIR+PROPS_FILE_NAME);
    downloadPolicy.load(in);
    in.close();
  }
  catch (IOException ex) {
    System.out.println( header + "loadProperties(): "+ex);
  }
}

/**
```

Deploying Existing Software

CHAPTER 6

169

6

DEPLOYING
EXISTING
SOFTWARE

LISTING 6.4   Continued

```
 * writes some related property values
 */
private void write(String client,
                   String policy,
                   String installedVersion,
                   String replaceItems,
                   String launchClass) {

  if (client==null)
    return;
  if (policy!=null)
    downloadPolicy.put(client+"-policy",policy);
  if (installedVersion!=null)
    downloadPolicy.put(client+"-installed",installedVersion);
  if (replaceItems!=null)
    downloadPolicy.getProperty(client+"-replace-items", replaceItems);
  if (launchClass!=null)
    downloadPolicy.getProperty(client+"-launch", launchClass);
}

/**
 * It reads some related property values
 */
private String[] read(String client){
  if (client==null)
    return null;
  String[] ret = new String[4];
  String policy =
    downloadPolicy.getProperty(client+"-policy",DEFAULT_POLICY);
  String installedVersion =
    downloadPolicy.getProperty(client+"-installed", "1.0");
  String replaceItems =
    downloadPolicy.getProperty(client+"-replace-items", "");
  String launchClass =
    downloadPolicy.getProperty(client+"-launch", "BankClient");

  ret[0] = policy;
  ret[1] = installedVersion;
  ret[2] = replaceItems;
  ret[3] = launchClass;
  return ret;
}

/**
```

LISTING 6.4 Continued

```
  * saves properties files
  */
 private void saveProperties(){
   try {
     FileOutputStream out = new FileOutputStream(SERVER_DIR+PROPS_FILE_NAME);
     downloadPolicy.store(out, "—-Bank Server download Policies file—-");
     out.close();
   }
   catch (IOException ex) {
     System.out.println( header + "saveProperties(): "+ex);
   }
   System.out.println( header + "save" );
 }

 /**
  * It launches the server
  */
 public static void main(String[] args) throws IOException {
   ServerSocket serverSocket = null;
   try {
     serverSocket = new ServerSocket(3333);
   } catch (IOException e) {
     System.out.println("BankServer - Could not listen on port: 3333: "+e);
     System.exit(-1);
   }
   System.out.println("BankServer - Waiting for Connections.");
   boolean listen = true;

   while(listen) {
     // connection started
     Thread t = new Thread(new BankServer(serverSocket.accept()));
     t.start();
   }
   serverSocket.close();
 }

}
```

The server uses a properties file to handle the CHECK command from clients. In this text file are stored the list of files that must be installed in the client cache. A simple example of such a file is shown in Listing 6.5.

Deploying Existing Software

CHAPTER 6

171

6

DEPLOYING
EXISTING
SOFTWARE

LISTING 6.5   An Example Of The `BankServer` Download Policies File

```
#— -Bank Server download Policies file— -
client0-replace-items=BankClient.class;Clazz.class;BankClientLoader.java
client0-installed=1.0
client0-policy=newest
client0-launch=com.marinilli.b2.c6.bank.BankClient
```

This property file states that regarding the "`client0`" client application, whenever it issues another CHECK command, the files listed at line 2 have to be sent to its cache when there are versions newer than 1.0 (that is recorded as the currently installed one). The main class to be launched the next time the application helper is executed is specified in line 5. This is quite a simplistic and unrealistic approach to resolution (as described in Chapter 2). Nevertheless, it gives a concrete idea of how servers could keep track of client-deployed configurations, allowing for total control over client applications.

Now let's have a look at what new applications will look like. Given our implementation, all old code still runs on our application helper (that is, the `OldBankClient` class in Listing 6.1) while newly designed applications are more rationally organized in a service provider class, `BankClientManager` (detailed in Listing 6.6) and various transaction-oriented classes as the one shown in Listing 6.7.

LISTING 6.6   The `BankClientManager` Class

```java
package com.marinilli.b2.c6.bank;

import java.lang.reflect.Method;
import java.lang.reflect.Constructor;
import java.io.*;
import java.net.MalformedURLException;
import java.net.Socket;

/**
 * Chapter 6 - This class encapsulates business-related utility services
 *
 * @author Mauro Marinilli
 * @version 1.0
 */

public class BankClientManager {
  private String[] arguments;
  private Socket socket = null;
  private DataOutputStream out = null;
  private DataInputStream in = null;
```

LISTING 6.6   Continued

```java
  private String thisClientId;

  /**
   * Class constructor
   *
   */
  public BankClientManager() {
    try {
      socket = new Socket("localhost", 3333);
      out = new DataOutputStream(socket.getOutputStream());
      in = new DataInputStream(socket.getInputStream());
    } catch (Exception e) {
      System.out.println("BankClientManager()- Couldn't work out the
connection: "+e);
      System.exit(1);
    }
    System.out.println("BankClientManager() - Connectiom established.");
  }

  /**
   * implements the POST Command
   */
  public void post(String data) throws IOException{
    sendCommand('p');
    out.writeUTF(data);
  }

  /**
   * implements the QUIT Command
   */
  public void quit() throws IOException{
    sendCommand('q');
    out.close();
    in.close();
    socket.close();
  }

  /**
   * implements the GET Command
   */
  public byte[] get(String serverFilename) throws IOException{
    sendCommand('g');
    out.writeUTF(serverFilename);
    int size = in.readInt();
    byte[] b = new byte[size];
    in.readFully(b);
```

Deploying Existing Software

CHAPTER 6

173

6

DEPLOYING
EXISTING
SOFTWARE

LISTING 6.6   Continued

```
    return b;
  }

  /**
   * sends a command to the server
   */
  private void sendCommand(char c){
    try {
      out.writeChar;
      System.out.println("BankClientManager- send command "+c);
    } catch (IOException exce) {
      System.out.println("BankClientManager- sendCommand()"+exce);
    }
  }
}
}1
```

In Listing 6.7, an example of a new client application is shown. It uses the commands from the `BankClientManager` class, and shows how classes and resources are provided transparently by the underlying `ApplicationHelper` execution.

LISTING 6.7   The `BankClient` Class

```
package com.marinilli.b2.c6.bank;

import java.io.*;
import java.net.Socket;

/**
 * Chapter 6 - The Client
 *
 * @author Mauro Marinilli
 * @version 1.0
 */

public class BankClient {
  Socket socket = null;
  private BankClientManager manager;

  public BankClient(BankClientManager mngr) {
    manager = mngr;
    try {
      executeTransaction();
      // dismiss connection
      manager.quit();
```

Listing 6.7   Continued

```
  } catch (Exception exce) {
    System.out.println("BankClient- executing transaction: "+exce);
  }
  System.out.println("BankClient- Client Log out.");
}

private void executeTransaction() throws Exception{

  System.out.println("BankClient- BankClient Executing.");
  InputStream is =
getClass().getClassLoader().getResourceAsStream("test.txt");
  int c;
  while((c = is.read())!=-1 )
    System.out.print((char)c);

  Class.forName("Clazz");

  manager.post("all OK.");
}

}
```

The method `executeTransaction` (lines 29–40 in Listing 6.7) loads a resource (in this case, a text file) from its classloader, printing out as a proof the file content. If this class is created by the `ApplicationHelper` (as it is supposed to be), the `BankClientLoader` will take charge of downloading the file if it is not present in cache. The same is true for the dynamic creation of a class, at line 37.

Running the Example

Having seen all the pieces separately, we will study a client-server session in which classes and resources are deployed transparently to the executing application and to the end-user.

Caution

When executing the `ApplicationHelper` configured to launch the `BankClient` application, be careful to not include the example class at line 37 in Listing 6.7 in your client classpath (this is possible especially if you use an IDE). In this case, the file "Clazz.class" won't appear in the client cache at the end of execution, indicating that the class was loaded by the super classloader instead. Just compile the class separately, and put the obtained file in the `serverdir` directory, from where the `BankServer` takes files for replying to clients.

Deploying Existing Software

CHAPTER 6

175

6

DEPLOYING
EXISTING
SOFTWARE

Let's see how these classes work. Before launching them, be sure to have the following directories in your work directory:

- `clientdir`. Contains the client properties file and the directory "`cached`" that holds all
  cached resources coming from the server.
- `serverdir`. Contains the deployment server properties file and all the files that the client
  can request. It is important to copy all the files here that are to be deployed, classes
  included; otherwise, the server will not find them.

First, we launch the `BankServer`, through its `main` method. Then, we invoke the
`ApplicationHelper` on the client computer.

At the end of the transaction, we can see in Listing 6.8 the output on the client, and we can see
the server output in Listing 6.9.

LISTING 6.8   The Client Output

```
ApplicationHelper- saved in cache: BankClient.class
ApplicationHelper- saved in cache: downloadPolicy.properties
ApplicationHelper- saved in cache: Clazz.class
ApplicationHelper- saved in cache: BankClientLoader.java
BankClientLoader- class: java.lang.Object loaded from super classloader
BankClientLoader- class: java.lang.Throwable loaded from super classloader
BankClientLoader- class: java.lang.Exception loaded from super classloader
BankClientLoader- class: com.marinilli.b2.c6.bank.
BankClientManager loaded from super classloader
BankClientManager() - Connectiom established.
BankClientLoader- class: java.lang.System loaded from super classloader
BankClientLoader- class: java.io.PrintStream loaded from super
classloaderBankClient- BankClient Executing.
BankClientLoader- class: java.lang.Class loaded from super classloader
BankClientLoader- class: java.lang.ClassLoader loaded from super classloader
BankClientLoader- getResource( test.txt ) EMPTY: look for it on the server
ApplicationHelper- saved in cache: test.txt
BankClientLoader- class: java.io.InputStream loaded from super classloader
hello
BankClientLoader- class: Clazz loaded from local cache
BankClientManager- send command p
BankClientManager- send command qBankClient- Client Log out.
ApplicationHelper- appl. launched creating:
    public com.marinilli.b2.c6.bank.BankClient(com.marinilli.b2.c6.bank.
➥BankClientManager)
ApplicationHelper-  closing application.
```

After the server is ready for accepting connections (line 1 in Listing 6.9), the
`ApplicationHelper` client connects, and the server forks a thread (line 2 in Listing 6.9).
Subsequently, the `ApplicationHelper` instance issues a CHECK command. Thus, the server
thread recognizes its client as a deployment client, and changes its thread name accordingly

(see lines 104–106 in Listing 6.4). This is only a cosmetics operation that will help us only to clarify the role of the two different server threads. Now, "Thread-0" in line 2 of Listing 6.9 becomes "Deployment-Thread-0" in the following lines.

In lines 3–11 of Listing 6.9, the CHECK command is carried out by the server. Consequently, the files sent by the server are saved in the client cache (lines 1–4 in Listing 6.8).

The client execution continues, and the application classes are loaded in, using our BankClientLoader (lines 5–8 in Listing 6.8). Then, the client application is launched (line 9 of Listing 6.8), and a connection with another server thread (only for business transactions) is established (line 12 of Listing 6.9). From now on, the BankClient class is executed (or, to be precise, created, as reported in lines 22–23 of Listing 6.8).

The example transaction is composed of three steps:

1. Requesting a resource from the classloader (that resource is not present in cache at first, so it has to be downloaded from the server, see lines 15, 16 of Listing 6.8). Then, the file content is printed on the output stream (line 18 of Listing 6.8).

2. A class is loaded using the Java dynamic loading feature (see line 37 in Listing 6.7). This was done essentially to fool the compiler during development time. Otherwise, it would have asked for the class Clazz, which would complicate the deployment stage because we should have had to separate this compiled class from the others.

3. Finally, a sample business command is issued at line 39 in Listing 6.7. The server receives the POST command at line 15 of Listing 6.9.

Then, after the BankClient class ends the transaction, all data structures are shut down, and the ApplicationHelper itself finishes execution (last line of Listing 6.8) while the server process will wait for accepting new connections.

Listing 6.9   The Server Output

```
BankServer - Waiting for Connections.
BankServer[Thread-0] - Connection Accepted.
BankServer[Deployment-Thread-0] - CHECK: for client: client0,
    policy: newest,
    installedVersion: 1.0,
    replaceItems=BankClient.class;downloadPolicy.properties;Clazz.class;
➥BankClientLoader.java,
    launchClass=com.marinilli.b2.c6.bank.BankClientBankServer[Deployment-
Thread-0] - sendToClient. BankClient.class
BankServer[Deployment-Thread-0] - sendToClient. downloadPolicy.properties
BankServer[Deployment-Thread-0] - sendToClient. Clazz.class
BankServer[Deployment-Thread-0] - sendToClient. BankClientLoader.java
```

Deploying Existing Software

CHAPTER 6

177

6

DEPLOYING
EXISTING
SOFTWARE

LISTING 6.9   Continued

```
BankServer[Thread-1] - Connection Accepted.
BankServer[Deployment-Thread-0] - Command: GET test.txt size:5
BankServer[Deployment-Thread-0] - sendToClient. test.txt
BankServer[Thread-1] - Command: POST (data="all OK.")
BankServer[Thread-1] - Command: QUIT.
BankServer[Thread-1] - Client closed session.
BankServer[Thread-1] - shutting down client connection
BankServer[Deployment-Thread-0] - Command: QUIT.
BankServer[Deployment-Thread-0] - Client closed session.
BankServer[Deployment-Thread-0] - shutting down client connection
```

Some Considerations

When developing mechanisms for the installation and update of existing code, some other considerations may apply.

Often, the common choice is to make the application helper module totally invisible to client (legacy) code. Although there are no strict criteria, it makes sense to provide handles for application helper services only to client software that is written explicitly to be run on that application helper. In our case, we will not provide any reference to our application helper, even if newer software may take advantage of it.

> **NOTE**
>
> The interested reader may look at Chapter 11, "Runtime Client Services," for an example of services provided by an application helper (in that case, a JNLP client) to its client applications.

In our case, there is no explicit way for a client application to tell whether it is running in a stand-alone fashion or if was launched by our application helper. A new application could try to check it out by inspecting the class type of its own classloader.

Generally speaking, after having added the deployment facilities (in our case, the ApplicationHelper and BankClientLoader classes), the remaining is often a matter of code reorganization.

This is a demonstration application. Clearly, although full-working, it is full of deficiencies. Our purpose was to keep it simple and with a code as short as possible to ease focusing on the most interesting aspects. Let's see the major limitations:

- Cache clearing is not implemented, together with selective cached files deletion. These can be done only manually.

- Conceptually, the use of the GET command in the retrieving of classes and resources by the ApplicationHelper class is a mistake. This subtle particular can reveal itself a problem as fully discussed later in this section.

- For simplicity, we designed both deployment services (GET, CHECK, QUIT) and business-related ones (GET, POST, QUIT) implemented in the same protocol. This could be a practical shortcoming, other than a conceptual overlook. A sounder design would have separated the two groups of commands.

- Classes with the same name but in different packages cannot coexist in the local cache. We didn't use the fully qualified names for informative reasons (that is, for keeping the cache contents more readable).

- There is no support for ZIP or JAR files. This has been avoided in order to keep the code simple and intuitive, but it is clear that such a feature (deploying groups of files at once) is highly desirable in a real-world deployment mechanism.

Getting Back to Our Abstract Model

Let's see how this simple deployment solution relates with the deployment model we introduced in Chapter 2. We refer to the model stages shown in Figure 2.5.

It is important to point out that the deployment solution we present here, although fully working and capable of a wide range of features, is a very simple one that is built mainly for demonstrative purposes. Hence, the implementation of the features covered in the abstract model is to be intended as a basic—not sophisticated—one, especially when compared against commercial products. Nevertheless, it could be useful to see even this simple system in the frame of the general abstract model proposed in Chapter 2.

- **Publication**. This phase is simplified because distributor and producer are the same organization. It is fulfilled by copying the files to be deployed (classes and other files) into the serverdir directory. In this way, resources are made available for deployment.

- **Application Helper Installation**. It is performed by the usual means, such as mail attachments, installer utilities, using deployment personnel, and so on.

- **Application Installation**. The first version of the client application comes bundled with the application helper package.

- **AH Check-Out**. It is performed during the CHECK command communications. The resolution phase is performed entirely on the server, by means of the downloadPolicy properties file.

- **Application Management**. It is an outcome of the CHECK command (that is issued for updating the application). A simple form of application configuration could be achieved by using properties files stored in the cache and updated by the server. There is no way to uninstall an application.

- **Application Helper Execution**. Some of the various steps in this phase are provided by our simple deployment solution.

  For the AH-application support, only the on-the-run update (taking advantage of the classloader mechanism) and resource distribution features are partially implemented. For the latter, for example, it is not possible to decide where, on the local file system, deployed resources are saved. Features not implemented are JRE preparation, debugging, and other types of on-the-run management.

  For the application helper management support, only the application helper configuration feature is supported using the `appHelper` properties file. This file in the current implementation has been kept outside the cache directory. Hence, it cannot be modified by server commands, making impossible to configure remotely the application helper through its property file. Features such as application helper update and other management are not implemented.

- **Deployment Server Management**. In this case, to manage the server for deployment it's enough to administer the `serverdir` directory and the `downloadPolicy` properties file.

Other notions used in our model (such as client environment and configurations, deployment policies, and so on) are poorly implemented in this system.

The Satellite Effect

As was mentioned in Chapter 4 (and will be pointed out in Chapter 7, "Building Your Own Deployment Solution"), inexperienced developers often tend to underestimate the freedom of update their solution provides when building a brand new deployment solution.

We called it the satellite effect because it is like the development and launch of a satellite into space. Once we try to update and manipulate it, we can discover that our design was flawed, and some unexpected parts of the system are out of reach. We cannot modify them without launching a new satellite (that is, redistributing the whole package).

Our `ApplicationHelper` suffers from this weakness, too. The parts that are "out-of-reach" are the two classes that compose the application helper. They are hard-wired, and cannot be modified by our deployment protocol. If we wanted to change them, we would have to redistribute a newer version of the application helper, with all the costs it would have.

However, what we can modify with a relatively small effort is the way CHECK commands are executed. Simply factoring out the `check` method and its related data in a new class (to be downloaded by our `BankClientLoader`, of course) will allow for easy startup deployment modifications. When we want to modify the CHECK command, we just download the new class that will implement the new startup deployment code. Unfortunately, we don't have the space to present this and other enhancements to the code presented here.

Another shortcoming in our design (already mentioned before) is regarding the GET command used by the `getRemoteFile` method beginning at line 163 in Listing 6.2. To download a file from the server (both for missing classes and resources), the `ApplicationHelper` uses the GET command. Given that the `ApplicationHelper` is not updateable anymore once it is installed on the client, we obtain that the GET command is hard-wired in the protocol. When we want to modify the GET command in our communication protocol in the future, we are forced to create another command, say GET2. If we modify the existing GET command, our application helpers installed on the clients won't work anymore. In this example, we must keep working legacy code that uses the GET command, so we have no choice. Anyway, in other situations this could reveal itself to be a problem in the long-term software maintenance.

This problem originated from the fact that we violated the design principle of keeping separated the business from the deployment layer. The GET command is a business command we used as for deployment.

Summary

Abstracting from the code reuse problem that motivated this deployment solution at first, there are several general aspects to point out here. For instance, all JNLP client implementations (as Java Web Start) could be thought of as a more sophisticated version of our architecture, in which application helpers parse special XML files in order to provide a wider range of deployment services.

The most interesting (and reusable) aspects of this solution are as follows:

- The classloader mechanism for implementing a full-fledged, 100% Java application helper.
- The overall software architecture: An application helper that uses a cache mechanism for providing deployment services to business classes. Clearly, a real-world application helper will employ several possibly optimized caches, other auxiliary data structures, etc.
- The software design process for reorganizing more rationally the existing code, and generally to better think classes relatively to their deployment.
- A mechanism for ensuring full compatibility of new deployment features with older software.

While other details such as the communication mechanism, the class and resources loading rules, and the cache implementation are all to be intended as demonstrative and limited to the current case only.

Building Your Own Deployment Solution

IN THIS CHAPTER

After having seen the deployment options for non-J2SE platforms (in Chapter 5, "Deployment Options for Non-J2SE Clients") and the issue of redesigning the deployment mechanism for already-deployed code (in Chapter 6, "Deploying Existing Software"), we focus again on the desktop front (J2SE and JDK 1.x) for discussing the available choices in those cases in which standard deployment solutions cannot be applied.

In this chapter, we will continue the discussion begun in Chapter 4, "Designing for Deployment," concentrating on deployment circuits built to fit particular purposes. We will switch from the design-oriented, general approach of Chapter 4 to a more practical, case-based one. The topic being discussed (building ad-hoc deployment solutions) makes it quite limiting to rely only on general considerations. The proposed examples range from very common situations (deploying applications via CD-ROMs or in a intranet scenario) to customizable architectures that will work in several different cases (the `deploylet` package).

Designing Ad-Hoc Deployment Solutions

Given the broad range of possible situations developers face in real-world cases, an exhaustive discussion of all the design choices is almost impossible.

Standard deployment technologies (such as JNLP, third-party deployment tools, and so on) may not apply for many reasons. In Chapter 4, we saw the limits of these technologies; we will discuss here how to set up effectively and economically a deployment circuit that will work in these limited scenarios as well.

There are three main reasons why developers resort to ad-hoc deployment solutions, depending on standard deployment technologies limits:

- Standard deployment technologies are incompatible with the given scenario.
- For some other non-technical reason, ad-hoc solutions are preferred over standard ones (for example, high licensing fees or corporate policy).
- Standard deployment technologies don't provide a particular service, so the only way to go is to customize some existing deployment technology or build it completely from scratch.

Choosing the Starting Point

After realizing that an ad-hoc deployment solution is needed, the next problem is from where to start building it. We already discussed deployment means in Chapter 4; in this chapter, we focus on situations in which not all the standard deployment technologies are available. In Figure 7.1, a deployment design box illustrates the possible choices given the following (fictitious) design constraints:

- J2SE cannot be used (see the gray box in Figure 7.1). There could be several practical situations that prevent the use of J2SE including the use of Java 1.x legacy code that would be too costly to reengineer (maybe because ill-documented or badly designed), the need of compatibility with older tools or libraries, the costs of acquiring new licenses, etc.

- Applets cannot be used (note that this constraint regards the client application, not the deployment infrastructure, so it cannot be represented in Figure 7.1).

- In our deployment circuit, we need to provide two services: automatic updates and a special version of the incremental updates service (line L1 in Figure 7.1).

We have the following available choices:

- Using JRE 1.x to develop from scratch a deployment solution that will work in our scenario (point A in Figure 7.1). Given the impossibility to use applets, we don't consider the JDK 1.0.x option.

- Choosing a third-party deployment solution—customizing it to fit our needs (point C in Figure 7.1).

- Employing a skilled workforce (point D)—although possible in theory, is quite inappropriate in this case.

NOTE

For an introduction to the diagrams such as Figure 7.1, see the discussion of Figures 4.1 and 4.3 in Chapter 4.

Of the three possible deployment means for implementing our deployment circuit (points A,C and D in Figure 7.1), we chose the Java 1.x solution. It requires some additional ad-hoc code (the arrow W in Figure 7.1) in order to provide the desired deployment services. The final deployment circuit (that is, JRE 1.x plus some specialized code) is represented in Figure 7.1 by the point B (that lies on line L1). This choice was motivated by the simplicity of the needed deployment services, that justifies the use of a potentially more expensive development effort when compared with the other available options. In fact, customizing a complex third-party deployment tool would require the prior study of its sophisticated developer APIs together with the license fee costs and may become more time-consuming than developing the deployment services from scratch using a more primitive but well-known starting base. In a different situation, when the needed deployment services are more complex, this choice (a simpler deployment means) could become too expensive to be adopted.

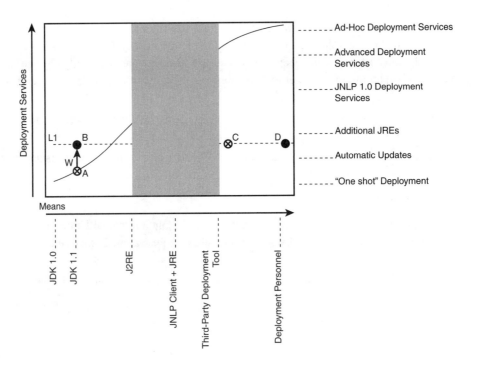

FIGURE 7.1

Choosing the deployment implementation starting point.

Such trade-offs are typical of the design of custom deployment solutions. Often, the best way is to customize an existing deployment solution, rather than building one totally from scratch. This choice needs experienced developers with that given technology and a clear view of the available design choices. What was said in Chapter 4 about general deployment design applies here as well.

To recap, when we need to implement an ad-hoc deployment circuit, we have to decide which deployment means (among one of those defined in Chapter 4) is best suited for implementing the base of our deployment circuit. In making this decision, we should consider the parameters used for customizing standard deployment technologies (license fees, end-user impact, etc.; see Chapter 4) plus our ability to effectively provide ad-hoc code built on top of the chosen deployment technology in order to implement the planned services. This latter aspect may involve considerations such as the level of experience with the given technology, time to market, and other useful software development figures.

AH and Deployment Server Design

Often, designing ad-hoc deployment solutions is a matter of client-server design. Many good books are available on such a broad topic, and we probably wouldn't add anything new to the field by discussing it here. Anyway, providing deployment services is a rather specialized, peculiar activity that deserves some observations.

- Designing a deployment solution gives great freedom of choice to developers, but (especially for this reason) can result in huge, unpractical deployment solutions. In fact, deployment services are often run behind the scenes in a transparent fashion. If they are not designed privileging this aspect, they can become bulky, complex systems when loaded with real applications.

- In real-world cases, Application Helpers are rarely employed—for several reasons. First of all, they are expensive to build and complex to manage remotely from a centralized server. Unfortunately, some design shortcomings become apparent only after the AHs are shipped to all remote clients, resembling the design shortcomings of the early pioneering satellites that couldn't be fixed after they were launched into orbit (thus generating huge economic losses). Although software is not so expensive to build, and thorough testing will solve most problems, the real-world test is always a risk for complex deployment scenarios. Furthermore, ad-hoc Application Helpers don't fit well in particular specialized situations, in which simpler solutions that take advantage of the given scenario peculiarities could be employed more effectively.

- Performance is always an issue when developing Java code, and even more when it comes to such "infrastructure" services such as deployment ones. This aspect favors developing fast, lightweight ad-hoc solutions in contrast with complete, heavy, and general ones. Of course, development costs should be taken into account, as we saw in Chapter 4 and mentioned briefly previously.

Having said that, we begin the most interesting part of the chapter with some examples that shed some light on different scenarios in which custom deployment is often needed.

Examples

In this section, we will see some real cases of Java implementations of ad-hoc deployment solutions. The code is illustrative, and may need to be polished or adapted in order to be used in your particular case. These examples assume that standard deployment solutions (installer utilities, JNLP, third-party solutions, simple applets) cannot be used or must be customized in order to achieve the particular need. This assumption justifies the choice of an ad-hoc, possibly expensive, deployment solution creation.

Installing from CD-ROMs

A common scenario is the installation of Java code from a CD-ROM physically delivered to end-users. Despite that, a variety of standard tools exist for this popular case; sometimes, various particular constraints don't allow for their use. In this example, we will see a simple implementation of a general-purpose installer utility.

Our CD-ROM Java installer features the basic one-shot installation service.

How It Works

The installation process sequence is the following:

1. A native executable is launched, either from a user's command or automatically. In our example, an automatically launched Windows script would start the installation when the CD-ROM is inserted into the CD reader.

2. The native executable launches our Java installer using a JRE on the CD-ROM. We assume that there is always room for such an auxiliary JRE on our installation CD-ROM. Note that we don't assume any JRE pre-installed on the client computer.

3. Our Java application works as a normal installer following the instructions contained in a given configuration file stored on the CD-ROM. By changing this file and modifying the proposed code it is possible to customize this example to handle a wide range of ad-hoc deployment cases.

In Figure 7.2, there is a screenshot from our installer at work.

FIGURE 7.2

The Installer application initial dialog box.

Users can decide the installation type among three choices: minimal, typical, and custom. The latter choice will prompt the user with the customization dialog box shown in Figure 7.3.

FIGURE 7.3

The Choose Application Components dialog box.

Whichever installation type the user chooses, when the install button is hit, another recapping dialog box is shown to the user (see Figure 7.4), so that any further options can be modified before the installation takes places.

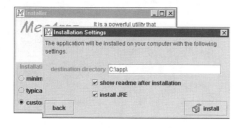

FIGURE 7.4

The Installation Summary dialog box.

When the user hits the install button in Figure 7.4, the installation begins. According to the user choice and depending on the particular platform, the proper JRE is installed. (In our simple case, we provided only Windows support: It is enough to launch the Sun's JRE native installer to perform the JRE installation on such a platform.) During the application installation (that is, basically copying files from the CD-ROM to the client's hard disk), a progress dialog box is shown to the user (see Figure 7.5).

Eventually, an instruction file is shown to the user when the installation is complete, as shown in Figure 7.6.

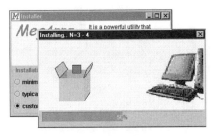

FIGURE 7.5

The progress dialog box shown to the user during the installation.

FIGURE 7.6

Finally an instruction text file is shown to the user.

As we will see in the next section, this is just the basic implementation of a CD-ROM installer that can be customized in many ways.

The Code

The following code (like all the code given in the other examples) is available on the Companion Web site for this book.

COMPANION
Web site For brevity, we will not show all the code here. Instead, we will focus on the deployment aspects and on the overall class structure. The package is composed of six classes:

- **CDLauncher**. The main class that is invoked by the native launcher. This class handles the whole installation process, eventually showing up other auxiliary dialogs to the user. These JDialogs subclasses form the remaining of the package. (The CDLauncher class is reported in Listing 7.1.)

- **InstallerDialog**. A convenience abstract class that perform some operations common to all CDLauncher's auxiliary dialogs.

- **CustomInstallDialog**. Used for modifying modules installation, shown at work in Figure 7.3. Its code is not reported here because of lack of interest.

- **InstallationProcessDialog**. Shown in Figure 7.5, its code is reported in Listing 7.3 and discussed right after it.

- **SummaryDialog**. A screenshot from an instance of this class is shown in Figure 7.4. Its code is not discussed here.

- **ReadDialog**. A simple dialog showing a text file at the end of the installation. A screenshot from an instance of this class is shown in Figure 7.6. Its code is not discussed here.

Listing 7.1 shows the CDLauncher class, the main class of our installer application.

LISTING 7.1   The CDLauncher Class

```
package com.marinilli.b2.c7.launcher;
import java.awt.event.*;
import java.util.Properties;
import java.util.ArrayList;
import java.util.StringTokenizer;
import java.io.IOException;
import java.io.FileInputStream;
import java.io.FileOutputStream;
import java.io.FileReader;
import java.io.File;
import javax.swing.*;
import java.awt.*;
import javax.swing.border.*;
import javax.swing.event.*;

/**
 * Chapter 7 - the main class for the CD-ROM installer
 *
 * @author Mauro Marinilli
 * @version 1.0
 */
public class CDLauncher extends JFrame implements Runnable {
  private final static String PROPS_FILENAME = "install.properties";
  public final static String SETUP_DIR = "setup/";
  public final static String SETUP_RES_DIR = SETUP_DIR + "res/";
  private String currentDir;
  private Properties installationSettings;
  private String appName;
```

LISTING 7.1   Continued

```java
private String appIconName;
private String appLargeIconName;
private int alreadyInstalledFiles;
private String destinationDir;
private String applDesc;
public static ImageIcon installIcon;

private String[] minInstallationFiles;
private String[] fullInstallationFiles;
private String[] fullInstallationDesc;
private String[] typicalInstallationFiles;
private boolean installJre = true;
private boolean showReadme = true;
private String[] resources;

//GUI stuff
JPanel jPanel1 = new JPanel();
JPanel jPanel2 = new JPanel();
JRadioButton jRadioMinimal = new JRadioButton();
JRadioButton jRadioCustom = new JRadioButton();
JRadioButton jRadioTypical = new JRadioButton();
JButton installButton = new JButton();
JLabel imageLabel = new JLabel();
JTextArea msgTextArea = new JTextArea();

/**
 *  Constructor
 */
public CDLauncher() {
  currentDir = System.getProperty("user.dir") + System.getProperty
➥ ("file.separator");
  loadProperties();

  // GUI setup
  setIconImage(new ImageIcon(appIconName).getImage());
  installIcon = new ImageIcon(SETUP_DIR + "icon.gif");
  Box box1 = Box.createVerticalBox();
  TitledBorder titledBorder1 =
      new TitledBorder(BorderFactory.createLineBorder(Color.lightGray,2)
➥ ,"Installation Options");
  setTitle("Installer");
  setDefaultCloseOperation(WindowConstants.DO_NOTHING_ON_CLOSE);
  addWindowListener(new java.awt.event.WindowAdapter() {
    public void windowClosing(WindowEvent e) {
```

LISTING 7.1 Continued

```
      quitInstallation();
   }
});
// radio buttons setting
jRadioMinimal.setText("minimal");
jRadioCustom.setText("custom");
jRadioTypical.setText("typical");
jRadioTypical.setSelected(true);//the default one
ButtonGroup group = new ButtonGroup();
installButton.addActionListener(new java.awt.event.ActionListener() {
   public void actionPerformed(ActionEvent e) {
      install();
   }
});
group.add(jRadioMinimal);
group.add(jRadioTypical);
group.add(jRadioCustom);

installButton.setText("Install");
installButton.setIcon(installIcon);
jPanel2.setBorder(titledBorder1);
jPanel2.setLayout(new BorderLayout());
imageLabel.setIcon(new ImageIcon(appLargeIconName));
jPanel1.setLayout(new BorderLayout());
msgTextArea.setPreferredSize(new Dimension(180,80));
msgTextArea.setBorder(BorderFactory.createEmptyBorder(4,6,4,6));
msgTextArea.setText(applDesc);
msgTextArea.setLineWrap(true);
msgTextArea.setEditable(false);
msgTextArea.setWrapStyleWord(true);

getContentPane().add(jPanel1, BorderLayout.CENTER);
jPanel1.add(imageLabel, BorderLayout.CENTER);
jPanel1.add(msgTextArea, BorderLayout.EAST);
jPanel1.setBackground(Color.white);
getContentPane().add(jPanel2, BorderLayout.SOUTH);
jPanel2.add(box1, BorderLayout.CENTER);
box1.add(jRadioMinimal, null);
box1.add(jRadioTypical, null);
box1.add(jRadioCustom, null);
jPanel2.add(installButton, BorderLayout.EAST);

//shows up
pack();
```

LISTING 7.1   Continued

```
   if (getSize().width < 256)
     setSize(400, 256);
   setVisible(true);
 }

 /**
  * Loads properties file
  */
 private void loadProperties(){
   try {
     installationSettings = new Properties();
     FileInputStream in = new FileInputStream(SETUP_DIR+PROPS_FILENAME);
     installationSettings.load(in);
     //now reads in all variables
     appName = installationSettings.getProperty
➥ ("application-name", "Application");
     appIconName = SETUP_DIR + installationSettings.getProperty
➥"application-icon", "");
     appLargeIconName = SETUP_DIR + installationSettings.getProperty
➥ ("application-large-icon", "");
     applDesc = installationSettings.getProperty
➥ ("application-desc", "");

     minInstallationFiles =
         getItems(installationSettings.getProperty
➥ ("application-minimal-set", ""));
     fullInstallationFiles =
         getItems(installationSettings.getProperty(
➥"application-full-set", "m.jar"));
     typicalInstallationFiles =
         getItems(installationSettings.getProperty
➥ ("application-typical-set", ""));
     destinationDir = installationSettings.getProperty
➥ ("destination-dir", "c:\\app\\");
     fullInstallationDesc =
         getItems(installationSettings.getProperty
➥ ("application-full-desc", "basic"));

     in.close();
   }
   catch (IOException ex) {
     System.out.println("ApplicationHelper- loadProperties(): " + ex);
   }
 }
```

LISTING 7.1   Continued

```
/**
 * It obtains tokens from a string
 */
private String[] getItems(String s){
  ArrayList result = new ArrayList();
  StringTokenizer st = new StringTokenizer(s,";:");
  while (st.hasMoreTokens()) {
    String w = st.nextToken();
    result.add(w);
  }
  String[] a = new String[result.size()];
  result.toArray(a);
  return a;
}

/**
 * Install the application
 */
public void install() {
  if (jRadioCustom.isSelected()) {
    // the custom option has been chosen
    CustomInstallDialog cid = new CustomInstallDialog(this);
    cid.setVisible(true);
    install(cid.getChosenResources());
  } else if (jRadioTypical.isSelected()) {
    //
    install(typicalInstallationFiles);
  } else if (jRadioMinimal.isSelected()) {
    //
    install(minInstallationFiles);
  }
}

/**
 * Install the specified set of files
 */
private void install(String[] res) {
  if (res == null)
    return;
  resources = res;
  SummaryDialog sd = new SummaryDialog(this);
  sd.setVisible(true);
  if (!sd.isInstallChoice())
    return;
```

LISTING 7.1   Continued

```
  alreadyInstalledFiles = 0;
  Thread t = new Thread(this);
  t.start();

  new InstallationProgressDialog(this);
}


/**
 * launch the installer thread
 */
public void run() {
  if (isInstallJre())
    installJre();
  // install chosen files
  File f = new File(destinationDir);
  f.mkdirs();

  File file;
  for (int i = 0; i < resources.length; i++) {
    alreadyInstalledFiles++;
    try {
      copy(resources[i]);
      Thread.currentThread().sleep(1000);//XXX only cosmetics: remove it!
    } catch (Exception ex) {
      System.out.println("During Installation: "+ex);
    }
  }
  installCustom();
  // installation finished
  alreadyInstalledFiles = -1;
  if (isShowReadme()) {
    ReadDialog rd = new ReadDialog(this);
  }
  installationFinished();
}

/**
 * performs the actual files copy
 */
private void copy (String from){
  try {
    File inputFile = new File(currentDir + SETUP_RES_DIR + from);
    File outputFile = new File(destinationDir + from);
```

LISTING 7.1 Continued

```
    System.out.println("from="+inputFile+" to="+outputFile);

    FileInputStream in = new FileInputStream(inputFile);
    FileOutputStream out = new FileOutputStream(outputFile);
    int c;

    while ((c = in.read()) != -1)
       out.write;
    in.close();
    out.close();
  }
  catch (Exception ex) {
    System.out.println("during file copy: "+ex);
  }
}

/**
 * installs the proper JRE depending the current OS
 */
private void installJre(){
  System.out.println("installJre()"+System.getProperty("os.name"));
  final String WIN_PATH = "jre\\win\\";
  if (System.getProperty("os.name").indexOf("Win")!=-1) {
    File f = new File(currentDir + WIN_PATH);
    String jres[] = f.list();
    System.out.println("Installing WIN JRE:" + jres[0]);
    try {
      Runtime.getRuntime().exec(currentDir + WIN_PATH + jres[0]);
    } catch (Exception ex) {
      System.out.println("Installing JRE: "+ex);
    }
    alreadyInstalledFiles ++;
  }
}

/**
 * performs some special-purpose code
 */
private void installCustom(){
  // add your code here, if needed
  // ...
  alreadyInstalledFiles ++;
}
```

7
BUILDING YOUR
OWN DEPLOYMENT
SOLUTION

LISTING 7.1   Continued

```java
/**
 * ask before leaving the installation
 */
public void quitInstallation() {
  int choice = JOptionPane.showConfirmDialog(this,
                              "Are You Sure?",
                              "Quit Installation",
                              JOptionPane.OK_CANCEL_OPTION,
                              JOptionPane.WARNING_MESSAGE);
  if (choice == JOptionPane.CANCEL_OPTION) {
    setVisible(true);
    return;
  }
  installationFinished();
}

/**
 * obtain the readme file
 */
public String getReadme(){
  StringBuffer s = new StringBuffer();
  try {
    FileReader fr = new FileReader(currentDir + SETUP_RES_DIR + "readme");

    char buffer[] = new char[512];
    int i;
    while((i = fr.read(buffer)) != -1)
      s.append(buffer,0,i);
  } catch (Exception ex) {
    System.out.println("during readme file read: "+ex);
  }
  return s.toString();
}

/**
 * invoked at the end of the installation
 */
public void installationFinished(){
  System.out.println("Installation Finished.");
  System.exit(0);
}
```

LISTING 7.1   Continued

```java
// accessory methods

public int getAlreadyInstalled(){
  return alreadyInstalledFiles;
}

public int getTotalItemsToInstall(){
  return resources.length;
}

public String getDestinationDir(){
  return destinationDir;
}

public void setDestinationDir(String dir){
  destinationDir = dir;
}

public void setInstallJre(boolean newInstallJre) {
  installJre = newInstallJre;
}

public boolean isInstallJre() {
  return installJre;
}

public void setShowReadme(boolean newShowReadme) {
  showReadme = newShowReadme;
}

public boolean isShowReadme() {
  return showReadme;
}

public String[] getFullInstallationFiles() {
  return fullInstallationFiles;
}

public String[] getFullInstallationDesc() {
  return fullInstallationDesc;
}
```

LISTING 7.1 Continued

```
/**
 * main method
 */
public static void main(String[] args) {
  CDLauncher CDLauncher1 = new CDLauncher();
}


}
```

From Listing 7.1 we can see that all the action takes place during the installer thread execution (the run method beginning at line 207). Such a thread is created and launched at lines 197-198.

The install method (beginning at line 169 in Listing 7.1) will begin the physical installation of the specified files. Depending on the selected options it can bring up a customization dialog in order to let the user directly choose the modules to be installed (see Figure 7.4). For simplicity, in such a dialog the first item is always intended to be necessary to every installation and it cannot de-selected (it is thought to be the core module). The physical installation is performed by the copy method, starting at line 236.

The installJre method (beginning at line 259 of Listing 7.1) takes care of executing the proper installation executable (located in a particular directory on the CD-ROM, depending on the supported platform). In this implementation only Windows machines are supported. For adding support to install the needed JRE on other platforms it is enough to extend the installJre method.

When needing some special installation activity, you can subclass the CDLauncher class providing your own implementation of the installCustom method at line 278 of Listing 7.1. In this way for example, platform-dependent installation directives could be enforced by means of native code invoked by this method (for example to write some application installation data in the Windows Registry). This method provides the flexibility you may need and that general-purpose installers (even if more sophisticated) may not have.

Method loadProperties (beginning at line 123 of Listing 7.1) loads the configuration file (install.properties, reported in Listing 7.4 below) that specifies the installation data.

Finally, note that the statement at line 219 of Listing 7.1 is not needed in production code and should be deleted.

> **CAUTION**
>
> In the provided example pack for the CD-ROM installer package, the JRE installation file and the whole tempjre directory content are omitted to save download time. In order to run this example, be sure to put a JRE installation executable for Windows in the "cdrom-root\jre\win" directory, such as "j2re-1_3_1-win.exe " from Sun (or newer). You can download it from http://java.sun.com/j2se/. Furthermore, a full-blown JRE (for Windows) file hierarchy has to be copied into the "cdrom-root\tempjre" directory. For simplicity, use the installed JRE you got from the previous step, or another one you have already installed.

The InstallerDialog class is shown in Listing 7.2.

LISTING 7.2 The InstallerDialog Class

```
package com.marinilli.b2.c7.launcher;
import java.awt.*;
import javax.swing.*;

/**
 * Chapter 7 - the Installer-dependent abstract dialog.
 * all installer sub-dialogs extends this one
 *
 * @author Mauro Marinilli
 * @version 1.0
 */
public abstract class InstallerDialog extends JDialog {
  protected CDLauncher installer;

  /**
   *  Constructor
   */
  public InstallerDialog(CDLauncher inst, String title) {
    super(inst, title , true);
    installer = inst;
    Point p = installer.getLocation();
    p.translate(60,40);
    setLocation(p);
    graphInit();
  }
```

LISTING 7.2 Continued

```
/**
 *   this method is implemented by subclasses
 */
abstract void graphInit();


}
```

The `InstallerDialog` class in Listing 7.3 is the common superclass of all auxiliary Installer dialogs and performs only GUI initialization tasks.

An interesting class is the one responsible for showing the installation progress to the user, the `InstallationProgressDialog` class shown in Listing 7.3.

LISTING 7.3 The `InstallationProgressDialog` Class

```
package com.marinilli.b2.c7.launcher;
import java.awt.*;
import javax.swing.*;
import javax.swing.border.Border;
import java.awt.event.*;

/**
 * Chapter 7 - shows the user the installation progress
 *
 * @author Mauro Marinilli
 * @version 1.0
 */
public class InstallationProgressDialog extends InstallerDialog {
  private final static String TITLE_HEADER = "Installing.. ";
  private JProgressBar progressBar;
  private Timer timer;

  /**
   *   Constructor
   */
  public InstallationProgressDialog(CDLauncher inst) {
    super(inst, TITLE_HEADER);
  }

  /**
   *   GUI initialization
   */
  void graphInit() {
    setModal(false);
```

LISTING 7.3   Continued

```
    JPanel panel1 = new JPanel();
    JLabel imageLabel = new JLabel();
    progressBar = new JProgressBar();
    progressBar.setBorder(BorderFactory.createEmptyBorder(2,6,10,6));
    progressBar.setStringPainted(true);
    int totalSteps = installer.getTotalItemsToInstall() + 1 ;//
➥last step for custom inst.
    if (installer.isInstallJre())
      totalSteps++;
    progressBar.setMaximum(totalSteps);
    ImageIcon img = new ImageIcon(CDLauncher.SETUP_DIR + "installer.gif");
    imageLabel.setIcon(img);
    panel1.setLayout(new BorderLayout());
    panel1.add(progressBar, BorderLayout.SOUTH);
    panel1.add(imageLabel, BorderLayout.CENTER);
    getContentPane().add(panel1);

    progressBar.setValue(0);
    timer = new Timer(1000, new ActionListener() {
      public void actionPerformed(ActionEvent evt) {
        int n = installer.getAlreadyInstalled();
        if (n < 0) {
          Toolkit.getDefaultToolkit().beep();
          timer.stop();
          dispose();
        }
        progressBar.setValue(n);
        setTitle(TITLE_HEADER +
        "N="+installer.getAlreadyInstalled()+" - "+installer
➥.getTotalItemsToInstall());
      }
    });

    pack();
    setVisible(true);
    setCursor(new Cursor(Cursor.WAIT_CURSOR));
    setResizable(false);
    // last, start the timer
    timer.start();
  }

}
```

7

**BUILDING YOUR
OWN DEPLOYMENT
SOLUTION**

It is interesting to see how the progress dialog is managed using a Swing Timer object, created as an anonymous class at line 48 in Listing 7.3. Such a timer is activated every second, and it refreshes the progress bar value (line 55 in Listing 7.3) according to the installation's current state. The progress dialog queries the CDLauncher to obtain the current installation progress state. Note that the timer is started automatically at the end of the dialog creation (line 66).

Another important file is the install.properties properties file that instructs the CDLauncher class how to customize the current application. An example of such a file is reported in Listing 7.4.

LISTING 7.4   The install.properties Text File

```
#----------------------------------------#
#
#  installation properties file
#
#----------------------------------------#


#
# the application title
#
application-name=MegAppz


#
# the application icon
#
application-icon=appicon.gif


#
# the application large icon
#
application-large-icon=applarge.gif


#
# the application description
#
application-desc=It\ is\ a\ powerful\ utility\ that\
➥provides\ full\ support\ for\ your\ work\ with\
➥ a\ simple\ and\ easy\ to\ use\ user\ interface.


#
# the application minimal installation set of files
#
application-minimal-set=a.jar
```

LISTING 7.4   Continued

```
#
# the application typical installation set of files
#
application-typical-set=a.jar;b.jar


#
# the application full installation set of files
#
application-full-set=a.jar;b.jar;c.jar;d.jar


#
# the short description for each installation file
#
application-full-desc=core\ GUI\ component;advanced\
➡engine;additional\ extra\ module;power\ pack


#
# the application destination directory
#
destination-dir=C:\\app\\
```

Finally, an example of a native executable that will launch our CDLauncher application is supplied in Listing 7.5. Such a batch file is only demonstrative, and could be invoked directly by the user or by some platform-dependent auto-launching mechanism, such as the one provided on Windows platforms by the autorun.inf file. Note that the path to the JVM executable is platform-dependent (\bin\java.exe on Windows platforms, for example). In this way, different native executables could refer to different temporary JREs.

LISTING 7.5   The launch-win.bat native batch file.

```
call tempjre\bin\java.exe -jar setup\launch.jar
```

File Settings

Our installer works thanks to a predefined file hierarchy on the CD-ROM. To run the examples, set your IDE preferences to make the "cdrom-root" directory the current working directory. This directory is supposed to be copied integrally on the CD-ROM in order for the installer to work. Then, refer to such a directory contents for the standard locations of installation items.

In particular, our simple installer uses the following items in a hard-wired fashion:

- Files in the `cdrom-root/setup/` directory.
- Items in the `cdrom-root/setup/res/` directory are the items to be installed on the client computer. Typically, all JAR/ZIP files and the "readme" file are stored in this directory.
- The `CDLauncher` will look for the "readme" file exclusively with the given name: `cdrom-root/setup/res/readme`.
- In the `cdrom-root/jre/` directory are listed all the JRE installation files organized in separated directories for the given OS.
- In the `cdrom-root/tempjre/`, the native executable will look for the auxiliary JRE needed to execute the `CDLauncher` application.

> **NOTE**
>
> This installer uses a temporary JRE interpreter, located in the `tempjre/` directory only to launch the `CDLauncher` Java application. This one in turn will properly install another JRE on the client computer, located in the `jre/` directory, while the content of the `tempjre/` directory is never copied on the local hard disk.

An Installer Applet

A simple example of ad-hoc deployment is represented by an installer applet. Such an applet is capable of saving some files on the local computer. This simple arrangement implements a one-shot installation deployment circuit with little effort, while also showing how the Plug-In could be used as an effective deployment means.

One common problem with applets is that they easily tend to get bulky, and their download can be rather tedious. In fact, one of the shortcomings of the applet model is the little control the developer has over the applet caching mechanism. Using this technique (that is, saving locally applet's resources), we can "install" some parts or even the whole program locally on the client hard disk. One can think of using the applet as a mere "installer" for opportunely placing files on the client hard disk. When implementing this technique, some problems need to be solved. The main hurdle is represented by the applet's security sandbox. We will use the Plug-In utility included in the J2SE JRE distributed freely by Sun. This will solve nicely the JRE installation problem (especially in an intranet environment, as we will see) from a developer's perspective, but will require the end-user to download the JRE installation file (around 5MB). Of course, one can use some alternative method, as shown in the previous example. The real problem is that such a technique is quite obtrusive, and end-users hardly will allow an external application to take control of their local hard disk.

Once we obtained the access on the client hard disk we will save the needed files and launch the "real" slimmed-down applet. In order to fool the applet container, we can use a custom classloader, as discussed in the previous chapter. This way, we can implement a "mixed-mode" deployment solution that will take advantage of the best of both worlds—applets and locally cached applications—in a fully transparent way. A number of enhancements are possible, such as some mechanism for detecting newer versions, for example (forcing to reload the local cache) or directly executing the application once installed, etc.

We are interested in showing a simple usage of the Plug-In utility, so we will not get into such details. Our basic installer applet is shown in Listing 7.6.

CAUTION

In the provided example pack for the applet installer package, the JRE installation file is omitted to save download time. In order to download the Plug-In in this example, be sure to put a JRE installation executable file for Windows substituting the fake "j2re-1_3_1-win.exe " file. You can use the same file as the CDLauncher example or, if you haven't already done so, you can download it from http://java.sun.com/ j2se/. If the Plug-In is already installed on your computer, you can skip the file substitution and run the example.

In order to run this example you should unzip the example pack in a directory installed on your Web server, likewise all other examples in this book that require a Web server support, and open up a Web browser pointing to the following address: "http://server/b2/c7/installer.html" (If your Web server address and directory structure are different than the one used in the example you will need to modify accordingly the supplied installer.html page).

LISTING 7.6 The InstallerApplet Class

```
package com.marinilli.b2.c7.installerapplet;
import java.awt.*;
import java.awt.event.*;
import java.applet.*;
import javax.swing.*;
import java.io.*;
import java.net.*;
import java.util.*;
```

LISTING 7.6 Continued

```
/**
 * Chapter 7 - The installer applet
 *
 * @author Mauro Marinilli
 * @version 1.0
 */
public class InstallerApplet extends JApplet {
  boolean isStandalone = false;
  JLabel titleLabel = new JLabel();
  JTextArea messagesArea = new JTextArea();

  /**Get a parameter value*/
  public String getParameter(String key) {
    if (isStandalone)
      return System.getProperty(key);
    return super.getParameter(key);
  }

  /**Construct the applet*/
  public InstallerApplet() {
  }

  /**Initialize the applet*/
  public void init() {
    titleLabel.setText("<html><body><b>"+
            "<i>"+getParameter("appname")+
            "</i> Installation Applet</b>");

    setSize(new Dimension(512,300));
    messagesArea.setForeground(Color.blue);
    messagesArea.setEditable(false);
    messagesArea.setText("Installation started..\n");
    getContentPane().add(titleLabel, BorderLayout.NORTH);
    getContentPane().add(new JScrollPane(messagesArea,
            JScrollPane.VERTICAL_SCROLLBAR_ALWAYS,
            JScrollPane.HORIZONTAL_SCROLLBAR_AS_NEEDED)
➥, BorderLayout.CENTER);
  }
  /**Start the applet*/
  public void start() {
    int choice = JOptionPane.showConfirmDialog(this,
                        "This will Install "+
                        getParameter("appname")+
                        " on your computer",
```

LISTING 7.6 Continued

```
                            "Continue with Installation?",
                        JOptionPane.OK_CANCEL_OPTION,
                        JOptionPane.WARNING_MESSAGE);
  if (choice == JOptionPane.OK_OPTION) {
    copy();
  } else {
    printMessage("User decided to abort installation.");
    printMessage("To restart the installation visit again this page.");
  }
}

/**Stop the applet*/
public void stop() {
}

/**Destroy the applet*/
public void destroy() {
}

/**
 * copies specified files on the specified local destination
 */
public void copy(){
  String[] resources = getItems( getParameter("resources") );
  String destDir = getParameter("destination");

  if (resources==null || destDir==null) {
    printMessage("Invalid Parameter Settings.\n Installation aborted.");
    return;
  }

  BufferedInputStream in = null;
  URL serverURL;
  byte[] buffer;
  try {
    for (int i = 0; i < resources.length; i++) {
      serverURL = new URL(getCodeBase(), resources[i]);
      URLConnection conn = serverURL.openConnection();
      in = new BufferedInputStream(conn.getInputStream());
      String res = destDir+System.getProperty("file.separator")+resources[i];
      new File(new File(res).getParent()).mkdirs();
      FileOutputStream out = new FileOutputStream(res);
      printMessage(" - copying from:"+serverURL+" to:"+res);
      buffer = new byte[2048];
```

LISTING 7.6 Continued

```
      int j;
      while((j = in.read(buffer)) != -1)
        out.write(buffer, 0, j);
    }//for
    printMessage("Installation finished.");

  } catch (Exception ex) {
    printMessage("copy: "+ex);
    printMessage("Installation aborted.");
  } finally {
      try {
        if(in != null)
          in.close();
      } catch (Exception ex) {
        printMessage("copy() closing InputStream "+ex);
      }
  }
}

/**
 * overwritten for application support
 */
public URL getCodeBase() {
  try {
    if (isStandalone)
      return new File(".").toURL();
  } catch (MalformedURLException mue) {
    System.out.println("getCodebase() "+mue);
  }

  return super.getCodeBase();
}

/**
 * tokenize a string
 */
private String[] getItems(String s){
  if (s==null)
    return null;
  ArrayList result = new ArrayList();
  StringTokenizer st = new StringTokenizer(s,";:,");
  while (st.hasMoreTokens()) {
    String w = st.nextToken();
    result.add(w);
```

LISTING 7.6 Continued

```
  }
  String[] a = new String[result.size()];
  result.toArray(a);
  return a;
}

/**
 * writes on the applet's message area
 */
private void printMessage(String msg){
  messagesArea.append(msg+"\n");
}

/**
 * main method
 */
static public void main(String[] args) {
  System.getProperties().put("resources","setup\\res\\a.jar");
  System.getProperties().put("destination","c:\\appzz");
  System.getProperties().put("appname","MegaAppz 1.0");
  InstallerApplet a = new InstallerApplet();
  a.isStandalone = true;

  JFrame f = new JFrame("Test Frame");
  f.addWindowListener(new WindowAdapter() {
    public void windowClosing(WindowEvent e) {
      System.exit(0);
    }
  });
  a.init();
  f.getContentPane().add(a);
  f.setSize(400,300);
  f.setVisible(true);
  a.start();
}

}
```

Note the code used to allow the applet to run as an application as well, especially the main method beginning at line 157 of Listing 7.6. The parameters and the getCodebase method (line 119 of Listing 7.6) supply directory change according to whether the InstallerApplet is run as an applet or an application (method getParameter at line 22 of Listing 7.6).

A screenshot from the installer applet launched as an application is shown in Figure 7.7.

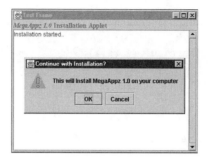

FIGURE 7.7

A screenshot from the installer applet launched as an application.

In order to run such an unsigned applet, we have three choices:

- Signing the JAR file containing the applet with the `jarsigner` tool if you own a valid certificate provided by some well-known certificate authority.

- Another option is to modify the policy file or provide your own, invoking the Java interpreter with the following command line option, for example:

  ```
  - Djava.security.policy=<full path to new policy file>
  ```

  Otherwise, the simplest thing to do (and the most potentially dangerous) is to modify the `java.policy` default policy file (on Windows JREs under the path `<jre_home>/lib/security/`); for example, adding the following line among the other permissions:

  ```
  grant {
        permission java.security.AllPermission;
  }
  ```

  This solution (modifying the default policy file), apart from being potentially highly dangerous, works only in limited situations and is infeasible for large client populations.

- Only for this applet, a `main` method has been added so that the same effect can be achieved running the `InstallerApplet` as a Java application.

NOTE

For more information on these topics, see the Java security FAQ or the SDK1.2 security trail in the Java Tutorial.

Another important piece is the HTML page, listed in Listing 7.7 below.

LISTING 7.7   The installer HTML Page

```html
<HTML>
<HEAD>
<META HTTP-EQUIV="Content-Type" CONTENT="text/html; charset=windows-1252">
<TITLE>
Installation Page
</TITLE>
</HEAD>
<BODY>
Welcome!<BR>
<OBJECT classid="clsid:8AD9C840-044E-11D1-B3E9-00805F499D93"
    width="512" height="300" align="baseline"
    codebase="http://server/b2/c7/j2re-1_3_1-win.exe#Version=1,3,0,0">
<PARAM NAME="archive" VALUE="plugin.jar">
<PARAM NAME="code" VALUE="com.marinilli.b2.c7.installerapplet.InstallerApplet">
<PARAM NAME="codebase" VALUE=".">
<PARAM NAME="type" VALUE="application/x-java-applet;version=1.3">
<PARAM NAME="resources" VALUE="a.jar">
<PARAM NAME="destination" VALUE="c:\\appz">
<PARAM NAME="appname" VALUE="Mega-Appz 1.0">
<COMMENT>
<EMBED type="application/x-java-applet;version=1.3" width="512" height="300"
        align="baseline"
code="com.marinilli.b2.c7.installerapplet.InstallerApplet" codebase="."
        archive="plugin.jar"
        resources="a.jar"
        destination="c:\\appz"
        appname="Mega-Appz 1.0"
        pluginspage="http://server/b2/c7/j2re-1_3_1-win.exe ">
    <NOEMBED></COMMENT>
        No JDK 1.3 support for APPLET!!
    </NOEMBED>
    </EMBED>
</OBJECT>
</BODY>
</HTML>
```

In Listing 7.7, it is interesting to notice the support both for MS Internet Explorer and for Netscape browsers. Note also, the location of the JRE installer file that is located on the intranet deployment server (see for example at line 12 of Listing 7.7, for IE browsers). It is stored locally, in the same directory together with the web page, the resources to install and the `plugin.jar` file. This avoids any firewall problem and it is an important benefit of the Plug-In deployment technology.

In some situations, the Plug-In solution can be quite useful. The applet model simplicity, together with the most up-to-date Java features provided by the Plug-In (see the related discussion in Chapter 2, "An Abstract Model for Deployment") make this technique perfectly suited for some deployment scenarios. In intranet environments, in which a reliable connection is available and users are willing (or required) to experience some little extra complexity (essentially, first-time activation costs), the Plug-In solutions become very valuable. Such an environment offers the following benefits, among the others:

- Support for the latest J2SE features.

- By means of security, fine-tuning is possible to run applets that exhibit all the features of full-fledged Java applications. These applets are particularly suited for trusted closed environments such as corporate intranets.

- Its automatic management of all basic deployment services (download, installation, and caching of needed resources and code, even for optional packages) makes it a very attractive deployment solution for developers.

- Such features favor the implementations of sophisticated deployment circuits built using the Plug-In features in an intranet environment.

As a proof of concept of what we said, we will introduce an extensible deployment framework based on such a technology in the next section.

A Complete Deployment Solution

Although we cannot have any direct control on the client AH (the applet container, provided by the Sun's Plug-In), we can achieve a quite sophisticated level of services building on top of the applet model deployment services in order to enforce our deployment policies. We saw at the beginning of this chapter that developers need to build ad-hoc Application Helpers rarely because of the inherent "unique" nature of their application domain (otherwise, they would resort to cheaper, more standard solutions). We will see that most deployment services can be achieved even without the support of a fully controlled AH installed on client platforms.

Let's introduce an example of the use of our deployment solution in order to introduce it more concretely. The internal IT development staff of a corporation releases several applications for internal use. One of such applications is an accounting utility. Applications intended for internal use only don't need to be so formalized and carefully crafted as those available on the market. On the other hand, the intranet facility could shorten up development times even more. We will see an example of our proposed framework that will provide (besides standard applet deployment services) a simple logging and debugging facility. This way, the accounting application could be released earlier, and detected bugs will be automatically reported back to the deployment server back to the IT developers. In this way, new enhanced releases will be available earlier to end-users (thanks to the applet's mechanism), and so on. The overall effect is a shorter development time, with fewer costs (the deployment circuit is set up only once for all the applications) and a higher software quality. Figure 7.8 shows a screenshot of its execution. In Listing 7.8, the code is supplied without the GUI building details in the `initApplication` method.

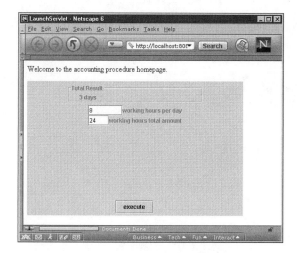

FIGURE 7.8

The accounting applet at work.

Essentially, we created a utility `Applet` subclass, `ClientDeploylet` (see Line 14 in Listing 7.8) that provides deployment services to our client applets. Such services are provided by means of some inherited methods. In this example scenario, we provided a logging and debugging service, called using the `log` methods (line 31 or 45 in Listing 7.8). But the most interesting aspect of this deployment framework is its client application lifecycle coverage, as we will see later.

LISTING 7.8 The `AccountApplet` Class

```
package com.marinilli.b2.c7.deploylet;
import java.awt.*;
import java.awt.event.*;
import java.applet.*;
import javax.swing.*;
import javax.swing.border.*;

/**
 * Chapter 7 -The example account applet
 *
```

LISTING 7.8   Continued

```
 * @author Mauro Marinilli
 * @version 1.0
 */
public class AccountApplet extends ClientDeploylet {
  JButton calcButton = new JButton();
  JTextField hoursTextField = new JTextField(4);
  JTextField hpdTextField = new JTextField(4);
  JLabel resultLabel = new JLabel();

  /**Construct the applet*/
  public AccountApplet() {
  }

  /**Initialize the applet*/
  public void initApplication() {
  //...
  }

  /**Start the applet*/
  public void startApplication() {
    log("account applet started");
  }

  /**
   * throws an exception
   */
  void calculate(ActionEvent e) {
    try {
      // hopefully we'll get an exception here
      int hours = Integer.valueOf(hoursTextField.getText()).intValue();
      int hpd   = Integer.valueOf(hpdTextField.getText()).intValue();
      resultLabel.setText(hours / hpd + " days");
    }
    catch (Exception ex) {
      log(ex);
    }
  }

}
```

Note that our `AccountApplet` doesn't implement the usual `start`, `stop`, and `init` methods, but similar methods with different names (`startApplication` at line 30 of Listing 7.8, `stopApplication` that we didn't implement in this applet, and `initApplication` at line 25).

With this mechanism, the `ClientDeploylet` applet will take charge of all client-server deployment communication in order to provide to our code the given deployment services. We also cover the very beginning of the applet lifecycle, thanks to a launching servlet (see Web address in Figure 7.8) that is discussed in the next sections.

If we input in our `AccountApplet` zero working hours per day, we'll obtain a division by zero exception that will be sent automatically to our deployment server (see Listing 7.8, line 45). Then, the IT development staff would have a recorded log like the following:

```
Processing Debug message:
message=Uncaught Exception: / by zero
Deploylet log=
 - *** logged: com.marinilli.b2.c7.deploylet.AccountApplet
with ServerDeploylet: //localhost/deploylet/127.0.0.1-0
 - init()
 - account applet started
Uncaught Exception trace:
java.lang.ArithmeticException: / by zero
     at com.marinilli.b2.c7.deploylet.AccountApplet.calculate(AccountApplet.
➥java:76)
     at com.marinilli.b2.c7.deploylet.AccountApplet$1.actionPerformed
➥(AccountApplet.java:33)
     at javax.swing.AbstractButton.fireActionPerformed(Unknown Source)
     at javax.swing.AbstractButton$ForwardActionEvents.actionPerformed(Unknown
➥Source)
     at javax.swing.DefaultButtonModel.fireActionPerformed(Unknown Source)
     at javax.swing.DefaultButtonModel.setPressed(Unknown Source)
     at javax.swing.plaf.basic.BasicButtonListener.mouseReleased(Unknown
➥Source)
     at java.awt.Component.processMouseEvent(Unknown Source)
     at java.awt.Component.processEvent(Unknown Source)
     at java.awt.Container.processEvent(Unknown Source)
     at java.awt.Component.dispatchEventImpl(Unknown Source)
     at java.awt.Container.dispatchEventImpl(Unknown Source)
     at java.awt.Component.dispatchEvent(Unknown Source)
     at java.awt.LightweightDispatcher.retargetMouseEvent(Unknown Source)
     at java.awt.LightweightDispatcher.processMouseEvent(Unknown Source)
     at java.awt.LightweightDispatcher.dispatchEvent(Unknown Source)
     at java.awt.Container.dispatchEventImpl(Unknown Source)
     at java.awt.Component.dispatchEvent(Unknown Source)
     at java.awt.EventQueue.dispatchEvent(Unknown Source)
     at java.awt.EventDispatchThread.pumpOneEventForHierarchy(Unknown Source)
     at java.awt.EventDispatchThread.pumpEventsForHierarchy(Unknown Source)
     at java.awt.EventDispatchThread.pumpEvents(Unknown Source)
     at java.awt.EventDispatchThread.run(Unknown Source)
```

Just before the stack trace, there is a log reporting some semantic messages that illustrates the program evolution in time. The server counterpart of our applet is reported, too (an instance of the `ServerDeploylet` we will see in the following), together with its server address. This mechanism could be refined to provide a helpful tool for offline code debugging. Developers study the error messages fixing up the `AccountApplet` bugs more efficiently because of the provided runtime deployment service. Note that we could also have provided server-side services to our framework.

This example was quite brief, and didn't show all the power of our deployment solution. To keep things simple, we implemented a rather coarse accounting program and an even simpler example of runtime service. We are interested in the concepts in our extensible deployment framework rather than providing particular services.

Deploylet Extensible Deployment Framework

In this section, we will cover the theory behind our deployment framework; in the next section, we will discuss its implementation. Nevertheless, for concreteness and clarity, we will mention some implementation details while covering the theory.

Our ad-hoc deployment solution builds on the Plug-In applet technology, and provides the following features:

- There is full coverage of the client application lifecycle (see note following).
- It is fully flexible and extensible, both as regards lifecycle issues and runtime services provided to client applications.
- Provides the possibility of the control fine-tuning of a client application. For example, first-time execution, installation, and dismissing can be tracked both on the client side and on the server side.

> **NOTE**
>
> When we refer to the term *client application*, we don't mean the network-related client side of an application. Instead, we refer to a whole business application (both on the client and on the server) that uses our deployment framework. So, such an application is a *client* of our class framework. In this way, the `AccountApplet` is a client of our deploylet framework.

A *deploylet* is a kind of application container that takes charge of providing deployment services to client executables. Thus, developers are freed to concentrate on the business aspects of their applications, leaving deployment plumbing to the underlying `deploylet` package. A deploylet is implemented as a two-parts entity: a client and a server act as one and are synchronized throughout the application lifecycle. For client-server communication, they use the RMI protocol. The client side is implemented as a Plug-In-enabled applet for taking advantage of its basic deployment features.

Figure 7.9 shows the deploylet activation sequence.

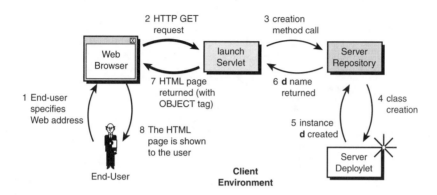

FIGURE 7.9

The deploylet activation sequence.

Referring to Figure 7.9, we can individuate the following steps:

1. An end-user points the browser to the account applet page, in which a launching servlet is activated.

2. The launch servlet requests the deploylet server-side creation service to a special RMI server, and returns an HTML page containing the client-side deploylet to the browser (implemented as an applet). From here on, the applet communicates directly with its server-side counterpart, and the launch servlet is not invoked any more.

3. The final end-user experience is an applet appearing in its Web browser. If the Plug-In is not installed on the client computer, a preliminary installation phase takes place (see preceding example for such details).

In Figures 7.9 and following Figure 7.10, the arrow shape indicates the kind of communication mechanism employed. Normal arrows indicate normal ("local") class reference or user interaction, thick arrows denote HTTP communication, and dotted arrows mean RMI invocation.

After the applet is activated, the Plug-In features are used (that is, full J2SE applet support), and the execution proceeds, as described in Figure 7.10.

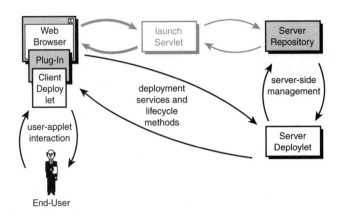

FIGURE 7.10

A deploylet runtime operation.

The client side and server side of the deploylet strictly interact (by means of the RMI proto-col). By using such an architecture, a variety of deployment services and advanced features are possible, even though we don't have a custom AH installed on the client platform (such as the ad-hoc deployment architecture presented in Chapter 6, "Deploying Existing Software"). Indeed, we can compare the two architectures, noting that this one is less "client-obtrusive," and the server needs to devote more resources than the other solution. Such an architecture is perfectly suited for intranet environments, in which clients are possibly fewer and available resources are greater (predictable connections, hardware resources, user population, and so on), allowing for more sophisticated services.

It is important to point out that this architecture provides advanced deployment services, while client applets are free to use any other business-related connection mechanism or code they need (such as database JDBC connections, other RMI connections, and so on), just like "nor-mal" Java code. Applets taking advantage of this framework could be developed faster and eas-ier than usual applets.

What is interesting to see here is how this mechanism could cover the whole deployment abstract model we discussed in Chapter 2.

Before getting any further, we anticipate some implementation details for clarity. The deploylet entity is implemented in two classes—ClientDeploylet and ServerDeploylet—that share a common Deploylet interface. ServerDeploylets are kept in an RMI-enabled server, imple-mented in the ServerRepositoryImpl class that administers them.

Figure 7.11 shows a simplified version of that deployment model regarding the lifecycle issue.

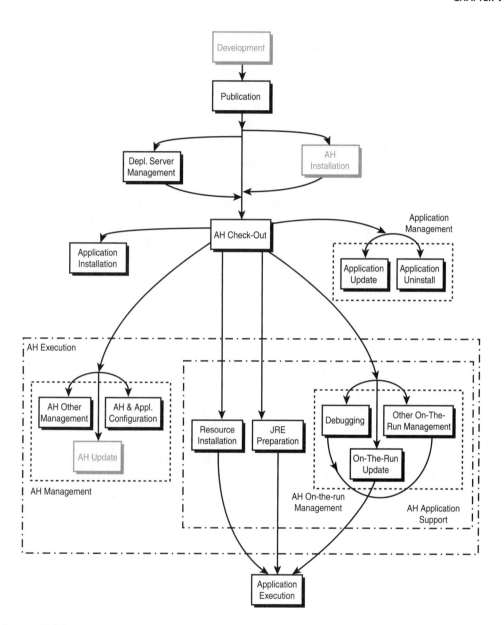

FIGURE 7.11

The deploylet underlying lifecycle deployment model.

The phases depicted in Figure 7.11 correspond to methods invoked on our deploylets. Such a correspondence is detailed in Table 7.1.

TABLE 7.1 Deploylet Lifecycle Implementation

Model Phase	Deploylet Method	Activation Sequence
Development	—	—
Publication	publish	—
DS Management	—	—
AH Install	—	—
AH Check-Out	resolve	c→s
Application Update	applicationUpdate	c→s
Application Installation	applicationInstallation	rep→s→c
Application Un-Installation	applicationUninstallation	c→s
AH Other Management	—	—
AH Update	—	—
AH And Application Configuration	applicationConfiguration	c→s
Resource Installation	resourceInstallation	c→s
JRE Preparation	jrePreparation	c→s
On-The-Run Update	*(see runtime services)*	c→s
Debugging	*(see runtime services)*	c→s
Other On-The-Run Management	*(see runtime services)*	c→s
Application Execution	initApplication/ startApplication/ StopApplication	c→s

The third column indicates the practical calls sequence performed in the Java classes implementation. By means of such method invocations, client and server sides of the same deploylet are kept consistent. "c" is the ClientDeploylet instance, and "s" is the ServerDeploylet counterpart. "rep" is the ServerDeploylet repository. For example, in the Application Installation (seventh) row of Table 7.1, the lifecycle-related applicationInstallation method is invoked by the ServerDeploylet repository (implemented in the ServerRepositoryImpl class) on the newly created ServerDeploylet instance. It will, in turn, invoke its ClientDeploylet instance respective method. All such details will be clearer when we will examine the source code.

Table 7.1 documents a practical implementation of a deployment lifecycle in Java. Similar to an Applet instance, when its init method is invoked, the code contained in the method is meant to perform the initialization, so each of these methods provides "hooks" for lifecycle-related actions. For example, by overriding the ServerDeploylet's stopApplication method, an application could register persistently some data (both on the client and on the server) or perform some logging mechanism, etc.

Also in Table 7.1, some lifecycle phases are mapped on runtime services ("*see runtime services*" in the second column). This means that in order to use a given deployment service, the client application should use the related runtime service. An example of this is given in the `log` method discussed in Listing 7.8.

After having mapped our abstract model to the deploylet class framework in a theoretical, top-down fashion, we are ready to see the code details.

The Implementation

First of all, let's see the `Deploylet` interface, shown in Listing 7.9. This interface captures the behavior of deploylet entities discussed before, and needs to be implemented both on the client side (by the `ClientDeploylet` class and all its subclasses) and on the server side (`ServerDeployment` and all its subclasses) in order for the deployment circuit to work.

LISTING 7.9 The `Deploylet` Interface

```
package com.marinilli.b2.c7.deploylet;
import java.rmi.*;

/**
 * Chapter 7 - Deployable interface
 *
 * This interface models the lifecycle of a deployable application,
 * abstracting from its client/server actual implementation.
 *
 * @author Mauro Marinilli
 * @version 1.0
 */
public interface Deploylet extends Remote {

  // lifecycle methods

  /**
   * triggers the publication phase
   */
  public void publish() throws RemoteException;

  /**
   * implements the resolution phase
   */
  public void resolve() throws RemoteException;
```

LISTING 7.9 Continued

```java
/**
 * implements the application update phase
 */
public void applicationUpdate() throws RemoteException;

/**
 * implements the application un-installation phase
 */
public void applicationUninstallation() throws RemoteException;

/**
 * implements the application installation phase
 */
public void applicationInstallation() throws RemoteException;

/**
 * implements the application configuration phase
 */
public void applicationConfiguration() throws RemoteException;

/**
 * implements the resources installation phase
 */
public void resoucesInstallation() throws RemoteException;

/**
 * implements the JRE prepaparation phase
 */
public void JREPreparation() throws RemoteException;


/**
 * triggered on the client (applet) by the start() method
 */
public void startApplication() throws RemoteException;

/**
 * triggered on the client (applet) by the stop() method
 */
public void stopApplication() throws RemoteException;

/**
 * implements the application initialization
 */
public void initApplication() throws RemoteException;
```

LISTING 7.9 Continued

```
//
// runtime services methods

/**
 * requests a service to its counterpart
 */
public ServiceResult requestService(DeploymentService ds) throws
➥ RemoteException;

//
// support methods

/**
 * get the server side of this deploylet (a servlet instance)
 */
public Deploylet getServer() throws RemoteException;

/**
 * get the client side of this deploylet (an applet instance)
 */
public Deploylet getClient() throws RemoteException;

/**
 * set the client side of this deploylet
 */
public void setClient(Deploylet d) throws RemoteException;

/**
 * set the server side of this deploylet
 */
public void setServer(Deploylet d) throws RemoteException;

/**
 * get the deploylet name (RMI address)
 */
public String getName() throws RemoteException;
}
```

The Deploylet interface implements what is detailed in Table 7.1 together with some
auxiliary methods and a general-purpose runtime service request mechanism (see method
requestService at line 79 of Listing 7.9). Regarding the requestService method, we will
not show the RequestService, DeploymentService, and DebugService classes. The support
methods are needed for client-server interaction.

In Listing 7.10, the `ClientDeploylet` applet is reported. This class is the base class for all client-side applications that use the deploylet framework.

LISTING 7.10   The ClientDeploylet Class

```
package com.marinilli.b2.c7.deploylet;
import java.awt.*;
import java.awt.event.*;
import java.applet.*;
import javax.swing.*;
import java.rmi.*;
import java.io.*;

/**
 * Chapter 7 - ClientDeploylet
 *
 * The client-side of the Deploylet interface .
 *
 * @author Mauro Marinilli
 * @version 1.0
 */
public abstract class ClientDeploylet extends JApplet implements Deploylet {
  private Deploylet server;

  //
  // Applet methods
  //

  /**Construct the applet*/
  public ClientDeploylet() {
  }

  /**Initialize the applet*/
  public final void init() {
    //
    try {
      String serverName = getParameter("name");
      server = (Deploylet) Naming.lookup(serverName);
      System.out.println("Deploylet-server="+server.getServer());
      log("*** logged: " + getClass().getName() + "\nwith ServerDeploylet:
" + serverName);
      log("init()");
      initApplication();
    } catch (Exception e) {
      System.out.println("ClientDeploylet during ServerDeploylet lookup: "+e);
    }
  }
```

LISTING 7.10   Continued

```
/**Start the client applet*/
public final void start() {
  try {
    resolve();
  } catch (Exception ex) {
    log(ex);
  }
}

/**Stop the applet*/
public final void stop() {
  // first stop client deploylet
  stopApplication();
  // then stop server deploylet
  try {
    server.stopApplication();
  } catch (Exception ex) {
    log(ex);
  }
}

/**Destroy the applet*/
public void destroy() {
}

/**Get Applet information*/
public String getAppletInfo() {
  return "Client Deploylet version 1.0";
}



//
// Deploylet methods
//

/** Implements the related Deploylet method */
public void publish() {
}

/** Implements the related Deploylet method */
public void resolve() {
  try {
    server.resolve();
```

LISTING 7.10   Continued

```
    } catch (Exception e) {
      log;
    }
    startApplication();
}

/** Implements the related Deploylet method */
public void applicationUpdate() {
}

/** Implements the related Deploylet method */
public void applicationUninstallation() {
}

/** Implements the related Deploylet method */
public void applicationInstallation() {
}

/** Implements the related Deploylet method */
public void applicationConfiguration() {
}

/** Implements the related Deploylet method */
public void resoucesInstallation() {
}

/** Implements the related Deploylet method */
public void JREPreparation() {
}

/** Implements the related Deploylet method */
public abstract void startApplication();

/** Implements the related Deploylet method */
public void stopApplication() {
}

/** Implements the related Deploylet method */
public ServiceResult requestService(DeploymentService ds) {
  return null;
}

/** Implements the related Deploylet method */
public Deploylet getServer() {
```

LISTING 7.10   Continued

```
      return null;
  }

  /** Implements the related Deploylet method */
  public Deploylet getClient() {
    return this;
  }

  /** Implements the related Deploylet method */
  public void setClient(Deploylet d) {
    //do nothing
  }

  /** Implements the related Deploylet method */
  public void setServer(Deploylet d) {
    server = d;
  }

  /** a convenience method for DebugService access */
  protected void log(String m){
//    DebugService.log("[" + new java.util.Date()+ "] " + m );
    DebugService.log(" - " + m );//shorter
  }

  /** a convenience method for DebugService access */
  protected void log(Exception e){
    try {
      // in case of an exception report it to the server
      CharArrayWriter caw = new CharArrayWriter();
      PrintWriter pw = new PrintWriter(caw);
      e.printStackTrace(pw);
      String s = new String(caw.toCharArray());
      DebugService.log("Uncaught Exception trace:\n");
      DebugService.log(s);
      server.requestService(new DebugService("Uncaught Exception:
"+e.getMessage())));
    } catch (Exception exc) {
      System.out.println("ClientDeploylet.log: "+exc);
    }
  }

}
```

Note that applet-related lifecycle methods (namely start, stop, and init) are declared final, so that client subclasses are forced to implement the Deploylet interface's corresponding methods. At line 30 of Listing 7.10, the connection with the ServerDeploylet is created and the logging service is initialized during the init method. After that, the initApplication method of the ClientDeploylet subclass is invoked for performing business code applet initialization, as reported in Listing 7.8. The stop method implementation is similar (starting at line 54).

In Listing 7.11, the ServerDeploylet class is listed. For simplicity, we kept the server-side deploylet pretty simple. We didn't subclass it or override its lifecycle methods for providing some special deployment functionalities on the server side.

LISTING 7.11 The ServerDeploylet Class

```
package com.marinilli.b2.c7.deploylet;
import java.rmi.*;
import java.rmi.server.*;
import java.rmi.registry.*;
import java.io.*;
import java.util.*;

/**
 * Chapter 7 - ServerDeploylet
 *
 * The server-side of the Deploylet interface.
 *
 * @author Mauro Marinilli
 * @version 1.0
 */
public class ServerDeploylet extends UnicastRemoteObject implements Deploylet {
  private Deploylet client;
  private String serverDeployletName;

  /** constructor */
  public ServerDeploylet(String deployletName) throws RemoteException {
    if (System.getSecurityManager() == null) {
      System.out.println("new RMISecurityManager()");
      System.setSecurityManager(new RMISecurityManager());
    }
    try {
      String name = "//localhost/deploylet/" + deployletName;
      Naming.rebind(name, this);
      System.out.println("ServerDeploylet bound with name \""+name+"\"");
      serverDeployletName = name;
    } catch (Exception e) {
```

LISTING 7.11 Continued

```
      System.err.println("ServerDeploylet - binding: " + e.toString() );
   }
}

//
// Deploylet methods
//

/** Implements the related Deploylet method */
public void publish() {
}

/** Implements the related Deploylet method */
public void resolve() {
}

/** Implements the related Deploylet method */
public void applicationUpdate() {
}

/** Implements the related Deploylet method */
public void applicationUninstallation() {
}

/** Implements the related Deploylet method */
public void applicationInstallation() {
   //client.applicationInstallation();
}

/** Implements the related Deploylet method */
public void applicationConfiguration() {
}

/** Implements the related Deploylet method */
public void resoucesInstallation() {
}

/** Implements the related Deploylet method */
public void JREPreparation() {
}

/** Implements the related Deploylet method */
public void startApplication() {
   //do nothing
}
```

7

BUILDING YOUR
OWN DEPLOYMENT
SOLUTION

LISTING 7.11   Continued

```
/** Implements the related Deploylet method */
public void stopApplication() {
  //
  try {
    String serverName = "rmi://localhost/deployletRepository";
    ServerRepository server = (ServerRepository)
➥ Naming.lookup(serverName);

    if (server!=null) {
      server.remove(this.getName());
    }
  } catch (Exception e) {
    System.out.println("ServerDeploylet during
➥ ServerRepository lookup: "+e);
  }
}

/** Implements the related Deploylet method */
public void initApplication() {
}

/** Implements the related Deploylet method */
public ServiceResult requestService(DeploymentService ds) {
  System.out.println("requestedService="+ds);
  if (ds instanceof DebugService) {
    //process debug service
    return processDebugService((DebugService)ds);
  }
  return null;
}

/**
 *
 */
private ServiceResult processDebugService(DebugService ds){
  Object[] s = ds.getContents();
  System.out.println("Processing Debug message:");
  System.out.println("message="+s[0].toString()+"\nDeploylet
➥ log=\n"+s[1].toString());
  return null;
}

/** Implements the related Deploylet method */
public Deploylet getServer() {
```

LISTING 7.11 Continued

```
    return this;
  }

  /** Implements the related Deploylet method */
  public Deploylet getClient() {
    return client;
  }

  /** Implements the related Deploylet method */
  public void setClient(Deploylet d) {
    client = d;
  }

  /** Implements the related Deploylet method */
  public void setServer(Deploylet d) {
    // do nothing
  }

  /** Implements the related Deploylet method */
  public String getName() {
    return serverDeployletName;
  }

}
```

Its implementation of the requestService method supports only DebugService requests (line 100 of Listing 7.11). The method processDebugService (beginning at line 110 of Listing 7.11) simply writes the DebugService argument on the standard output. In a real-world application, it could save its content (that reports an exception fired on the relative client applet) on a text file for successive use. At line 79 of Listing 7.11, the serverDeploylet is dismissed when the related client-side applet is stopped. In the constructor (lines 21–34 of Listing 7.11), the newly created ServerDeploylet instance is published on the RMI registry with the name obtained at line 27.

Another important piece in our framework is represented by the servlet that dynamically responds to Web browser's requests and supplies Plug-In-enabled applets. In Listing 7.12, the LaunchServlet class is shown.

LISTING 7.12 The LaunchServlet Class

```
package com.marinilli.b2.c7.deploylet;
import javax.servlet.*;
import javax.servlet.http.*;
import java.io.*;
import java.util.*;
```

LISTING 7.12   Continued

```java
import java.rmi.*;
public class LaunchServlet extends HttpServlet {
  private ServerRepository server;
  private static final String CONTENT_TYPE = "text/html";
  /**Initialize global variables*/
  public void init(ServletConfig config) throws ServletException {
    super.init(config);
    deployletRepositoryLookup();
  }
  /**Process the HTTP Get request*/
  public void doGet(HttpServletRequest request,
    HttpServletResponse response) throws ServletException, IOException {
    response.setContentType(CONTENT_TYPE);
    PrintWriter out = response.getWriter();
    out.println("<html>");
    out.println("<head><title>LaunchServlet</title></head>");
    out.println("<body>");
    out.println("<p>Welcome to the accounting procedure homepage.</p>");

    String dName = request.getRemoteHost();
    System.out.println("Deploylet-server="+server.getDeployletName(dName));
    Deploylet serverDeploylet = server.getServerDeploylet(dName);

    ...

    out.println("</body></html>");
  }
  /**Clean up resources*/
  public void destroy() {
  }

  /**
   * lookup the server repository
   */
  private void deployletRepositoryLookup(){
    //
    try {
      String serverName = "rmi://localhost/deployletRepository";
      server = (ServerRepository) Naming.lookup(serverName);
    } catch (Exception e) {
      System.out.println("LaunchServlet during ServerRepository lookup: "+e);
    }
  }
}
```

For brevity, we didn't list the whole servlet code for the creation of the HTML page (see the ellipsis in the doGet method). It is important to know that the servlet embeds in the OBJECT tag (needed for the Plug-In support) a special applet parameter ("name"), whose value is used by the client deploylet applet to look up its related server-side deploylet (such a value is fetched by the client deploylet at line 33 in Listing 7.10). For more details on the embedded code produced by the LaunchServlet, see the source code provided on the Companion Web site for this book.

The deployletRepositoryLookup method (starting at line 39 of Listing 7.12) performs the RMI server lookup, and it is invoked during servlet initialization. Afterward, when a Web browser requests the AccountApplet page (in this simple implementation, the LaunchServlet serves only such an applet independently from the client's request parameters), the servlet prepares the HTML page, and requests the ServerRepositoryImpl RMI server to create a new ServerDeploylet instance (line 27).

We used servlet technology here (rather than other, better-suited server-side technologies such as JSP) because it was used extensively throughout all the rest of the book.

In Listing 7.13, the ServerRepositoryImpl class is shown. This class implements a simple RMI-based management server for centralizing ServerDeploylets control. It is required to be successfully running when the LaunchServlet is requested for an applet Web page.

LISTING 7.13 The ServerRepositoryImpl Class

```
package com.marinilli.b2.c7.deploylet;
import java.rmi.*;
import java.rmi.server.*;
import java.rmi.registry.*;
import java.util.*;

/**
 * Chapter 7 - ServerDeploylet manager server
 * Don't forget:  -Djava.security.policy=<full path to new policy file>
 *
 * @author Mauro Marinilli
 * @version 1.0
 */
public class ServerRepositoryImpl extends UnicastRemoteObject implements
ServerRepository{
  private HashMap repository = new HashMap();

  /**
   * Constructor
   */
```

LISTING 7.13   Continued

```
public ServerRepositoryImpl() throws RemoteException {
  if (System.getSecurityManager() == null) {
    System.out.println("new RMISecurityManager()");
    System.setSecurityManager(new RMISecurityManager());
  }
  try {
    String name = "rmi://localhost/deployletRepository";
    Naming.rebind(name, this);
    System.out.println("Server bound with name \""+name+"\"");
  } catch (Exception e) {
    System.err.println("ServerRepositoryImpl - binding: " + e.toString() );
  }
}

/**
 * creates the server deploylet name based on its client counterpart address
 */
public String getDeployletName(String clientHost) {
  return clientHost;
}

/**
 * return the specified server deploylet or create it
 */
public Deploylet getServerDeploylet(String deployletName) {
  if (repository.containsKey(deployletName) )
    return (Deploylet)repository.get(deployletName);
  // create it from scratch
  ServerDeploylet sd = null;
  try {
    String name = deployletName + "-" + repository.keySet().size();
    sd = new ServerDeploylet(name);
    sd.applicationInstallation();
    System.out.println("ServerRepositoryImpl - added");
  } catch (Exception e) {
    System.err.println("creating ServerDeploylet: " + deployletName);
  }
  repository.put(deployletName, sd);
  return sd;
}

/**
 * remove the given server deploylet
 */
```

LISTING 7.13 Continued

```
public void remove(String clientHost) throws RemoteException {
  //removes it from the repository
  repository.remove(clientHost);
  System.out.println("ServerRepositoryImpl - removed: "+clientHost);
}

/**
 * Server Repository Main
 */
static public void main(String[] args) {
  try {
    ServerRepositoryImpl sri = new ServerRepositoryImpl();
  } catch (Exception e) {
    System.err.println("main(): " + e.toString() );
  }
}
}
```

The `ServerRepositoryImpl` server implements the remote `ServerRepository` interface (for brevity, we do not list it here). Its implementation is simple and rather fragile. Note that the `ServerDeploylet` repository is implemented with a `HashMap` instance. See the following RMI recommendations before launching this server class.

For simplicity, we didn't implement server-to-client communication, which is needed to complete the communication flow between the client and the server deploylet. Thus, the deployment-related communication is only unidirectional—from client to server—and not all the invocation sequences detailed in Table 7.1 are implemented. For example, see the commented client invocation at line 51 of Listing 7.11.

Setting Up the Deployment Circuit and Executing the Code

As you have seen, implementing a full-fledged, complete deployment circuit over a real-world network environment is not that simple. Before Java, it would have taken not a single chapter, but a whole book to describe it.

We have employed several Java technologies to implement this framework:

- The Plug-In technology, to provide full-fledged J2SE applet support. If you have run the previous example successfully, you don't need to do other configuration settings on your JRE (this example, too, needs to have unrestricted security access).

- A Web server that features a servlet container able to run our `LaunchServlet`. We used Tomcat. For details on how to set up such a servlet container (that acts as a basic Web server, too), see Chapter 12, "Server-Side Deployment Support."

- The RMI API, which is used between the client and the server parts and for intraserver communication between the `LaunchServlet` and the `ServerRepositoryImpl` discussed in the next item.

- Finally, a home-grown `ServerDeploylet`'s little server (`ServerRepositoryImpl`), for centralized deploylets server-side management. It is accessed only from server-side objects (the `LaunchServlet` and `ServerDeploylets`).

Therefore, in order to run this example on our environment, we need to accomplish these steps:

1. Install our `LaunchServlet`, and launch our favorite servlet container. (See Chapter 5 for J2EE deployment details.)

2. Launch the `Rmiregistry` tool on the server platform. (Such a tool is shipped with any JRE package, and is located in the same directory as the JVM executable.)

3. Then, launch our `ServerRepositoryImpl` mini-server. Read the following note if it is your first time with J2SE's RMI. At this point, the Web server is waiting for client requests, and the mini-RMI server is waiting for `LaunchServlet`'s requests.

4. Open up a browser window that provides the intranet address where we registered our servlet. In the provided example, pack the address as "`http://localhost:8080/deploylet/server`".

5. Finally, inspect what is going on. Regarding the server, look at the `ServerRepositoryImpl` standard output, while you may open up the Java Plug-In console to see if everything is OK on the client side. (On Windows 9x machines, double-click the Duke icon in the process tray)

Running this example needs some extra care, both for running Plug-In applets without security restrictions (see what was said for the previous example) and for enabling RMI to locate the remotely exposed classes stubs. In order to do the latter, you need to supply a correct value for the `java.rmi.server.codebase` property. The easiest way is to provide the local file system path to the `deploylet` package classes. In order to do so, launch the `ServerRepositoryImpl` class with the following command line:

```
java -Djava.rmi.server.codebase=file:///C:/[classes]/
➥com.marinilli.b2.c7.deploylet.ServerRepositoryImpl
```

Adapted with the current path to the Java root classes directory on your hard disk (substitute it in `[classes]` in the previous example). For more information about technical RMI details, consult the JDK 1.3 documentation; for a general overview, see the related section of the java Tutorial.

For brevity, we don't give advice on how to compile locally the provided code. The interested reader will find all the source files (together with `rmic`'s generated class stubs) in the example pack.

Again, note that the JRE installation file is not provided with the example pack in order to save space, as in the preceding Plug-In examples.

Summary

After a brief general introduction to the issues related to designing and building ad-hoc deployment solutions, we focused on some particular scenarios. We tried to provide a useful mix of common cases and advanced scenarios that will hopefully inspire developers facing complex real-world deployment challenges.

With this chapter, we finish the second part of this book. Chapter 8, "A JNLP Quick Launch," begins Part III, "JNLP," which will cover exclusively the Java Network Launching Protocol.

JNLP

PART
III

IN THIS PART

A JNLP Quick Launch

IN THIS CHAPTER

After having been introduced to the theory and practical design of software deployment in general, and Java deployment in particular, we will delve into more details by describing a particular Java deployment solution, the *Java Network Launching Protocol (JNLP)*. This third part of the book has been designed to be immediately accessible to programmers who need quick and practical advice on JNLP technology. Although it is the natural complement to the first two parts of the book, the discussion has been kept focused on programming details in this third part, reducing the importance of any previous knowledge of the other (more design-oriented) parts of the book.

This chapter introduces the technology using practical examples. Chapter 9, "The Protocol," discusses the protocol from a top-down perspective; whereas Chapter 10, "Defining the Client Environment," describes the XML elements in JNLP files. Chapter 11, "Runtime Client Services," illustrates the JNLP API that offers services to JNLP-launched applications. Chapter 12, "Server-side Support," gives details about the server-side support of the protocol. Finally, Chapter 13, "A Complete Example," discusses a complete real-world example. In Appendix A, "A Little Handbook for Deployment," there is a part dedicated to JNLP adoption; whereas the entire Appendix B, "The JNLP Specification," is devoted to the Java Network Launching Protocol specification.

An Introduction For Developers

Before starting our journey into the JNLP world, it is important to point out some basic things that will probably save you a lot of time and frustration in the near future.

As with any deployment technology (and JNLP is no exception), one can identify three different environments. The *production* environment is where developers build their programs. The *deployment* environment is where others, helped by deployment servers (we will use normal Web servers such as Apache), will put developers' programs packed for distribution. Finally, the third environment consists of *clients*, the end-users who run the applications on their computers.

Let's better examine these environments as they pertain to software development:

- **Development**. You will probably use an Integrated Development Tool (IDE) for developing Java code and JAR files—such as Kawa, JBuilder, Forte, VisualAge, and so on. Of course, you can always use the standard JDK, possibly with the help of some scripts. In this case, you will need some Java libraries, other application-specific resources such as icons, plus the `jarsigner` tool (or something similar) in order to sign JAR files should you need to develop trusted applications.

- **Deployment**. This step requires a Web server with upload access and with at least some administrator control on it. The code in these chapters, when not otherwise specified, works with a standard Web server (that is, no extra CGI or servlet support required). In Chapters 12 and 13, we will need some special support from the Web server.

- **Client**. For the client environment, we need a Web Browser plus a Web connection, configured proxy servers, and so on; and a JNLP client installed (for example, Sun's Java Web Start) that comes shipped with a J2SE JRE.

The typical development iteration is as follows:

1. Compile your classes; and stuff them with your icons, property files, native libraries, and miscellaneous items into some JAR files. Move those JAR files to the deployment server (that is, your Web server).

2. Write down your JNLP files pointing to the JAR files (accessible from the Web server) that you created in the previous step. Move the JNLP files to the correct directory on the Web server. Now your clients are ready to download your application.

3. Go to the client computer, and launch your application via an URL pointing to the desired JNLP file.

What does all this mean for developers? To begin with, it means that their production and testing environment is quite sophisticated and needs some extra care.

For example, a common problem that novices encounter with this kind of development is cache management. We have at least three distinct caches to be aware of:

- JNLP Client's cache. Even if our application did not work, it could have remained cached somewhere in the JNLP Client. For Java Web Start cache management, see this chapter's last section, "Java Web Start".

- Some other latencies along the processing pipe. Once compiled, classes and other files must be packed into JAR files and shipped to the Deployment Server. Be aware of all the needed steps and their possible twists, especially if some IDE is doing them for you.

- Browser's cache. Did you modify your JNLP file, but it didn't work out? Probably the browser is still using an old version of your launching file. Don't forget the Refresh button on your browser when modifying your JNLP files. (Netscape users may use the Shift+Refresh combination for completely reloading the current page).

What Is JNLP?

JNLP is a technology that enables the launching of remote Java 2, Standard Edition programs. Naturally, the JRE and all the needed resources (JAR files, extensions, and so on) must be installed locally before launching the program. Therefore, JNLP is *not* a deployment technology per se; rather, it is a remote launching protocol with some extra features. These extra features, apart from being able to execute a Java program from a given URL are (i)offering a client environment to launched programs, (ii) ensuring a secure environment to clients, and (iii)taking care of all the behind-the-scenes deployment issues. Of course, there are other features offered by this technology, and we will see them later. However, it is useful to focus on the main characteristics first.

The kind of Java programs that can be launched by JNLP clients are Java applets and applications written for the J2SE (Java 2 Standard Edition). Given the many implementation details (such as the extensive use of custom class loaders, for example) and the security model adopted for the protocol, Java 1.1 legacy executables have to be re-engineered in order to be employed. Furthermore, JNLP-deployed applications have to comply with some simple rules, such as running in a restricted environment if not authenticated, or accessing resources (images, property files, etc.) that are contained only in the downloaded JAR files. These are not severe limitations at all, but it is important to point them out at first. Figure 8.1 synthesizes this aspect.

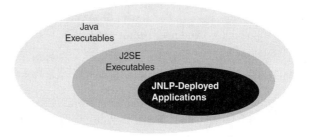

FIGURE 8.1
The set of Java executables that can be deployed via JNLP.

How JNLP Works

The basic steps in any Java applet/application (from now on, we'll use *application* for brevity) deployed with JNLP are as follows (see Figure 8.2 below):

1. Execution of the JNLP client with a JNLP file.

2. The JNLP Client takes care of retrieving and automatically caching all the pieces needed by the application, following the instructions contained in the JNLP file. The next time there will be no need to download them again. It even checks for new versions eventually available on the server.

3. When this is done, the JNLP client launches the Java application, waiting in the background to offer some runtime services, just as Web browsers do with applets. When the application exits, so does the JNLP Client.

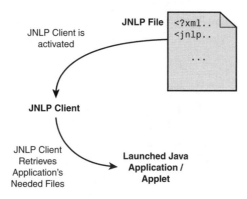

FIGURE 8.2

JNLP basic mechanism.

If you want to harness the power of JNLP, you will use it on a Web-enabled desktop. In this case, the Web browser becomes a powerful *mediator* between the JNLP Client and your application. By means of a browser, JNLP files can be given to the JNLP Client just by clicking a normal link in a Web page.

One may say that the JNLP idea is a crossbreed of the best of applet and plug-in ideas. Applets, in that JNLP defines a container, not like a mere application. (Despite this, developers can also use JNLP for common applications without taking advantage of the richer runtime environment.) Plug-ins, in that JNLP exploits the same mechanism in order to be invoked from a Web browser. We will better see these similarities in a moment.

Getting a bit more formal and precise, by taking advantage of the model described in Chapter 2, "An Abstract Model for Deployment," we can say that a JNLP Client is a particular kind of Application Helper that we called an Application Container. Just like an applet container or a J2EE bean container, it supports our applications even after it launches them.

In the first part of this book, we saw many deployment methods. In particular, the applet concept can resemble the JNLP approach.

The similarities with the applet model are:

- There is an external container (refer to Chapter 2) that manages the application, just like the browser does with the applet, providing several services to the launched application via the Java APIs.

- The security model is similar, but in JNLP it is much more flexible. There are two main levels of security: for trusted applications and for un-trusted ones that may still access local resources, but only after the end-user gave her explicit permission. Have a look at Chapter 10 for details.

- An application deployed with JNLP could be launched from a Web page or, to be more precise, from a URL eventually pointed at by another Web page.

Some differences with the applet model are useful to point out as well.

- The applet lifecycle is rigidly defined once and for all, with little or no control on the details. On the other hand, the JNLP protocol uses XML files, which allows a much richer definition of a great number of details.

- Applications launched with JNLP are first downloaded locally, cached opportunely, and then executed (all automatically). Applets instead are part of the Web page currently viewed in the browser, and are generally much more limited in their execution environment.

- Of course, the biggest difference from a developer's viewpoint is that JNLP-launched applications are full-fledged Java applications, with very little restrictions on how to retrieve resources like icons or files.

> **Note**
>
> We said that JNLP is a Web-centered protocol. What does this mean exactly? It means that all the items are identified by URLs. Java itself isn't as Web-centered as one may think. Take the classpath concept, for instance. It is a list of local files and directories in which the JVM and applications can find their resources. There are no URLs, only entries in the local file system. It should be no surprise that the classpath mechanism is not supported in the JNLP protocol, even when specified in JAR files.

Some Examples

Now it is time for some examples that will introduce the JNLP technology. The next chapters will dig into the details, both with technical advice and with practical code.

Setting Up the Book Examples

Go to the companion Web site, and download the whole example pack; or do the examples chapter by chapter, if you like. You will find JAR files and "b2" directories containing both sources and needed resource files.

Directories, examples, and Java sources are organized by chapters. The chapters are rooted in the b2 directory. In the examples, the Web server has been brilliantly called "server". If something doesn't work on your local configuration, just open up a JNLP file, and study its href attributes or modify them. If you encounter problems with proxy settings, try to have a look at the end of the "Java Web Start" section in this chapter.

So, to recap: At the end you'll have a directory named "b2" in your document home directory. Then, inside it there are the directories c8,c9,c10,c11,c12, and c13. The examples in this chapter are in the c8 directory. As it happens sometimes, the first examples are somewhat elementary. If you want to see something interesting, feel free to point your Web browser at Chapters 11–13, but before leaping ahead, I suggest you follow the advice in the following examples.

A First Example

Let's launch our first application with JNLP. In this first example, we will limit ourselves to the very essential: no icons or other gadgets, not even a Web connection. We will work only with local files.

The very first thing to do is to install Java Web Start, if you haven't already done so. You can download it from Sun's site at http://java.sun.com/products/javawebstart/. We will see at the end of this chapter how to set up the reference JNLP Client (Sun's Java Web Start).

Preparation

In order to set up our first application deployed with JNLP, we have to perform the following steps, having already installed Web Start or another JNLP Client:

1. Compile sources, and pack them into the JAR file (or use the one given on the companion Web site).

2. Copy the JNLP file and the JAR file on the local disk. In the original JNLP file, the test directory has to be located at "c:/". If you haven't the permissions to write there, just modify the JNLP file as needed. Note that even if you downloaded the examples, you still have to manually copy the test directory.

3. Double-click the JNLP file.

NOTE

For this very first example, we will cover all the steps up to the final execution. In the following examples, we will skip some basic operations such as source compilation, and so on.

For this little experiment, we need the following pieces:

- A JNLP file—an XML file that will contain all the details.
- One JAR file, containing a simple Java class. This will represent our application.

COMPANION Website All of the following files are available on the companion Web site for this book. They are organized under the `test` directory. Copy it onto your local hard disk under the `c:/` path.

Listing 8.1 is on the Companion Web site for this book.

LISTING 8.1 The Test JNLP File

```
<?xml version="1.0" encoding="UTF-8"?>
<jnlp spec="1.0+"
  codebase="file:///c:/test/"
  href="test.jnlp">
  <information>
    <title>Hello JNLP</title>
    <homepage href="" />
    <vendor>Mauro's Workshop</vendor>
    <offline/>
  </information>
  <resources>
    <j2se version="1.2+" />
    <jar href="bin/test.jar" />
  </resources>
  <application-desc />
</jnlp>
```

This XML file instructs the JNLP Client on several things.

- Where the resources are located (on the local file system, see the protocol "`file:///`" in line 3).
- Where to find the JNLP file itself, so that the application it represents can be cached in the application manager, and so on.
- Some information about the application: its title, vendor, and the Web page in which you can look for updates.
- The resources needed by the application. In this case, a single JAR file will suffice. Note the `<j2se>` element, which informs the JNLP Client about the version of J2SE needed to run that application. The string "`1.2+`" means J2SE version 1.2 or any higher.

Note that no main class has been specified in the JNLP file. It is declared in the manifest file into the file `test.jar`; otherwise, the launch process would fail.

Listing 8.2 supplies the `Test` class. It pops up a little dialog box, informing the user that the application was successfully launched, and exits after 10 seconds.

LISTING 8.2   The Test Java Class

```java
import javax.swing.*;
public class Test {
  public Test() throws Exception {
    JDialog jd = new JDialog();
    jd.setSize(200,100);
    jd.setLocation(100,100);
    jd.setTitle("Hello JNLP!");
    jd.getContentPane().add(new JLabel("Launching Test Successful."));
    jd.setVisible(true);
    Thread.currentThread().sleep(10000);
    System.exit(0);
  }
  public static void main(String[] args) throws Exception {
    Test test1 = new Test();
  }
}
```

The remainder of this subsection is intended for novice programmers. Please feel free to skip it to proceed to the execution subsection.

You can use the included `run.bat` script for Windows machines if you prefer to compile the `Test` class on your computer.

Then, prepare the JAR file with the following command:

```
jar cvfm test.jar manifest.txt *.class
```

You need the compiled `Test.class` file and the `manifest.txt` file shown in Listing 8.3.

LISTING 8.3   The Manifest File for the Test.jar File

```
Manifest-Version: 1.0
Main-Class: Test
```

8

A JNLP QUICK
LAUNCH

Execution

After you have copied the test.jar file into the c:/test/bin/ directory and the test.jnlp file in the c:/test/ directory, you are ready to launch the test application. Just double-click the test.jnlp file. Web Start or another installed JNLP Client will be invoked, and the dialog box will pop up for ten seconds, signaling that the launch was successful. Depending on your settings, the JNLP Client will create other launching facilities such as shortcuts, aliases, or other platform-dependent helpers for an easier application launch next time.

When you've finished with the example, remove the whole test directory. In Figure 8.3, there is a screen shot from the execution of Test class launched via JNLP.

FIGURE 8.3
Breaking the ice with JNLP.

In this first simple case, we saw how a basic JNLP file can trigger an application. Now that we have broken the ice with JNLP, it is time for something more interesting.

A More Detailed Example

Now, we are ready for launching something more interesting. First of all, let's move into the wide-open sea: the Internet. We need to set up a Web server, as we have already explained, in order to do so. Nevertheless, in the previous example, we saw how to deploy local JNLP applications, so if you don't want to get bothered with all these details, you can always adapt this and the next examples to run locally with no Web server support at all. For this example, we will deploy a little text editor application...well, a very minimal one.

Setting Up the Web Server MIME Type

What we need now is a basic Web server, accessible through the Internet or an intranet. In Chapter 12, we will see how to set up a full-fledged JNLP-enabled Web server. Right now, we are interested in showing the protocol with less overhead, so installing a Web server such as Apache locally on your development platform will be OK. There is only one little trick you need to do once the server is installed. You have to add a new MIME type on your Web server, if it is not present yet. Check for the "application/x-java-jnlp-file" MIME type associated with .jnlp files. In Apache, for example, just check the types file in the conf directory. If not present, add the new MIME type, being careful to correctly type the MIME type string.

> **NOTE**
>
> If you don't have a Web server for development, you can download the Apache Web server free of charge from the following address: http://www.apache.org/

Once you have added this new MIME type, the server can send JNLP files as files of the JNLP type, not plain text files. The browser will invoke the proper plug-in program (our JNLP Client) to execute the JNLP file.

Preparation

We will use many of the tricks JNLP can offer to better integrate our applications in the client computer. Furthermore, we want to add cute icons to our application and also read some configuration files as well. All this has to be packed into JAR files that will be magically ready to be used by our application on the Client, thanks to the JNLP Client.

What is new in the editor1.jnlp file (see Listing 8.4) is the presence of the description element. This informs the JNLP Client of the text to show to users and of the icon element that points to the application's icons.

LISTING 8.4   The editor1.jnlp File

```
<?xml version="1.0" encoding="utf-8"?>
<jnlp spec="1.0+"
      codebase="http://server/b2/c8/editor1/"
      href="editor1.jnlp">
 <information>
    <title>A Text Editor</title>
    <vendor>Mauro Inc.</vendor>
    <homepage href="home.html"/>
    <description>Load, edit and save any text file quickly and
effectively!</description>
    <description kind="short">A simple Java text editor</description>
    <description kind="tooltip">A text Editor</description>
    <icon href="img/logo.gif"/>
    <offline-allowed/>
  </information>
  <resources>
    <j2se version="1.3"/>
    <jar href="editor1.jar"/>
  </resources>
  <application-desc main-class="com.marinilli.b2.c8.editor1.Editor1"/>
</jnlp>
```

Listing 8.5 shows the launched Java class. It is a simple JFrame that contains a dummy toolbar and a TextArea.

LISTING 8.5   The Editor1 Java Class

```
package com.marinilli.b2.c8.editor1;

import javax.swing.*;
import java.awt.*;
import java.awt.event.*;

/**
 * A Simple Text Editor
 *
 * @author Mauro Marinilli
 * @version 1.0
 */

public class Editor1 extends JFrame {
  ClassLoader loader;
  public Editor1() {
```

LISTING 8.5 Continued

```java
    loader = getClass().getClassLoader();
    getContentPane().setLayout(new BorderLayout());
    getContentPane().add(getToolBar(), BorderLayout.NORTH);
    getContentPane().add(new TextArea(), BorderLayout.CENTER);
    setTitle("A Text Editor");
    setIconImage(new
ImageIcon(loader.getResource("images/Logo24.gif")).getImage());
    addWindowListener(new java.awt.event.WindowAdapter() {
      public void windowClosing(WindowEvent e) {
        exit();
      }
    });
    setSize(400,300);
    setVisible(true);
  }

  private JToolBar getToolBar() {
    JToolBar jt = new JToolBar();
    Icon saveIcon  = new ImageIcon(loader.getResource("images/Save16.gif"));
    Icon findIcon  = new ImageIcon(loader.getResource("images/Find16.gif"));
    jt.add(new JButton(saveIcon));
    jt.add(new JButton(findIcon));
    return jt;
  }

  private void exit() {
    System.exit(0);
  }

  public static void main(String[] a) {
    Editor1 ed1 = new Editor1();
  }
}
```

The most important thing to note here is how items contained in the delivered resources are accessed by the application. At line 22 in Listing 8.5, an icon is created that accesses a GIF file in the editor1 JAR file. This is the simplest way to access items in application resources. Note also that to access items, we need to use the JFrame's classloader (see lines 15 and 17 in Listing 8.5).

CAUTION

Generally speaking, don't use the `Classloader.loadSystemResources()` or related methods to retrieve icons or other items from application JAR files. JNLP Clients use their own classloader implementations, so ask the current (JNLP-launched) class or the main thread for its classloader, and use that one instead.

Remember that developers don't have to worry about where JAR files are located in the local file system because the JNLP Client took care of downloading them, installing them in its cache, and making them available in the application environment.

TIP

In Chapter 10, the resource issue (accessing items into JAR files, and so on) is fully detailed, with ready-to-use utility Java classes.

Finally, the application home page, in which users can refer to when needed, is shown in Listing 8.6.

LISTING 8.6   The Home Page of the editor1 Application

```html
<html>

<head>
  <meta http-equiv="Content-Type" content="text/html; charset=iso-8859-1">
  <title>Chapter 8. A Simple text Editor</title>
</head>

<body bgcolor="#FFFFFF">

<h1>Text Editor #1 !</h1>

<p>A Simple Text Editor</p>
This is the Home page of the simple text editor.

<ul>
    <li><a href="c8/editor1/editor1.jnlp">A Simple text Editor</a></li>
</ul>
```

LISTING 8.6   Continued

```
<hr>
</body>
</html>
```

> **NOTE**
>
> Even in this first example, in which the home page is quite bare, the JNLP technology demonstrates the potential for these services, and the application home page to become a service portal, blurring the borders of traditional software applications. These concepts are explained in further detail in Chapter 1, "Deploying Java," and Chapter 2, "An Abstract Model for Deployment," which explains the transformation of new-generation software towards more abstract services).

Execution

When you click the URL pointing to the editor1.jnlp file through a browser, the installed JNLP Client displays its splash window, taking control of the launch process. In Figure 8.4, we can see Java Web Start while downloading our editor. Note the icon we specified in the JNLP file, at line 12 of Listing 8.4.

FIGURE 8.4

The JNLP download window during JAR transfer.

When the download is finished and the JVM is properly initialized, our application is executed by invoking the main() method.

8

A JNLP QUICK
LAUNCH

> **NOTE**
>
> JNLP Clients always launch an application from the specified `main()` method, and only from that. Note also that a JVM runs only one launched application per time.

In Figure 8.5, we can see our text editor in all of its splendor. The application from now on is executed like a normal Java application.

FIGURE 8.5
Our powerful text editor is ready to be used.

When launching an application via a JNLP file, a JNLP Client is always behind the scenes. If we want, we can launch applications from its console without passing through the browser. The Java Web Start window (with our editor application cached in) is shown in Figure 8.6.

FIGURE 8.6
Java Web Start, showing the application cached locally.

Depending on the JNLP Client, we can use some platform-dependent facilities such as setting shortcuts or something similar in order to ease the application launch. As a default, Java Web Start asks the user the second time the application is launched whether to create such facilities, as shown in Figure 8.7.

FIGURE 8.7
Web Start prompts the user for shortcuts (on Windows) the second time we launch our editor.

Now that we have a more precise idea of what a typical JNLP-launched application looks like, it's time to explore some of the other features JNLP makes available to developers.

An Installer

A very interesting and commonly used feature of JNLP allows you to take control of the installation process with our Java code that substitutes the JNLP Client job. This example will provide a simple reusable component (a JNLP-aware splash window), an example of a JNLP file that specifies an installer, plus a practical example of how to use the runtime services offered by the JNLP Client environment (this will be fully discussed in Chapter 11).

We want to use our own installer code, both because we want to enforce our own deployment rules (for example, given the user type, we want to install only basic functionalities and not the full application), or because we simply want to hide the JNLP Client's splash window (see the next section) with our own in order to avoid end-user disorientation, to offer a better product, or for some other reason. The splash window class can be adapted to a variety of situations, but now let's see how it works.

When we launch the `app.jnlp` file, the following events happen:

1. The JNLP Client (that is, Java Web Start) will start, loading the `app.jnlp` file and interpreting it as a normal JNLP file.

2. Because the `app.jnlp` file includes a link to our custom installer, the JNLP Client stops installing the application and retrieves the installer JNLP file, namely `splash.jnlp`.

3. The JNLP Client parses the `splash` JNLP file, and launches its related code (note that the application has not been launched yet). The installer code (class `Splash.java` contained in the `splash.jar` file) then performs the rest of the application installation.

4. Lastly, when the installer has finished, the application (class App.java contained in the app.jar file) is executed, using items contained in the resources our installer downloaded.

Preparation

For this example, we have two JNLP files and two Java classes plus some JAR files.

First, we examine the main JNLP file, app.jnlp, shown in Listing 8.7. It declares in lines 18–21 that it needs four JAR resources (namely, the files app.jar, first.jar, second.jar, third.jar), plus a custom installer (described in the other JNLP) named splash.jnlp (lines 14–17 in Listing 8.7).

LISTING 8.7   The app.jnlp File

```
<?xml version="1.0" encoding="utf-8"?>
<jnlp spec="1.0+"
      codebase="http://server/b2/c8/splash/">
  <information>
    <title>A User-Friendly App</title>
    <vendor>Mauro Inc.</vendor>
    <homepage href="home.html"/>
    <description>Install Your programs via the Web, quickly and
effectively!</description>
    <description kind="short">An example of a simple Java-launched
Installator</description>
    <offline-allowed/>
  </information>
  <resources>
    <j2se version="1.3+"/>
    <extension
      name="Splash Window"
      href="splash.jnlp">
    </extension>
    <jar href="app.jar"/>
    <jar href="first.jar"/>
    <jar href="second.jar"/>
    <jar href="third.jar"/>
  </resources>
  <application-desc/>
</jnlp>
```

The splash.jnlp file is interestingly new. It is called an *extension descriptor* (line 16 in Listing 8.8), in that it doesn't describe an application—like app.jnlp—rather, it describes an *extension* to that application—in this case, a custom installer. We will see these type of JNLP files in detail in Chapter 9, "The Protocol." For the rest, it is pretty similar to the app.jnlp main file.

LISTING 8.8   The splash.jnlp File

```
<?xml version="1.0" encoding="utf-8"?>
<jnlp spec="1.0+"
      codebase="http://server/b2/c8/splash/">
  <information>
    <title>A User-Friendly Splash Window</title>
    <vendor>Mauro Inc.</vendor>
    <homepage href="home.html"/>
    <description>Install Your programs via the Web, quickly and
effectively!</description>
    <description kind="short">A simple Java-launched Installator</description>
    <offline-allowed/>
  </information>
  <resources>
    <j2se version="1.3+"/>
    <jar href="splash.jar"/>
  </resources>
  <installer-desc main-class="com.marinilli.b2.c8.splash.Splash"/>
</jnlp>
```

NOTE

Different from the other examples, here the jnlp element does not have an href attribute. This is intentional. In this way, the JNLP Client doesn't put the application in its list of available applications, and doesn't offer integration with the client OS. However, it still continues to cache the application.

TIP

The next time you launch the app.jnlp, you'll discover that the splash window doesn't show up any more. Because it is an installer extension, the JNLP Client knows that the application has been already installed, so it doesn't invoke the splash.jnlp file any more. You need to manually locate the JNLP Client cache in the file system and delete the cached files; then, the installation splash window will pop up again. Note that this is the only way to go because the JNLP Client won't show the application in the list of registered applications; thus, it is impossible to *selectively* clear the cache.

We arrived at the installer class, invoked by the `splash.jnlp` extension descriptor. The Splash class is shown in Listing 8.9.

LISTING 8.9   The Splash class

```
package com.marinilli.b2.c8.splash;

import java.awt.*;
import javax.swing.*;
import javax.jnlp.*;
import java.net.URL;
/**
 * Chapter 8 - Splash
 * @author Mauro Marinilli
 * @version 1.0
 */

public class Splash extends JWindow implements Runnable{
  //class members
  private ClassLoader loader;
  private static ExtensionInstallerService extensionInstaller;

  //graphics widgets
  private JLabel ImageLabel;
20:  private JLabel MessageLabel  = new JLabel();
  private JLabel animLabel;
  private JLabel resourceLabel  = new JLabel();
  private static Splash splash;

  //data
  private String[] jarSequence= {"first.jar", "second.jar", "third.jar"};
  private String[] msgSequence= {
    "Now Even More Powerful!",
    "Incredibly Fast And Reliable!",
    "Ready To Go?"};
  private String codebase = "http://server/b2/c8/splash/";

  /**
   * Private Constructor - Implements the Singleton Design Pattern
   */
  private Splash() {
    super();
    loader = getClass().getClassLoader();
    //prepare UI
40:    ImageLabel = new JLabel(new
ImageIcon(loader.getResource("images/background.jpg")));
```

LISTING 8.9 Continued

```
    animLabel = new JLabel(new
ImageIcon(loader.getResource("images/working.gif")));
    resourceLabel.setBorder(BorderFactory.createEmptyBorder(6,6,6,6));
    ImageLabel.setLayout(new BorderLayout());
    ImageLabel.setBorder(BorderFactory.createRaisedBevelBorder());
    ImageLabel.add(resourceLabel, BorderLayout.NORTH);
    ImageLabel.add(MessageLabel, BorderLayout.SOUTH);
    ImageLabel.add(animLabel, BorderLayout.CENTER);
    getContentPane().setLayout(new BorderLayout());
    getContentPane().add(ImageLabel, BorderLayout.CENTER);
    pack();

    //Centers the window
    Dimension size = getSize();
    Dimension screenSize = Toolkit.getDefaultToolkit().getScreenSize();
    if (size.height > screenSize.height) {
      size.height = screenSize.height;
    }
    if (size.width > screenSize.width) {
      size.width = screenSize.width;
60:    }
    setLocation((screenSize.width - size.width) / 2, (screenSize.height -
size.height) / 2);
  }

  /**
   * Implements the Singleton Design Pattern
   *
   */
  public static Splash getInstance(){
    if (splash == null)
      splash = new Splash();
    return splash;
  }

  /**
   * Sets a message visible at the bottom
   * @param text Text to show
   */
  public static void setMessage(String text) {
    if (splash != null)
80:      splash.MessageLabel.setText("    " + text);
  }
```

LISTING 8.9 Continued

```
/**
 * Sets a message visible at the top showing the
 * currently downloading resource file
 * @param rsr Text to show
 */
public static void setLoadingResource(String rsr) {
  if (splash != null) {
    splash.resourceLabel.setText("Downloading: "+rsr);
  }
}

/**
 * Shows up the splash window or destroys it
 * @param show
 */
public static void showUp(boolean show) {
  if (splash == null)
100:    return;
  splash.setVisible(show);
  if (show == false) {
    splash.setCursor(Cursor.getDefaultCursor());
    splash = null;
  } else {
    splash.setCursor(new Cursor(Cursor.WAIT_CURSOR));
    try {
      // Lookup the Service
      extensionInstaller =

(ExtensionInstallerService)ServiceManager.lookup("javax.jnlp.ExtensionInstaller
Service");
      // Hide JNLP Client's download window
      extensionInstaller.hideStatusWindow();
    } catch(UnavailableServiceException use) {
      System.out.println("Service not supported: "+use);
    }
  }
}

/**
120:  * Takes charge of all the JAR delivery
 */
public void run() {
  //downloads all the needed resources
  DownloadService ds;
```

LISTING 8.9   Continued

```
      int jarNumber = jarSequence.length;
      try {
        ds =
(DownloadService)ServiceManager.lookup("javax.jnlp.DownloadService");
      } catch (UnavailableServiceException use) {
        ds = null;
        System.out.println("Service is not supported: "+use);
      }//once have a ds you can do a lot of things

      //begin downloading jars
      for (int i=0;i<jarNumber;i++){
        if (ds != null) {
          processJar(ds,i);
        }
        //take a breath
        try {
140:          Thread.currentThread().sleep(3000);//IT'S ONLY COSMETICS!
//          Thread.currentThread().yield();
        } catch (Exception e) {
          System.out.println("Synchronization Exception: "+e);
        }
      }//-for
      showUp(false);//all the needed JARs have been processed
      extensionInstaller.installSucceeded(true);//we're optimistic
  }

  /**
   * A fancy method that finds out if a JAR is cached and removes it.
   * substitute it with your code.
   */
  private void processJar(DownloadService ds, int i){
    try {
      // determine if a particular resource is cached
      URL url =
        new URL(codebase + jarSequence[i]);
      boolean cached = ds.isResourceCached(url, null);
160:      // remove the resource from the cache, just for fun
      if (cached) {
       ds.removeResource(url, null);
      }

      // reload the resource into the cache, yes!
      setMessage(msgSequence[i]);
      setLoadingResource(jarSequence[i]);
```

LISTING 8.9   Continued

```
        DownloadServiceListener dsl = ds.getDefaultProgressWindow();
        ds.loadResource(url, null, dsl);
      } catch (Exception e) {
        System.out.println("Loading Resource: " + e);
      }
   }

   public static void main(String[] args) {
      Splash splash1 = Splash.getInstance();
      splash1.showUp(true);
      splash1.run();
   }
180:}
```

First of all, we should discuss some design considerations. Given its nature, a splash window is inherently a singleton; that is, a class that could have at most one instance at time (see Chapter 11 for some details on this design pattern). Inevitably, many details have been omitted. Given the space we have here, we necessarily have to limit features to the essential ones. It is up to you to expand the proposed code, as needed. Chapter 13 describes a whole application in detail.

The singleton is implemented, as usual, via a private constructor and a getInstance() static method. Note that the window pop-up and thread run have been kept separate for more flexibility.

> **TIP**
>
> If you want to make the class threaded, add the following line in the main method, just before invoking the run method:
>
> ```
> Thread t = new Thread(splash1);
> ```
>
> We omitted it for simplicity because the example is so simple that it doesn't really need any multithreaded support. Anyway, real-world installers often extensively use threads for improving performances.

Something that has been kept sketched in the code is the way data is passed on to the installer, by means of static arrays. One can figure out more flexible mechanisms, such as main() parameters or system properties (as illustrated in other code examples), which are less hard-wired and modifiable from outside the Java class. Also, the initialization of the codebase variable at line 31 has been sketched to keep the listing simple. In other examples, you can see how to obtain that value from the `BasicService` JNLP runtime object (see Chapter 11).

At line 140, a fake delay has been added in order to see the effect of the resources being downloaded, one after the other, in a local development environment. In real-world cases, always use line 141 for synchronizing threads, instead.

The `processJar()` method is included only for demonstration. Depending on your needs, you can modify it or even remove it, as needed. One important thing to see here is how runtime services are obtained by applications.

In lines 109–110, for example, an `ExtensionInstallerService` object is obtained, requesting its fully qualified name string to the `ServiceManager` and casting the resulting `Object` to the needed service class, as in the following lines of code:

```
extensionInstaller =

(ExtensionInstallerService)ServiceManager.lookup("javax.jnlp.ExtensionInstaller
Service");
```

By means of this service, it is possible, among other things, to hide JNLP Client's status window, as of line 112.

The launched application (see Listing 8.10) is much more simple than the installer class. It is a mere example of an application. It uses a resource contained in one of the JAR files downloaded by the `Splash` class, and nothing else.

LISTING 8.10   The App class

```java
package com.marinilli.b2.c8.splash;

import java.awt.*;
import javax.swing.*;
import java.awt.event.*;

/**
 * Chapter 8 - An Application installed by the Splash class
 * @author Mauro Marinilli
 * @version 1.0
 */
public class App extends JFrame {

  public App() {
    ImageIcon img =
      new ImageIcon(getClass().getClassLoader().getResource("back.jpg"));
    JLabel aLabel = new JLabel(img);
```

LISTING 8.10 Continued

```
    aLabel.setLayout(new BorderLayout());
    aLabel.add(new JLabel("An Application.."));
    getContentPane().add(aLabel);
    addWindowListener( new java.awt.event.WindowAdapter() {
      public void windowClosing(WindowEvent e) {
        System.exit(0);
      }
    });
    pack();
    setVisible(true);
  }

  public static void main(String[] args) {
    App app = new App();
  }
}
```

Execution

Now that we've had a look at the source, it is time to see some action. First of all, as evident from Figure 8.8, pardon my UI design skills; I'm sure you'll be able to design better splash windows!

FIGURE 8.8

Our splash window at work.

After the splash window entertained users during the program deployment, the application is finally launched, as shown in Figure 8.9.

FIGURE 8.9

After all the resources are downloaded, the application starts.

Java Web Start

Java Web Start is the reference implementation for the Client of the Java Network Launching Protocol. It provides four ways to launch an application:

- Directly from the Web, passing through the Web browser.
- Directly from pointing to the related JNLP file. Under Windows, for example, by double-clicking on a JNLP file, or
- From the included Application Manager utility, part of the `javaws` executable.
- From platform-dependent mechanisms (items such as the Start menu or desktop short-cuts in Windows).

Now, we will briefly discuss some aspects of Web Start from a developer's perspective.

Installation

Installing the JNLP Client is sometimes the biggest hurdle encountered in real-world situations, especially the first time when no Java Runtime Environment is installed yet.

There are a variety of options for solving the Java Web Start's first installation problem (future upgrades are less traumatic, thanks to the "check for updates" option in the Application Manager's console). The simplest option is to put a link directly to the Java Web Start homepage at Sun: `http://www.javasoft.com/products/javawebstart`.

Another useful URL made available from Sun is the following: `http://java.sun.com/cgi-bin/javawebstart-platform.sh?`, which launches directly the Java Web Start installation procedure without passing through the product's page.

Otherwise, you can wrap the Web Start installer together with your application in your installer program. This, in turn, will install Web Start first and then launch it with your JNLP file and resources, and so on. Another useful option is to use the `silent` command-line option of the Web Start installer executable file to perform a silent installation. This installs Java Web Start, without any user intervention, in a completely unobtrusive way.

Another option is to use some script inside HTML pages to tell whether Java Web Start is installed or not, so as to dynamically modify the Web page according to the given user, as shown in Listing 8.11.

LISTING 8.11 HTML Snippet for Launching JNLP Applications

```
<HTML><HEAD></HEAD>
<BODY>
  <SCRIPT LANGUAGE="Javascript">
    var isJWSInstalled = 0;
    var jWSHome = "http://www.javasoft.com/products/javaWebstart";
```

LISTING 8.11 Continued

```
    isIE = "false";
    if (navigator.mimeTypes && navigator.mimeTypes.length) {
      x = navigator.mimeTypes['application/x-java-jnlp-file'];
      if (x) isJWSInstalled = 1;
      } else {
        isIE = "true";
      }
      function insertLink(jnlpUrl, text) {
        if (isJWSInstalled) {
        document.write("<a href=" + jnlpUrl + ">"  + text + "</a>");
        } else {
          document.write("<a href=" + jWSHome +
">Before launching the application click here to install Java Web Start</a>");
        }
      }
    </SCRIPT>
    <SCRIPT LANGUAGE="VBScript">
      on error resume next
      If isIE = "true" Then
        If Not(IsObject(CreateObject("JavaWebStart.IsInstalled"))) Then
          isJWSInstalled = 0
        Else
          isJWSInstalled = 1
        End If
      End If
    </SCRIPT>
    <H1>Launch Page</H1>
    Try Out our application!
    <SCRIPT LANGUAGE="Javascript">
      insertLink("myApp.jnlp","Launch myApp")
    </SCRIPT>
</BODY></HTML>
```

End-User Considerations

We are going to shortly touch on some important points commonly encountered by end-users and developers dealing with Java Web Start.

Splash Windows Extravaganza

A common problem experienced by end-users with JNLP-launched applications is the fragmented experience perceived by them when observing several windows appearing one after the other during installation, and even during usual execution. Less-experienced users feel confused by the different vendor's banners, whereas developers want Java Web Start to be fully transparent to their customers. On the other side, people at Sun think that showing the Web Start banner is a warranty of reliability and security for users actually promoting the success of the JNLP technology.

We already mentioned this inconvenience in the first part of the book. Now, we can propose some concrete remedies. The more straightforward is to take control of the installation process as soon as possible by proposing a custom splash window, which is the same one used when the application is preparing to execute (already deployed locally). In order to do so, Listing 8.9 proposes a useful starting point for programmers.

Preferences

As we discuss here, the sophisticated Web Start UI was designed as a trade-off between inexperienced users on one side and developers on the other side. Depending on the kind of user population your application will have and the level of control you can enforce on them, it would be a good idea to describe in the help documentation the kind of settings users are encouraged to modify and those that are not. Often, less-experienced users find it difficult to realize that you coded only the application, and that you are not responsible for the launching program.

One last word about proxy settings. Proxy settings aren't usually a problem whenever a standard proxy is employed (standard in that it uses the BASIC authentication protocol). Some other proxy servers (most notably Microsoft's ones) use a proprietary authentication protocol, NTLM, which is not supported by JNLP Clients. In this case, you can resort to switching authentication off, or find yourself a compatible JNLP Client or a proxy server that uses the BASIC protocol for authentication.

Using Web Start in a Production Environment

Java Web Start is also commonly used by developers to test their products. This is an important aspect that puzzled engineers at Sun, and forced them to balance the two aspects—ease of use for the end-user and richness of control for the developer—all in the same product.

When testing programs with Java Web Start, developers (or advanced users) can use the following preference settings:

- Displaying the Java console, in which application's output streams are redirected for debugging.

- Setting a log file, in which the application's output is recorded. Non-existing log files are created on-the-fly.

- Flushing the cache. When developing applications, it is often necessary to force the clearing of the cache because when applications don't finish their work correctly, Java

Web Start could cache them without showing the related hooks in the UI. Therefore, further attempts to launch the same application fail because Web Start incorrectly resorts to cached (old) resources with unpredictable results. Advanced developers might selectively purge the cache directly by deleting related files from the root directory showed in the cache options area in the preferences panel.

- Launching the Java Web Start application from a command line and inspecting the process' outputs can help in particularly nasty situations.

- Wandering around into the Java Web Start working directories and configuration files (being careful not to damage anything) can help sometimes. However, remember that undocumented configuration options are likely to be unsupported in future releases.

Finally, a great deal of information can be found at Sun's site, through documentation, discussion newsgroups, and so forth.

Summary

In this chapter we introduced the JNLP technology through several examples. The proposed examples are useful to illustrate the various features of JNLP and could serve as a basis for creating your own deployment solutions.

- The first example (Listing 8.1) shows how to use JNLP with local files, without requiring a web connection.

- Listing 8.4 shows a more detailed example that resemble closely a real application launched through JNLP. It uses a web connection and some of the JNLP basic features.

- Listings 8.7 and 8.8 propose an application that is installed by a custom installer. The code proposed in this example can be adapted to real-world custom installers.

The next two chapters will discuss the JNLP protocol more systematically and comprehensively. In particular, Chapter 9 will deal with the structure of JNLP files and the main concepts behind JNLP technology.

The JNLP Protocol

IN THIS CHAPTER

As we saw from the examples in the previous chapter, there are a few simple concepts associated with the JNLP technology. We will examine many of them in detail here in this chapter, while leaving those related to the client environment definition (refer to Chapter 2, "An Abstract Model for Deployment") for Chapter 10, "Defining the Client Environment."

Let's introduce the principal concepts we will see in this chapter.

- *Resources*. With this term are gathered together four types of objects: system properties, extensions, native libraries, and of course, application JAR files. We will cover them in Chapter 10.

- *Descriptors*. Every JNLP file is a descriptor, describing the type and attributes of the pieces to be assembled together on the client platform. There are conceptually two kinds of descriptors and four different JNLP descriptors.

- *Extension Descriptors*. In JNLP terminology, extensions are either *installers* (that is, Java code run only once for installing particular executables) or *components* (that is, reusable groups of JAR files needed for the application being launched).

- *Application Descriptors*. There are two types of application descriptors: *applet* and *application* descriptors.

Figure 9.1 clarifies the role of extension and application descriptors regarding the basic structure (what a JNLP file basic syntax looks like).

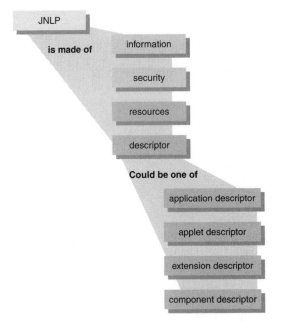

FIGURE 9.1
Basic static structure of JNLP files.

To recap, a JNLP file must contain a descriptor element that could be one of four possible types only. It always contains three other types of elements: an information element, a security element(that is optional; it is described in Chapter 10), and many resources elements as needed.

Before diving into JNLP details, it is important to briefly clarify situations in which this technology would be used.

When Adopting JNLP Technology Makes Sense

Generally speaking, when adopting the JNLP technology for your solution, all the considerations regarding Java technology still apply. They apply in particular for the J2SE case (that is, good RAM memory resources available on client machines, relatively new installed hardware, and so on).

A strong motivation for choosing the JNLP solution is to improve an existing Java application or to migrate an applet to a JNLP-deployed application.

It is essential to plan the JNLP Client deployment strategy in advance. Explicitly, how do you intend to install the JNLP Client (for example, Java Web Start) on client platforms if it is not already present? The capability to accomplish this task effectively is the real hurdle in adopting the JNLP technology.

Server-side considerations also have to be taken into account. We require a certain control over the deployment Web server, especially for the protocol's advanced features such as incremental updates of JAR files.

When is it not a good idea to take it on? Regarding this aspect, all the considerations described in the second chapter apply to the JNLP deployment technology too…in particular, when the first-time launch cost is too high. In terms of bandwidth (using Java Web Start as an example), we see that the JNLP client occupies roughly 6MB (almost 5.5MB for the J2SE JRE non-localized and .5 MB for the Web Start non-localized executable). Adding in an average application (say around .5 MB), the result is a total of 6.5MB (counting installer code, too).

Another important factor is whether end-users are willing to pay the JNLP Client installation cost in terms of complexity, time, and so on. This is often the case in organizations that produce the software they use.

Let's spend some time discussing what JNLP technology provides developers. Although it takes care of deployment, resource versioning in a secure end-user environment, and giving extra runtime services, the technology is limited in some ways. First of all, security is at a basic level, and authentication is limited to JAR files only. These are not severe limitations, but they leave developers of advanced applications with some work to do. Regarding security and other issues, such as per-user authentication, probably the best way to proceed is with in-house development. However, for other kinds of services such as example debugging or logging, some standard support would be quite useful, especially when interoperability features are desired. Despite that, JNLP technology is quite useful and, after all, still needs some time to mature.

Having seen some aspects concerning the adoption of the JNLP technology, it is now time to get into the details.

The Stages

In this section, we will explore the protocol steps sequence in detail.

First of all, a JNLP Client must be installed on the client computer. Then, we need a JNLP root file, that is, the main JNLP file that describes all the needed pieces and how to use them. By following directives in the main JNLP file and in the other extension files, the application can be launched. The dynamic structure (that is, how the file is interpreted by a JNLP Client at run-time) is depicted in Figure 9.2. Here, the main file points to its installer extension, its JAR resources that made up the application itself (files myApp, myIcons), and a set of libraries organized in a component extension.

When the JNLP Client has retrieved the main JNLP file, it begins the launch procedure by parsing the file interpreting the XML elements. First of all, the client launcher makes sure that it has the right JRE available, eventually downloading it. Then, for each extension descriptor found in the JNLP file (`<component-desc>` and `<installer-desc>` elements), it retrieves all the needed resources. In the case of extension descriptors contained in other extension descriptors, it downloads them recursively.

When they are all loaded, it begins executing the installers, as we saw in the splash window example of Chapter 8, "A Quick Launch." Finally, when the installers give the green light, it launches the application.

To recap what was said, in Figure 9.3 there is a picture of the steps involved in launching a Java application with JNLP.

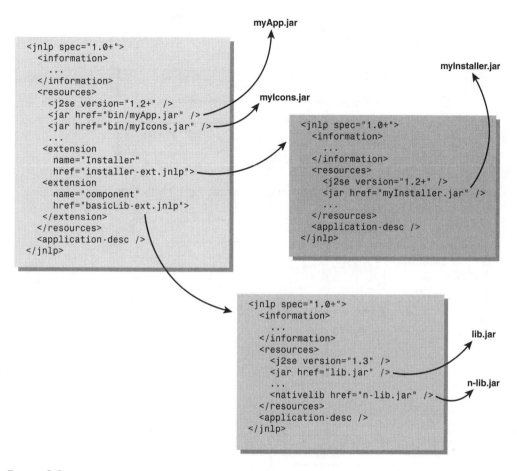

FIGURE 9.2

The dynamic structure of an example JNLP file.

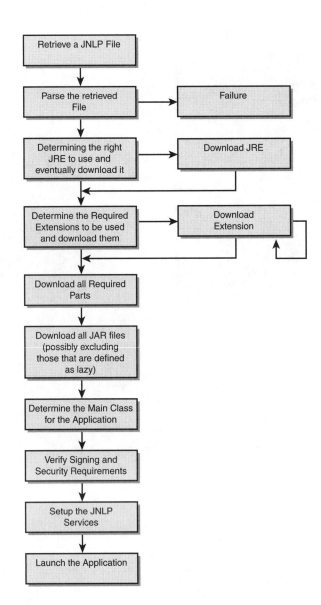

FIGURE 9.3
Flow chart for the basic JNLP launch procedure.

The JNLP File Structure

A basic template of a JNLP file for describing applications is shown in Listing 9.1. Extension descriptors' structure is very close to the application descriptors' structure. This template can be used as a starting point when creating your own JNLP main file.

LISTING 9.1   A JNLP Application Descriptor Template

```
<?xml version="1.0" encoding="UTF-8"?>
<jnlp spec="1.0+" codebase="http://www.mysite.com/application/" ...>
  <information> ... </information>
  <security> ... </security>
  <resources> ... </resources>
  <application-desc> ... </application-desc>
</jnlp>
```

Once the JNLP technology seems viable for solving your problem, the following decisions have to be made when writing JNLP files:

- Whether JNLP extension files are needed (that is, if some control over the installation is needed). Without custom installers, JAR files will be automatically downloaded and saved in the JNLP Client's cache. Also, determine whether libraries should be factored out in component descriptors.

- Which operations your application need to perform, in relation to security. If it has to access local disks or use native libraries, and so on. This will define the kind of security setting in the JNLP file. Note that if you need a custom installer (see the previous item in this list) that will write on the local disk, you need an unrestricted security environment (see Chapter 10).

- Whether to take advantage of the runtime services offered by the JNLP Client. This could result in an inability to run the application outside the JNLP Client's container. We will see a Java library that addresses this problem. This utility library will be used in the example in Chapter 13 and its code is discussed in Appendix D.

NOTE

These decisions will also affect your Java code, not only JNLP files. For loading items in resource JAR files or for accessing runtime services, you could need to modify your existing code.

Describing Applications and Applets

As we saw in the preceding section, there are essentially two different uses of JNLP files. One for describing applications (or applets) to be launched, and another one that specifies other necessary pieces that are too complex to be described as mere resources. Here, we will focus on the first type of descriptors.

An application descriptor is always needed, whereas extension descriptors are used for particular needs, such as the installation of new JREs, native libraries, and so on.

Describing Applications

A JNLP Client can launch two types of executables: applets and applications. In reality, one may think of something like a third type of applications that can be launched: those applications which take advantage of the JNLP Client runtime services, and couldn't otherwise run in a normal JRE basic environment. Runtime issues will be the subject of Chapter 11, "Runtime Client Services"; here, we are only interested in defining executables by using JNLP files.

Application descriptor JNLP files describe core information about the executables to be launched. An application descriptor must be supplied in the input to the JNLP Client to start the launch procedure. In any JNLP file describing applications, there are five types of data that can be specified:

- Management data needed for the JNLP Client in order to handle properly the JNLP files, such as specifying security restrictions, and so on.
- Basic information about the application, such as the application home page, icons, and so on.
- Various resources, in the form of JAR files.
- Needed extensions. Specified within the `resources` element.
- Application- or applet-specific data, such as input parameters, and so on.

Listing 9.2 shows an example of the `application-desc` element at work.

LISTING 9.2   An Example of the Application-Desc Element

```
<application-desc main-class="com.myCompany.MyMainClass">
  <argument>CommandLineArg1</argument>
  <argument>CommandLineArg2</argument>
  <argument>CommandLineArg3</argument>
</application-desc>
```

The fragment of the JNLP file in Listing 9.2 gives the following information to the JNLP Client:

- The JNLP file being processed is an application descriptor.
- The program execution starts by executing the main(..) method of the MyMainClass class in the main JAR file. The main JAR file is a specially defined JAR in the JNLP file intended to contain the main() method for the application.
- The parameters for the main() method are the <argument> values, in the same order as in the JNLP file. So Listing 9.2 causes the JNLP Client to execute the following:

```
com.myCompany.MyMainClass.main(
{ "CommandLineArg1","CommandLineArg1","CommandLineArg1" }
);
```

We saw some application descriptor JNLP files in Chapter 8, and we will see many more in the following chapters.

Now, let's see something interesting. Many programmers approaching JNLP technology often confuse the role of the installer and that of the application. In the JNLP terminology, these words refer only to the JNLP Client and how it has to treat the specified Java executables. When we specify a JNLP file (and all its resource elements) as an installer descriptor, it will only be executed the first time that code is launched, in order to prepare the environment for the application described in the application descriptor JNLP file. Then what the launched application does, is beyond the scope of the JNLP Client that finishes its job launching the application and supporting it with runtime services.

As an example of that, let's examine a Java class that is treated like a normal application by the JNLP Client, but once launched, it launches a native executable. In other words, it works much like an installer itself.

Retrieving and Executing a Native Installer

An interesting case that happens often in real situations is to execute a native installer. Often, it is the quickest way to deploy our legacy code (we used to deploy our applications to our customers with a big setup.exe file), or we can have some code that needs special native support each time the application is launched.

Naturally, this example can be adapted to also launch any kind of native files.

Let's examine the JNLP file shown in Listing 9.3.

LISTING 9.3   The install-win JNLP File

```xml
<?xml version="1.0" encoding="utf-8"?>
<jnlp spec="1.0+"
      codebase="http://server/b2/c9/install-win/">
  <information>
    <title>An Installer Launched via JNLP</title>
    <vendor>Mauro Inc.</vendor>
    <description>An Installer Launched via JNLP..</description>
  </information>
  <security><all-permissions/></security>
  <resources>
    <j2se version="1.3+"/>
    <jar href="install-win.jar" os="Windows"/>
  </resources>
  <application-desc main-class="com.marinilli.b2.c9.InstallWin"/>
</jnlp>
```

There are a few things to note:

- As already said, JNLP treats this code as a typical application, not an installer. We described it as an application in line 14.

- We need an unrestricted environment to run this example, as was requested at line 9 of Listing 9.3. For more on security, see Chapter 10.

- Naturally, our code is platform-dependent. This can be gracefully enforced in the JNLP file itself, saving developers the code to detect the current platform we are running on. See Chapter 10 for a discussion of this issue and for the resource element in general.

- Lastly, we mentioned only one resource to make up our application, the install-win.jar file at line 12. So where is our native installer? In this case, we have two choices. We can download it by ourselves from our remote server; or we can put it in our only JAR, so that the JNLP Client will do the delivery for us. We followed the latter solution in this example. One could imagine to look where the JNLP Client caches files and access it from there, but it would be a useless complication because we must always wrap resources in a JAR file, anyway, in order to let them be handled by the JNLP Client.

The native executable has been kept to a minimal size. Probably one of the barest batch files ever is listed in Listing 9.4. Of course, you can substitute it with your .exe file, .sh for Unix, and so on.

LISTING 9.4   The Native Windows Executable

```
echo Installing..
echo Installed.
```

When preparing this example, remember that the JAR must contain both the Java class (in the right path) and the `install.bat` executable too. The JAR file has to be signed; otherwise, the JNLP Client will deny its execution. After all, we are requesting to save a file on the client filesystem a file and then execute it. Your customers should really trust you to allow this on their computers!

Now let's see Listing 9.5, which supplies the `InstallWin` Java class.

LISTING 9.5   The InstallWin class

```java
package com.marinilli.b2.c9;
import javax.jnlp.*;
import java.io.*;
import java.net.URL;
/**
 * Chapter 10 - Installs native code and executes it
 * @author Mauro Marinilli
 * @version 1.0
 */
public class InstallWin {
  static ClassLoader loader;
  static boolean deleteTempFile = true;
  static final String tempFileName = "temp.bat";

  public static void main(String[] args) {
    if (args.length>0) {//checks whether to remove the temp file
      if (args[0].equalsIgnoreCase("leaveTempFile"))
        deleteTempFile = false;
    }
    loader = Thread.currentThread().getContextClassLoader();
    extractNativeResource("install.bat");
    executeNativeResource(tempFileName);

    if (deleteTempFile) {
      deleteTempFile(tempFileName);
    }
    System.out.println("installation terminated.");
    System.exit(0);
  }
```

LISTING 9.5   Continued

```
private static void extractNativeResource(String resourceName) {
  InputStream is = loader.getResourceAsStream(resourceName);
  FileOutputStream fos = null;
  try {
    fos = new FileOutputStream(tempFileName);
  } catch (IOException ioe) {
    System.out.println("creating temp file: "+ioe);
  }
  int c;
  try {
    while ((c = is.read()) != -1)
      fos.write(c);
    is.close();
    fos.close();
  } catch (IOException ioe) {
    System.out.println("extracting installer: "+ioe);
  }
}

private static void executeNativeResource(String fileName){
  try {
    Runtime.getRuntime().exec(fileName);
  } catch (IOException ioe) {
    System.out.println("executing installer: "+ioe);
  }
}

private static void deleteTempFile(String fileName){
    try {
      File f = new File(fileName);
      f.delete();
      System.out.println("temp file deleted.");
    } catch (Exception ioe) {
      System.out.println("deleting temp file: "+ioe);
    }
}

}
```

After reading the input parameters, the main() method (lines 15–30 of Listing 9.5) extracts
the native file to a temporary location, executes it, and then cleans up, leaving the temp.bat
file or not, as specified from the input parameter.

The method `extractNativeResource()` extracts a resource with the given name from the loaded JAR files (installed by the JNLP Client, specified in the `install-win` JNLP file in Listing 9.3) locally.

The method `executeNativeResource()` simply executes the file passed as the argument while the method `deleteTempFile()` removes the temp file.

Resources are loaded via the currently installed classloader, obtained at line 20. We will see all this in detail in Chapter 11.

NOTE

This code is intended only as an example of the use of JNLP technology, to be adapted to real cases as needed.

When executing the `install-win` JNLP file with Java Web Start, we are asked for permission to run it, as shown in Figure 9.4.

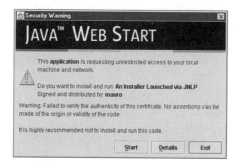

FIGURE 9.4
Java Web Start warns the user before executing intrusive code.

Given the low level of trustworthiness of our certificate (home-made only for testing, as described in Chapter 10), Java Web Start is rather suspicious but leaves the final decision to the user (security issues and the underlying philosophy are discussed in the next chapter). After having allowed the execution, we obtain the output in Listing 9.6.

LISTING 9.6   The Java Web Start Log File After the Execution

```
Java Web Start Console, started Mon Apr 16 11:23:49 GMT+02:00 2001
Java 2 Runtime Environment: Version 1.3.0 by Sun Microsystems Inc.
Logging to file: D:\Documents\myprojects\log.txt
temp file deleted.
installation terminated.
```

As an aside, the JNLP file that launches the native installer without removing the temporary file is shown in Listing 9.7. The only difference is in line 15, where the leaveTempFile string is passed as a parameter to the main() method.

LISTING 9.7   The install-win2 JNLP File

```
<?xml version="1.0" encoding="utf-8"?>
<jnlp spec="1.0+"
      codebase="http://server/b2/c9/install-win/">
  <information>
    <title>An Installer Launched via JNLP</title>
    <vendor>Mauro Inc.</vendor>
    <description>An Installer Launched via JNLP..</description>
  </information>
  <security><all-permissions/></security>
  <resources>
    <j2se version="1.3+"/>
    <jar href="install-win.jar" os="Windows"/>
  </resources>
  <application-desc main-class="com.marinilli.b2.c9.InstallWin">
    <argument>leaveTempFile</argument>
  <application-desc/>
</jnlp>
```

> **NOTE**
>
> Listing 9.7 is also a very simple example of how different behavior can be accomplished without modifying the code (the JAR files) by using different JNLP launch files.

Describing Applets

Applets are defined by mimicking the syntax of the HTML <applet> tag. Listing 9.8 shows an example of a JNLP file snippet describing an applet.

LISTING 9.8   An Example of the Applet-Desc Element

```
<applet-desc
  main-class="com.myCompany.MyAppletClass"
  documentbase="index.htm"
  name="MyAppletClass"
  width="300"
  height="300">
```

LISTING 9.8 Continued

```
  <param name="Param1" value="Value1"/>
  <param name="Param2" value="Value2"/>
</applet-desc>
```

The main use of this kind of JNLP file is for taking advantage of the JNLP Client environment (deployment and runtime services) for existing applets. Generally speaking, previous to a JNLP introduction, developers sometimes made improper use of applets, trying to address problems that were too complex for the applet model. In this case, a complete rewriting of the code to transform the old applet in a JNLP-launched application is probably the best solution. Otherwise, if your code conforms nicely to the applet model, don't forget the Sun Plug-In shipped with the JRE, which still remains the best choice for running applets.

We can see a JNLP file describing an applet in Listing 9.9.

LISTING 9.9 An Example of a JNLP File Describing an Applet

```
<?xml version="1.0" encoding="UTF-8"?>
<jnlp spec="1.0+"
  codebase="http://server/b2/c9/">
  <information>
    <title>1 applet</title>
    <vendor>Mauro's Workshop</vendor>
    <offline/>
  </information>
  <resources>
    <j2se version="1.2+" />
    <jar href="applet.jar" />
  </resources>
  <applet-desc
    main-class="com.marinilli.b2.c9.AnApplet"
    name="jnlp applet"
    width=220
    height=100>
      <param name="name" value="gus"/>
  </applet-desc>
</jnlp>
```

9

THE JNLP PROTOCOL

NOTE

Despite being quite simple, the JNLP support for applets allows developers to specify the JRE environment needed for running the applet.

The applet class is shown in Listing 9.10.

LISTING 9.10   The AnApplet Applet Class

```
package com.marinilli.b2.c9;
import java.awt.*;
import java.awt.event.*;
import java.applet.*;
import javax.swing.*;
public class AnApplet extends JApplet {
  String name;
  JLabel jLabel = new JLabel();
  JButton jButton = new JButton();
  public AnApplet() {
  }
  public void init() {
    try {
      name = getParameter("name");
      if (name==null)
        name="a param.";
      jLabel.setForeground(Color.yellow);
      jLabel.setText("Hello Applet");
      jButton.setForeground(Color.red);
      jButton.setText("I am a Button");
      setBackground(SystemColor.desktop);
      getContentPane().setLayout(new FlowLayout());
      getContentPane().add(jLabel, null);
      getContentPane().add(jButton, null);
      getContentPane().add(new JLabel(name), null);
    }
    catch(Exception e) {
      e.printStackTrace();
    }
  }
  public void start() {
  }
  public void stop() {
  }
  public void destroy() {
  }
  public String getAppletInfo() {
    return "Some Applet Information";
  }
}
```

> **NOTE**
>
> As one can see, the applet support in JNLP is quite straightforward, even if tools such as the Sun Plug-In will suffice in most cases when deploying applets.

Describing Extensions And Installers

When deploying Java code with JNLP, you will be dealing with application descriptors most of the time. Despite that, there are several common situations where extension descriptors come into play, as follows:

- When the basic installation procedure accomplished by a JNLP Client is not adequate. In these cases, a proprietary installer (that is, code written by you) is needed. In Chapter 8, we saw an example of how to launch a custom installer by means of JNLP. For installing native resources—device drivers, native code or native libraries, and so on—an installer descriptor JNLP file is needed.

- When our application relies on other libraries, and we prefer to keep those libraries explicitly separated from the application JAR files. For example, let's imagine we work for a games producer company, and our programs use some general-purpose graphics and sound libraries. We package them into a set of JAR files on our Web server, so that all our programs can access them. Our installer code for these libraries is launched to install them properly. In these cases, a component descriptor JNLP file is needed.

Components

Component descriptors are the analog of libraries in JNLP technology. We can even think of component descriptor JNLP files as another way of deploying Java technology-based *libraries*, not (strictly-speaking) application code. Note that we can also specify native libraries, preferred JRE environments, and so on in a component descriptor.

Listing 9.11 shows the `<component-desc>` element.

LISTING 9.11   The Component-Desc Element

```
<jnlp>
  ...
  <resources>
    <jar href="http://www.mysite.com/my-component/A.jar"/>
    <jar href="http://www.mysite.com/my-component/B.jar"/>
    ...
  </resources>
  <component-desc/>
</jnlp>
```

9

THE JNLP
PROTOCOL

Therefore, changing the descriptor part of the JNLP file makes it behave like a component descriptor. Note that all the elements described for application descriptors, together with their attributes, still apply for component descriptors JNLP files as well. In order to use component descriptors, you have to reference them from your main JNLP file or its subordinate JNLP files (such as extensions, and so on). In Chapter 13, "A Complete Example," we will see an example of this.

Regarding the preparation of component descriptor files, some general considerations may apply:

- When factoring out JAR files for component descriptors, reusability must be taken into account. The time spent in writing an effective JNLP-deployed library must be repaid in terms of its use.

- Component descriptors have the interesting side effect of keeping your resource environment tidy for deployment. That could be enough to adopt it even for relatively small (but complex) projects.

- As with writing code libraries, a series of guidelines should be kept in mind. All possible cases should be thought out in advance from a long-run usage perspective, providing platform-aware `resources` elements and locale-specific ones when appropriate.

Installers

Installer descriptors are used when there is some extra work to do before an application is launched. There are essentially two different reasons for using custom installers:

- For installation considerations. If you have to put some resource file in some places on the local filesystem, or if you have to connect back to some remote server before starting the installation, etc., you need to provide your own installer code.

- For end-user considerations regarding the GUI. For example, to reduce the number of splash windows proposed to users, or to offer a more recognizable product, and so on. In these situations, the standard JNLP Client window, even if customizable, may be inappropriate.

Listing 9.12 shows the `installer-desc` element.

LISTING 9.12   The Installer-Desc Element

```
<jnlp>
  ...
  <resources>
    <jar href="http://www.mysite.com/my-installer/installer.jar"/>
    ...
```

LISTING 9.12   Continued

```
  </resources>
  <installer-desc main-class="com.mysite.installer.Main"/>
</jnlp>
```

Let's examine a simple recapping example about installers. In Chapter 8, we already saw an example of a JNLP application that hid the standard JNLP downloading window in order to show its own splash screen. Now, we see how the same result can be achieved by customizing the JNLP Client's download window, through the use of the `ExtensionInstaller` class, as described in Chapter 11.

In our example, we have a main JNLP file launching our application by means of a custom installer, specified in the `extension` element, at lines 12–15 of Listing 9.13.

LISTING 9.13   The `jnlpinstaller-main` JNLP File

```
<?xml version="1.0" encoding="UTF-8"?>
<jnlp spec="1.0+"
  codebase="http://server/b2/c9/">
  <information>
    <title>Installer Template</title>
    <vendor>Mauro's Workshop</vendor>
    <offline/>
  </information>
  <resources>
    <j2se version="1.2+" />

    <extension
      name="Installer"
      href="jnlpinstaller-ext.jnlp">
    </extension>

    <jar href="anapp.jar" />
  </resources>
  <application-desc main-class="com.marinilli.b2.c9.AnApp" />
</jnlp>
```

In Listing 9.14, we can see the JNLP extension file that describes the installer.

LISTING 9.14   The jnlpinstaller-ext JNLP File

```
<?xml version="1.0" encoding="UTF-8"?>
<jnlp spec="1.0+"
  codebase="http://server/b2/c9/">
```

9

THE JNLP
PROTOCOL

LISTING 9.14   Continued

```
<information>
  <title>Installer Template</title>
  <vendor>Mauro's Workshop</vendor>
  <offline/>
</information>
<resources>
  <j2se version="1.2+" />
  <jar href="jnlpinstaller.jar" />
</resources>
<installer-desc main-class="com.marinilli.b2.c9.JNLPInstaller" />
</jnlp>
```

Now, let's have a look at the Java classes involved. The installer is shown in Listing 9.15. It is a typical example of using the ExtensionInstallerService class. It simply modifies the look of the standard JNLP Client's download window, presenting a download procedure to the user—only illustrative. Note that in the previously mentioned example (Listing 9.9), we hide the standard JNLP download window; whereas here, we are customizing it for our application. Depending on your needs and on the experience you want to transmit to users, you can decide to display your own download window or to use the standard one that is more recognizable by users. It requires less code to be handled, but can be less flexible in some situations.

LISTING 9.15   The jnlpinstaller-ext JNLP File

```
package com.marinilli.b2.c9;
import javax.jnlp.*;
/**
 * Chapter 9 - Customizing the standard download window
 * @author Mauro Marinilli
 * @version 1.0
 */

public class JNLPInstaller {
  ExtensionInstallerService eis;
  public JNLPInstaller() {
    try {
      eis =
(ExtensionInstallerService)ServiceManager.lookup("javax.jnlp.ExtensionInstaller
Service");
    } catch(UnavailableServiceException use) {
      System.out.println("Service not supported: "+use);
    }
    if (eis!=null) {
```

LISTING 9.15 Continued

```
    eis.setHeading("Just An Heading..");
    eis.setStatus("Here we Go!");
    for (int i=0; i<100; i++) {
      eis.updateProgress(i);
      try {
        Thread.currentThread().sleep(100);
      } catch (Exception e) {
        System.out.println(""+e);
      }
    }
    eis.setHeading("Installation Finished.");
    eis.hideProgressBar();
    try {
      Thread.currentThread().sleep(400);
    } catch (Exception e) {
      System.out.println(""+e);
    }
    boolean rebootAfterInstallation = false;
    eis.installSucceeded(rebootAfterInstallation);
  }
}
public static void main(String[] args) {
  JNLPInstaller JNLPInstaller1 = new JNLPInstaller();
}
```

Chapter 11 supplies an example of the way a custom installer class installs an optional package in the standard lib/ext/ JRE directory. There, you will find information on how to write installer code using the JNLP client API.

Summary

In this chapter we introduced JNLP from a more theoretical viewpoint than Chapter 8. In particular, we discussed some considerations regarding the adoption of such a deployment technology. Then we explored the protocol main stages and the basic JNLP file structure, covering the two main types of descriptors, for extensions and applications. After having completed a first, overall picture of the JNLP protocol, we are now ready to examine its details. The next chapter will describe how the Client Environment (we introduced such a concept in Chapter 2) can be described using the JNLP protocol.

9

THE JNLP
PROTOCOL

Defining the Client Environment

IN THIS CHAPTER

In Chapter 2, "An Abstract Model for Deployment," we saw that an important part of the deployment process is what we called the resolution phase. Within this phase, the quality of the client environment definition is crucial to the quality of the overall deployment process. As we will see, JNLP covers just a part of all the possible properties for a client environment. The rest is up to the developer.

In Chapter 9, "The JNLP Protocol," we discussed the protocol from a top-down perspective, illustrating extension and application descriptors. It is now time to examine the other three elements of the JNLP file, as shown in Figure 9.1: describing information, resources and security.

Application Basics

Applications need to be integrated into the client environment. For example, on the Windows platform, shortcuts can be created both on the desktop and on the Start menu. Icons and text descriptions can enhance the application usability and can be left to the JNLP Client, instead of developers writing lots of platform-dependent code to perform that integration.

The `information` element fulfills this need by providing basic application information such as title, home page, and so on. Listing 10.1 shows part of a JNLP file that instructs the JNLP Client how to integrate the application on the desktop using locale-specific data for the supported platforms and default data for all the remaining ones.

LISTING 10.1   Example of Use of the Information Element

```
<jnlp>
  <information>
    <title> DefaultTitle </title>
    <vendor> Myself</vendor>
    <description> Lengthy Description </description>
    <description kind="tooltip"> it does something </description>
    <icon href="img/icon.gif"/>
    <offline-allowed/>
  </information>
...
  <information locale="it_IT">
    <title> Titolo Italiano </title>
    <vendor> </vendor>
    <description> Descrizione </description>
    <description kind="tooltip"> Descrizione </description>
    <icon href=""/>
    <offline-allowed/>
  </information>
</jnlp>
```

> **CAUTION**
>
> The `vendor` and `title` elements need to be specified in every JNLP file. As a consequence, the `information` element also has to be specified for every JNLP file. Otherwise, the JNLP Client will produce an error.

The following data can be specified in an `information` element.

- The locale the `information` element refers to
- The application title
- The name of the application's vendor
- The application home page
- The description element, which can consist of three different kinds: one-line, short, or tooltip
- The application icon
- Whether the application can run in offline mode or not

See Appendix B, "The JNLP Specification," for all the details.

> **NOTE**
>
> Icons, when not specified, are assumed to be 32x32 pixels with a color depth of 8 bits (256 colors).

Resources

We have discussed the main rules of our game, but we still miss the counters and how they move. In the JNLP game, pawns are represented by *resources*. As we know, JAR files, native libraries, and system properties are described within the `resources` element; and are mentioned as application extensions (which we introduced in the previous chapter).

Taming Resources Management

Before diving into the JNLP resources sea of details, it could help to see things from a different perspective. What is your need?

10

- If you need to access your JAR files only for their content, and you don't care about their physical position, the usual `resources` element will work perfectly. This is the most common case, by far. You will see dozens of these cases in this book. The same thing applies to native libraries that need only to be loaded by the JVM (by means of the `System.loadLibrary` method) to be usable by the launched application. For this latter requirement, use the `nativelib` element as described later.

- Installing the so-called *optional packages* is a quite common need. What are they? Once they were called standard extensions; they could be a mix of Java code and native libraries required to extend the JRE. Typical examples are input methods for non-Latin alphabets, products such as Java Advanced Imaging, Java3D, Java Secure Socket Extension (JSSE), and so on. If you are in need of installing something like that for your JNLP-launched application, Listing 11.6 does just that. Have a look at the Java reference documentation for optional package details.

- If your application requires the installation of native libraries—that is, non-JAR files in some defined locations on the local file system—you can resort to a custom installer. Take a look listings 8.7, 8.8, and 8.9 in Chapter 8, "A JNLP Quick Launch," for some concrete Java code that does it with JNLP. Another similar case involves needing to know where downloaded executable files are, in order to launch them or to manipulate them in some way. With this technique, native installers and in particular native libraries could be installed via JNLP. If this is your requirement, be sure to make use of Listings 9.3, 9.4, and 9.5 in Chapter 9. Also, Chapter 13, "A Complete Example," has some useful code concerning this aspect.

- Something helpful is to organize your libraries into a set of JAR files with their own installer code arranged like an individual unit, so that different programs could use them by means of a single link without having to always rebundle those six-or-so JAR libraries together with your single JAR of application code. If this is what you are looking for, you should try the JNLP `component-desc` element, described later in this chapter.

NOTE

Generally speaking, before writing all the code to download your resources in a custom installer from scratch, you should try to figure out how the JNLP technology could help you. After all, this is what downloading and automatically caching your resources is all about...hopefully minimizing developers' efforts in the process.

Focusing on the JNLP file, there are six possible subelements for the `<resources>` element: `<jar>` and `<nativelib>`, which describe code resources; `<j2se>`, `<property>`, `<package>`, and

`<extension>`, which point to other external JNLP files. We are going to describe them in the following section.

Defining Resources

The `resources` element (subelement of the root element `jnlp`) informs the JNLP Client about the pieces to be downloaded, installed by the Client, and used by the launching application. For any resources, we can define some properties for which the resources element should be considered.

There are actually three properties that could be specified within a JNLP file for any resource.

- *Operating system.* The OS the resource is designed for. It could be specified by means of the os attribute. For example:

```
<resources os="Windows">
   ...
</resources>
```

Possible values for this attribute are coded with the strings `Windows`, `SunOS`, `Aix`, `MacOS`, and so on. See Appendix B for more details.

- Underlying *hardware architecture.* OSs are platform-specific, (for example, Sun Solaris) and are available both for SPARC and x86 architectures. This is useful in some cases.

- *Locale.* The given resource is locale-specific. As an example:

```
<resources locale="it_IT">
   ...
</resources>
```

The locale identification and matching is the same as for the `information` element. This would spare some download time. Nowadays, applications often come bundled with all the locale-specific data, where only one locale will be used by the client.

As a general rule, multiple values can be specified by separating them with spaces.

CAUTION

Be sure of using the '\' character to avoid accidentally separating the values. For example, to specify three different values for the Windows OS use the following string:

```
"Windows\ 98 Windows\ ME Windows\ 2000"
```

The simple space character works as a separator, while the '\' \ escape sequence is intended as a character part of the value string.

10

DEFINING THE
CLIENT
ENVIRONMENT

To recap, when parsing the XML file, it is as if the JNLP Client would compare those specified values against the current ones. In the case when one of them doesn't match the current values for that computer, the whole `resources` element is ignored.

> **NOTE**
>
> When one of the properties above is not specified, the given resource is meant to be used with all the possible values.

As a practical rule of thumb, it is a good idea to always include some default resource elements and then provide their specializations for locale data, platform-dependent parts, and so on.

Code Resources

There are two types of code resources that can be described in the JNLP protocol: JAR files and native libraries. Although they are both JAR files, one contains only Java code and other application files, whereas the native library JAR files also contain shared libraries such as Windows' `DLL` or UNIX's so files. The latter code resource type has to be treated differently from plain JAR files because it is specific for some platforms only, and needs to be loaded differently into the JVM.

JAR files

The `jar` element is used to add JAR files to the application's classpath, such as in the following line:

```
<jar href="com.mycompany.myjar.jar"/>
```

Although a less-frequent case, it is possible that some JAR files contain platform-specific code. In this situation, the resources attributes (`os` and `arch`) need to be specified for these resources as well.

For a JAR resource, we can specify different properties:

- Physical location on the deployment server. Using the `href` attribute, relative to the `codebase` assigned in the `<information>` element, just like a normal relative Web link.
- The current *version* of the JAR file.
- How the JNLP Client has to *download* the JAR file. Using the download attribute with two possible values: `lazy` (the JAR file is downloaded when needed) and `eager` (together with all other eager resources, at JRE initialization time).

- The *part* the JAR file belongs to. Parts are id strings (whose definition scope is local to the current JNLP file only) that group together resources for download. Whenever a code resource with a specified part attribute is downloaded, all the resources with the same part are downloaded as well.

- Whether it is the *main* JAR file or not. If the main attribute is present with `"true"` as a value, as in the following, the JAR file is the one that contains the class to be launched through its `main(..)` method in order to execute the application:

```
<jar href="" main="true"/>
```

Otherwise, if `"false"` or no main attribute is specified at all, the JAR file isn't the main one.

The only exception to this is when no JAR file is specified as the main one. In this case, the JNLP Client assumes the first one mentioned in the JNLP file as main.

TIP

To avoid confusion and unintended behavior when modifying a JNLP file, it is always a good idea to specify a JAR file as the main one, without relying on the line ordering in the JNLP file.

Lazy resources are loaded when the JVM needs them by means of the custom classloader installed by the JNLP Client.

To recap, Listing 10.2 shows a JNLP file example.

LISTING 10.2   Example of Use of the Information Element

```
<jnlp>
<?xml version="1.0" encoding="UTF-8"?>
<jnlp spec="1.0+"
  codebase="http://server/b2/c10/"
  href="jnlpexample.jnlp">
  <information>
    <title>A JNLP Example File</title>
    <vendor>Mauro's Workshop</vendor>
    <description>Welcome !</description>
    <description kind="tooltip">a brief description</description>
    <homepage href="default.html" />
  </information>
  <information locale="it">
```

LISTING 10.2   Continued

```
    <title>Un Esempio di File JNLP</title>
    <vendor>Il Lab. di Mauro</vendor>
    <description>Benvenuti !</description>
    <homepage href="italian.html" />
  </information>
  <resources os="Windows">
    <j2se version="1.3.0" />
    <jar href="lazyeditor/lazyeditor.jar" download="eager"/>
    <jar href="sec-test.jar" version="1.0"/>
    <jar href="lazyeditor/draw-module.jar" download="lazy"/>
  </resources>
  <resources os="Aix">
    <j2se version="1.4+" />
    <jar href="lazyeditor/lazyeditor.jar" download="eager"/>
  </resources>
  <application-desc/>
</jnlp>
```

> **NOTE**
>
> Lazy download is not mandatory in the JNLP Client specification. That is, JNLP Clients often happily ignore that suggestion and download all resources as eager.

Let's see a simple example of lazy resources management with JNLP technology. The launch JNLP file is shown in Listing 10.3.

LISTING 10.3   The lazyeditor.jnlp File

```
<?xml version="1.0" encoding="UTF-8"?>
<jnlp spec="1.0+"
  codebase="http://server/b2/c10/lazyeditor/"
  href="lazyeditor.jnlp">
  <information>
    <title>A Lazy Editor</title>
    <vendor>Mauro's Workshop</vendor>
    <offline/>
  </information>
  <resources>
    <j2se version="1.2+" />
    <jar href="lazyeditor.jar" />
    <jar href="draw-module.jar" download="lazy"/>
```

LISTING 10.3   Continued

```
  </resources>
  <application-desc/>
</jnlp>
```

In Listing 10.4, a very simple word processor is proposed. Among its commands, the draw option launches a pop-up dialog box, intended as a plug-in of the main program, for editing draws. This is a typical scenario for sophisticated applications deployed over the Web, where secondary functionalities are downloaded only when needed. This way, if the user never utilizes that function, there will be a resource saving, especially during the first-time installation process.

To obtain this behavior with JNLP technology, just define as lazy the resources that are part of the secondary programs and be sure to mention those classes only when needed in your main program.

The LazyEditor Java class representing the main application is shown in Listing 10.4.

LISTING 10.4   The LazyEditor Class.

```
package com.marinilli.b2.c10;
import javax.swing.*;
import java.awt.*;
import javax.jnlp.*;
import java.awt.event.*;
/**
 * Chapter 10 - A Simple Lazy Text Editor
 * @author Mauro Marinilli
 * @version 1.0
 */
public class LazyEditor extends JFrame {
  ClassLoader loader;
  JButton drawButton = new JButton();
  JButton otherButton = new JButton();
  JButton anotherButton = new JButton();
  public LazyEditor() {
    loader = getClass().getClassLoader();
    getContentPane().setLayout(new BorderLayout());
    getContentPane().add(getToolBar(), BorderLayout.NORTH);
    getContentPane().add(new TextArea(), BorderLayout.CENTER);
    setTitle("A Lazy Text Editor");
    addWindowListener(new java.awt.event.WindowAdapter() {
      public void windowClosing(WindowEvent e) {
        exit();
```

Listing 10.4 Continued

```
        }
    });
    setSize(400,300);
    setVisible(true);
}

private void showDrawEditor() {
    DrawEditor de = new DrawEditor(this);
}

private JToolBar getToolBar() {
    JToolBar jt = new JToolBar();
    drawButton.addActionListener(new java.awt.event.ActionListener() {
        public void actionPerformed(ActionEvent e) {
            showDrawEditor();
        }
    });
    drawButton.setText("draw");
    otherButton.setText("other");
    anotherButton.setText("open");
    this.addWindowListener(new java.awt.event.WindowAdapter() {
        public void windowClosing(WindowEvent e) {
            System.exit(0);
        }
    });
    jt.add(anotherButton);
    jt.add(otherButton);
    jt.add(drawButton);
    return jt;
}
private void exit() {
    System.exit(0);
}
public static void main(String[] a) {
    LazyEditor led = new LazyEditor();
}
}
```

Note in Listing 10.4 that when the "draw" button is activated, the DrawEditor class is created for managing the drawing plug-in.

The DrawEditor class is illustrated in Listing 10.5.

LISTING 10.5 The DrawEditor Class

```java
package com.marinilli.b2.c10;
import javax.swing.*;
import java.awt.*;
import java.awt.event.*;
/**
 * Chapter 10 - Drawing extension
 * @author Mauro Marinilli
 * @version 1.0
 */
public class DrawEditor extends JDialog {
  JPanel jPanel1 = new JPanel();
  JButton closeButton = new JButton();

  public DrawEditor(JFrame jf) {
    super(jf);
    setTitle("Drawing Editor Plug-in");
    closeButton.setText("close");
    closeButton.addActionListener(new java.awt.event.ActionListener() {
      public void actionPerformed(ActionEvent e) {
        dispose();
      }
    });
    this.getContentPane().setBackground(Color.white);
    this.getContentPane().add(jPanel1, BorderLayout.SOUTH);
    jPanel1.add(closeButton, null);
    setSize(200,220);
    setVisible(true);
  }
}
```

All the noteworthy work is done by the JNLP file (at line 13 of Listing 10.3), where the draw-module JAR file is declared lazy. To try out the application, launch the JNLP file and then open up the JNLP Client cache for inspecting where cached JAR files regarding the LazyEditor application are created. Once you have found them, just push the "draw" button, and magically the draw-module.jar file will appear in the cache. Be sure to clear up the cache before you perform this experiment.

In Figures 10.1 and 10.2, you can see what appears before and after the activation of the "draw" button.

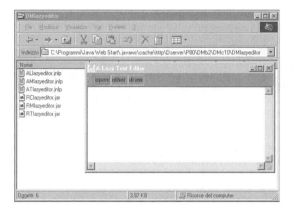

FIGURE 10.1

Before the invocation of the DrawEditor class, there is only the main application JAR in the cache.

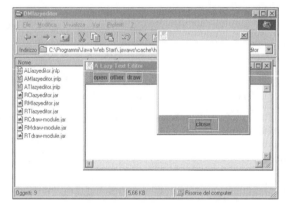

FIGURE 10.2

After having invoked the missing class, the JNLP Client downloads it on-the-fly.

NOTE

This behavior is possible thanks to the expandable lazy Classloader mechanism introduced in the Java 2 platform.

Let's repeat: lazy resources support is not mandatory according to the JNLP specifications. Hence, not all the JNLP Clients will behave the expected way. If JNLP Clients don't support lazy resources, they will download all of them eagerly (but in no cases will they throw java.lang.NoClassDefFoundErrors when programs are trying to invoke still unloaded classes on an online connection). Java Web Start supports lazy download, and this example will run correctly.

> **NOTE**
>
> With IDE JAR packagers (those development tools that analyze dependencies and include mechanically all the needed items in a JAR file), this little experiment may not work because the tool automatically puts the lazy resources into the main JAR file, eliminating all our testing efforts. A way to work around this, if it happens to be a problem, is to invoke classes by means of Class.forName(); that is, the dynamic loading of Java classes to fool dependency compilers. Anyway, it should be avoided if not really needed because it could produce more troubles than those it solves. This trouble could appear both at compile time, when the benefits of static type-checking are reduced, and during execution, when extensive (and unnecessary) dynamic class loading degrades performances.

Finally, what happens when the application is run offline? The even more powerful JNLP Client will throw a java.lang.NoClassDefFoundError. Every technology has its own limits.

Specifying Packages

When we declare the download type of a given resource as *lazy*, we don't tell the JNLP Client in which JAR file to look for given classes when they are needed. This could be very handy and can be obtained using the package element, which instructs the JNLP Client which classes are in which JAR files.

The package element has three attributes:

- name. The Java fully qualified name of a single class or a package. It specifies what is inside the JAR files that makes up that given part. For example, the following line tells the JNLP Client that the package "com.myCompany.jnlp.*" is in one of the JAR files of the "part1" part:

  ```
  <package name="com.myCompany.jnlp.*" part="part1">
  ```

  Whenever the JNLP Client needs a class from that package, it knows which JAR files to download.

- part. The part that contains the given class or packages specified in the name attribute.

- recursive. It can have only Boolean values. When set to true, this value tells the JNLP Client that subpackages also have to be considered.

Native Libraries

When instructing JNLP Clients to use native libraries, it is important to specify which platform they are intended to be used on. The three attributes of the <resource> element are suited for this. A typical native library JNLP definition looks like the following:

```
<resources os="Windows" arch="x86">
  <nativelib href="libraries/winlib.jar" />
</resources>
```

When this level of definition is not enough (for example, when more detailed information is needed on already installed native libraries) developers need to explicitly write the code to perform the installation.

> **TIP**
>
> To invoke the installation of native libraries from Java code, use the `System.loadLibrary(..)` method (which is not available for unsigned applications). See the "Security" section later in this chapter.

There is a little problem when trying to lazily download a native library. Using the `download` attribute won't work because according to the JVM specification, the classloader is not invoked when a native library is missing and needs to be retrieved. The only way to accomplish the lazy download behavior is to synchronize the download using the `part` attribute:

```
<resources>
  <jar href="a.jar" part="part1" kind="lazy"/>
</resources>
<resources os="AIX">
  <nativelib href="libraries/aixlib.jar" part="part1" kind="lazy"/>
</resources>
```

In this way, the loading of the `a.jar` resource will trigger the download and installation of the `aixlib.jar` native library, whenever the first happens.

System Properties

Adding the following line into a `resources` element causes the JRE to set the property to that given value. Just as in the command-line "D"-definitions, the JNLP XML code looks like the following:

```
<property name="???" value="???"/>
```

See the section about security for the properties accessible to the various level of security.

JRE

It is also possible to define the JRE intended for that application elements within a resources element.

The `jnlp` element might have three different attributes:

- `version`. Describes the J2SE JRE versions suited for the application to be launched.
- `initial-heap-size`. Instructs the JNLP Client on the initial JVM heap size.
- `max-heap-size`. Indicates the maximum JVM heap size.

Another feature regarding the `jnlp` element is that it can contain nested `resources` elements. However, the nesting is considered by JNLP Clients only at its first iteration. Further nested `resources` elements are ignored. This behavior is shown in Listing 10.6.

LISTING 10.6   Example of Nested Resources in a j2se Element

```
<?xml version="1.0" encoding="UTF-8"?>
<jnlp spec="1.0+"
  codebase="http://server/b2/c10/"
  href="nestedres.jnlp">
  <information>
    <title>Example Of Nested Resources JNLP File</title>
    <vendor>Mauro's Workshop</vendor>
  </information>
  <resources>
    <j2se version="1.3 1.2.1 1.4*" />
    <resources>
      <jar href="lazyeditor/draw-module.jar" download="eager"/>
    </resources>
    <jar href="lazyeditor/lazyeditor.jar" />
    <jar href="sec-test.jar" download="lazy"/>
  </resources>
  <application-desc/>
</jnlp>
```

JRE String Identification

Often, programmers need to specify which JRE their application is intended to run, both in the Java platform version and also for their own resources.

There are two ways of specifying JREs with JNLP. The first is to identify a given platform version, like this:

```
<j2se version="1.4"/>
```

10

A platform version is a version of the J2SE platform. Platform versions are "1.2.2", "1.3", "1.4", and so on (both "x.y" and "x.y.z"). If you want to obtain the exact platform version string you are using for your code, just extract it from the system property "java.specification.version".

The other way of specifying a JRE is to specify exactly where it is located by providing a URL to the vendor's site. This kind of version is called a *product version* because it is the version of a particular implementation of a J2SE platform version.

The system property to query for the current product version is "java.version". When using this kind of JRE specification, the line in the JNLP file should look like this:

```
<j2se href="http://vendor.com/jres/j2se" version="1.2"/>
```

Some constraints on the JRE product versions can be specified by means of the + sign. (For example, "1.3.2+" means greater than or equal to the "1.3.2" product version.) You can also use the asterisk (*). (For example, "1.4.*" means any J2SE JRE having 1.4 as a product version.)

CAUTION

It is always a bit dangerous to specify exactly one version only because if that version is superseded or the vendor retires it, your applications run the risk of being unable to execute anymore.

Security

When designing your application, you have to decide whether it runs in an unrestricted environment or not. The security mechanism adopted in JNLP resembles the applet's. If your code is not signed, your program will run in a restricted environment (also known as a sandbox); otherwise, it will have access at all the resources. A third modality can be set using the security element switched to the so-called *J2EE application client environment* security value.

We will examine the differences of these modalities, but before we get into details, let's have a look at the most commonly used permissions. In Table 10.1, Yes means that the action is always allowed, whereas No means that is never allowed. Ask User means that the JNLP Client presents an authorization window to the user before allowing the action.

TABLE 10.1 Main Permissions At a Glance

Action	Untrusted	All-Permissions	J2EE Application Client
Access Local File System	Ask User	Yes	Yes
Download resources in Codebase	Yes	Yes	Yes
Download application JARs from other Web servers	No	Yes	Yes
Download JREs and extensions from any Web server	Yes	Yes	Yes
Exiting the JVM and thread management	Yes	Yes	Yes
nativelib allowed	No	Yes	Yes
Access system Clipboard	Ask User	Yes	Yes

Authenticated Applications

Also known as *signed applications*, *authenticated applications* verify the following properties.

- All JAR files (for `jar` and `nativelib` elements) must be signed. A JAR file is considered signed when all its entries are signed with the same certificate (except of course of standard files in the META-INF directory).

- To simplify user interaction, only one certificate is used to sign all JAR files mentioned in a single JNLP file. This means that users are asked for authorization only once.

- If the certificate used to sign JAR files is signed itself, it must be verified against a set of root certificates, from the major certificate authorities. This set of root certificates usually comes bundled with the JNLP Client.

Furthermore, JNLP files can be optionally signed; that is, when a copy of the main JNLP file is included in the main (signed) JAR file with the name "JNLP-INF/APPLICATION.JNLP", and the two copies match byte-wise. Then, the JNLP file is considered to be signed. Note that this feature is only optional, and signing applications as defined above will suffice.

In order to be run in a trusted environment (J2EE Application Client or All-Permission), the application must be signed as defined above. It must also be explicitly authorized by the user by means of an authorization window shown just before allowing the potentially dangerous action.

10

DEFINING THE CLIENT ENVIRONMENT

> **TIP**
>
> If an application uses JAR files signed with different certificates, a solution is to separate them in one JNLP application-descriptor file, and the rest of JAR files are in another JNLP component-descriptor file, so that each JNLP file contains all the JAR files signed with the same certificate.

Untrusted Environment

When our application is not signed, and the JNLP file doesn't specify a `security` element, the application is run in an untrusted environment, also known as the JNLP Client sandbox.

In such an environment, the following actions are allowed only after explicit user authorization:

- Attempt to access the local file system using the standard JNLP services, both in read and write.
- Use of the JNLP Clipboard service for both reading and writing.
- Attempt to send a job to the printer using that JNLP service.

Using the `nativelib` element, installing a `SecurityManager`, accessing other remote servers different from the one from where the application was downloaded, or silently accessing the file system or the system Clipboard is always denied.

Therefore, accessing the system Clipboard, printer, or local file system for untrusted applications is possible only via JNLP runtime services that will cause the JNLP Client to ask for permission from the user.

> **NOTE**
>
> The JNLP Client sandbox is slightly more relaxed than the applet sandbox, in that it allows the calling of `System.exit()` and the access to `ThreadGroup` objects because any JNLP-launched application runs in its own exclusive JVM.

A complete list of all the (unconditionally) allowed permissions follows.

Security Permission	Description
`java.lang.RuntimePermission`	Exit the JVM
`java.net.SocketPermission`	Connect, accept from the download host

Security Permission	Description
java.net.SocketPermission	Listen to localhost:1024
java.util.PropertyPermission	(Only) read property: java.version
java.util.PropertyPermission	Read java.vendor
java.util.PropertyPermission	Read java.vendor.url
java.util.PropertyPermission	Read java.class.version
java.util.PropertyPermission	Read os.version
java.util.PropertyPermission	Read os.name
java.util.PropertyPermission	Read os.arch
java.util.PropertyPermission	Read path.separator
java.util.PropertyPermission	Read file.separator
java.util.PropertyPermission	Read line.separator
java.util.PropertyPermission	Read java.specification.vendor
java.util.PropertyPermission	Read java.specification.name
java.util.PropertyPermission	Read java.specification.version
java.util.PropertyPermission	Read java.vm.specification.name
java.util.PropertyPermission	Read java.vm.specification.vendor
java.util.PropertyPermission	Read java.vm.version
java.util.PropertyPermission	Read java.vm.vendor
java.util.PropertyPermission	Read java.vm.name
java.awt.AWTPermission	showWindowWithoutWarningBanner
java.lang.RuntimePermission	Stop a thread

Properties not listed here are not allowed for this security level.

All-Permissions Trusted Environment

Because there are no limitations to the All-Permissions trusted environment, the JNLP Client will prompt the user with a warning dialog box at application startup, like the one shown in Figure 9.4. JNLP Clients always warn users when a signed application requests unrestricted access to the local environment.

J2EE Application Client Trusted Environment

The J2EE Application Client Trusted Environment is in-between the first two security modalities. The allowed permissions are listed in the following table.

Security Permission	Description
`java.awt.AWTPermission`	Access `Clipboard`
`java.awt.AWTPermission`	Access `EventQueue`
`java.awt.AWTPermission`	Show `WindowWithoutWarningBanner`
`java.lang.RuntimePermission`	Access `System.exit`
`java.lang.RuntimePermission`	Access `loadLibrary`
`java.lang.RuntimePermission`	Access `queuePrintJob`
`java.net.SocketPermission`	Connect
`java.net.SocketPermission`	Listen, accept from `localhost:1024`

For more information on this level of security, consult the J2EE specification documentation.

A Class Testing JNLP Security

The `SecurityTester` class allows the user to launch any of the runtime services with different security levels. It is also a first example of how to use JNLP runtime services. We will see them in detail in Chapter 11, "Runtime Client Services."

In Listing 10.7, you see the JNLP file for the `all-permissions` modality.

LISTING 10.7   JNLP File for Launching the Security Testing Application With All-Permissions

```
<?xml version="1.0" encoding="utf-8"?>
<jnlp spec="1.0+"
      codebase="http://server/b2/c10/">
  <information>
    <title>A Security Test</title>
    <vendor>Mauro Inc.</vendor>
    <description>A Security Test</description>
    <offline-allowed/>
  </information>
  <security><all-permissions/></security>
  <resources>
    <j2se version="1.3+"/>
    <jar href="sec-test.jar"/>
  </resources>
  <application-desc main-class="com.marinilli.b2.c10.SecurityTester"/>
</jnlp>
```

Changing the kind of permissions while still launching the same application will show the differences in the three security modalities.

A screenshot of the little testing program at work is given in Figure 10.3.

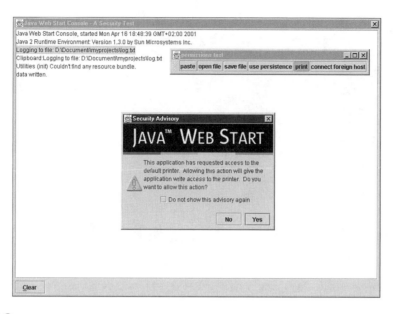

FIGURE 10.3

In a restricted environment, when trying to use services such as printing, the JNLP Client asks for authorization from the user.

COMPANION **Web site** In Listing 10.8, the class `SecurityTester` is shown, minus its lengthy graphic constructor. For the full listing, please see the companion Web site. We will see how runtime services can be used in Chapter 11.

LISTING 10.8   The `SecurityTester` Java Class

```
package com.marinilli.b2.c10;
import com.marinilli.b2.c11.util.*;
import javax.swing.*;
import java.awt.event.*;
import javax.jnlp.*;
import java.net.*;
import java.io.*;
import java.util.Iterator;
import java.awt.*;
import java.awt.print.*;
/**
 * Chapter 10 - JNLP Security - Try it Out Yourself
 * @author Mauro Marinilli
 * @version 1.0
 */
```

LISTING 10.8 Continued

```java
public class SecurityTester extends JFrame{
  public SecurityTester() {
    //boring GUI init
  }
  private void usePersistence(){
    PersistentStorage pst = new PersistentStorage();
    pst.write("key","value");
    System.out.println("data written.");
  }
  private String getClipboardContent() {
    String s = "";
    ClipboardService cbs =
      (ClipboardService)Utilities.getService("javax.jnlp.ClipboardService");
    try {
      if (cbs.getContents()!=null)

s=(String)cbs.getContents().getTransferData(java.awt.datatransfer.DataFlavor.st
ringFlavor);
    } catch (Exception e) {
      e.printStackTrace();
    }
    return s;
  }
  public void openFile() {
    FileContents file = null;
    FileOpenService fs =
      (FileOpenService)Utilities.getService("javax.jnlp.FileOpenService");
    if (fs!=null) {
      try {
        file = fs.openFileDialog(null,null);
      } catch (Exception e) {
        System.out.println("openFile: "+e);
      }
    }
  }
  public void saveFile() {
    FileContents file = null;
    FileOpenService fo =
      (FileOpenService)Utilities.getService("javax.jnlp.FileOpenService");
    FileSaveService fs =
      (FileSaveService)Utilities.getService("javax.jnlp.FileSaveService");
    if (fs!=null) {
      try {
        file = fo.openFileDialog(null, null);
```

LISTING 10.8 Continued

```
        FileContents savedFile = fs.saveAsFileDialog(null, null, file);
      } catch (Exception e) {
        System.out.println("openFile: "+e);
      }
    }
  }
  public void connectForeignHost(String url) {
    try {
      FileOutputStream fos = new FileOutputStream("aFile.html");
      URL anURL = new URL(url);
      URLConnection anURLConn = anURL.openConnection();
      InputStream is = anURLConn.getInputStream();
      int q;
      while ((q = is.read()) != -1)
        fos.write(q);
      is.close();
      fos.close();
    } catch (Exception e) {
      System.out.println("connectForeignHost "+e);
    }
  }
  public class PrintableExample implements Printable {
    public int print(Graphics graphics, PageFormat pageFormat, int pageIndex){
      Graphics2D g2d = (Graphics2D)graphics;
      g2d.setPaint(Color.blue);
      g2d.drawString("Print Test",200,200);
      return PAGE_EXISTS;
    }
  }
  public static void main(String[] args) {
    SecurityTester securityTester1 = new SecurityTester();
  }
}
```

It is important to reiterate that without using the JNLP runtime services, it would be impossible to access local resources such as the printer, the system Clipboard, or local files for an untrusted application.

It is interesting to try connecting to hosts different from the one the application was downloaded from. The method connectForeignHost (lines 64–78 of Listing 10.8) tries just that, writing the output on a local file. For untrusted applications, the operation is immediately blocked by the throwing of an exception.

We will discuss code like this extensively in the Chapter 11.

CAUTION

The classes `PersistentStorage` and `Utilities` are not part of the JNLP API, but they are utility classes developed for this book, freely available to readers. These classes and other utility code relating to the client side of the JNLP technology will be discussed in the next chapter.

Signing JAR Files with the `Jarsigner` Tool

Most JNLP Clients, including Web Start, use the security API in the Java 2 platform. The Java 2 SE JRE 1.2.x supports code signing with the SHA-with-SDA algorithm. J2SE JRE 1.3 also supports MD2withRSA and MD5withRSA.

The steps to sign your JAR files with auto-certificates (useful only for development purposes) are as follows:

1. Prepare the directory in which you want to store your keys, and remember to have the Java signing tools in the path, located in the bin directory of any J2SE JDK distribution.

2. Create a test key store; that is, "`testks`".

   ```
   keytool -genkey -keystore testks -alias myself
   ```

   The keytool utility will start asking information about yourself to be used in the certificate. It will take awhile. When the program asks for the user password, you should type only the "return" key so to use the same password as the one entered for key store.

3. Then, to create a test certificate, type the following:

   ```
   keytool -selfcert -keystore testks -alias myself
   ```

4. After awhile, the key store will be ready. To use it for testing your JAR files, launch the following command with `myResource.jar` as the JAR file name:

   ```
   jarsigner -keystore testks myResource.jar myself
   ```

   This will sign the JAR file that will be considered signed by the JNLP Client.

If you have your own certificate anyway, just follow the last step to digitally sign your JAR files. The result of the digital signing will be two files stored in the META-INF directory of the signed JAR file.

TIP

You can move or copy the obtained `testks` file (the key store) for signing your JAR files.

For more details on code signing and certificates in general, you can visit certification authorities Web sites for companies such as Cybertrust, VeriSign, Thawte, or others. Other useful tools for signing and certificate operations are provided by Netscape, so visit their site at `http://developer.netscape.com/software/`.

Finally, for details on the Sun's `jarsigner` tool, you can browse the documentation at

`http://java.sun.com/j2se/1.3/docs/tooldocs/win32/jarsigner.html`

> **Caution**
>
> Auto-signed certificates are useful only for testing. They are not usable in commercial applications, both because of their expiration time and because they are not released by a certification authority.

Summary

In this chapter we discussed how developers can describe the client environment using the JNLP deployment technology. We saw here three elements (with all their sub elements):

- `information`
- `resources`
- `security`

The next chapter will discuss another important set of features provided by JNLP Clients to launched applications. This is the ability to invoke special runtime services not available for usual, stand-alone applications.

10

DEFINING THE
CLIENT
ENVIRONMENT

Runtime Client Services

IN THIS CHAPTER

In this chapter, we will examine the runtime services offered by a JNLP Client to its launched applications.

Introduction

To compile the code in this chapter, you need to add the `javax.jnlp` library (released from Sun) in your classpath. It is freely available through the Java Developer Connection or more quickly from the Java Web Start product page at `http://www.javasoft.com/products/javaWebstart`.

The services offered by the JNLP Client to launched applications are always invoked by obtaining a service object from the `javax.jnlp.ServiceManager` class (as shown in the following code):

```
service =
(ExtensionInstallerService)ServiceManager.lookup("javax.jnlp.ExtensionInstaller
Service");
```

Once obtained, the particular service object clients can use it as needed. We won't discuss the API details here (have a look at Appendix B, "The JNLP Specification," or at the `jnlp` package documentation); instead, we will give practical code that is useful in real-world situations.

Figure 11.1 depicts a UML class diagram showing the `javax.jnlp` package classes.

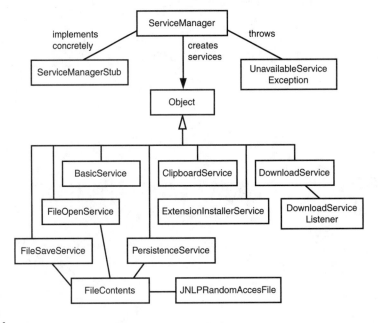

FIGURE 11.1

The class diagram for the JNLP classes.

The `ServiceManager` class

The ServiceManager class provides the means for obtaining services from the JNLP Client through the use of the lookup() method. This method is called by passing it a string with the fully qualified class name. To discover all the available services, use the method getServiceNames. The method setServiceManagerStub is used only by the JNLP Client to install its implementation of the services factory.

> **NOTE**
>
> The superclass of all the service classes is Object (see Figure 11.1).

The `BasicService` class

To begin with, we will study the BasicService class, the most general-purpose service of all the JNLP services. It provides four methods:

- getCodebase(). Returns the codebase URL as specified in the main JNLP file.
- isOffline(). Useful for applications or installers that need to determine whether the client computer is currently connected.
- showDocument(). Launches the installed Web browser to the specified URL. Used, for example, in the JNLPLabel class in this chapter.
- isWebBrowserSupported(). Useful to know whether a Web browser is currently installed on the given OS.

A Utility class

We already saw the Utilities class in the previous chapter. This class helped us keep the code short and meaningful. It is a singleton (see note below), with two instantiation methods, namely getInstance() and getInstance(String). The latter initializes the class with a specified resource bundle for dealing with multilingual applications (but it is always a good idea to use it). These initialization methods are not required. If we call a static method without prior initialization:

```
Utilities.getService("javax.jnlp.ClipboardService");
```

The Utilities class is able to initialize itself transparently.

Listing 11.1 illustrates the various aspects of the javax.jnlp API as it pertains to the client side.

LISTING 11.1   The Utilities Class

```
package com.marinilli.b2.c11.util;
import javax.swing.ImageIcon;
import java.awt.image.BufferedImage;
import java.net.URL;
import javax.jnlp.UnavailableServiceException;
import javax.jnlp.ServiceManager;
import javax.jnlp.BasicService;
import java.util.ResourceBundle;
/**
 * Chapter 11 - Utilities
 * @author Mauro Marinilli
 * @version 1.0
 */
public class Utilities {
  private static Utilities util;
  private static ClassLoader loader;
  private static BasicService basicService;
  private static ImageIcon EMPTY_ICON =
    new ImageIcon(new BufferedImage(24,24,BufferedImage.TYPE_INT_RGB));
  private ResourceBundle msg;
  private static String bundleFilename = "messages";
  private Utilities() {
    loader = getClass().getClassLoader();
    basicService =
      (BasicService)getService("javax.jnlp.BasicService");
    initializeDefaultResources();
    try {
      msg = ResourceBundle.getBundle(bundleFilename);
    } catch (java.util.MissingResourceException mre) {
      msg = null;
      System.out.println("Utilities (init)
➥ Couldn't find any resource bundle.");
```

LISTING 11.1 Continued

```
    }
  }
  private void initializeDefaultResources() {
    //initializes the empty icon
    java.awt.Graphics g = EMPTY_ICON.getImage().getGraphics();
    g.drawLine(8,8,16,16);
    g.drawLine(8,16,16,8);
  }
  public static ClassLoader getClassLoader(){
    if (util==null)
      getInstance();
    return loader;
  }
  public static ImageIcon getImageIcon(String name){
    if (util==null)
      getInstance();
    URL res = loader.getResource(name);
    if (res!=null)
      return new ImageIcon(res);
    return EMPTY_ICON;
  }
  public static Object getService(String fullyQName){
    Object service = null;
    try {
      service = ServiceManager.lookup(fullyQName);
    } catch (UnavailableServiceException use) {
      System.out.println(util.getClass()+"getService("+ fullyQName +") "+use);
    }
    return service;
  }
  public static BasicService getBasicService(){
    if (util==null)
      getInstance();
    return basicService;
  }
  public static String getMsg(String key){
    if (util==null)
      getInstance();
    if (util.msg!=null) {
      String m = util.msg.getString(key);
      if (m!=null)
        return m;
    }
    return "";
```

LISTING 11.1   Continued

```
  }
  public static Utilities getInstance(){
    if (util==null)
      util = new Utilities();
    return util;
  }
  public static Utilities getInstance(String resourceBundleName){
    bundleFilename = resourceBundleName;
    if (util==null)
      getInstance();
    else
      System.out.println(
          util.getClass()+" getInstance must be invoked as initializator.");
    return util;
  }
}
```

This class provides several services added on top of the JNLP API:

- Robust resources retrieval. For icons and resource bundles, if the given item is not found, a default value is always returned. For messages, an empty string is returned in case of a missing value.

- For icons, a default icon is always provided by creating it in code, so that NullPointerException messages for inexistent icons are never thrown. See lines 18–19 and the initializeDefaultResources method at lines 34–38.

- It saves programmers from lengthy try-catch constructs in standard services creation code. Note also that an instance of the BasicService class is always created because it is usually the most often used service.

The Utilities class has been kept simple to serve a didactic purpose as well. You can always expand it as needed.

A Hypertext Swing Label Class

To see a simple and interesting example of how it is possible to take advantage of the JNLP Client API and the Utilities class, let's use a very simple Jlabel component that can be clicked just like a hyperlink in a Web page. When this action is completed, a Web browser will open, pointing to the given URL. Listing 11.2 shows the code.

LISTING 11.2   The JNLPLabel Class

```java
package com.marinilli.b2.c11.util;
import javax.swing.JLabel;
import java.awt.event.*;
import java.util.*;
import java.awt.Cursor;
import java.net.URL;
import javax.swing.event.*;
/**
 * Chapter 11 - A Label that launches a browser
 * @author Mauro Marinilli
 * @version 1.0
 */
public class JNLPLabel extends JLabel implements MouseListener {
  private String text = "";
  private URL url= null;
  private static final String COLOR_BEFORE_CLICKING = "blue";
  private static final String COLOR_AFTER_CLICKING  = "purple";
  private boolean alreadyClicked = false;
  private transient Vector hListeners;

  public JNLPLabel() {
    addMouseListener(this);
  }
  public void mouseClicked(MouseEvent e) {
    alreadyClicked=true;
    java.awt.Toolkit.getDefaultToolkit().beep();
    fireHyperlinkUpdate(new HyperlinkEvent
➡ (this, HyperlinkEvent.EventType.ACTIVATED,url));
    Utilities.getBasicService().showDocument(url);
  }
  public void mousePressed(MouseEvent e) {
  }
  public void mouseReleased(MouseEvent e) {
  }
  public void mouseDragged(MouseEvent e) {
  }
  public void mouseMoved(MouseEvent e) {
  }
  public void mouseEntered(MouseEvent e) {
    if (!alreadyClicked)
      super.setText("<html><font color="+COLOR_BEFORE_CLICKING+" >
➡<u>"+text+"</u></font>");
    else
      super.setText("<html><font color="+COLOR_AFTER_CLICKING+" >
➡<u>"+text+"</u></font>");
```

LISTING 11.2   Continued

```
      setCursor(Cursor.getPredefinedCursor(Cursor.HAND_CURSOR));
  }
  public void mouseExited(MouseEvent e) {
    setText("<html><body>"+text+"");
  }
  public void setText(String txt) {
    text=txt;
      super.setText("<html><font color="+COLOR_BEFORE_CLICKING+" >
➡<u>"+text+"</u></font>");
  }
  public void setURL(URL u) {
    url=u;
    setToolTipText("view in browser "+url);
  }
  public void setURL(String u) {
    try {
      setURL(new URL(u));
    } catch (Exception exc) {
      System.out.println(getClass()+"setURL: "+ exc);
    }
  }
  public synchronized void removeHyperlinkListener(HyperlinkListener l) {
    if (hListeners != null && hListeners.contains(l)) {
      Vector v = (Vector) hListeners.clone();
      v.removeElement(l);
      hListeners = v;
    }
  }
  public synchronized void addHyperlinkListener(HyperlinkListener l) {
    Vector v;
    if (hListeners == null)
      v = new Vector(2);
    else v = (Vector) hListeners.clone();
    if (!v.contains(l)) {
      v.addElement(l);
      hListeners = v;
    }
  }
  protected void fireHyperlinkUpdate(HyperlinkEvent e) {
    if (hListeners != null) {
      Vector listeners = hListeners;
      int count = listeners.size();
      for (int i = 0; i < count; i++) {
        ((HyperlinkListener) listeners.elementAt(i)).hyperlinkUpdate;
```

LISTING 11.2   Continued

```
        }
      }
    }
}
```

Note that the Hyperlink events code (methods `removeHyperlinkListener`, `addHyperlinkListener`, `fireHyperlinkUpdate`) is useful for listening to launch events from other classes. It could be safely dropped if we use our label only for launching a Web browser.

The most interesting line is probably line 28, in which the browser is pointed to the given URL using the `BasicService` JNLP class. This can be as simple as the following line of code:

```
Utilities.getBasicService().showDocument(url);
```

In order to use it in your code, just set the text to be displayed, like a normal `JLabel`, plus the URL to point to.

This little component could be very handy when used to create professional looking About dialogs, for instance.

File Management

Handling files with the JNLP API requires the use of the following classes:

- `FileContents`. This class represents a file, both for reading and for writing, using the usual input and output streams. It is metered; that is, only a given amount of space (bytes) can be allocated for a file in order to allow JNLP Clients to maintain control on the local resources allocated to launched applications. Note that path information is absent. This means that applications obtaining this object (by means of one of the following three services: `FileOpenService`, `FileSaveService` and `PersistenceService`) can examine only the file contents.

- `FileOpenService`. Applications wanting to access files on the local system should use this service. For untrusted applications, it is the only way to access local files (which is, of course, subject to user authorization). This will pop up a File Open dialog box for choosing a file.

- `FileSaveService`. This class is similar to the FileOpenService, but this time the `JfileChooser` dialog box will save a file (represented as a `FileContents` object).

- `JNLPRandomAccessFile`. The JNLP API implementation of a random access file (a file treated as an array of bytes).

Any attempt to use other means than those four classes to access local files for untrusted applications is not permitted. Listing 11.3 shows an example of these classes used to obtain files and then process them.

LISTING 11.3   The FileContentsExample Class

```java
package com.marinilli.b2.c11;
import com.marinilli.b2.c11.util.*;
import javax.jnlp.*;
import java.io.*;
/**
 * Chapter 11
 * @author Mauro Marinilli
 * @version 1.0
 */
public class FileContentsExample {
  public FileContentsExample() {
    testRead();
    testWrite();
    writeAsRAF();
    System.exit(0);
  }
  private void testRead() {
    FileContents file = null;
    FileOpenService fs =
     (FileOpenService)Utilities.getService("javax.jnlp.FileOpenService");
    if (fs!=null) {
      try {
        file = fs.openFileDialog(null, null);
      } catch (Exception e) {
        System.out.println("openFile: "+e);
      }
    }
    if (file!=null) {
      process(file);
      readLines(file);
    }
    System.out.println("finished.");
  }
  private void testWrite() {
    System.out.println("testWrite()");
    FileContents file = null;
    FileSaveService fs =
     (FileSaveService)Utilities.getService("javax.jnlp.FileSaveService");
    if (fs!=null) {
```

LISTING 11.3   Continued

```
    try {
      file =
       ((FileOpenService)Utilities.getService("javax.jnlp.FileOpenService"))
          .openFileDialog(null, null);
      FileContents outcome = fs.saveAsFileDialog(null,null,file);
      System.out.println("outcome "+outcome);
    } catch (Exception e) {
      System.out.println("openFile: "+e);
    }
  }
  if (file!=null) {
    writeData(file);
  }
}
private void testWrite2() {
  FileContents file = null;
  FileSaveService fs =
   (FileSaveService)Utilities.getService("javax.jnlp.FileSaveService");
  if (fs!=null) {
    try {
      FileContents outcome = fs.saveAsFileDialog(null,null,file);
    } catch (Exception e) {
      System.out.println("openFile: "+e);
    }
  }
  if (file!=null) {
    writeData(file);
  }
}
public void readLines(FileContents file){
  try {
    InputStream input = file.getInputStream();
    BufferedReader reader = new BufferedReader(new InputStreamReader(input));
    String s = "";
    while ((s = reader.readLine()) != null) {
      System.out.println("\""+s+"\"");
    }
  } catch (Exception e) {
    e.printStackTrace();
  }
}
public byte[] readBytes(FileContents file){
  byte [] buffer = null;
  try {
```

LISTING 11.3   Continued

```
      InputStream input = file.getInputStream();
      buffer = new byte[(int)file.getLength()];
      input.read(buffer);
      input.close();
    } catch (Exception e) {
      e.printStackTrace();
    }
    return buffer;
  }
  public void process(FileContents file){
    try {
      InputStream input = file.getInputStream();
      int c;
      while ((c = input.read())!= -1) {
          System.out.write;
      }
      input.close();
    } catch (Exception e) {
      e.printStackTrace();
    }
  }
  public void writeData(FileContents file){
    try {
      if (file.canWrite()) {
        DataOutputStream dos = new DataOutputStream
➥(file.getOutputStream(false));
        dos.writeInt(123);
        dos.writeFloat(123F);
        dos.close();
      }
    } catch (Exception e) {
      e.printStackTrace();
    }
  }
  public void writeAsRAF(){
    FileContents file = null;
    FileOpenService fs =
      (FileOpenService)Utilities.getService("javax.jnlp.FileOpenService");
    if (fs!=null) {
      try {
        file=fs.openFileDialog(null,null);
        if (file.canWrite()) {
          enlargeFile(file, 2028);
          if (file.getMaxLength() > file.getLength() ) {
```

LISTING 11.3 Continued

```
                JNLPRandomAccessFile raf = file.getRandomAccessFile("rw");
                raf.seek(raf.length() - 1);
                raf.writeUTF("Last In file.");
                raf.close();
            }
        }
    } catch (Exception e) {
        e.printStackTrace();
    }
  }
}
private long enlargeFile(FileContents file, int extraLength){
  long length = 0L;
  if (file!=null)
    try {
      length = file.getLength();
      if (length + extraLength > file.getMaxLength()) {
          length = file.setMaxLength(length + 1024);
      }
    } catch (Exception e) {
      e.printStackTrace();
    }
  return length;
}
public static void main(String[] args) {
  FileContentsExample fileContentsExample1 = new FileContentsExample();
}
}
```

Let's discuss some aspects of this code.

- The constructor (lines 12–15) calls some example methods that manipulate files on the local file system. Note that if your application is trusted (as described in Chapter 10, "Defining the Client Environment"), you do not need to pass through the JNLP services to access local files.

- The method `testRead` tries to open up a File dialog box for accessing a file on local disks. The method `process` (lines 93–99) does some simple processing on the opened file, by copying it four bytes at a time onto the standard output. The method `readLines` reads it as a text file, line by line.

- The method `testWrite` at lines 34–53—after having obtained a reference on a local file and having asked to save its own file on the file system—invokes the `writeData` method, beginning at line 105. This method, after checking the permissions on the given file, treats it as a data file, writing some numerical data into it.

- The method writeAsRAF treats the file like a random access file and, after having enlarged it, writes a string at the end of the file. The general-purpose enlargeFile method tries to enlarge specified files whenever allowed by the JNLP Client.

- Finally, the method testWrite2 is similar to testWrite, but asks for a saveAsFileDialog. The method readBytes at line 81 returns the specified file as a big chunk of bytes in memory.

Resource Management

The DownloadService and DownloadServiceListener classes are dedicated to the download and caching of resources, and are often used together with the ExtensionInstallerService.

The DownloadService can return information about cached parts (refer to Chapter 10), parts of extensions, or simple JAR files. This information can be returned only for items belonging to the application currently running. In other words, the information can be returned only for items that are mentioned in the main JNLP file or in referenced JNLP files.

A JAR file, a part, or an extension part could be loaded using the methods loadResource, loadPart, and loadExtensionPart. The DownloadServiceListener is used as an argument in these methods in order to track the download process.

When removing cached items with these methods, resources are rarely deleted immediately. Rather, JNLP Clients would regard them as no longer needed, and that they should be released when required in the future.

As an example of cache control, see Listing 11.4.

LISTING 11.4 An Example Of Cache Control

```
package com.marinilli.b2.c11;
import com.marinilli.b2.c11.util.*;
import javax.jnlp.*;
import java.net.URL;
import java.io.*;
/**
 * Chapter 11 - Example of DownloadService
 * @author Mauro Marinilli
 * @version 1.0
 */
public class DownloadExample {
  public DownloadExample() {
    removeFromJNLPCache("anapp.jar");
  }
  public static void removeFromJNLPCache(String resourceName){
```

LISTING 11.4   Continued

```
      DownloadService ds = null;
      ds = (DownloadService)Utilities.getService("javax.jnlp.DownloadService");
      URL url = null;
      try {
        url = new URL(Utilities.getBasicService().getCodeBase(), resourceName);
      } catch(IOException exc) {
        System.out.println("Creating URL: "+exc);
      }
      try {
        ds.removeResource(url ,null);
        System.out.println("Resource "+url+" removed from JNLP cache.");
      } catch(IOException exc) {
        System.out.println("removing resource from JNLP cache: "+exc);
      }
    }
  }
}
```

Persistence

Persistence services are achieved through the use of a `PersistenceService` class that saves `FileContents` objects given a URL as a key. The local file system works like a cache for this data that is always thought of as being a copy of data stored on the server. The whole concept is inspired by the cookies mechanism; the primary difference being that the space allowed on the disk is bigger and more flexible.

The URL-keys work hierarchically. That is, common directories are shared by applications sharing portions of their codebase.

For example, two applications having codebases can see each other application's data at locations `http://www.asite.org/pub/` and `http://www.asite.org/`:

- `http://www.asite.org/pub/app1/`
- `http://www.asite.org/pub/app2/`

Therefore, common data can be organized following remote paths on a Web server.

Each single entry (a pair of a URL as a key and a `FileContents` as a value) can be tagged regarding its relationship with the server-side data cache. Tags are represented as `int`s that can be accessed via the accessory methods `setTag()` and `getTag()`. We can have three possible states for data stored locally:

Tag Value	Meaning
dirty	Server doesn't have an up-to-date copy of the data
cached	Server has an up-to-date copy
temporary	Data that can always be recreated

These states are read by the JNLP Client when it needs to clear the cache. The deletion order is: `temporary` files first; then `cached` data; and, finally, items tagged as `dirty`.

A Persistence Utility Class

Another utility class provided with this book, the `PersistenceStorage` class, is a wrapper of the `PersistenceService` object, so that you don't have to deal with `FileContents` or all the details typical of the new `jnlp` API. Instead, the interface of this utility class is very simple to use, and there is no additional knowledge of the `PersistenceService` API required in order to use it. Of course, if you need particular operations, you can always extract the wrapped `PersistenceService` object and manage it as required. However, this class will help in the majority of real cases.

It is useful for storing Java objects locally with a given key. It works much like a Hash table, saving objects and retrieving them by means of a key (a string or a full URL). The key string is used to create a URL based on the `codebase` value (see the `getUrl()` method at lines 102–111) in Listing 11.5.

To save a serializable object, just use the following code:

```
persistenceStorage1.write("key", serializableObject);
```

to read the following value:

```
Object serializableObject = persistenceStorage1.read("key");
```

Then, cast the obtained object as needed.

LISTING 11.5 The `PersistenceStorage` Utility Class

```
package com.marinilli.b2.c11.util;
import com.marinilli.b2.c11.util.Utilities;
import javax.jnlp.*;
import java.net.URL;
import java.io.*;
import java.util.*;
/**
 * Chapter 11 - utility wrapper for PersistenceService
 * @author Mauro Marinilli
 * @version 1.0
```

LISTING 11.5   Continued

```
 */
public class PersistentStorage {
  private PersistenceService persistenceService;
  private long DEFAULT_SIZE = 2048L;
  public PersistentStorage() {
    persistenceService =

(PersistenceService)Utilities.getService("javax.jnlp.PersistenceService");
  }
  public PersistentStorage(PersistenceService ps) {
    persistenceService = ps;
  }
  public void write(String keyString, Object value) {
    write(keyString, value, DEFAULT_SIZE);
  }
  public void write(String keyString, Object value, long maxLength) {
    write(getUrl(keyString), value, DEFAULT_SIZE);
  }
  public void write(URL url, Object value, long maxLength) {
    if (exists(url))
      removeEntry(url);
    try {
      persistenceService.create(url, maxLength);
      FileContents fc = persistenceService.get(url);
      ObjectOutputStream oos =
        new ObjectOutputStream(fc.getOutputStream(false));
      oos.writeObject(value);
      oos.close();
    } catch (IOException ioe) {
      System.out.println(getClass()+".write("+url+", "+value+"): "+ioe);
    }
  }
  public Object read(String keyString) {
    return read(getUrl(keyString));
  }
  public Object read(URL url) {
    if (!exists(url))
      return null;
    Object object = null;
    try {
      FileContents fc = persistenceService.get(url);
      ObjectInputStream ois = new ObjectInputStream(fc.getInputStream());
      object = ois.readObject();
    } catch (Exception e) {
```

LISTING 11.5   Continued

```
      System.out.println(getClass()+".read("+url+"): "+e);
    }
    return object;
  }
  public boolean exists(URL url){
    try {
      if (persistenceService.getNames(url).length>0)
        return true;
    } catch (Exception e) {
      System.out.println(getClass()+".exists("+url+"): "+e);
    }
    return false;
  }
  public void synchronize(String keyString) {
    synchronize(getUrl(keyString));
  }
  public void synchronize(URL url) {
    try {
      if (persistenceService.getTag(url)==PersistenceService.DIRTY)
      persistenceService.setTag(url, persistenceService.CACHED);
    } catch (Exception e) {
      System.out.println(getClass()+".synchronize("+url+"): "+e);
    }
  }
  public void removeEntry(URL url) {
    try {
      persistenceService.delete(url);
    } catch (Exception e) {
      System.out.println(getClass()+".remove("+url+"): "+e);
    }
  }
  public List getEntries(String keyString) {
    return getEntries(getUrl(keyString));
  }
  public List getEntries(URL url) {
    List list =null;
    try {
      list=
        Collections.unmodifiableList(
          Arrays.asList(persistenceService.getNames(url)));
    } catch (Exception e) {
      System.out.println(getClass()+".getEntries("+url+"): "+e);
    }
    return list;
```

LISTING 11.5 Continued

```
  }
  public PersistenceService getPersistenceService() {
    return persistenceService;
  }
  public URL getUrl(String keyString) {
    URL codebase = Utilities.getBasicService().getCodeBase();
    URL  url = null;
    try {
      url = new URL(codebase,keyString);
    } catch (IOException ioe) {
      System.out.println(getClass()+".getUrl("+keyString+"): "+ioe);
    }
    return url;
  }
}
```

This class provides the following wrapper methods:

- `public void write(String keyString, Object value)`. It persistently saves the given object at the given key location.

- `public void write(String keyString, Object value, long maxLength)`. The same as the previous method, but it also specifies the maximum space allocable to the object serialized on disk.

- `public void write(URL url, Object value, long maxLength)`. The same as the preceding method, but a URL is supplied to identify the resource. Note that if the URL is not based on the `codebase` value (that is, it is not rooted on the Web server that deployed the application), the service won't work.

- `public Object read(String keyString)` and `public Object read(URL url)`. Will return an object given a key, expressed as a string or a complete URL.

- `public boolean exists(URL url)`. Returns `true` if there are some data cached with that URL as a key.

- `public void synchronize(String keyString)` and `public void synchronize(URL url)`. Synchronize the data, tagging it as explained before.

- `public void removeEntry(URL url)`. Remove the given entry from the local cache.

- `public List getEntries(String keyString)`. Returns a List collection for all the entries stored at the given URL.

- public PersistenceService getPersistenceService(). Obtains the wrapped persistence service.

- public URL getUrl(String keyString). It is the method used by the PersistenceStorage class to translate the key strings in URLs.

Controlling Installations

The API for controlling the installation of resources (and applications) comprises the DownloadService, DownloadServiceListener, and ExtensionInstallerService. We have already seen many examples of these classes at work. In Chapter 13, "A Complete Example," there are also some examples of these classes in use.

In Listing 11.6, we present an interesting example of an installer that puts downloaded JAR files into a specified directory—here the lib/ext/ directory of the currently installed JRE.

LISTING 11.6 An Optional Packages Installer Example

```
package com.marinilli.b2.c11;
import com.marinilli.b2.c11.util.Utilities;
import javax.swing.*;
import java.awt.print.*;
import javax.jnlp.*;
import java.awt.*;
import java.io.*;
import java.net.*;
/**
 * Chapter 11 - Another Installer Example
 * @author Mauro Marinilli
 * @version 1.0
 */
public class InstallerExample implements Runnable {
  ExtensionInstallerService eis;
  public InstallerExample() {
    Utilities.getInstance("installer-msgs");
    eis = (ExtensionInstallerService)Utilities.getService(
➥"javax.jnlp.ExtensionInstallerService");
    Thread t = new Thread(this);
    t.start();
  }
  public void run() {
    setupDownloadWindow();
    doResourcesDownload();
    installationCompleted(true, false);
  }
```

LISTING 11.6   Continued

```
public void setupDownloadWindow() {
  eis.setHeading(Utilities.getMsg("heading1"));
  eis.setStatus(Utilities.getMsg("sometext"));
}
public void doResourcesDownload(){
  installOptionalPackage();
}
public void installationCompleted(boolean success, boolean reboot){
  if (success){
    if (reboot){
      //handle some reboot preparation
    }
    eis.installSucceeded(reboot);
  } else {
    //handle failure
    eis.installFailed();
  }
}
public void installOptionalPackage(){
  String optionalPackagesJARDirWin = "\\lib\\ext\\";//see Sun docs
  String jarName = "anapp.jar";
  String jarServerPath = "http://server/b2/c11/"+jarName;
  URL jreURL = null;
  try {
    jreURL = new
URL("http://jsp.java.sun.com/servlet/javawsExtensionServer");
  } catch (Exception e) {
    System.out.println("creating URL: "+e);
  }
  String jrePath = eis.getInstalledJRE(jreURL,"1.3.0");
  File javaFile = new File(jrePath);//where java is located
  String jreRoot = javaFile.getParentFile().getParent();
  File libDir = new File(jreRoot+optionalPackagesJARDirWin);
  if (!libDir.exists())
    libDir.mkdirs();
  File jarFile = new File(jreRoot + optionalPackagesJARDirWin +jarName);
  try {
    FileOutputStream fos = new FileOutputStream(jarFile);
    URL jarURL = new URL(jarServerPath);
    URLConnection jarConn = jarURL.openConnection();
    InputStream is = jarConn.getInputStream();
    int q;
    while ((q = is.read()) != -1)
      fos.write(q);
```

LISTING 11.6 Continued

```
        is.close();
        fos.close();
    } catch (Exception e) {
        System.out.println("creating & writing "+jarName+": "+e);
    }
  }
  public static void main(String[] args) {
    InstallerExample installer = new InstallerExample();
  }
}
```

There are some interesting things to notice in this listing:

- First, notice the *sequence* of actions that an installer usually follows. First, it obtains the ExtensionInstallerService (line 17–18); then, it prepares the GUI, both creating it by itself or adapting the JNLP Client's one, using methods of the previously obtained ExtensionInstallerService (method setupDownloadWindow at lines 27–30). Then, it performs its operations in the method doResourcesDownload (lines 31–33), eventually calling setJREInfo or setNativeLibraryInfo for notifying changes to the JRE, and finally concludes the installation procedure, as in method installationCompleted at lines 34–44.

- Also, notice how to locate the directory where a JRE is currently installed, by using the following, as shown in Line 55:

  extensionInstallerService.getInstalledJRE(jreURL,VersionString);.

  Note that the JRE URL is the vendor's URL, and it can be determined together with the exact version string directly from the Preferences control panel of Java Web Start or in an analogous way for other JNLP Clients.

- The method installOptionalPackage beginning at line 45 first tries to determine where the JRE Java executable is located. Then, it creates the proper path where the resources are intended to be downloaded.

- Lastly, just a note on threads. Despite the fact that they are not needed in this simple example, they are commonly used by installers that want to reduce the total installation time.

The JNLP main file (namely installer-main.jnlp) shown in Listing 11.7 declares its own application JAR files and the installer extension, as reported in Listing 11.8.

LISTING 11.7 The Main JNLP file for the Optional Packages Installer Example

```
<?xml version="1.0" encoding="UTF-8"?>
<jnlp spec="1.0+"
  codebase="http://server/b2/c11/">
  <information>
    <title>Optional Pkg. Install.</title>
    <vendor>Mauro's Workshop</vendor>
    <offline/>
  </information>
  <resources>
    <j2se version="1.2+" />
    <extension
      name="Installer"
      href="installer-ext.jnlp">
    </extension>
    <jar href="dummy-app.jar" />
  </resources>
  <application-desc main-class="com.marinilli.b2.c11.DummyApp" />
</jnlp>
```

The JNLP extension descriptor file is listed below in Listing 11.8. Note that to access the file system, we require signed installers specifying trusted permissions (that is, all-permissions or j2see-application-client-permissions values) and that optional packages are located in different directories within a JRE environment, depending on the platform. Consequently, the platform-specific code has to be specified in the resources element, or the Java code should be able to tell the difference. See the J2SE documentation on optional packages for more details. For simplicity, we assumed a JRE exists that is compliant with the Windows environment.

LISTING 11.8 The Extension Descriptor JNLP file for the Optional Packages Installer Example

```
<?xml version="1.0" encoding="UTF-8"?>
<jnlp spec="1.0+"
  codebase="http://server/b2/c11/">
  <information>
    <title>Installer Example</title>
    <vendor>Mauro's Workshop</vendor>
    <offline/>
  </information>
  <security><all-permissions/></security>
  <resources>
    <j2se version="1.2+" />
```

LISTING 11.8   Continued

```
    <jar href="installer-signed.jar" />
  </resources>
  <installer-desc main-class="com.marinilli.b2.c11.InstallerExample" />
</jnlp>
```

NOTE

Using the JNLP API, installers may even ask a JNLP Client to reboot the computer to finish the installation. Refer to line 39 in Listing 11.6.

In order to install a new JRE, the procedure is similar to the InstallerExample previously discussed. However, the method setJREInfo must be called by the installer, providing the absolute path to the java executable of the installed JRE. Likewise, when installing a native library in a particular directory in the local file system, it is necessary to invoke the setNativeLibraryInfo to inform the JNLP Client from where to download the native libraries.

Other Services

JNLP also offers implementations of printing and Clipboard access services, much as in the case of file-related services. This allows untrusted applications to have a chance to access the given services.

Accessing the System Clipboard

Untrusted applications cannot access the system Clipboard without passing through this service. See the AnApplication class (Listing 11.10) for an example of usage of this service. In particular, examine lines 75–86 of Listing 11.10.

Queuing Jobs to the Printer

For printing applications via the JNLP API (for unsigned applications as well) use the PrintService. See Listing 11.9 for an example usage of this service.

LISTING 11.9   An Example Of Printing with the JNLP API

```
package com.marinilli.b2.c11;
import com.marinilli.b2.c11.util.Utilities;
import java.awt.print.*;
```

LISTING 11.9 Continued

```
import javax.jnlp.*;
import java.awt.*;
/**
 * Chapter 11 - An example of printing via JNLP API
 * @author Mauro Marinilli
 * @version 1.0
 */
public class PrintServiceExample {
  public PrintServiceExample() {
    PrintService ps =
      (PrintService)Utilities.getService("javax.jnlp.PrintService");
    ps.print(new PrintableExample());
    System.exit(0);
  }
  public class PrintableExample implements Printable {
    public int print(Graphics graphics, PageFormat pageFormat, int pageIndex){
      Graphics2D g2d = (Graphics2D)graphics;
      g2d.setPaint(Color.black);
      g2d.drawString("A JNLP Print",100,100);
      return PAGE_EXISTS;
    }
  }
  public static void main(String[] args) {
    PrintServiceExample printServiceExample1 = new PrintServiceExample();
  }
}
```

An Example Application

As a recapping example of what said, let's take a look at Listing 11.10, in which an application uses many of the things discussed in this chapter. As we can see, we are constantly moving toward a full-fledged application, such as the one presented in Chapter 13.

LISTING 11.10 A Recapping Example of JNLP Runtime Services at Work

```
package com.marinilli.b2.c11;
import com.marinilli.b2.c11.util.*;
import javax.swing.*;
import java.awt.event.*;
import javax.jnlp.*;
import java.net.URL;
import java.io.*;
import java.util.Iterator;
```

LISTING 11.10   Continued

```java
import java.awt.*;
/**
 * Chapter 11 A test application
 * @author Mauro Marinilli
 * @version 1.0
 */
public class AnApplication extends JFrame {
  JPanel centerPanel = new JPanel();
  JButton pasteButton = new JButton();
  JLabel southLabel = new JLabel();
  JLabel centerLabel = new JLabel();
  JPanel northPanel = new JPanel();
  JNLPLabel northLabel = new JNLPLabel();
  JButton openFileButton = new JButton();
  public AnApplication() {
    setTitle(Utilities.getMsg("title"));
    setIconImage(Utilities.getImageIcon("bubu").getImage());
    this.getContentPane().setLayout(new BorderLayout());
    this.addWindowListener(new java.awt.event.WindowAdapter() {
      public void windowClosing(WindowEvent e) {
        System.exit(0);
      }
    });
    centerPanel.setLayout(new BorderLayout());
    pasteButton.setText("Paste");
    pasteButton.addActionListener(new java.awt.event.ActionListener() {
      public void actionPerformed(ActionEvent e) {
        centerLabel.setText(pasteClipboardContent());
      }
    });
    southLabel.setText(Utilities.getMsg("hello"));
    centerLabel.setIcon(Utilities.getImageIcon("anIcon.gif"));
    northLabel.setText("please click here!");
    northLabel.setURL("http://server/b2/index.html");
    openFileButton.setIcon(Utilities.getImageIcon("open.gif"));
    openFileButton.addActionListener(new java.awt.event.ActionListener() {
      public void actionPerformed(ActionEvent e) {
        openFile();
      }
    });
    this.getContentPane().add(centerPanel, BorderLayout.CENTER);
    centerPanel.add(pasteButton, BorderLayout.EAST);
    centerPanel.add(centerLabel, BorderLayout.CENTER);
    centerPanel.add(northPanel, BorderLayout.NORTH);
```

LISTING 11.10 Continued

```
      northPanel.add(openFileButton, null);
      northPanel.add(northLabel, null);
      this.getContentPane().add(southLabel, BorderLayout.SOUTH);
      PersistenceService ps =
(PersistenceService)Utilities.getService("javax.jnlp.PersistenceService");
      if (ps!=null) {
        doSomething(ps);
      }
      setSize(300,200);
      setVisible(true);
  }
  private void doSomething(PersistenceService ps){
    PersistentStorage pst = new PersistentStorage();
    pst.write("url0","salve");
    pst.synchronize("url0");

    Iterator iter = pst.getEntries("url0").iterator();
    while (iter.hasNext()) {
      Object obj = iter.next();
      System.out.println("item="+obj);
    }
  }
  private String pasteClipboardContent() {
    String s = "";
    ClipboardService cbs =
     (ClipboardService)Utilities.getService("javax.jnlp.ClipboardService");
    try {
      if (cbs.getContents()!=null)
s=(String)cbs.getContents().getTransferData(java.awt.datatransfer.DataFlavor.st
ringFlavor);
    } catch (Exception e) {
      e.printStackTrace();
    }
    return s;
  }
  public void openFile() {
    String[] suffixes = {"txt","jnlp","jar","java"};
    FileContents file = null;
    FileOpenService fs =
     (FileOpenService)Utilities.getService("javax.jnlp.FileOpenService");
    if (fs!=null) {
      try {
```

LISTING 11.10 Continued

```
        file = fs.openFileDialog("mydir", suffixes);
      } catch (Exception e) {
        System.out.println("openFile: "+e);
      }
    }
  }
}
  public static void main(String[] args) {
    AnApplication anApplication1 = new AnApplication();
  }
}
```

Figure 11.2 presents a screenshot from the test application running.

Production direc-
tive said to crop
this. Okay?

FIGURE 11.2

A screenshot from the test application.

In Figure 11.2, we see several different things:

- Locale-specific data, both in the title and in the bottom label. If you try to run the program on a computer with a Locale other than Italian, you'll see English text instead
  (provided as default; see following).

- Icons loaded and icons not found in the JAR file. The JFrame icon hasn't been found so
  the Utilities class provides a default one without firing any exception.

- The JNLPLabel at work, showing the pointed URL as a tooltip (the hand cursor is not
  shown).

- Clicking the Paste button will activate the Clipboard, which will prompt for authorization
  because the application is not signed. The button with the open file icon, instead, will
  prompt to open a file from the local file system.

Note that, besides the launching JNLP file (anapp.jnlp), there is the anapp.jar JAR file containing the following items:

- Two properties files, messages.properties and messages_it.properties, specifying text for the two supported locales.
- Java classes needed to run the application.
- Eventually, the META-INF/MANIFEST.MF, necessary if the main class has not been specified in the JNLP file.
- Some graphic icons.

See Chapter 13 for more examples of use of the JNLP API.

Summary

In this chapter, we examined the runtime services offered by JNLP client to its applications. The heart of these services lies within the javax.jnlp.ServiceManager class. In Chapter 12, we will study how JNLP is supported by a remote server which acts as a deployment server, as described in Chapter 2.

Server-Side Deployment Support

IN THIS CHAPTER

In this chapter, we will study how JNLP is supported by a remote Server, which acts as a deployment server, as described in Chapter 2, "An Abstract Model for Deployment." We already discussed some server side deployment in Chapter 5, "Deployment Options for Non-J2SE Clients;" here, we will focus on servlet deployment adapted to support JNLP clients.

An implementation of the server-side JNLP protocol that makes use of servlet technology (and thus can be used in any servlet container) has been provided by the author and is freely available for downloads at this address:
`http://www.marinilli.com/projects/juniper/juniper.html`.

Readers interested in providing version-based download or other non-basic JNLP server support to their JNLP applications, or are simply interested in the details of a JNLP server should read this chapter.

Overview

In this section, we discuss the differences between basic and full JNLP server support. For brevity, we will imply that a server is a JNLP-enabled Web server that can accomplish successfully all the requests formulated by a JNLP client (from here on, the client).

Table 12.1 shows the main JNLP features and the required server support. With basic support, we mean simple file download via a Web server. With advanced support instead, we refer to servlets and other server-side code (CGI, scripting, and so on) beside basic file download capabilities.

TABLE 12.1. Server-side Support Needed for the Main JNLP Features.

JNLP Feature	Basic Support	Advanced Support
Simple JAR Download	Yes	Yes
Version-Based Download	No	Yes
Extension Download	Limited	Full
Attribute-Based Download	No	Yes

Indeed, attribute-based and version-based downloads are basically the same kind of requests to the server (a request for a file accompanied by a series of attributes that identify the needed resource). We distinguish them because the version-based download needs an elaborate version description, whereas other attributes have simpler values.

To summarize Table 12.1, we can say that the advanced support comprises all attribute-based requests: versioned downloads, JAR file differencing, and extensions download.

For example, a basic server can only support this kind of request from a JNLP client:

```
http://www.mybasicserver.com/downloadpath/file.jar
```

While a full JNLP server can reply to more sophisticated requests like the following:

```
http://www.myjnlpserver.com/servletpath/file.jar?version-
➥id=3.1.2*+3.4*&os="windows"&current-version-id=2.8.2
```

Note that posing these kind of requests to a basic Web server will generally cause an error on the JNLP client. This is not a problem anyway, as long as your JNLP files (that ultimately trigger client requests) are written for and tested on the server you are going to use.

Deploying Resources to the Server

In this section, we will see how to prepare the server environment for enabling full support of the JNLP protocol.

We will refer to a servlet implementation of the JNLP server as the one provided by Sun (that is intended only for development) or the Juniper project implementation.

Practically, those interested in providing full JNLP support should install one of the servlet-based solutions available to developers. See the Sun Web Start page for some further details.

As for servlet deployment, there are some practical notes in Chapter 5 as well.

Server-Side Resource Management

In the preceding chapters, we concentrated on the client-side of the protocol, assuming basic support on the server. Files are treated like passive resources that are sent back to the requesting client, like the usual behavior of a static Web server.

In this scenario, each file is uniquely identified by its URL path. The JNLP client (or simply client, for brevity) may request files specifying some given attributes value as well. The attributes JNLP supports are the following:

- **Versions**. The version of the given resource. Versions are encoded with strings, as we will see later.
- **Supported OS**. The operating systems that the given resource is designed to run on.
- **Supported Architectures**. Beyond the OS, the underlying hardware architecture also matters sometimes.
- **Locales**. The job of localizing resources (that is, dividing them in groups depending on the supported languages) can be left to the protocol, to avoid huge all-can-do JAR files that support dozens of languages. The benefits are twofold: reduced download bandwidth and easier management during the development lifecycle.

We have already seen how these attributes can be specified in a JNLP file. But without proper server-side support, they would be ignored or—even worse—cause a blocking error.

At this point, it could be useful to distinguish between physical resources (concrete files) and logical ones (that is, requests that clients solicit to the server, as follows) :

- **Logical Resource**. An abstract, sometimes vague resource definition, issued by the client. The server job is to transform a client request in a file to be sent back to the client. If there were no attributes to be specified for a resource, there would be no difference between logical and physical resources, and a simple Web server would suffice.
- **Physical Resource**. A physical file present on the server repository. Such a file may have attached a number of attribute values that define its exact version, the lists of supported OS, hardware architectures and locales, whereas an abstract resource may indicate them only vaguely.

For example:

```
name="file.jar", version-id="1.2+", OS="Windows"
```

is a logical resource, expressed for instance by the following client HTTP request:

```
http://www.myserver.com/mypath/file.jar?version-id=1.2%2B&os=Windows
```

that can be matched by the file (physical resource):

```
"/JNLPRepository/App1/Win/file__v1.2.0.2-rc.jar".
```

Note that the server is able to associate some attributes values to a physical file in a given directory (presumably in a given WAR file). The way this association is created depends on the server, and it is the focus of the next section.

Specifying Attribute Values for Server Files

Sun proposed two mechanisms for defining attribute values for resource files to be managed by servers. One is a simple naming convention for files. All the attributes are encoded in the file-name, as follows.

There are four possible attributes to be specified:

- Locales. Appending many times as needed the "__L" + locale strings to the resource file-name.
- Versions. Using (one time only per resource) the "__V" + version id to the resource file-name.
- Os. Appending the "__O" + os names to the resource filename.
- Architectures. Appending the "__A" + architecture names to the resource filename.

The value for each attribute is described in Chapter 10, "Defining the Client Environment."

For example:

```
application__V1.2__Len_US__Len.jar
```

It instructs the JNLP server that the given resource is a named application, has a version "1.2", and supports two locales: American English and default English.

These files should be kept within the WAR file of the deployment servlet (see the Chapter 5 section on J2EE deployment for some detail on WAR files).

Another convention is to use an XML file in every directory we want to specify attribute values for the contained files. These files always have the standard name "version.xml".

`jnlp-versions` within the root element can be only two possible elements: `resource` and `platform`. The former is used for describing all the attribute values for a given physical resource (that is, a file), whereas the latter is used to specify resources with a platform version id. The elements `pattern` and `file` can be specified for any resource or platform giving attribute values.

For example, Listing 12.1 shows a simple `version.xml` file that instructs the JNLP server that `file1.jar` is the concrete file for the resource named `resource1`, supporting three different languages, and with a current version "0.1.2".

LISTING 12.1 An Example of the `version.xml` File

```xml
<jnlp-versions>
  <resource>
    <pattern>
      <name>resource1 </name>
      <version-id>0.1.2</version-id>
      <locale>en</locale>
      <locale>it</locale>
      <locale>es_ES</locale>
    </pattern>
    <file>file1.jar</file>
  </resource>
</jnlp-versions>
```

Listing 12.2 proposes another example of version.xml file that shows the equivalence of the two notations mechanism: that one based on the filename only, and this one based on XML files.

LISTING 12.2   An Example of the `version.xml` File Showing the Equivalence of the Two Specification Mechanisms

```
<jnlp-versions>
  <resource>
    <pattern>
      <name>application.jar</name>
      <version-id>1.2</version-id>
      <locale>en_US</locale>
      <locale>it</locale>
    </pattern>
    <file>application__V1_2__Len_us__Lit.jar</file>
  </resource>
</jnlp-versions>
```

Behind the Scenes of a JNLP Server

Now we will see some of the details of a JNLP server implementation. We don't have the space needed to cover all the aspects of such an implementation. Instead, we will provide commented code for the more particular aspects of the protocol, such as version management, while leaving out servlet implementation details. Those interested may refer to the Juniper home page for the source code of a complete, up-to-date, and robust JNLP server implementation.

We will begin with HTTP details.

HTTP Implementation

The JNLP protocol builds on top of the HTTP protocol. All JNLP requests are special HTTP GET requests.

In the following table are listed all the new MIME types that a Web server fully supporting JNLP needs to use.

MIME type	Description
Application/x-java-archive	JAR file
Application/x-java-archive-diff	JARDiff file
Application/x-java-jnlp-file	JNLP file
Application/x-java-jnlp-error	Generic JNLP-related error

In case of a JNLP-error response type, the following error codes are used by the server.

Server-Side Deployment Support

CHAPTER 12

355

12

SERVER-SIDE
DEPLOYMENT
SUPPORT

Error Code	Description
10	Could Not Locate Resource
11	Could Not Locate Requested Version
20	Unsupported Operating System
21	Unsupported Architecture
22	Unsupported Locale
23	Unsupported JRE Version
99	Unknown error

Checking for New Versions

As we know from Chapter 9, "The JNLP Protocol," an application can be registered for updates by specifying the URL where the main JNLP file can be found using the `href` attribute of the `jnlp` element.

In this case, the JNLP client uses the `last-modified` field of the HTTP header of the referenced file to discover new versions of the same application, even if the JNLP main file didn't change.

In this way, simply "touching" (that is, refreshing the `last-modified` file attribute of) the JNLP main file for that application, developers may indicate to remote clients that a new release has been published. This phase is what we called the Publication phase, in the abstract model of Chapter 2. As an example, see Figure 2.5.

Extension Download Protocol

JNLP clients can request extensions (that are either JREs or JNLP extensions, as described in Chapter 9) to the server. In this case, a special type of the version-based download protocol is used.

For example, the following snippet of JNLP file:

```
<resources os="Windows" locale="de">
  <extension name="ext1" href="http://www.site.com/ext1.jnlp" version="1.2" />
</resources>
```

will cause the JNLP client to issue the following request to the server:

```
http://www.site.com/ext1.jnlp?arch=x86&os=Windows&locale=de&version-
id=1.2&known-platforms=1.3.1+1.4
```

We assumed that on the client machine there are two JREs already installed, with versions
`1.3.1` and `1.4`.

Note the `known-platform` field in the HTTP request. It defines the J2SE JRE already installed on the client machine. It must be always specified when requesting an extension.

Also note that all the usual attributes (`arch`, `os`, `locale`) together with the above mentioned `known-platform` one, must be specified for any request.

Anyway, for allowing a minimal extension support also for basic Web servers, when the `version` field is not specified, the extension request is handled like a normal file request, and the client will accept and use the downloaded JNLP extension files.

Finally, let's see how new JREs can be downloaded using the extension mechanism provided by JNLP.

The attribute responsible for specifying JREs in the JNLP file is `j2se`. It can be used to specify a particular URL from where a JRE can be downloaded, if not already present on the client machine. Of course, the URL should point to a servlet or other code able to satisfy the JNLP extension request.

For example, given the following line in the JNLP file:

```
<j2se version="1.4" href="http://www.jrevendorsite.com/jnlpjre/" />
```

the JNLP client will issue the following HTTP `GET` request (assuming to have a Windows 2000 client with JRE version 1.3.1 already installed):

```
http://www.jrevendorsite.com/jnlpjre?arch=x86&os=Windows+2000&locale=en_US&vers
ion-id=1.4&known-platforms=1.3.1
```

Otherwise, the URL can be omitted; in this case, the client is responsible for knowing the URL where the given JRE could be downloaded. Clients such as Java Web Start typically will point to Sun's JREs.

Providing Incremental Updates For JAR Files

JARDiff files are a special type of JAR files that describe the differences between two JAR files. They are useful to save bandwidth during downloads.

Clients do not explicitly request JARDiff files. Instead, clients simply add the currently installed version for that JAR resource to the request, together with the usual requested version. Then, it is up to the server to decide whether to return a version-compatible JAR resource or a JARDiff file that contains the pieces to be added to the JAR file currently installed on the client, together with the instruction to assemble them.

Figure 12.1 depicts the mechanism for incremental updates.

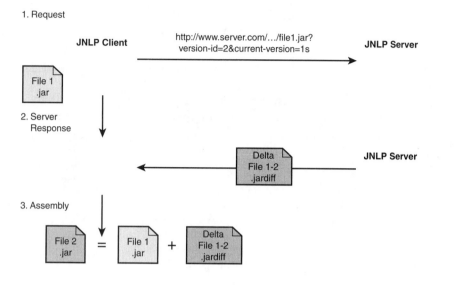

FIGURE 12.1
The JARDiff working mechanism.

After a JAR file is requested, specifying the already installed version, the JNLP server may return a JARDiff file, and the JNLP client will take care to build the new file from assembling the JARDiff with the installed old JAR file.

NOTE

As of version 1.0 of the JNLP specification, JARDiff files are an optional feature. They don't embody a conceptual characteristic in the protocol; rather they are just an implementation-level enhancement.

The granularity level (that is, the smallest piece that can be handled) of differencing with JARDiff files is class-level for code, and generally of a file entry inside the JAR file. To see it in a slightly different way, it's like we could be able to patch JAR files, and our patches could be no littler than Java classes items (contained into JAR files).

Getting back to Part I of this book, we saw that some Java deployment solutions allow for finer granularity levels (for instance, DeployDirector permits byte-level differences. This is to say that it allows patching single classes).

The finer the granularity level, the greater are the bandwidth savings we can have. Anyway, a level of granularity of a file entry inside a JAR file is perfectly suited for most real cases.

> **TIP**
>
> As you already imagined, class size counts here. If we created our application as a single big class, updating it incrementally via a JARDiff file will be ineffectual.
>
> Instead, orient yourself to design a greater number of smaller classes, as well-known, common-sense OO practices suggest.

A JARDiff file is a JAR file named "INDEX.JD" that contains the new files and an index file in the META-INF directory, in which all the changes to be performed on the old JAR file are listed.

For more details on JARDiff files, see Appendix B, "JNLP (Java Network Launcher Protocol) Specification."

Specifying Versions

Versions are different from the other attributes (namely OS, architectures, and locales) because they have a more sophisticated definition.

As we saw in Chapter 9, "The JNLP Protocol," the version attribute is used to specify a version in a JNLP file. This attribute is used in the following elements:

- jar
- extension
- nativelib
- icon
- j2se

> **NOTE**
>
> Only for the j2se element is it mandatory to specify a version; for the other JNLP elements, it is optional.

When specifying a version string in a JNLP, file, we can use one or more versions separated by a space, like the following:

```
<jar href="..." version="2.1.1.9 2.2.1+ 2.3*" />
```

Now, we will introduce an implementation of versions as described in the JNLP specification document, version 1.0.

Our demonstration implementation is composed of seven classes, including one class that allow for some interactive testing.

- `Versionable`. The abstract superclass.
- `VersionString`. Implements a version string; for example: "1.2 1.1+ 1.0.02-final"
- `VersionId`. Implements a single version id, such as "1.0.2".
- `PlusVersion`. Implements a set of version ids that comprises all the versions greater than or equal to the specified one; for example: "1.2+"
- `StarVersion`. Implements a so-called *prefix match*. In this case, a version id matches one of these objects when they match their initial subversions, like for example "1.2.3" and "1.2", which both match the object represented by "1.3*" or "1.1.003" and "1.1*".
- `UnspecifiedVersion`. Denotes an unspecified version.
- `Test`. A GUI for interactive version input.

A code similar to this is probably running on your JNLP server implementation. Anyway, if you are not interested in server-side JNLP implementations, you can skip the following code and run the Test class to get familiar with version strings in JNLP.

Listing 12.3 shows the `Versionable` class. This abstract class is the superclass of all version classes, and includes some general-purpose code such as a factory method (beginning at line 22) for creating the proper object directly from the representing string.

LISTING 12.3   The `Versionable` Class

```
package com.marinilli.b2.c12;

/**
 * Chapter 12 - abstract class for all the kinds of Version objects
 *
 * @author Mauro Marinilli
 * @version 1.0
 */

public abstract class Versionable {

  /**
   * Factory method for <code>Versionable</code> types
   *
```

LISTING 12.3 Continued

```
 * Depending on the string passed in creates the appropriate type, among:
 * <code>VersionId</code><br>
 * <code>StarVersion</code><br>
 * <code>PlusVersion</code><br>
 * <code>VersionString</code><br>
 *
 */
public static Versionable createVersionable(String vers) {
  if (vers==null)
    return new UnspecifiedVersion();
  if (vers.indexOf(' ')!=-1)
    return new VersionString(vers);
  if (vers.indexOf('+')!=-1)
    return new PlusVersion(vers);
  if (vers.indexOf('*')!=-1)
    return new StarVersion(vers);
  if ((VersionId.isNumber(vers)) || (vers.indexOf(VersionId.DOT_CHAR)!=-1))
    return new VersionId(vers);

  return new UnspecifiedVersion();//in all other cases
}

/**
 * Factory method for VersionId types
 */
public static VersionId createVersionId(String vers) {
  if (vers==null)
    return new UnspecifiedVersion();
  Versionable v = createVersionable(vers);
  if (v instanceof VersionId)
    return (VersionId)v;
  return new UnspecifiedVersion();
}

/**
 * exact match
 */
public abstract boolean match(Versionable v);

}
```

Listing 12.4 shows the VersionId class that represents exact version labels for resources. Note that such versions can be sorted using the Comparable interface. In this way, the cache of a

JNLP server can keep in memory the sorted list of different versions of the same logical resource to minimize handling operations.

Note also at lines 68–91 the `compareToVersionId` method that compares two `VersionId` instances. The normalization step (lines 72,73) ensures that the array of strings composing the `VersionId` element can be effectively compared, both in their length and in neutralizing possible problems with padding zeros (so "`1.002`" correctly matches "`1.2`").

LISTING 12.4   The `VersionId` Class

```
package com.marinilli.b2.c12;
import java.util.*;

/**
 * Chapter 12 - VersionIds representations
 *
 * A VersionId as defined in the JNLP specs. from Sun.
 * An example is represented by the string '1.2.2-ea'.
 *
 * @author Mauro Marinilli
 * @version 1.0
 */

public class VersionId extends Versionable implements Comparable {
  public final static char DOT_CHAR = '.';
  public final static String SEPARATORS = DOT_CHAR+"-_";//
➥see JNLP specs. Appendix A
  private String[] singleValues;//see JNLP specs. Appendix A

  /**
   * Creates a new Version Id.
   * @param String s the string representing the version
   */
  protected VersionId(String s) {
    if (s==null)
      return;
    ArrayList arraylist = new ArrayList();
    int i = 0;
    for(int j = 0; j < s.length(); j++)
      if(SEPARATORS.indexOf(s.charAt(j)) !=-1) {
        if(i < j) {
          String s1 = s.substring(i, j);
          arraylist.add(s1);
        }
        i = j + 1;
      }
```

LISTING 12.4 Continued

```
    if(i < s.length())
        arraylist.add(s.substring(i, s.length()));
    singleValues = new String[arraylist.size()];
    arraylist.toArray(singleValues);
}

/**
 * The exact match between two Versions
 */
public boolean match(Versionable v) {
  if(v == null)
    return false;
  // to be refined
  if (v instanceof StarVersion)
    return ((StarVersion)v).contains(this);
  if (v instanceof PlusVersion)
    return ((PlusVersion)v).contains(this);
  if(v instanceof UnspecifiedVersion)
    return false;
  if(v instanceof VersionString) {
    return ((VersionString)v).contains(this);
  }
  if(!(v instanceof VersionId))
    return false;
  VersionId vid = (VersionId)v;
  return (compareToVersionId(vid)==0);
}

/**
 * compare a VersionId against another
 */
public int compareToVersionId(VersionId vid) {
  if (vid instanceof UnspecifiedVersion )
    return 0;
  // normalize one against the other
  String as[] = normalize(singleValues, vid.getSingleValues().length);
  String as1[] = normalize(vid.getSingleValues(), singleValues.length);

  // then scan each single value against the respective one
  for(int i = 0; i < as.length; i++) {
    if(!as[i].equals(as1[i]))
      if (isNumber(as[i]) && isNumber(as1[i])) {
        int v1 = Integer.parseInt(as[i]);
        int v2 = Integer.parseInt(as1[i]);
```

LISTING 12.4   Continued

```
             if (v1!=v2)
                return v1 - v2;
          } else {
             // we have at least a non-number, so compare them lexicographically
             // see JNLP specs, Appendix A
             return as[i].compareTo(as1[i]);
          }
       }//-for
       // if we arrive here the two versionIds are logically equal
       return 0;
    }

    public static boolean isNumber(String s){
       try {
          Integer.valueOf(s);
          return true;
       }
       catch(NumberFormatException _ex) {
          //don't care
       }
       return false;
    }

    /**
     * Implements the superclass method
     */
    public int compareTo(Object obj) {
       Versionable value = null;
       if (obj instanceof String)
         value = createVersionable((String)obj);
       if (obj instanceof Versionable)
         value = (Versionable)obj;
       if (value==null) {
         throw new ClassCastException("Cannot cast to Versionable or
➥ String classes");
       }

       //begins comparation
       //   remember that
       //   <0 : this < value
       //   =0 : this = value
       //   >0 : this > value
```

LISTING 12.4 Continued

```java
    if (value instanceof VersionId)
      return compareToVersionId((VersionId) value);
    if (value instanceof StarVersion)
      return -1;

    return 0;
  }

  /**
   * An utility method when comparing VersionIds.
   * See JNLP  Specs. Appendix A.
   */
  protected String[] normalize(String pieces[], int maxLen) {
    if (pieces.length >= maxLen)
      return pieces;
    String normalized[] = new String[maxLen];
    System.arraycopy(pieces, 0, normalized, 0, pieces.length);
    Arrays.fill(normalized, pieces.length, maxLen, "0");
    return normalized;
  }

  public String[] getSingleValues(){
    return singleValues;
  }

  /**
   * Returns a human-readable representation of the versionId
   */
  public String toString() {
    StringBuffer stringbuffer = new StringBuffer();
    for(int i = 0; i < singleValues.length - 1; i++) {
      stringbuffer.append(singleValues[i]);
      stringbuffer.append(DOT_CHAR);
    }
    if(singleValues.length > 0)
      stringbuffer.append(singleValues[singleValues.length - 1]);
    return stringbuffer.toString();
  }

  /**
   * By now VersionIds are considered equals when they have the same
   * string representation. THIS IS NOT ALWAYS TRUE !
   *
   */
```

LISTING 12.4 Continued

```java
public boolean equals(Object object) {
  /** @todo refine it better: THIS IS BUGGY!!*/
  if (!(object instanceof VersionId))
    return false;
  if (object instanceof UnspecifiedVersion)
    return false;
  VersionId other = (VersionId) object;
  return toString().equals(other.toString());
  }
}
```

Listing 12.5 shows the VersionString class.

LISTING 12.5 The VersionString Class

```java
package com.marinilli.b2.c12;

import java.util.*;

/**
 * Chapter 12 - A VErsionString implementation
 *
 * A set of three possible types:
 * <ul>
 *    <li><code>VersionId</code></li>
 *    <li><code>PlusVersion</code></li>
 *    <li><code>StarVersion</code></li>
 * </ul>
 *
 * @author Mauro Marinilli
 * @version 1.0
 */
public class VersionString extends Versionable{
  private ArrayList versionables;

  /**
   * the Constructor
   */
  public VersionString(String s) {
    versionables = new ArrayList();
    if(s != null) {
      StringTokenizer stringtokenizer = new StringTokenizer(s, " ", false);
      for(; stringtokenizer.hasMoreElements();)
        addVersionable( createVersionable(stringtokenizer.nextToken()) );
```

LISTING 12.5   Continued

```
    }
  }

  /**
   * Implements the superclass method
   */
  public boolean match(Versionable v) {
    return false;
  }

  /**
   * Adds a new Versionable (but not a VersionString itself!) to the
   * Version string.
   */
  public boolean addVersionable(Versionable v){
    if (v instanceof VersionString)
      return false;//it is not possible to have versionStrings
➥ containing other VersionStrings!
    return versionables.add(v);
  }

  /**
   * Returns a human-readable representation of the versionString
   */
  public String toString() {
    StringBuffer stringbuffer = new StringBuffer();
    for(int i= 0; i< versionables.size(); i++) {
      stringbuffer.append(versionables.get(i).toString());
      stringbuffer.append(' ');
    }
    return stringbuffer.toString();
  }


  /**
   * return true if the given VersionId is contained
   */
  public boolean contains(VersionId vid) {
    Iterator iter = versionables.iterator();
    while (iter.hasNext()) {
      Versionable item = (Versionable)iter.next();
      if (vid.match(item))
        return true;
    }
```

LISTING 12.5 Continued

```
    return false;
  }
}
```

Instances of the VersionString class will be typically created to represent client requests. They will contain StarVersion or PlusVersion instances, together with simple VersionIds.

Listing 12.6 shows the StarVersion class.

LISTING 12.6 The StarVersion Class

```java
package com.marinilli.b2.c12;

/**
 * Chapter 12 - A StarVersion implementation
 *
 * A 'star' single version string.
 * An example of 'star' version is '1.2*'
 *
 * @author Mauro Marinilli
 * @version 1.0
 */

public class StarVersion extends Versionable implements Comparable {
  public final static String STAR_SYMBOL = "*";
  private VersionId versionId;

  /**
   * The Constructor.
   * @param the string representing the version
   */
  public StarVersion(String s) {
    String trimmed = s.trim();
    if (trimmed.endsWith(STAR_SYMBOL))
      versionId = new VersionId(trimmed.substring(0,trimmed.length()-1));
  }

  /**
   * Implements the superclass method
   */
  public boolean match(Versionable v) {
    return false;
  }
```

LISTING 12.6 Continued

```java
public int compareTo(Object o) {
  /**@todo: Implement this java.lang.Comparable method*/
  throw new java.lang.UnsupportedOperationException("Method compareTo()
➥ not yet implemented.");
}

public String toString() {
  return versionId.toString()+STAR_SYMBOL;
}

public VersionId getVersionId() {
  return versionId;
}
/**
 * StarVersion are considered equals when they have the same string
 * representation.
 *
 */
public boolean equals(Object object) {
  if (!(object instanceof StarVersion))
    return false;
  return toString().equals( ((StarVersion)object).toString() );
}

/**
 * return true if the given VersionId is contained
 */
public boolean contains(VersionId vid) {
  String mine[] = versionId.normalize( versionId.getSingleValues()
➥, versionId.getSingleValues().length);
  String yours[] = versionId.normalize(vid.getSingleValues()
➥, versionId.getSingleValues().length);
  int length = Math.min(versionId.getSingleValues()
➥.length, vid.getSingleValues().length);

  for(int i = 0; i < length; i++) {
    if(!mine[i].equals(yours[i]))
      if (VersionId.isNumber(mine[i]) && VersionId.isNumber(yours[i])) {
        int v1 = Integer.parseInt(mine[i]);
        int v2 = Integer.parseInt(yours[i]);
        if (v1!=v2)
          return false;
      } else {
        return mine[i].equals(yours[i]);
```

LISTING 12.6   Continued

```
      }
    }//-for
    return true;
  }
}
```

From Listing 12.6, we can see how the contains() method (see lines 60–77) performs all the needed operations to test whether a given version-id is contained.

Finally, we can see the Test class in Listing 12.7. This class is useful for testing interactively version definitions, as represented in JNLP.

LISTING 12.7   The Test Class

```
package com.marinilli.b2.c12;
import javax.swing.*;
import java.awt.*;
import java.awt.event.*;

/**
 * Chapter 12 - A version test class
 *
 * @author Mauro Marinilli
 * @version 1.0
 */

public class Test extends JFrame {
  JPanel jPanel2 = new JPanel();
  JPanel jPanel1 = new JPanel();
  FlowLayout flowLayout1 = new FlowLayout();
  JLabel jLabel1 = new JLabel();
  JTextField versionStringTextField = new JTextField(12);
  JLabel jLabel2 = new JLabel();
  JTextField versionIdTextField = new JTextField(8);
  JPanel jPanel3 = new JPanel();
  JButton matchButton = new JButton();
  JLabel outcomeLabel = new JLabel();

  public Test() {
    getContentPane().setLayout(flowLayout1);
    jLabel1.setText("VersionString");
    jLabel2.setText("VersionId");
    matchButton.setText("match");
```

LISTING 12.7   Continued

```
    matchButton.addActionListener(new java.awt.event.ActionListener() {
      public void actionPerformed(ActionEvent e) {
        // the "match" button has been pushed
        Versionable v1 = Versionable.createVersionId
➡(versionIdTextField.getText());
        versionIdTextField.setText(v1.toString());

        Versionable v2 = Versionable.createVersionable
➡(versionStringTextField.getText());
        versionStringTextField.setText(v2.toString());

        outcomeLabel.setText("  result: " + v1.match(v2)+"  ");
      }
    });
    addWindowListener(new java.awt.event.WindowAdapter() {
      public void windowClosing(WindowEvent e) {
        System.exit(0);
      }
    });
    getContentPane().add(jPanel2, null);
    jPanel1.add(jLabel1, null);
    jPanel1.add(versionStringTextField, null);
    getContentPane().add(jPanel3, null);
    jPanel3.add(matchButton, null);
    getContentPane().add(jPanel1, null);
    jPanel2.add(jLabel2, null);
    jPanel2.add(versionIdTextField, null);
    outcomeLabel.setBorder(BorderFactory.createEtchedBorder());
    outcomeLabel.setText("comparison result");
    getContentPane().add(outcomeLabel, null);
    setSize(224,192);
    setTitle("Version Strings Test");
    setVisible(true);
  }

  /**
   * launch this class to start the GUI interactive version testing
   */
  public static void main(String[] args) {
    Test test1 = new Test();
  }

}
```

The most interesting lines of Listing 12.7 are lines 33–39, in which version objects are created and matched interactively.

We don't report the `PlusVersion` and `UndefinedVersion` classes here because of their little interest. Instead, let's examine a screenshot of the `Test` class at work.

FIGURE 12.2

A screenshot from the test class.

Summary

In this chapter, we have studied how JNLP is supported by a remote server which acts as a deployment server, as described in Chapter 2. Chapter 13 will conclude our journey with a comprehensive example that will tie together all the topics covered in this book.

A Complete Example

IN THIS CHAPTER

In this chapter, we will examine a simple application that can be deployed with JNLP.

In the previous chapters of Part III, we saw all the different aspects of JNLP technology in detail; now we will put all the pieces together to assemble a complete application. We will see a typical, pure Java application that implements an expandable text editor.

We will also expand the themes outlined in Chapter 4, "Designing for Deployment," from a practical viewpoint. We will discuss the practical organization of modules and the overall deployment illustrating it with this concrete case.

Design

We choose a well-known application domain that fits nicely with the features provided by JNLP. Our application—that we will call (with great imagination) *Textuale*—is easily organized into a set of software modules, using a functional decomposition of the provided features.

For simplicity, we will supply just one of those "add-on" features, a graphical editor for embedding simple draws in our text. A screenshot of a document processed with our text editor is proposed in Figure 13.1.

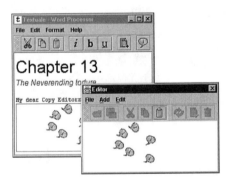

FIGURE 13.1
Our application at work.

Before we illustrate the implementation of our application, we take the remainder of this section to review the mechanisms of JNLP technology. After a recapping digression about JNLP usage, we will apply the observations found to our particular case.

JNLP support is achieved using the following means:

- JNLP files that organize coherently the resources to be deployed.
- An optional icon that is used both at download time and for integrating the application on the client platform, depending on JNLP Client's features.

- An optional HTML page that users can refer to for support.

- Some optional Java classes that will take advantage of the runtime services supplied by the JNLP Client. In our example, we used a simple installer class that takes charge of the whole first-time installation process.

A Procedure for JNLP Deployment

Let's recap the main steps necessary to deploy an application using the JNLP technology. We will take advantage of Chapter 4 for general advice. To deploy an application using JNLP, the deployment engineer (see Chapter 2, "An Abstract Model for Deployment") should perform the following activities:

1. Produce a complete catalog of all needed application resources.

2. Organize such application resources in deployment units, called *modules*.

3. Implement the obtained modules in JNLP constructs that will form the JNLP files of our application.

4. Create the proper JNLP resources (creating JAR files, writing the application homepage, and so on).

5. Deploy the JNLP files and JNLP resources with the proper file hierarchy on the Deployment Server. (This corresponds to the Producer To Distributor Publication Step in the abstract model of Chapter 2).

Note that this possible procedure may be modified as needed or made iterative (that is, alternating a first simpler JNLP file, trying it out, and then refining it again) especially if it is the first time you use this technology or if your application is quite complex.

Let's examine these steps in detail.

List All Application Resources

Usually, the resources employed in an application fall into one of the following categories.

- Java classes

- Other files (images, properties files, and so on)

- Third-party libraries (help support, JDBC drivers, and so on)

- Optional packages (previously known as *extensions*)

- The required J2SE JRE version

- Other resources (native libraries, special executables, and so on)

Map Application Resources in Modules

This step consists of decomposing the resources mentioned above into a coherent set of *modules*. We discussed this issue in Chapter 4.

13

A COMPLETE
EXAMPLE

Implement Modules in JNLP

The modules obtained in the previous step must be translated into JNLP constructs.

This usually involves the specification of language and platform information for the involved resources.

Optional packages have to be installed by custom installers; hence, an installer extension is needed. When deploying reusable libraries, a component extension is needed (though it is not necessary). The required JRE can be defined through the j2se element.

The following table describes the most frequent cases. Note that this table recaps imprecisely what was said before; for example, when we mention the installer-desc JNLP element, we mean the proper creation of an extension installer descriptor file, and so on.

Type Of Application Resource	Final JNLP Element
Java classes and other files	jar
Third-party and other reusable libraries	component-desc
Optional packages	installer-desc
JRE	j2se
Other resources	nativelib, jar

This is a basic procedure, and it is not exhaustive. Special cases will require ad-hoc installer classes, and so on.

Create JNLP Resources

This step involves the preparation of the following items, for example in the following order:

1. JNLP resources. They are created by properly packaging the application resources, eventually signing the resulting JAR files. JNLP resources include all the items mentioned by JNLP files, including icons, HTML pages, and so on.

2. The hierarchical structure of the JNLP resources obtained in the previous step is carefully thought out, in order to access such resources through URLs.

3. Finally, JNLP files creation can be concluded because all URLs are defined, and only little details such as the attributes of the main JNLP file information element are left. Also, all other details needed to finish the JNLP files are defined now (such as the setting of system properties).

Note that this is just one possible order to accomplish the creation of JNLP resources; feel free to follow your own style. What is important is to obtain all the final pieces ready to be deployed on the server.

Deploy on the Server JNLP Files and Resources

This step consists of copying all the JNLP resources obtained in the previous step and the JNLP files on the deployment server with the planned hierarchical structure. The particular arrangement will depend on the given JNLP server used. Usually, this one is implemented as a servlet; in this case, the JNLP resources can be packaged in a WAR file, as discussed in Chapter 5, "Deployment Options for Non-J2SE Clients." Consult your JNLP server documentation for details.

Some Considerations on the First-time Activation Cost

A full-fledged application could be large, even by Java standards. The simple word processor proposed in this chapter could use several localization packages (and their correspondent input methods) for each supported language, and it may use other optional packages for other add-ons (not to mention the JavaHelp executables and the related JAR data files). Anyway, excluding bulky optional packages, an average Java application could be considered to be less than 1MB in size, in most cases. Adding the other required libraries (such as JDBC drivers, specialized libraries, and so on) can take up more space (for example, Java Advanced Imaging for Windows platforms, an optional package, takes up 4.6MB). This will greatly increase the total size of the resources to install. As a simple example, see the following table.

Module	Average File Size
Core executables	0.5MB
Help library and data	0.4MB
Other libraries	1MB
Optional packages	5MB
JRE with a JNLP Client	5.5MB
Total size	**12.4MB**

Most applications will not reach such sizes, although a few will get even bigger!

In real-world situations, core executables have a predictable size. The most important source of size increase is caused by third-party libraries and the optional packages used.

The strategies we can employ for solving the problem of transferring such files to client computers were outlined in Chapter 4. Here, we will adapt them to the JNLP technology.

The most important solution to reduce the first-time activation cost (in terms of download time, see Chapter 2) is to split the size of the resources into several parts, to be transferred at different times. Of course, the JNLP Client and the J2SE JRE must be transferred first. Then comes the core module (for simplicity, we will consider only one core module) that comprises all the needed libraries and optional packages.

The installation logical sequence is always the following one:

1. JRE and JNLP Application Helper (for example, Java Web Start)
2. The core module
3. Add-on modules

> **NOTE**
>
> We are focusing only on the first-time activation, so updates and other deployment services costs are not considered now.

Provided that our JNLP Client supports lazy resources downloads, we have to decide how to distribute the resources weight between steps 2 and 3 of the previous list.

Another important and popular technique to generally reduce transfer costs is to include only the required resources in the planned client configurations. As we saw in Chapter 4, often applications come shipped with unneeded locale-specific data, or other platform-specific data that is never used during application execution. In order to take the maximum advantage from such JNLP features, developers have to divide platform-specific data in different JAR files and then prepare JNLP files in order to take advantage of such arrangement. This could be time consuming (often, locale-specific data is split in different files, for example), and if the obtained JAR files are too small, it could even be not worth the cost. You should also consider maintenance issues because the application evolves after the first release. Much will depend on the tools you have for administering this (the packaging and creation of the JNLP resources from your application resources).

Our Example

The resources decomposition in modules is straightforward in our case. We have only two modules: the core and the draw editor add-on.

The core module contains the core executables and their resources, plus third-party libraries. In this case, we use a standard set of icons for Swing applications provided by Sun. For concreteness, we can map modules with JAR files, obtaining the following association.

Module	JAR File
core	`textuale.jar; jlfgr-1_0.jar`
draw add-on	`draw.jar`

The following table shows the non-code resources used in our application and the belonging JNLP resource (that is JAR file).

Resource	JAR File
Application icon	`textuale.jar`
Other special icons	`textuale.jar; draw.jar`
Support properties files	`textuale.jar`
Java Swing standard icons	`jlfgr-1_0.jar`

The support properties files are used by the utility library that will be introduced in the "A JNLP Utility Library" section right before the chapter's summary.

Now, let's see the source code.

Implementation

The code shown here is available for download at the Companion Web site for this book.

COMPANION
Website Let's begin with the main JNLP file, (namely `textuale-main.jnlp`) shown in Listing 13.1.

13

LISTING 13.1   The application main JNLP file

```xml
<?xml version="1.0" encoding="UTF-8"?>
<jnlp spec="1.0+"
  codebase="http://server/b2/c13/"
  href="textuale-main.jnlp">
  <information>
    <title>Textuale Application</title>
    <vendor>Mauro's Workshop</vendor>
    <homepage href="home.html"/>
    <description kind="short">A simple expandable Java text
editor</description>
    <description kind="tooltip">A text Editor</description>
    <icon href="textuale-big.gif"/>
    <offline-allowed/>
  </information>
  <security><all-permissions/></security>
  <resources>
    <j2se version="1.3+" />

    <extension
      name="Installer"
      href="textuale-ext.jnlp">
    </extension>
```

LISTING 13.1   Continued

```
    <jar href="textuale.jar" part="core" />
    <jar href="jlfgr-1_0.jar" part="core" />
    <jar href="textuale-draw.jar" part="draw" download="lazy"/>
    <package name="com.marinilli.b2.c13.draw.*" part="draw" />
    <property name="application.parts" value="core;draw;etc"/>
    <property name="application.parts.desc" value="basic
functionalities;drawing add-on; — -"/>

  </resources>
  <application-desc main-class="com.marinilli.b2.c13.MainFrame" />
</jnlp>
```

In Listing 13.1, we can see the resources defined for the application: the core module (part "core" at lines 23–25) that is composed of two JAR files, and the "draw" part that can be downloaded when needed. Note also the optional package element at line 26, which suggests where to find the given classes to the JNLP file. The extension installer defined at lines 18–21 of Listing 13.1 is invoked for installing (and uninstalling) the application. The corresponding JNLP file is reported in Listing 13.2.

LISTING 13.2   The Application Installer Extension: the `textuale-ext` JNLP File

```
<?xml version="1.0" encoding="UTF-8"?>
<jnlp spec="1.0+"
  codebase="http://server/b2/c13/"
  href="textuale-ext.jnlp">
  <information>
    <title>Installing Textuale</title>
    <vendor>Mauro's Workshop</vendor>
    <icon href="textuale-big.gif"/>
    <offline/>
  </information>
  <security><all-permissions/></security>
  <resources>
    <j2se version="1.3+" />
    <jar href="textuale-installer.jar" />
  </resources>
  <installer-desc main-class="com.marinilli.b2.c13.Installer" />
</jnlp>
```

> **NOTE**
>
> Note that we requested an unrestricted security environment, so all JAR files used must be signed, including the third-party icon file.

In Listing 13.3, our application's main class is listed, abridged of some uninteresting code for menu creation (method populate at line 85).

LISTING 13.3 The MainFrame Class

```
package com.marinilli.b2.c13;
import com.marinilli.b2.c13.draw.EmbeddedDraw;
import com.marinilli.b2.ad.util.*;
import javax.swing.*;
import java.awt.*;
import java.awt.event.*;
import javax.swing.text.*;
import java.util.*;
import com.marinilli.b2.c13.util.*;

/**
 * Chapter 13 - Main class for the Textuale application
 *
 * @author Mauro Marinilli
 * @version 1.0
 */
public class MainFrame extends JFrame {
  StyledEditorKit editor;
  JScrollPane jScrollPane1 = new JScrollPane();
  JTextPane textPane = new JTextPane();
  BorderLayout borderLayout1 = new BorderLayout();
  JToolBar toolbar = new JToolBar();
  JMenuBar menubar = new JMenuBar();
  JButton addImageButton = new JButton();
  JButton infoButton = new JButton();

  // GUI-related initialization
  private Hashtable actionTable = new Hashtable();
  private String[] cutCopyPasteActionNames = new String[] {
          DefaultEditorKit.cutAction, "Cut",
"toolbarButtonGraphics/general/Cut24.gif",
          DefaultEditorKit.copyAction, "Copy",
"toolbarButtonGraphics/general/Copy24.gif",
```

LISTING 13.3 Continued

```
        DefaultEditorKit.pasteAction, "Paste",
"toolbarButtonGraphics/general/Paste24.gif",
  };

  private String[] familyActionNames = new String[] {
        "font-family-SansSerif", "SanSerif",
        "font-family-Monospaced", "Monospaced",
        "font-family-Serif", "Serif",
  };
  private String[] styleActionNames = new String[] {
        "font-italic", "Italic", "toolbarButtonGraphics/text/Italic24.gif",
        "font-bold", "Bold", "toolbarButtonGraphics/text/Bold24.gif",
        "font-underline", "Underline",
"toolbarButtonGraphics/text/Underline24.gif",
  };
  private String[] sizeActionNames = new String[] {
        "font-size-8",  "8",   "font-size-10", "10",
        "font-size-12", "12", "font-size-14", "14",
        "font-size-16", "16", "font-size-18", "18",
        "font-size-24", "24", "font-size-36", "36",
        "font-size-48", "48",
  };

  /**
   * Constructor
   */
  public MainFrame() {
    setTitle(GeneralUtilities.getMsg("application.title"));

setIconImage(GeneralUtilities.getImageIcon("images/textuale16.gif").getImage())
;

addImageButton.setIcon(GeneralUtilities.getImageIcon("images/AddDraw24.gif"));

    editor = new StyledEditorKit();
    editor.install(textPane);

    getContentPane().setLayout(borderLayout1);
    addWindowListener(new java.awt.event.WindowAdapter() {
      public void windowClosing(WindowEvent e) {
        close();
      }
    });
    getContentPane().add(jScrollPane1, BorderLayout.CENTER);
```

LISTING 13.3   Continued

```
  getContentPane().add(toolbar, BorderLayout.NORTH);
  jScrollPane1.getViewport().add(textPane, null);
  loadActionTable();
  populate();
  setJMenuBar(menubar);

  setSize(400,300);
  setVisible(true);
}


/**
 * fill up menus and actions
 */
private void populate() {
  // ...
}

/**
 * fill up action table
 */
private void loadActionTable() {
  Action[] actions = textPane.getActions();
  for(int i=0; i < actions.length; ++i) {
    actionTable.put(actions[i].getValue(Action.NAME), actions[i]);
  }
}

/**
 * quits the application
 */
private void close() {
  System.exit(0);
}

/**
 * return an action
 */
private Action getAction(String name) {
  return (Action)actionTable.get(name);
}

/**
 * shows up the about dialog
```

LISTING 13.3   Continued

```
   */
  private void showAboutDialog() {
    new AboutDialog(this);
  }

  /**
   * insert a new draw into the document
   */
  private void addComponent() {
    int userSays = JOptionPane.YES_OPTION;
    if (!GeneralUtilities.isModuleInstalled("draw"))
      userSays = JOptionPane.showConfirmDialog(this,
                                "This will install a new Module.
Continue?",
                                "Draw Editor Installation",
                                JOptionPane.YES_NO_OPTION);

    if (userSays==JOptionPane.YES_OPTION) {
      textPane.insertComponent(new EmbeddedDraw());
    }
  }

  /**
   * inner class for the "show about box" action
   */
  public final class About extends AbstractAction {
    public About() {
      super("about");
    }
    public void actionPerformed(ActionEvent e) {
      showAboutDialog();
    }
  }

  /**
   * to be launched as a simple application
   */
  public static void main(String[] args) {
    MainFrame frame = new MainFrame();
  }

}
```

What is interesting to see is the control performed before creating a new document—embedded draw in method addComponent (lines 123–134 of Listing 13.3). This warns the user before using this functionality if not already cached because it requires the download of some JAR files through JNLP. Figure 13.2 shows what happens the first time the user adds a draw to the document (assuming that the draw add-on module is not already installed).

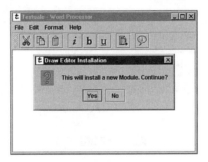

FIGURE 13.2

Our application requires the user authorization before using a feature that will imply a resources download.

> **NOTE**
>
> The "lazy" download of resources is not supported as mandatory in the JNLP specification, so this feature may not even be implemented on some JNLP Clients, or it may be implemented in different ways (for example, resources smaller than a given size are downloaded eagerly). Hence, depending on your JNLP Client, the confirmation window may not appear at all. For more details on such a feature, see Chapter 10, "Defining the Client Environment."

After the first authorization, the add draw button will not cause the confirmation dialog box to appear anymore, and the drawing functionalities are available to the user, as shown in Figure 13.3.

An interesting use of JNLP runtime services is provided by the "about" dialog box, shown in Figure 13.4. In Listing 13.4, its code is presented. This JDialog subclass is activated at line 116 of Listing 13.5.

13

A COMPLETE EXAMPLE

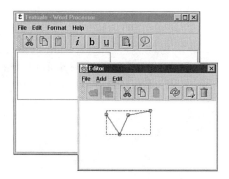

FIGURE 13.3

The drawing editor add-on opened by a user's double-click on the draw after first-download authorization.

FIGURE 13.4

The application "about" dialog box.

In the proposed about box, the interesting aspect (apart from the URL-like component that will bring up a Web browser pointing to that page that we presented in Chapter 11, "Runtime Client Services") is the listing of the currently installed modules. This is achieved by another component, a simple subclass of the `JTable` Swing class, detailed in Listing 13.3.

LISTING 13.4   The `AboutDialog` Class

```
package com.marinilli.b2.c13.util;
import java.awt.*;
import javax.swing.*;
import javax.swing.border.*;
import java.awt.event.*;
import java.util.*;
import com.marinilli.b2.c11.util.JNLPLabel;

/**
```

LISTING 13.4 Continued

```
 * Chapter 13 -
 *
 * @author Mauro Marinilli
 * @version 1.0
 */
public class AboutDialog extends JDialog {
  JButton closeButton = new JButton();
  JNLPLabel homepageLink = new JNLPLabel();
  AboutTable aboutTable;
  private final static String DEFAULT_APP_NAME = "Textuale 1.0";
  private final static String PARTS_PROP = "application.parts";
  private final static String PARTS_DESC = "application.parts.desc";
  private final static String REFERENCE_URL = "http://www.marinilli.com";

  /**
   * constructor
   */
  public AboutDialog(Frame frame) {
    super(frame, "Info", true);
    //initializes the about table
    aboutTable =
        new AboutTable(getItems(
System.getProperties().getProperty(PARTS_PROP)),
                       getItems(
System.getProperties().getProperty(PARTS_DESC)) );

    //GUI initialization
    JPanel mainPanel = new JPanel();
    JPanel centerPanel = new JPanel();
    JPanel southPanel = new JPanel();
    homepageLink.setURL(REFERENCE_URL);
    homepageLink.setText(REFERENCE_URL);
    JPanel p = new JPanel();
    p.add(homepageLink);

    JLabel titleLabel = new JLabel("<html><body><font size=\"+3\"><b>"+
        System.getProperties().getProperty("app.name", DEFAULT_APP_NAME));
    JLabel subTitleLabel1 = new JLabel("<html><body><font size=\"+1\">&copy;
2001 (M) Inc.");
    JLabel subTitleLabel2 = new JLabel("<html><body><font size=\"-1\">"+
        "Java "+
        System.getProperties().getProperty("java.version")+" on "+
        System.getProperties().getProperty("os.name"));
```

LISTING 13.4 Continued

```
JLabel subTitleLabel3 = new JLabel("<html><body><font size=\"+1\">"+
    "Loaded Modules:");
Box b = Box.createVerticalBox();
b.add(titleLabel);
b.add(subTitleLabel1);
b.add(subTitleLabel2);
b.add(subTitleLabel3);
mainPanel.setLayout(new BorderLayout());
closeButton.setText("close");
closeButton.addActionListener(new java.awt.event.ActionListener() {
  public void actionPerformed(ActionEvent e) {
    dispose();
  }
});
centerPanel.setBorder(BorderFactory.createEmptyBorder(4,4,4,4));
centerPanel.setLayout(new BorderLayout());
getContentPane().add(mainPanel);
mainPanel.add(centerPanel, BorderLayout.CENTER);
centerPanel.add(b, BorderLayout.NORTH);
centerPanel.add(new JScrollPane(aboutTable), BorderLayout.CENTER);
centerPanel.add(p, BorderLayout.SOUTH);
mainPanel.add(southPanel, BorderLayout.SOUTH);
southPanel.add(closeButton, null);

setSize(216,260);
setVisible(true);
}

/**
 * return a tokenized input string
 */
private String[] getItems(String s){
  if (s==null)
    s="";
  ArrayList result = new ArrayList();
  StringTokenizer st = new StringTokenizer(s,";:");
  while (st.hasMoreTokens()) {
    String w = st.nextToken();
    result.add(w);
  }
  String[] a = new String[result.size()];
  result.toArray(a);
  return a;
}

}
```

In line 28 of Listing 13.5, a DownloadService object is obtained and is then queried in order to discover the modules (implemented as JNLP *parts*) that are currently cached locally (line 31 of Listing 13.5).

LISTING 13.5 The AboutTable class.

```
package com.marinilli.b2.c13.util;
import javax.swing.*;
import javax.jnlp.*;
import javax.swing.table.*;
import java.util.*;
import com.marinilli.b2.ad.util.*;

/**
 * Chapter 13 - utility component to be shown in the about dialog
 *
 * @author Mauro Marinilli
 * @version 1.0
 */
public class AboutTable extends JTable {

  /**
   * constructor - creates the table model and populates it
   */
  public AboutTable(String[] parts, String[] desc) {
    Vector data = new Vector();
    Vector columnNames = new Vector(2);
    columnNames.add("name");
    columnNames.add("description");
    setRowSelectionAllowed(true);
    setColumnSelectionAllowed(false);
    setSelectionMode(ListSelectionModel.SINGLE_SELECTION);
    DownloadService ds =

(DownloadService)GeneralUtilities.getService("javax.jnlp.DownloadService");
    for (int i = 0; i < parts.length; i++) {
      Vector row = new Vector();
      if (ds.isPartCached(parts[i])) {
        row.add(parts[i]);
        row.add(desc[i]);
        data.add(row);
      }
    }
    setSelectionBackground(java.awt.Color.pink);
    setBackground(java.awt.Color.orange);
```

LISTING 13.5 Continued

```
      AboutTableModel atm = new AboutTableModel(data,columnNames);
      setModel(atm);
   }

   /**
    * inner class for table model
    */
   private static class AboutTableModel extends DefaultTableModel {
      public AboutTableModel(Vector d, Vector c) {
         super(d,c);
      }

      public boolean isCellEditable(int row, int col) {
         return false;
      }
   }
}
```

The list of all application modules and their description is available through the `AboutDialog` class (lines 30–32 in Listing 13.4) using the system properties set in the main JNLP file (lines 27–28 in Listing 13.1). Note that thanks to the support library discussed as follows (used by the `GeneralUtilites` class) the same mechanism is available to normal applications as well, as will be explained in Appendix D, "A JNLP Utility Library".

Finally, in Listing 13.6, the custom installer we used to take control of the whole application installation is listed. It can be modified to perform the installation of optional packages or other special resources, as suggested at the beginning of this chapter.

LISTING 13.6 The `Installer` Class

```
package com.marinilli.b2.c13;
import javax.jnlp.*;
import com.marinilli.b2.ad.util.*;

/**
 * Chapter 13 - textuale installer
 * @author Mauro Marinilli
 * @version 1.0
 */
public class Installer {
  ExtensionInstallerService eis;

  /**
```

LISTING 13.6   Continued

```
 * indirectly invoked by the JNLP Client for uninstallation
 */
private void uninstall (){
  System.out.println("Textuale uninstalled.");
}

/**
 * indirectly invoked by the JNLP Client for installation
 */
private void install (){
  eis = (ExtensionInstallerService)
        GeneralUtilities.getService("javax.jnlp.ExtensionInstallerService");
  if (eis!=null) {
    eis.setHeading("Textuale - Text Editor");
    eis.setStatus("Installing..");
    // in case of input methods or other needed optional packages
    // put here custom code expanding Listing 11.6
    for (int i=0; i<10; i++) {
      eis.updateProgress(i*10);
      try {
        Thread.currentThread().sleep(100);
      } catch (Exception e) {
        System.out.println(""+e);
      }
    }
    eis.installSucceeded(false);
  }
}

/**
 * launch the installer - used by the JNLP Client
 */
static public void main(String[] args) {
  String command = args[0];
  Installer inst = new Installer();
  if (command.equals("install"))
    inst.install();
  else if (command.equals("uninstall"))
    inst.uninstall();
}

}
```

13

> **Technical Note**
>
> Unfortunately, the installer was much more complex, involving the installation of the JAI opt. Package, used by the draw module. But the severe instability of such a feature in Web Start and the upcoming (soon after summer it seems) release of new facilities from Sun about optional packages obliged me to cut it down drastically, to what you can see now.

Note at line 46 in Listing 13.6 that the `Installer` class is managed by the JNLP Client through its `main` method, both for installation and uninstallation. Figure 13.5 depicts a screen shot from the first-time installation procedure.

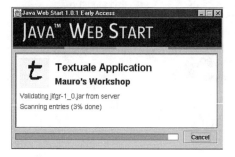

FIGURE 13.5

The installation process performed by Java Web Start.

Finally, we will not discuss the `draw` package that implements the draw editor module. Such a package is used here only as an example (you can see that it is rather fragile). It would take too long to discuss it...indeed, it could take another whole book to discuss it properly!

A JNLP Utility Library

The Textuale application uses a JNLP utility library, presented in Appendix D, "A JNLP Support Library". This library provides some service classes, such as those discussed in Chapter 11 plus some new ones. The old classes (for example `GeneralUtilities` that replaces the Utilities class presented in Chapter 11) were essentially retrofitted and expanded to fully integrate with the proposed framework in Appendix D.

We chose this approach (partial duplication of code and possible confusion on which class to use) for two reasons. On one hand, an incremental introduction has the advantage of flattening the learning curve, and on the other side separating "lightweight" and "fully-integrated" utility code allows for more freedom of choice.

Developers who want to use the single utilities classes proposed in this chapter and the other of this part of the book can do so without importing many classes. On the other side, developers can always take advantage of the utility library proposed in Appendix D. Here, we will discuss the additional services this library provides apart from those supplied by the `utility` class in Chapter 11. In this way, we will explain the code in this chapter as well.

When taking advantage of JNLP runtime services (for instance, the persistence service), developers make the implicit choice to run their applications on a JNLP Client. This could potentially tamper the portability of their Java code. In such a case, a common technique is to provide a thin implementation of those runtime services that will work even if the application is launched without an assisting JNLP Client. We provide a set of classes that "emulates" a JNLP Client—providing persistence, printing, and the other JNLP runtime services.

Of course, this technique has its shortcomings. In order to be lightweight (we don't want to reimplement a JNLP Client from scratch), it must be implemented as a pure Java library to be added with our deployed code. This way, our replacement mechanism for a JNLP Client cannot have access to data such as JNLP files, system-dependent resources, and so on. Furthermore, it may turn out to be incompatible with some real-world JNLP Clients. For example, some data saved with our library cannot be restored by Java Web Start or OpenJNLP clients. Indeed, such interoperability issues happen between different JNLP Clients as well, as we observed in Chapter 2. Nevertheless, this library has many advantages:

- It can be used for limited testing within a development environment without setting up the complete execution scenario for every minimal test.

- Even at execution time, a properly designed application can be run seamlessly as a common application or through a JNLP Client without renouncing to JNLP runtime services in both modalities. This will ease application development because there is no need to produce two different versions of the same code (a costly and complex solution)—one to be run from a JNLP client and the other one to be run as a simple command-line-based application.

- The library implementation may be modified and fine-tuned to handle special cases as needed.

We will not discuss here the details of such a library that are presented and discussed in Appendix D.

As a little example of the facilities provided by the support library, there is the localization feature (for instance, see line 57 in Listing 13.3) shown in the window title of Figure 13.6—the Textuale application is running on an Italian locale.

13

A COMPLETE
EXAMPLE

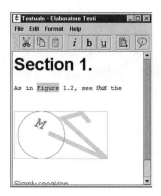

FIGURE 13.6

An example of the utility features provided by the support library. The Textuale application is running on an Italian locale.

Summary

In this chapter, we recapped much of what has already been said about JNLP technology through the use of a concrete example. We also used this application as a way to discuss the design options involved in deploying a complete application using the JNLP technology.

You can consult Appendix B for a JNLP 1.0 specification summary and Appendix D for the discussion of a general utility library used by the code in this example.

Appendixes

IN THIS PART

A Little Handbook for Java Deployment

IN THIS APPENDIX

This appendix contains some useful reference material for this book's contents and for practical reference.

It is useful for a fast lookup when in need of some practical advice for solving a deployment problem. It is not a substitute for the book contents; instead, it is a succinct, alternative organization of the book material structured in a hands-on fashion.

The first section is a very short summary of what was provided in Chapter 4, "Designing for Deployment." The second section proposes several useful categorizations of the many examples proposed in this book. The third section provides some details about the Unified Modeling Language (UML) formalism for documenting deployed software artifacts. Finally, the last section discusses some legal material involved with the redistribution and usage of third-party software modules, a common practice for Java developers.

Deployment Design in a Nutshell

This section succinctly summarizes what was discussed in Chapter 4 and other chapters of this book. It assumes a previous reading of the whole book.

To design a deployment circuit for a Java application is a complex task that involves many considerations. Here, we will describe briefly the main decisions involved. For a complete discussion, see the chapters of Part II, "Deployment Engineering," especially Chapter 4.

Three-Step Procedure

To reduce it to the bare essentials, we can think of the deployment design activity as a three-step sequence, in which deployment engineers have to define exactly the wanted deployment services, how to implement them in Java, and implement the planned deployment circuit using the chosen Java technologies.

1. Define the Required Deployment Services

The first step is to clearly determine which deployment services will be required by client applications. Chapter 4 defines a standard list of the most common deployment services.

2. Decide on the Deployment Technology

When choosing the deployment technology, two choices are possible: choosing a standard deployment technology (JNLP, applets, or some third-party deployment tools) or building your own deployment means. This latter choice is much more complex and expensive than customizing a general-purpose, ready-to-use deployment technology.

In order to make this decision, a deployment engineer should determine whether a given deployment policy is applicable on its particular application scenario. A comparison of some deployment technologies is shown in Table 6.1 of Chapter 6, "Deploying Existing Software." If no standard deployment tool can be employed, the only solution is to implement in-house the required deployment circuit.

In the following table (an extreme summing up of several considerations in Part II), the major shortcomings for some of the main deployment technologies are summarized. The ☺ symbol represents a high end-user burden, whereas the $ symbol represents the attendance of license fees in order to use that deployment technology.

Technology	Shortcomings
Installer Utilities	$, ☺
JNLP 1.0	mainly technical, see below
Applet	limited deploym. services
Third-Party Deployment Solutions	$, ☺

NOTE

Although the Sun Plug-In provided the capability to deploy full-fledged J2SE applets, developers should be aware that the applet model itself, though very handy on the deployment side, could appear limited in many cases. Applets are document-bounded (by the document hosting the Web page), and little control over the lifecycle could be enforced by developers. For this and other reasons, they don't work very well when implementing complex applications.

An even simpler approach, valid for many cases, is the following.

First of all, if the planned deployment circuit features only simple one-shot deployment, installer utilities could be used for installing the given software. Analogously, if our executables could be sensibly implemented as an applet, the deployment choice is clear.

If none of these apply, it is left to see whether the JNLP technology may be utilized for the given application deployment. If it doesn't apply, for technical or other reasons (see Chapter 4 or Chapter 7, "Building Your Own Deployment Solution," for the possible reasons behind a deployment means choice), developers could resort to advanced third-party deployment solutions (some examples of such tools are presented in Chapter 3, "Existing Solutions") or to self-implemented deployment means.

Regarding JNLP technology, two technical limitations need to be explicitly mentioned:

- JNLP Clients can communicate with their deployment servers only through a Web connection. No communication protocols other than HTTP are supported.
- Only J2SE applications can be deployed with JNLP.

When such requirements cannot be matched, other deployment solutions should be investigated. In particular, when no Web connection (that is, the HTTP protocol) is available, only ad-hoc deployment options (see the example in Chapter 6 or the whole Chapter 7) or some third-party deployment tools are left. A careful use of the JNLP technology can reduce the end-user burden to the minimum (the so-called "one-click" installations).

3. Implement the Planned Deployment Circuit
See Chapter 4 for more details. For JNLP-specific advice, Chapter 13, "A Complete Example," provides a recapping, practical discussion.

A Roadmap to the Source Code in This Book

This section provides some useful classifications of the source code provided in this book for future reference. This section is intended as an alternative fast track to the code resources provided throughout this book, which can be used as practical help.

The next subsection lists all the code examples provided in this book, whereas the following subsections classify such examples for an easier lookup.

Code Example Complete List

Table A.1 lists all the major code examples proposed in this book, in order of appearance.

TABLE A.1. All Examples Provided in This Book

Name	Listing	Description
AMIDlet	5.1–3	MIDlet deployment
LicenseServlet	5.4,5.11,5.12	Additional deployment service for MIDlets
Card test	5.5–10	JavaCard deployment
bank	6.1–5	Complete deployment solution with AH
CDROM Installer	7.1–5	CD-ROM installer
Installer applet	7.6–7	J2SE applet installer
deploylet suite	7.8–13	Complete deployment solution without AH

A Little Handbook for Java Deployment

APPENDIX A

401

A

A LITTLE
HANDBOOK FOR
JAVA DEPLOYMENT

TABLE A.1. Continued

Name	Listing	Description
editor1	8.4–6	Sample JNLP application
splash package	8.7–11	JNLP custom installer
test	8.1–3	JNLP for local files
installwin	9.3–7	JNLP native installer
AnApplet	9.8–10	Simple demo applet
JNLPinstaller	9.14–15	JNLP installer customizing standard download window
LazyEditor	10.3–5	JNLP lazy resources installation
Security tester	10.7–8	JNLP security demo
Utilities	11.1	Simple JNLP utility class
JNLPLabel	11.2	JNLP URL launcher widget
FileContentsExample	11.3	JNLP file runtime access services example
DownloadExample	11.4	JNLP download runtime service example
PersistenceStorage	11.5	JNLP persistence runtime service example
InstallerExample	11.6–8	JNLP optional package installer
PrintServiceExample	11.9	JNLP printing runtime service example
AnApplication	11.10	A demo application
VersionManagement	12.3–7	Complete package for JNLP versioning implementation
Textuale	13.1–3,13.6	Complete JNLP application (features: ad-hoc installer, lazy modules)
AboutDialog	13.4–5	JNLP utility widget
JNLP utility library	D.*	JNLP utility library

Code Examples Organized per Most Common Scenarios

Here, we categorize the major autonomous examples provided in this book into three main categories: intranet, Internet, and all other scenarios. When developers are in need of some deployment examples for such a situation, they can reference one of the reported examples.

Intranet Deployment

In this section are collected all the examples suitable to be used for intranet deployment.

- Installer applet (Listings 7.6–7) for installing files using a signed applet.
- "The Bank" package (Listings 6.1–5) for an example of a complete deployment circuit.
- The Deploylet package (Listings 7.8–13) for an example of a complete deployment solution build on top of the Plug-In deployment means.

Web Deployment

In this section are collected all the examples suitable to be used for Internet deployment.

- The deployment examples for J2EE and J2ME (MID Profile) presented in Chapter 5, "Deployment Options for Non-J2SE Clients."
- All the JNLP-related examples (see the "Code Examples Organized per Deployment Service" section below)
- Also, the bank example could be used effectively over an Internet connection.

Other Deployment Examples

This section lists the most important examples that don't fit into the previous two categories.

- CD-ROM and multiple means deployment through the CDLauncher example (Listings 7.1–5).
- The JavaCard applet example (Listings 5.5–10).

Code Examples Organized per Deployment Service

For the reference list of deployment services, see Chapter 4.

Figure A.1 graphically illustrates the organization of the examples in this book. For an introduction to the diagram in Figure A.1, see Chapter 4.

The following paragraphs discuss the supplied examples organized on the basis of the provided deployment services.

One-Shot Installation

The code examples that implement this basic deployment service (the capability of delivering and installing a given client application) are listed as follows.

- The CD-ROM launcher package in Chapter 7 (Listings 7.1–5) covers the use of Java technology for packaging a custom installer together with the application to deploy on a CD-ROM support.

A Little Handbook for Java Deployment

APPENDIX A

403

A

A LITTLE
HANDBOOK FOR
JAVA DEPLOYMENT

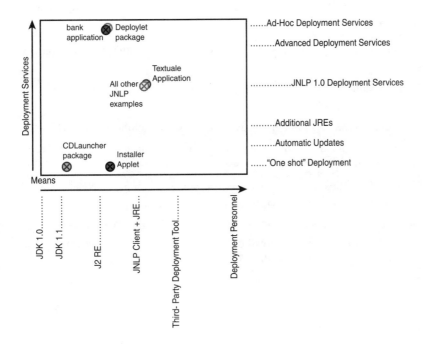

FIGURE A.1

The code examples graphically described.

- The InstallerApplet in Chapter 7 (Listings 7.6–7) shows how an application can be downloaded and installed via a Web page by using a Java applet. It relies upon the Plug-In technology that comes bundled with Sun's JRE installation package.
- Code provided in Chapter 5 shows how to install Java executables for some non-J2SE platforms (J2ME MIDlet profile, JavaCard, and J2EE are covered).

Note that all the code examples reported in the following sections provide such a deployment service.

Automatic Updates and Additional JREs

The code samples in this book that implement such a deployment feature are included in the following two sections.

JNLP 1.0

The following code samples show some uses of JNLP deployment technology. They are organized in three lists for quicker access.

General JNLP examples:

- `Test` application (Listings 8.1–3) shows how to use local file system resources with JNLP.
- A simple example of a basic yet complete JNLP deployment is provided in the `editor1` application (Listings 8.4–6).
- An example of lazy resource usage is the `LazyEditor` application (Listings 10.3–5).
- The security demo shown in Listings 10.7–8 provides an example of the security model of JNLP 1.0. It uses JNLP runtime services as well.
- The *Textuale* application (see Chapter 13) provides a complete JNLP application deployment example, featuring among the others: ad-hoc installer support, lazy resources.
- Version management classes (see Chapter 12, "Server-side Deployment Support") provide a package for implementing version-based management. They could be used within a servlet environment for providing JNLP versioned download. A front-end test GUI class is supplied for direct testing.

Examples of the use of JNLP runtime services are the following:

- Splash window (Listings 8.7–11).
- Native code installer (Listings 9.3–7).
- Customize the JNLP Client's download window (Listings 9.14–15).
- `FileContents` manipulation (Listing 11.3).
- `DownloadService` example (Listing 11.4).
- Printing example via JNLP (Listing 11.9).
- The *Textuale* application (see Chapter 13) provides another installer example, similar to the download window customization example of Chapter 9, "The JNLP Protocol."
- Optional packages installation example (Listings 11.6–8).

JNLP general utility, reusable code:

- The `Utilities` class (Listing 11.1). A "lightweight" utility class that provides simpler JNLP runtime services access, internationalization support, and robust icon and resource acquisition services. It doesn't automatically handle standalone application execution (it doesn't require the utility package in Appendix D).
- A JNLP label (Listing 11.2). A Swing component that shows a clickable URL-like label that brings up a Web browser window. The label text and URL address are separated.
- A persistence wrapper class (Listing 11.5). It wraps JNLP persistence services, providing—among other services—a serialization-like interface for reading and writing objects identified with simple strings or complete URLs.

A Little Handbook for Java Deployment

APPENDIX A

405

A

A LITTLE
HANDBOOK FOR
JAVA DEPLOYMENT

- An about dialog utility JDialog subclass (Listings 13.4—5). Useful for implementing the application about box, it provides a built-in mechanism for inspecting the currently installed application modules. It uses the JNLP Label widget.

- The utility package in Appendix D discusses a general purpose JNLP utility library ready to be used in JNLP-deployed applications. Such a library emulates to some extent the JNLP runtime environment client that applications use. In this way, programs could be launched seamlessly via JNLP or as standalone applications. It includes an extended version of the Utilities class presented in Chapter 11, "Runtime Client Services."

Advanced Ad-Hoc Deployment Services

For deployment engineers who cannot resort to the previous examples or standard deployment solutions, this book also provides examples of complete deployment solutions to be adapted to the given situation. Such packages are inherently complex, and differ from the code described in the preceding subsections because these are intended as complete, self-standing deployment solutions—not episodic, circumscribed code examples. Following this line, source code is accompanied with architecture discussions and other considerations.

The following two solutions can be adapted to practically meet any deployment needs. They differ (apart from the scenario) in that the first example is built totally from scratch, and the second relies upon the applet model's basic deployment services.

- The bank package (see Chapter 6) provides a full-blown deployment solution using a custom Application Helper. It shows the widely used classloader mechanism, as well.

- The deploylet package (see Chapter 7) supplies a full-blown deployment solution that doesn't require an Application Helper. It uses the Plug-In technology for J2SE applets.

Using UML for Deployment Documentation

In this section, we will see the Unified Modeling Language (UML) formalism for software deployment. Like deployment itself, UML deployment diagrams are often overlooked by technical writers and developers, who prefer to concentrate their efforts on more "popular" UML model diagrams, such as static class, use-case, and scenario diagrams. The so-called UML "physical" diagrams are of two types:

- Deployment diagrams. They show the physical relationships among software and hardware components in the installed system. They are composed of *nodes*, representing some type of computational item, often a hardware unit (from a back-end server to an embedded device). Then, we may have *connections* among nodes, showing the communications paths over which the application communicates with the other nodes.

- Component diagrams. They zoom into the system, describing the various *components* it is made up of and their *interactions*. In Java components, JAR files are often physically deployed on the client machine (but not necessarily present locally), and dependencies could range from compilation and compatibility relationships (for example: "JAR file 'A' version 2.1 cannot work with JAR files 'B' older than 1.0") or communication relationships.

These diagrams are used to document the final deployed software system, and are intended mainly for system management on the client machines and maintenance developers reading. An often-overlooked aspect of such diagrams is their utility as a design tool for clarifying the overall deployment mechanisms in a design phase. Unfortunately, such diagrams (when written at all) are used for documenting the implemented scenario when everything is laid out definitively (mistakes included) after the development phase has finished.

Often the two diagrams are mixed together to provide a more intuitive view of the deployed system. Figure A.2 shows the graphical notations for the main entities (component, node, objects, and their relationships) used in these diagrams.

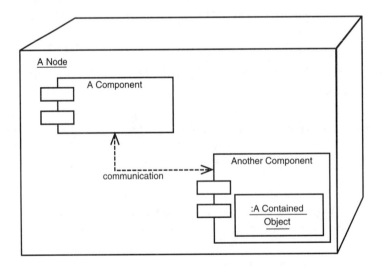

FIGURE A.2

The main pieces of deployment and component UML diagrams.

We conclude this section with an example of a little system documented with such diagrams, reported in Figure A.3. The proposed system is a JNLP-deployed application composed of two JAR files (core.jar and extra.jar) installed in the JNLP Client cache. The JNLP Client communicates with a deployment servlet, located on a remote host called the Deployment Server. The application communicates with another remote host, called the Business Server, via a JDBC connection, in order to provide business transactions on a remote database.

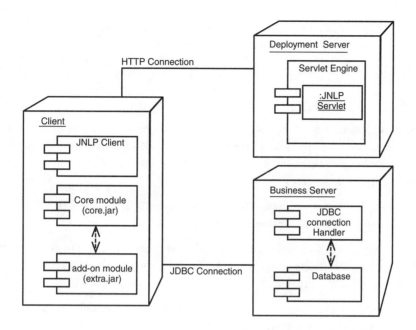

FIGURE A.3
An example of deployment and component UML diagrams mixed together to describe a real system.

Legal Notes

An often-overlooked aspect of deployment is its legal side as involves the redistribution of third-party software needed for our application. We will focus only on deployment-related issues here.

Commercial Third-Party Redistributables

Given the huge number of slightly different contracts each vendor establishes, we are forced to discuss only the main features of such contracts.

Generally speaking, there could be three types of inclusion of a third-party library in your application:

- Including the vendor's provided JAR files.
- As individual class files (that is, unjarring the related JAR files).
- As class files included in your application JAR files.

Often, the most important issue for developers is the ability to "break" the provided (large) JAR files in order to selectively use only the needed classes. This feature is not always accorded to third-party libraries licensees. In this case, developers have to include in their distribution the provided JAR files without any modifications.

Consult vendor's redistribution policy documents or contact them directly for any inquiry.

Open Source Libraries

Given the possible confusion that could arise for open source contracts, we discuss here this increasingly common case. The kind of use that can be made of such libraries is basically of two types: including the libraries in your applications and (wherever the sources are available) eventually modifying the sources.

For a handy list of all the major open source licenses, visit the following URL: `http://www.opensource.org/licenses/`.

There are a large variety of open source licenses. It may be of some help to briefly mention the main types, as regards software deployment. All the following license types permit to redistribute software at no cost and provide to developers the source codes as well.

- Royalty-free libraries that can be used freely, but cannot be modified by user programmers, even if sources are publicly available.

- Licenses that allow for source modifications, such as the BSD licensing model. BSD-style licenses allow for open source software to be combined with proprietary software and be licensed with no restrictions (that is, also as proprietary software itself). It requires a citation of Licensing Authority in any derivative use. The Apache licensing model permits public check-ins to the core libraries as well.

- Finally, licenses that allow for sources modifications, public check-in of code, and impose the constraint that all derivatives must be free. The General Public License (GPL) used for example for GNU or Linux licensing. Under the GPL, you can distribute the original work or its derivatives to whomever you like, as long as you make readily available the source to the original work, the modifications you obtained, and any modifications you made. Any licenses you give must also follow the GPL restrictions.

Be aware of the type of open-source license with which your executables come shipped. Depending on the particular license, often you may only distribute the software and the modifications in a compiled form as long as some added value is provided (for example, IBM's XML4J package commercial license).

A brief mention about the so-called "Viral Clause" used among the others by the GPL license. This clause requires that software incorporating fragments of GPL-licensed code be licensed (in its entirety) under the GPL. A compromise version, the Library GPL (LGPL), permits other software to use (and redistribute) a LGPL-licensed library without itself being under the GPL.

Note finally that the Java Community Source License doesn't allow for code modifications (apart from research purposes only), as we will see in the next section.

A Note on the Sun JRE distribution Package

The Sun licenses for both SDK and JRE products are quite articulate. We will cover here only the technical details. We assume that developers are familiar with the main provisions the license imposes. For any other detail, see the license text (file "LICENSE" in the JRE's root directory).

When redistributing Sun's JRE, the following two constraints have to be observed.

- Any modification of the Java 2 Runtime Environment is prohibited.

- In your application's product license, the conditions stated in the Sun Binary License Agreement must be included.

Furthermore, some files and directories in the JRE redistribution can be omitted, as discussed below.

Files that Can Be Omitted from the JRE Distribution Package

When not needed by the particular application, the following files may be omitted by the redistributed JRE package.

- Localized applications. The character conversion classes and all other locale support: `lib/i18n.jar`.

- RMI-related tools. The Java RMI activation system daemon: `bin/rmid`, the Java Remote Object Registry: `bin/rmiregistry`, and the Java IDL name server: `bin/tnameserv`.

- Security-related tools. The key and certificate management tool: `bin/keytool`, and the policy file creation and management tool: `bin/policytool`.

- The extension directory: `lib/ext/`.

Files from the Java 2 SDK that Can be Redistributed

Some files of the Java 2 SDK, Standard Edition (that cannot be redistributed) can be included in JRE redistributions when needed for the given applications. Such files are listed as follows.

All paths are relative to the top-level directory of the SDK, whose `jre/` is a subdirectory.

- All additional font files: `jre/lib/fonts/*.tff`. The default font contained in the file `LucidaSansRegular.ttf` is contained in the JRE distribution.

- Color map conversions with Java2D API. `jre/lib/cmm/PYCC.pf`. Color-management profile.

- MIDI soundbank support, present in the Java 2 SDK, but removed from the JRE. File: `jre/lib/audio/soundbank.gm`.

JNLP (Java Network Launching Protocol) Specification

IN THIS APPENDIX

This appendix covers the specification and reference material for the JNLP protocol implementation. It refers to version 1.0.

It is divided into two parts: the client- and the server-side specifications.

Client

The client side of the JNLP specification refers to the JNLP file elements and attributes, the runtime services API and other details of the JNLP protocol.

JNLP File

All the allowed XML elements and their attributes, organized in sections, are gathered here for reference—based on the main elements and all their subelements clustered together.

Table B.1 helps you locate quickly the information about the elements in the JNLP file. For example, to know more about the homepage element, consult the information element section.

TABLE B.1 Elements for the JNLP file

Element Name	Subelement of
jnlp	-
information	jnlp
title	information
vendor	information
homepage	information
description	information
icon	information
offline-allowed	information
security	jnlp
all-permissions	security
j2ee-application-client-permissions	security
resources	jnlp
j2se	resources
jar	resources
nativelib	resources
property	resources
value	property
package	jnlp

TABLE B.1 Continued

Element Name	Subelement of
application-desc	jnlp
argument	application-desc
applet-desc	jnlp
param	applet-desc
component-desc	jnlp
installer-desc	jnlp
extension	resources
ext-download	extension

JNLP Root Element

The `jnlp` element is the root element in JNLP files. It can have the following attributes:

- `spec`: Specifies the version.

- `codebase`: Specifies the location of the root of all the relative external resources used in the JNLP file. An example of a relative external resource is `jnlp/resources.jar`.

Information Element

The *information element* lists all the information needed by the JNLP Client to manage the launched application regarding the OS and/or the end-user.

Its only attribute, `locale`, specifies the `Locales` (separated by a space) that should be in use on the client platform in order to consider the data in that information element. If the current `Locale` doesn't match any of the `Locales` specified in this attribute, all the `information` element data is ignored. `Locale` definitions and matching are standard Java. For details, have a look at the Java internationalization trial tutorial at `http://java.sun.com/docs/books/tutorial/i18n/index.html`.

TIP

All the data contained in an `information` element without a locale attribute is considered to be locale-independent. Always put a locale-independent `information` element first, in order to supply default values. Then, use locale-specific `information` elements for the various languages supported by the application.

Allowed subelements are described in the following sections.

title Subelement

The title subelement specifies the name of the application to be launched.

vendor Subelement

The vendor subelement specifies the application's vendor.

homepage Subelement

The homepage subelement has only one attribute, href, which specifies the Web page where end-users will find more information about the application.

icon Subelement

The icon subelement specifies the application's icon. There are five possible attributes, all optional:

- width: Specifies the image width in pixels.
- height: Specifies the image height in pixels.
- kind: Specifies the intended type of icon, among the following possible values: default, selected, disabled, rollover.
- depth: Specifies the number of possible colors in that image.
- size: Specifies the size of the icon file to be downloaded.

offline-allowed Subelement

The offline-allowed subelement specifies whether the application should be launched by the JNLP Client, even when the client system is not connected to the network. If this element is omitted, the application will not run in offline mode.

description Subelement

The description subelement gives a brief description of the application. It has one attribute that can have one of the three values:

- tooltip: The description string will be used as a tooltip by the JNLP Client and/or the client OS.
- short: The description string will be used for text descriptions longer than a single line.
- one-line: The description string will be used for brief list-like descriptions.

For longer descriptions, it is better to use a Web page pointed to by the homepage element.

security Element

The security element defines the security level needed for the application. There are two empty subelements of this element.

all-permissions Empty Subelement

When used with a trusted application (that is, signed and accepted by the user), this subelement grants all the permissions to the client application.

j2ee-application-client-permissions Empty Subelement

When used with a trusted application (that is, signed and explicitly accepted by the user), this subelement grants the permissions shown in Table B.2 to the client application.

TABLE B.2   Permissions

Affected Permission String	Semantics
java.awt.AWTPermission	access system Clipboard
java.awt.AWTPermission	access event queue
java.awt.AWTPermission	show window without warning banner
java.lang.RuntimePermission	exit JVM
java.lang.RuntimePermission	load library
java.lang.RuntimePermission	queue print job
java.net.Socket.Permission	socket connection
java.io.FilePermission	read/write files
java.util.PropertyPermission	read properties

package Element

The package element maps Java packages to JAR files, which is useful only for lazily down-loaded JARs. Using this, the JNLP Client knows where the needed classes are, and waits until the right moment to download only the necessary files.

The package element can have three different attributes:

- name: String that identifies a set of Java classes based on their package. This string closely resembles the syntax of the import statement in Java, particularly the use of the ".*" construct.
- part: Specifies the classes in the name attribute.
- recursive: Maximum heap size, a JVM parameter. It makes sense only for non-exact part values; that is, that contain ".*". It is an optional attribute.

resources Element

Describes a logical component of the resources needed by the application. It has six subelements and three optional attributes:

- os: The given resource can be used only if the os value matches the beginning of the os.name Java System property string. To specify the space character in the string, use '\ '.
- arch: The given resource can be used only if the arch value matches the beginning of the os.arch Java System property string.
- locale: Specifies the Locale for that resource. See the information element.

property Subelement

Specifies Java System properties. It has two mandatory attributes:

- key: The key for that property.
- value: The value associated with that key. It overwrites previously set values.

jar Subelement

The jar element specifies a JAR file to be loaded by the JNLP Client through its ClassLoader.

Attributes allowed for this element are as follows:

- version: An optional attribute that uniquely identifies (together with the href attribute) the JAR file. See the versioning section for details.
- href: The URL (only the HTTP protocol is allowed) that points to the JAR file on the server. This is a required attribute.
- size: An optional attribute that specifies the size of the JAR file, measured in bytes.
- download: Specifies when it must be loaded by the JNLP Client. It has two possible values: eager or lazy.
- part: An optional attribute for grouping together resources. Parts are local to the JNLP file. Specifications of this attribute also influence the downloading. All resources with the same part attribute are downloaded together.
- main: The JAR that contains the class to be launched through its main(..) method. Only one main attribute can be used for a JNLP file. If no main attribute is specified, the first jar element encountered in the JNLP file is used as the main JAR.

nativelib Subelement

Specifies a JAR file that contains native libraries. The loading is left to the launched application (through the System.loadLibrary method). Attributes allowed for this element are as follows:

- version: An optional attribute that uniquely identifies (together with the href attribute) the JAR file. See the versioning section for details.

- href: The URL (only the HTTP protocol is allowed) that points to the JAR file on the server. This is a required attribute.

- size: An optional attribute that specifies the size of the JAR file, measured in bytes.

- part: An optional attribute that specifies the part the JAR file belongs to. (The same as the jar element.)

- download: Specifies when it must be loaded by the JNLP Client. It has two possible values: eager or lazy.

extension Subelement

The extension element specifies information about the extension to be included in the including resources element.

The extension element has three attributes:

- name: The name of the extension.

- version: An optional attribute that uniquely identifies (together with the href attribute) the extension.

- href: The URL that launches the extension-downloading procedure.

ext-download Subelement

The extension element can contain other subelements of the ext-download type. These elements specify when different parts of an extension should be downloaded by the JNLP Client. It synchronizes parts (that is, applications) with component extensions for a better optimization of their download.

This element has three attributes:

- ext-part: Name of the extension part.

- download: Specifies when it must be loaded by the JNLP Client. It has two possible values: eager or lazy.

- part: Specifies a part defined in the JNLP file.

j2se Subelement

The j2se element specifies information about the Java runtime environment to use with that resource.

The j2se element can contain nested resources elements. This nesting is meaningful only at the first level. j2se elements that are nested in such resources elements are ignored. The information in nested `resources` elements is used only if the client JNLP uses the specified JRE; otherwise, the data are ignored.

Three attributes are used:

- `version`: Version string that specifies the supported versions of the JRE. See section about versioning identification.
- `initial-heap-size`: Initial heap size, a JVM parameter. Modifiers allowed are "m" ("64m" is the same as "67108864" because it is equal to 64 * 1024 * 1024) and "k" ("256k" is the same as "262144"—that is, 256 * 1024). Modifiers are not case-sensitive.
- `max-heap-size`: Maximum heap size, a JVM parameter. Modifiers are defined as in the `initial-heap-size` attribute.

`application-desc` Empty Element

This element describes the resources needed to launch the application. It has an optional attribute, `main-class`, which specifies the Java class containing the `main` method. The resolution of the `main-class` is described in the launch mechanism section.

`argument` Subelement

Only one subelement is allowed for the `application-desc` element. The `argument` element describes the command line arguments passed to the main method of the class to be launched.

CAUTION

The order of the `argument` elements in the JNLP file is meaningful. It is with this same order that arguments are passed to the invoked `main(argv)` method.

`applet-desc` Empty Element

This element identifies all the resources needed to launch the applet. Resources are loaded from the `resources` elements. The attributes are as follows:

- `main-class`: The main applet class to be launched.
- `width`: The applet's width, in pixels.
- `height`: The applet's height, in pixels.
- `name`: Specifies the applet name.

param **Subelement**

This element specifies information to be passed to the applet. Two attributes are used that mimic closely the applet tag in HTML:

- name: The name of the parameter to be set in the applet.
- value: The current value for the applet parameter.

component-desc **Empty Element**

In large applications, it could be useful to identify software components to reuse in different applications. When this empty element is present, the resources in the JNLP file are considered to belong to the defined component. It has no attributes.

installer-desc **Empty Element**

When this element is present, the JNLP file is meant to describe a so-called installer extension. That is, an application is launched only once—the first time the JNLP file is used. It has only one attribute, the optional main-class attribute, which specifies the class to be launched through its main(..) method.

Client Application Environment

A number of classes offer different services to the applications launched by a JNLP Client. In order to do so, the launched applications must have the proper permissions.

Class ServiceManager

The ServiceManager class is an abstract class from which all services offered to launched applications derive.

The ServiceManager provides static methods to look up JNLP services. Because this class is abstract and final, it cannot be instantiated.

Requests are delegated to a ServiceManagerStub object, which must be set up by the JNLP Client on startup using the setServiceManagerStub method.

- static String[] getServiceNames()

  Returns the names of all services implemented by the JNLP Client.

- static Object lookup(String serviceName) throws
  UnavailableServiceException

  Asks the JNLP Client for a service with a given name.

- static void setServiceManagerStub(ServiceManagerStub stub)

  Sets the object that all lookup and getServiceNames methods are delegated to.

Interface `ServiceManagerStub`

This interface is a stub for the `ServiceManager`'s methods. It is implemented by the JNLP Client with a concrete class and then registered with the `ServiceManager.setServiceManagerStub` method. `ServiceManagerStub` wraps a hashtable containing the implemented services ready to be returned as needed to launched applications.

- `String[] getServiceNames()`

  Returns the names of all services as implemented by the JNLP Client.

- `Object lookup(String name)`

  Asks the JNLP Client for a service with the given `name`. The method is meant to always return the same instance. Note that the type of the returned service can be any class, that is, the service interfaces do not extend to a common service super-type.

Interface `BasicService`

The `BasicService` interface provides access to the `codebase` of the application. It also offers simple interaction with the native browser eventually present on the given platform.

- `java.net.URL getCodeBase()`

  Returns the codebase for the application.

- `boolean isOffline()`

  Returns `true` if the client is offline at that moment.

- `boolean isWebBrowserSupported()`

  Returns `true` if a Web browser that is supported by the client JNLP is present on the client platform.

- `boolean showDocument(java.net.URL url)`

  Points the Web browser to the specified URL. Returns `false` if the client platform or the JNLP Client doesn't support a Web browser.

Interface `FileContents`

The `FileContents` interface wraps up the contents of a file to be read by the launched applications with adequate permissions.

- `boolean canRead()`

  Returns `true` if the file can be read.

- `boolean canWrite()`

  Returns `true` if the file can be (over)written.

- `java.io.InputStream getInputStream()`

Gets an `InputStream` from the file.

- `long getLength()`

  Returns the file length.

- `long getMaxLength()`

  Returns the maximum file length for the file, as previously set by the creator of this object.

- `String getName()`

  Returns the filename.

- `java.io.OutputStream getOutputStream(boolean append)`

  Returns an `OutputStream` to the file (see the `java.io.OutputStream` class for more details).

- `JNLPRandomAccessFile getRandomAccessFile(String mode)`

  Returns a `JNLPRandomAccessFile` proxy to the file's contents.

- `long setMaxLength(long maxlength)`

  Sets the maximum file length for the file.

Interface `FileOpenService`

The `FileOpenService` exposes the capability to open files from the client's local disks to launched applications.

- `FileContents openFileDialog(String pathHint, String[] extensions)`

  Asks (through the use of a dialog box) the user to choose a single file.

- `FileContents[] openMultiFileDialog(String pathHint, String[] extensions)`

  Asks the user to choose one or more files from a GUI dialog box.

Interface `FileSaveService`

Models the capability from launched applications to perform file modifications on the client's local disk.

- `FileContents saveAsFileDialog(String pathHint, String[] extensions, FileContents contents)`

  Asks the user to save a file.

- `FileContents saveFileDialog(String pathHint, String[] extensions, java.io.InputStream stream, String name)`

  Asks the user to save a file.

Interface `PersistenceService`

The `PersistenceService` interface offers methods for storing entries on the client side persistently. Entries have URLs as keys. Offers a service similar to the cookie mechanism on Web browsers.

- Static fields: `int CACHED` (the server has an up-to-date copy of the entry), `DIRTY` (the opposite of `CACHED`), `TEMPORARY` (the file can be re-created at any moment).

- `long create(java.net.URL url, long maxsize)`

  Creates a new entry in the persistent cache, with the specified URL as a key and a maxsize size.

- `void delete(java.net.URL url)`

  Removes the stream associated with the given URL from the client-side data persistence store.

- `FileContents get(java.net.URL url)`

  Returns a `FileContents` object representing the file's content.

- `String[] getNames(java.net.URL url)`

  Returns an array of strings containing the names of all the entries for a given URL.

- `int getTag(java.net.URL url)`

  Returns an `int` corresponding to the current value of the tag for the persistent data store entry associated with the given URL. The returned value surrogates are enumerated with the following possible values: `CACHED`, `DIRTY`, `TEMPORARY`.

- `void setTag(java.net.URL url, int tag)`

  Associates the given URL with the given tag value, having the following possible values: `CACHED`, `DIRTY`, `TEMPORARY`.

Interface `ClipboardService`

The `ClipboardService` interface provides basic interaction (`set` and `get`) with the client platform's Clipboard. It is always assumed that the client system supports a Clipboard.

- `java.awt.datatransfer.Transferable getContents()`

  Returns a `Transferable` object representing the current contents of the Clipboard.

- `void setContents(java.awt.datatransfer.Transferable contents)`

  Assigns the current contents of the Clipboard to the given `Transferable` object.

Interface `DownloadService`

Offers downloading services to the launched applications.

- DownloadServiceListener getDefaultProgressWindow()

  Returns a default DownloadServiceListener implementation. When passed to a load method, it should pop up and update a progress window as the load progresses.

- boolean isExtensionPartCached(java.net.URL ref, String version, String part)

  Returns true if the given part of the given extension is cached, and the extension and part are mentioned in the JNLP file for the application.

- boolean isExtensionPartCached(java.net.URL ref, String version, String[] parts)

  Returns true if the given parts of the given extension are cached, and the extension and parts are mentioned in the JNLP file for the application.

- boolean isPartCached(String part)

  Returns true if the part referred to by the given string is cached, and that part is mentioned in the JNLP file for the application.

- boolean isPartCached(String[] parts)

  Returns true if the parts referred to by the given array are cached, and those parts are mentioned in the JNLP file for the application.

- boolean isResourceCached(java.net.URL ref, String version)

  Returns true if the resource is correctly mentioned in the JNLP file, is referred to by the given URL and version, and is currently cached.

- void loadExtensionPart(java.net.URL ref, String version, String[] parts, DownloadServiceListener progress)

  Downloads the given parts of the given extension if the parts and the extension are mentioned in the JNLP file for the application.

- void loadExtensionPart(java.net.URL ref, String version, String part, DownloadServiceListener progress)

  If the part and the extension are correctly mentioned in the JNLP file for the application, it downloads the given part of the given extension.

- void loadPart(String[] parts, DownloadServiceListener progress)

  If the parts are present in the application's JNLP file, it downloads them.

- void loadPart(String part, DownloadServiceListener progress)

  If the part is present in the application's JNLP file, it downloads it.

- void loadResource(java.net.URL ref, String version, DownloadServiceListener progress)

Downloads the given resource if the resource is mentioned in the JNLP file for the application.

- `void removeExtensionPart(java.net.URL ref, String version, String part)`

  Removes the given part of the given extension from the cache, given that the part and the extension are mentioned in the JNLP file for the application.

- `void removeExtensionPart(java.net.URL ref, String version, String[] parts)`

  Removes the given parts of the given extension from the cache, given that the parts and the extension are correctly mentioned in the JNLP file for the application.

- `void removePart(String part)`

  If the part is correctly mentioned in the JNLP file, it removes it from the cache.

- `void removePart(String[] parts)`

  Removes the given parts from the cache.

- `void removeResource(java.net.URL ref, String version)`

  Removes the given resource from the cache.

Interface `DownloadServiceListener`

A listener specialized in downloading events in order to better track the downloading process.

- `void downloadFailed(java.net.URL url, String version)`

  A JNLP Client's `DownloadService` implementation should call this method if a download fails or aborts unexpectedly.

- `void progress(java.net.URL url, String version, long readSoFar, long total, int overallPercent)`

  A JNLP Client's `DownloadService` implementation has to call this method during a download, repeatedly, to notice the download progress.

- `void upgradingArchive(java.net.URL url, String version, int patchPercent, int overallPercent)`

  A JNLP Client's `DownloadService` implementation should call this method at least several times when applying an incremental update to an in-cache resource by means of the JARDiff protocol.

- `void validating(java.net.URL url, String version, long entry, long total, int overallPercent)`

  Implementations of `DownloadService` should call this method at least several times during validation of a download.

Class `UnavailableServiceException`

The `UnavailableServiceException` exception is thrown by the `ServiceManager` and its `ServiceManagerStub` (because an exception extends `java.lang.Exception`).

- `UnavailableServiceException()`

  Constructs an `UnavailableServiceException` with `null` as its error detail message.

- `UnavailableServiceException(String msg)`

  Constructs an `UnavailableServiceException` with the specified detail message.

Interface `JNLPRandomAccessFile`

Extends both `java.io.DataInput` and `java.io.DataOutput`. It offers a random access-like interface to files.

- `void close()`

  Closes this random access filestream, and releases any system resources associated with it.

- `long getFilePointer()`

  Returns the current offset in this file.

- `long length()`

  Returns the file length.

- `int read()`

  Reads an `int` from this file.

- `int read(byte[] b)`

  Reads up to `b.length` bytes of data from this file into an array of bytes.

- `int read(byte[] b, int off, int len)`

  Reads up to `len` bytes of data from this file into an array of bytes.

- `boolean readBoolean()`

  Reads a `boolean` from this file.

- `byte readByte()`

  Reads a byte from the file.

- `char readChar()`

  Reads a Unicode character from this file.

- `double readDouble()`

  Reads a double.

- `float readFloat()`

Reads a float.

- void readFully(byte[] b)

Reads b.length bytes from this file into the byte array.

- void readFully(byte[] b, int off, int len)

Reads exactly len bytes from this file into the byte array.

- int readInt()

Reads an integer from this file (four bytes, two complement).

- String readLine()

Reads the next line of text from the file.

- long readLong()

Reads a signed long.

- short readShort()

Reads a signed short.

- int readUnsignedByte()

Reads an unsigned byte.

- int readUnsignedShort()

Reads an unsigned short.

- String readUTF()

Reads a String.

- void seek(long pos)

Sets the file-pointer offset.

- void setLength(long newLength)

Sets the file length.

- int skipBytes(int n)

Attempts to skip over n bytes of input, discarding the skipped bytes.

- void write(byte[] b)

Writes b.length bytes from the specified byte array.

- void write(byte[] b, int off, int len)

Writes len bytes from the specified byte array, starting at offset off to this file.

- void write(int b)

Writes the specified byte.

- void writeBoolean(boolean v)

Writes a `boolean` as a one-byte value into the file.

- void writeByte(int v)

Writes a byte to the file as a one-byte value.

- void writeBytes(String s)

Writes the string s to the file as a sequence of bytes.

- void writeChar(int v)

Writes a Unicode char as a two-byte value, high byte first on to the file.

- void writeChars(String s)

Writes a `String` as a sequence of characters to the file.

- void writeDouble(double v)

Converts the `double` argument to a `long` using the `doubleToLongBits` method in class `Double` and then writes that `long` value as an eight-byte quantity, high byte first.

- void writeFloat(float v)

Converts the `float` argument to an `int` using the `floatToIntBits` method in class `Float` and then writes that `int` value to the file as a four-byte quantity, high byte first.

- void writeInt(int v)

Writes an `int` as four bytes, high byte first.

- void writeLong(long v)

Writes a `long` as eight bytes, high byte first onto the file.

- void writeShort(int v)

Writes a `short` as two bytes, high byte first.

- void writeUTF(String str)

Writes a `String` into the file using standard UTF-8 encoding.

Interface `ExtensionInstallerService`

The `ExtensionInstallerService` interface handles the service install procedure.

- java.net.URL getExtensionLocation()

Returns the URL representing the location of the extension being installed.

- String getExtensionVersion()

Returns the `String` representing the version of the extension being installed.

- String getInstalledJRE(java.net.URL url, String version)

Returns the `String` representing the path to the executable for the given JRE.

- String getInstallPath()

Returns the String representing the path to the directory where the installer is recommended to install the extension in.

- `void hideProgressBar()`

  Hides the progress bar.

- `void hideStatusWindow()`

  Hides the status window.

- `void installFailed()`

  Installer classes should invoke this method if the install fails for any reason.

- `void installSucceeded(boolean needsReboot)`

  Installer classes should invoke this method after a successful extension installation.

- `void setHeading(String heading)`

  Updates the status of the installer process with a new `heading`.

- `void setJREInfo(String platformVersion, String jrePath)`

  Sets the JNLP Client path to the executable for the JRE (if the `jrePath` argument string points to a JRE installer). It also informs the JNLP Client about the platform-version of this JRE.

- `void setNativeLibraryInfo(String path)`

  Informs the JNLP Client of a directory in which it should search for native libraries.

- `void setStatus(String status)`

  Updates the status of the installer process.

- `void updateProgress(int value)`

  Updates the progress bar.

Interface PrintService

Handles printing passing through the JNLP Client.

- `java.awt.print.PageFormat getDefaultPage()`

  Creates a new `PageFormat` instance, and sets it to the default size and orientation.

- `boolean print(java.awt.print.Pageable document)`

  Prints a document using the given document.

- `boolean print(java.awt.print.Printable painter)`

Prints a document using the given `Printable` object instead of a `Pageable` one.

- `java.awt.print.PageFormat showPageFormatDialog(java.awt.print.PageFormat page)`

  Displays the properties dialog box of a `PageFormat` object, returning it modified by the user.

JARDiff Format

The JARDiff format is a way to perform incremental updates to a JAR file. It is composed of a special JAR file sent to the client, which describes the differences between two JAR files, say `OldJAR` and `NewJAR`.

The differencing information is stored in the "`META-INF/INDEX.JD`" text file, and describes the copies of new or changed files in the `NewJAR` file relative to the `OldJAR` file.

The file is composed of lines `<command> space <value>`. The first line describes the JARDiff format version (currently 1.0):

`version <version>`

And following are lines of two types:

- `remove <fully qualified class in OldJar but not in NewJAR>`
- `move <fully qualified class in OldJAR> <fully qualified class in NewJAR >`.

That describes the differences between the already-installed `OldJAR` file and to-be-installed `NewJAR` file.

Versioning Notation

This section covers the versioning notation. It is implemented in the JNLP protocol as strings conforming to given rules. See Chapter 12, "Server-Side Deployment Support," for the classes that concretely implement these algorithms in Java.

Throughout this section, given two strings of all-ASCII characters representing Version Ids v1, v2, we represent them in the following way:

`v1 = v1H+v1T; v2 = v2H + v2T`

where vxH is the substring up to the first occurrence of the separator characters and vxT is all the rest (the tail).

Furthermore, in the following algorithms, the version ids are thought of as being divided into tuples, and are normalized to have the same number of elements. For example, 1.4 and 1.2.2.008, when compared, become respectively (1,4,0,0) and (1,2,2,008).

Exact Match

The algorithm for the exact match is intended to function as follows:

The first parts, v1H and v2H, must be the same (that is, as in the String's equals(..) method), and v1T matches exactly v2T, or they are both empty (v1T==V2T=="").

Prefix Match

Similarly, the algorithm for prefix match is defined as follows:

The first parts, v1H and v2H, must be the same, and

v1T is a prefix match of v2T, or v1T is empty (v1T=="").

Version Ids Ordering

For the ordering of two different Version Ids, the algorithm is as follows:

v1 > v2 if at least one of the following is true:

- v1H > v2H,
- v1H == v2H and v1T !="" and v2T !="",
- v1H == v2H and v1T > v2T recursively.

Server

The server-side of the JNLP specification describes the protocol involved in sending the requested material to the JNLP Client. The protocol is greatly simplified by relying completely on the HTTP protocol. Basically, the server reacts to GET requests from JNLP Clients.

General Response

Due to the different kinds of requests, the JNLP protocol encourages the use of error codes for the more common problems, as reported in the following table.

Error Code	Error Description
10	Resource Not Found(HTTP error 404)
11	Could Not Locate Requested Version
99	Unknown Error

In case of an error, the response must be a string composed as follows:

```
String Response = errorCode + ' ' + errorDescription + "\n";
```

The returned MIME type is JNLP Error ("`application/x-java-jnlp-error`").

Basic Download

In the basic download case of the JNLP protocol, a normal Web server could be used. Resources are available for HTTP GET requests as normal, static Web pages.

Return types allowed are the following:

- Icons having the MIME types "`image/jpeg`" or "`image/gif`".
- JAR files having MIME type "`application/x-java-archive`" requested in the JNLP file with `jar` or `nativelib` elements.
- JNLP files having the MIME type: "`application/x-java-jnlp-file`".
- JNLP Error having the MIME type: "`application/x-java-jnlp-error`".

Version-Based Download

Version-Based downloads require more advanced server support in order to respond to requests in the form of a GET operation:

```
URL?version-id=...&main=...
```

Return types allowed are:

- Icons having the MIME types: "`image/jpeg`" or "`image/gif`". Requested in the JNLP file with `icon` elements.
- JAR files having the MIME type: "`application/x-java-archive`". Requested in the JNLP file with `jar` or `nativelib` elements.
- JARDiff files having the MIME type: "`application/x-java-archive-diff`". Requested in the JNLP file with `jar` or `nativelib` elements.
- JNLP Error having the MIME type: "`application/x-java-jnlp-error`".

For Java code that implements the version-based JNLP protocol on the server side, see Chapter 10, "Defining the Client Environment."

Extension Download

This kind of download is used for JNLP files that contain the `extension-desc` empty element.

Only the JNLP file return type is allowed with the MIME type "`application/x-java-jnlp-file`". In the HTTP header, the field "`x-java-jnlp-version-id`" must be set with the current exact version returned by the server in response to the version string requested by the JNLP Client.

There are specialized error codes for this case of the JNLP protocol, as reported in the following table.

Error Code	Error Description
20	Unsupported Operating System
21	Unsupported Architecture
22	Unsupported Locale
23	Unsupported JRE Version

Other Deployment Technologies

IN THIS APPENDIX

We discussed Java-related deployment technologies throughout the book. Here, we gather some material loosely related to Java software deployment and other deployment-related services and concepts. Particularly, we give references to some of the projects aimed at providing languages for describing software systems' constraints, configurations and dependencies. Such languages are needed in automatic software deployment, as we saw in Chapter 2, "An Abstract Model for Deployment."

OSD

The Open Software Description format is a standard proposed by Marimba and Microsoft to the W3C consortium for automatic software distribution. For more details, the reader can look at `http://www.w3.org/TR/NOTE-OSD.html`.

OSD is implemented with XML files. For describing the dependencies among software packages, the concept of directed graph is used. Nodes represent software packages, and arcs represent the dependencies among them. An OSD file can reference another OSD file (pointing to its URL), creating large dependency graphs. OSD files can be used in HTML pages as well, embedding an `object` or `applet` tag pointing to the OSD file in the Web page.

Also the Channel Definition Format (CDF) used for "push" Web channels technology takes advantage of OSD files to describe software packages and their interrelationships.

DTMF Initiatives

The Distributed Management Task Force (DMTF) is a not-for-profit organization dedicated to promoting systems management and interoperability. It is the source of many initiatives within the software management industry. Here, we will mention briefly the CIM initiative. For more information, the user can visit the DMTF Web site at: `http://www.dtmf.org`.

DTMF proposed a Conceptual Information Model (CIM) for describing management in an implementation-independent way, so that management information can be exchanged between different management systems and applications. Management systems include Microsoft's SMS, Compaq's Insite Manager, HP's OpenView, Tivoli's Management Software, and so on. Also important is the Management Information Format (MIF) initiative that we will not describe here.

Other Deployment Technologies

The sheer number of commercial software deployment and management solutions makes it impossible to provide even a shallow reference here. For an interesting but slightly outdated look at other options, HP's white paper on the deployment of desktop and software management and other related material one can be obtained at `http://www.hp.com/go/overview`.

Other examples of a complete management solution include InstallShield's NetInstall suite (`http://www.installshield.com`) or Microsoft's System Management Server (SMS, available at `http://www.microsoft.com/smsmgmt/default.asp`).

Academic and Open-Source Initiatives

There are many interesting deployment frameworks. We will cite just a few. Although we don't have the space to discuss them in detail, the interested reader may follow the provided references.

Such languages and tools provide, at various levels, the ability to model the hardware, software, and (often) documentation data together with the relationships between them. Here, we present only two of them.

- PCL is a configuration language for describing the architecture of multiple versions of computer-based systems. It can describe the following concepts: sets of versions for a single (hardware/software/documentation) component, version descriptors, building tool descriptors, classification definitions (used to define classification terms among sets of component versions), relation definitions among sets of component versions and other entities, and attribute type definitions.

  Further information material is available via anonymous ftp: `ftp://ftp.comp.lancs.ac.uk/pub/proteus/PCL`.

- The Software Dock architecture is a software deployment architecture supporting a great number of the activities involved in software deployment. It is implemented using several specialized agents. For more information, visit `http://www.cs.colorado.edu/serl/cm/dock.html`.

A JNLP Utility Library

IN THIS APPENDIX

This appendix illustrates a JNLP utility library that can be used in any JNLP-launched application. We used it in the application example of Chapter 13, "A Complete Example."

After a brief introduction of the main features provided by this library, we will examine its implementation and finally discuss a simple example of use.

The example is quite simple, given that the library aims at emulating the runtime services provided by a JNLP Client, so that the code may be left the same for the two modalities (standalone, usual application, or JNLP-launched execution) without any "two-case" additional code provided for distinguishing the two execution modalities (within a JNLP Client container or as a standalone application).

COMPANION **Web site** Naturally, the library JAR file must be bundled with your application. See the example pack provided on the Companion Web site for this appendix. In the package to be downloaded are both sources and a JAR file containing the compiled executables, ready to be deployed with your code. This package can be used like any other third-party library by using its executables without prior source compilation or modifying the provided source in order to adapt it to your particular needs.

The package associated with this appendix includes the following source code classes:

- `AServiceManagerStub`. An implementation of the JNLP ServiceManagerStub class.
- `BasicServiceImpl`. An implementation of the JNLP `BasicService` class.
- `ClipboardServiceImpl`. An implementation of the JNLP `ClipboardService` class.
- `DownloadServiceImpl`. An implementation of the JNLP `DownloadService` class.
- `FileContentsImpl`. An implementation of the JNLP `FileContentsService` class.
- `FileOpenServiceImpl`. An implementation of the JNLP `FileOpenService` class.
- `FileSaveServiceImpl`. An implementation of the JNLP `FileSaveService` class.
- `GeneralUtilities`. A utility class.
- `PersistenceServiceImpl`. An implementation of the JNLP `PersistenceService` class.
- `PrintServiceImpl`. An implementation of the JNLP `PrintService` class.
- `Test`. A sample test class that shows how the library can be used. Not to be included in your code.

Each class will be discussed in the following sections.

Introduction

This library provides the following services:

- It allows applications to be launched seamlessly via a JNLP Client (like Java Web Start, for example) or as a standalone application.

- It permits an easier testing and a simpler development of the application. Developers don't have to package everything and deploy it every time they need to test even a little detail of their applications.

- Providing the source code, developers can modify the implementation for handling particular cases.

In particular, the present version of this library supports the following:

- Persistence services are supported, hence, even standalone application can use them consistently like JNLP-launched applications.

- File-related services are supported, with the exception of random access files.

- Clipboard and printing services are also supported.

The `DownloadService` is only partially supported, but cannot practically be used (that is, installer applications cannot be tested effectively).

All the code here is supposed to provide a basic implementation of JNLP 1.0 runtime services, and it is not meant to substitute the JNLP Client execution environment in a full-fledged operative scenario.

Implementation

The current implementation is provided in the following sections. Check the Companion Web site for this book or the author's Web site (`http://www.marinilli.com`) for updates to the code provided here.

GeneralUtilities

The `GeneralUtilities` class is reported in Listing D.1.

It uses the following files (but it can operate even without any of them):

- JNLP property file used to supply the same properties set by the launching JNLP file when the application is run standalone.

- Locale-specific message bundles that are automatically loaded at initialization.

D

A JNLP UTILITY
LIBRARY

LISTING D.1 The GeneralUtilities Class

```java
package com.marinilli.b2.ad.util;
import javax.swing.ImageIcon;
import java.awt.image.BufferedImage;
import java.net.URL;
import javax.jnlp.UnavailableServiceException;
import javax.jnlp.ServiceManager;
import javax.jnlp.DownloadService;
import javax.jnlp.BasicService;
import java.util.ResourceBundle;
import java.util.Properties;

/**
 * Appendix D - general utilities class
 *
 * @author Mauro Marinilli
 * @version 1.0
 */
public class GeneralUtilities {
  private static GeneralUtilities util;
  private static ClassLoader loader;
  private static BasicService basicService;
  private static ImageIcon EMPTY_ICON =
      new ImageIcon(new BufferedImage(24,24,BufferedImage.TYPE_INT_RGB));
  private ResourceBundle msg;
  private static String bundleFilename = "messages";
  private final static String JNLP_PROPERTIES = "jnlp.properties";

  /**
   * creates the only instance for this singleton class
   */
  private GeneralUtilities() {
    loader = getClass().getClassLoader();
    basicService =
      (BasicService)getService("javax.jnlp.BasicService");
    if (basicService==null){
      AServiceManagerStub sms = new AServiceManagerStub();
      ServiceManager.setServiceManagerStub(sms);
      basicService =
        (BasicService)getService("javax.jnlp.BasicService");
      try {
        Properties p = System.getProperties();
        URL up = loader.getResource(JNLP_PROPERTIES);
        System.out.println("url="+up);
        if (up!=null) {
```

LISTING D.1   Continued

```
            p.load(loader.getResourceAsStream(JNLP_PROPERTIES));
            System.setProperties(p);
            System.out.println("jnlp properties loaded.");
        }
    } catch (Exception ex) {
        System.out.println("setting JNLP properties: "+ex);
    }
}
initializeDefaultResources();
try {
    msg = ResourceBundle.getBundle(bundleFilename);
} catch (java.util.MissingResourceException mre) {
    msg = null;
    System.out.println("GeneralUtilities (init) Couldn't find any resource
bundle.");
    }
}

/**
 * initializes default resources
 */
private void initializeDefaultResources() {
    //initializes the empty icon
    java.awt.Graphics g = EMPTY_ICON.getImage().getGraphics();
    g.drawLine(8,8,16,16);
    g.drawLine(8,16,16,8);
}

/**
 * return the given class loader
 */
public static ClassLoader getClassLoader(){
    if (util==null)
        getInstance();
    return loader;
}

/**
 * return resource as an ImageIcon
 */
public static ImageIcon getImageIcon(String name){
    if (util==null)
        getInstance();
    URL res = loader.getResource(name);
```

LISTING D.1   Continued

```java
    if (res!=null)
      return new ImageIcon(res);
    System.out.println("GeneralUtilities.getImageIcon(\""+name+"\") Couldn't
find any resource.");
    return EMPTY_ICON;
  }

  /**
   * return the requested service
   */
  public static Object getService(String fullyQName){
    Object service = null;
    try {
      service = ServiceManager.lookup(fullyQName);
    } catch (UnavailableServiceException use) {
      System.out.println("GeneralUtilities.getService("+ fullyQName +") "+use);
    }
    return service;
  }

  /**
   * return the basic service
   */
  public static BasicService getBasicService(){
    if (util==null)
      getInstance();
    return basicService;
  }

  /**
   * return a localized message string
   */
  public static String getMsg(String key){
    if (util==null)
      getInstance();
    if (util.msg!=null) {
      String m = util.msg.getString(key);
      if (m!=null)
        return m;
    }
    return "";
  }

  /**
```

LISTING D.1 Continued

```
    * return true if the given module is installed
    */
  public static boolean isModuleInstalled(String part){
    if (util==null)
      getInstance();
    DownloadService ds =
      (DownloadService)getService("javax.jnlp.DownloadService");
    return ds.isPartCached(part);
  }

  /**
    * default Singleton initialization.
    * It is performed automatically by all methods.
    */
  public static GeneralUtilities getInstance(){
    if (util==null)
      util = new GeneralUtilities();
    return util;
  }

  /**
    * Singleton initialization with a given resource bundle
    */
  public static GeneralUtilities getInstance(String resourceBundleName){
    bundleFilename = resourceBundleName;
    if (util==null)
      getInstance();
    else
      System.out.println(
          util.getClass()+" getInstance must be invoked at initialization
time.");
    return util;
  }

}
```

Note that the GeneralUtilities can tell the different execution modality (whether launched as a standalone application or by a JNLP Client) by obtaining a JNLP service (line 35 in Listing D.1). If that service is null, the utility library's AServiceManagerStub is installed; otherwise, the application is assumed to be running within a JNLP Client container.

The net effect from the client application is always the same. In the following listings in this appendix, we will see how the various JNLP runtime services are implemented in order to be provided to applications launched without JNLP support in a standalone way.

Note that some implementation differences may arise, especially on the details of how the various services are implemented.

AServiceManagerStub

This class implements our JNLP runtime services provider. It is shown in Listing D.2. It makes use of a hashtable for supplying the requested service implementations.

LISTING D.2   The `AServiceManagerStub` Class

```
package com.marinilli.b2.ad.util;
import javax.jnlp.ServiceManagerStub;
import java.util.*;

/**
 * Appendix D - Implementation of the corresponding JNLP runtime stub
 *
 * @author Mauro Marinilli
 * @version 1.0
 */
public class AServiceManagerStub implements ServiceManagerStub {
  private HashMap hash;

  /**
   * Constructor
   */
  public AServiceManagerStub() {
    hash = new HashMap();
    //fill up the hashtable with the supported services
    hash.put("javax.jnlp.BasicService", new BasicServiceImpl());
    hash.put("javax.jnlp.ClipboardService", new ClipboardServiceImpl());
    hash.put("javax.jnlp.PrintService", new PrintServiceImpl());
    hash.put("javax.jnlp.FileSaveService", new FileSaveServiceImpl());
    hash.put("javax.jnlp.FileOpenService", new FileOpenServiceImpl());
    hash.put("javax.jnlp.DownloadService", new DownloadServiceImpl());
    hash.put("javax.jnlp.PersistenceService", new PersistenceServiceImpl());
  }

  /**
   * return service all names
   */
  public String[] getServiceNames() {
    String result[] = new String[hash.keySet().size()];
    hash.keySet().toArray(result);
    return result;
  }
```

LISTING D.2   Continued

```
  /**
   * return the correspondednt service instance
   */
  public Object lookup(String fullyQName) throws
javax.jnlp.UnavailableServiceException {
    Object result = hash.get(fullyQName);
    return result;
  }


}
```

BasicServiceImpl

This service implementation provides only the Internet Explorer browser support on Windows platforms. It is reported in Listing D.3. It can be invoked to bring up a Web browser window pointing to a given URL.

LISTING D.3   The BasicServiceImpl Class

```
package com.marinilli.b2.ad.util;
import javax.jnlp.*;
import java.net.URL;

/**
 * Appendix D - Implementation of the corresponding JNLP runtime service
 *
 * @author Mauro Marinilli
 * @version 1.0
 */
public class BasicServiceImpl implements BasicService{
  boolean isBrowserSupported = false;
  String browser = "";

  /**
   * This class supports only basic Windows platforms
   * (MS IE only)
   *
   */
  public BasicServiceImpl() {
    //detect browser
    String os = System.getProperties().getProperty("os.name");
    if (os.indexOf("Windows")!=-1) {
      isBrowserSupported = true;
```

D

LISTING D.3   Continued

```
      String windDir = System.getProperties().getProperty("user.home");
      browser = windDir+"\\"+"explorer ";
    }
  }

  /**
   * return the codebase. Not supported
   */
  public URL getCodeBase(){
    return null;
  }

  /**
   * whether is offline or not
   * (trivially implemented: always return false)
   */
  public boolean isOffline(){
    return false;
  }

  /**
   * whether a web browser is supported
   */
  public boolean isWebBrowserSupported(){
    return isBrowserSupported;
  }

  /**
   * bring up a Web browser window
   */
  public boolean showDocument(URL url){
    //
    try {
      Runtime.getRuntime().exec(browser + url);
    } catch (Exception ex) {
      System.out.println("executing "+browser+": "+ex);
    }
    return true;
  }

}
```

ClipboardServiceImpl

This service implementation provides read-only access to the system Clipboard, as detailed in
Listing D.4.

LISTING D.4 The ClipboardServiceImpl Class

```
package com.marinilli.b2.ad.util;
import javax.jnlp.ClipboardService;
import java.awt.datatransfer.Transferable;
import java.awt.*;

/**
 * Appendix D - Implementation of the corresponding JNLP runtime service
 *
 * @author Mauro Marinilli
 * @version 1.0
 */
public class ClipboardServiceImpl implements ClipboardService {

  /**
   * Constructor
   */
  public ClipboardServiceImpl() {
  }

  /**
   * return clipboard contents
   */
  public Transferable getContents() {
    return Toolkit.getDefaultToolkit().getSystemClipboard().getContents(this);
  }

  /**
   * sets clipboard contents
   * (Not implemented)
   */
  public void setContents(Transferable parm1) {
    System.out.println("Method setContents() not implemented.");

  }

}
```

D

DownloadServiceImpl

This service (see the class implementation in Listing D.5) has been included only for enabling stub-like support; any use beyond that it is not supported.

LISTING D.5 The DownloadServiceImpl Class

```java
package com.marinilli.b2.ad.util;
import javax.jnlp.DownloadServiceListener;
import java.net.URL;
import javax.jnlp.DownloadService;

/**
 * Appendix D - Implementation of the corresponding JNLP runtime service
 *
 * This class does not support any DownloadService features.
 *
 * @author Mauro Marinilli
 * @version 1.0
 */
public class DownloadServiceImpl implements DownloadService {

  /**
   * Constructor
   */
  public DownloadServiceImpl() {
  }

  /**
   * Not implemented
   */
  public DownloadServiceListener getDefaultProgressWindow() {
    return null;
  }

  /**
   * always return false
   */
  public boolean isExtensionPartCached(URL parm1, String parm2, String parm3) {
    return false;
  }

  /**
   * always return true (assumes a standalone application installation)
   */
  public boolean isExtensionPartCached(URL parm1, String parm2, String[] parm3)
```

LISTING D.5 Continued

```
{
    return true;
  }

  /**
   * always return true (assumes a standalone application installation)
   */
  public boolean isPartCached(String parm1) {
    return true;
  }

  /**
   * always return true (assumes a standalone application installation)
   */
  public boolean isPartCached(String[] parm1) {
    return true;
  }

  /**
   * always return true (assumes a standalone application installation)
   */
  public boolean isResourceCached(URL parm1, String parm2) {
    return true;
  }

  /**
   * Not supported
   */
  public void loadExtensionPart(URL parm1, String parm2, String parm3,
DownloadServiceListener parm4) throws java.io.IOException {
    throw new java.io.IOException("not supported.");
  }

  /**
   * Not supported
   */
  public void loadExtensionPart(URL parm1, String parm2, String[] parm3,
DownloadServiceListener parm4) throws java.io.IOException {
    throw new java.io.IOException("not supported.");
  }

  /**
   * Not supported
   */
```

LISTING D.5 Continued

```
public void loadPart(String parm1, DownloadServiceListener parm2) throws
java.io.IOException {
   throw new java.io.IOException("not supported.");
}

/**
 * Not supported
 */
public void loadPart(String[] parm1, DownloadServiceListener parm2) throws
java.io.IOException {
   throw new java.io.IOException("not supported.");
}

/**
 * Not supported
 */
public void loadResource(URL parm1, String parm2, DownloadServiceListener
parm3) throws java.io.IOException {
   throw new java.io.IOException("not supported.");
}

/**
 * Not supported
 */
public void removeExtensionPart(URL parm1, String parm2, String parm3) throws
java.io.IOException {
   throw new java.io.IOException("not supported.");
}

/**
 * Not supported
 */
public void removeExtensionPart(URL parm1, String parm2, String[] parm3)
throws java.io.IOException {
   throw new java.io.IOException("not supported.");
}

/**
 * Not supported
 */
public void removePart(String parm1) throws java.io.IOException {
   throw new java.io.IOException("not supported.");
}
```

LISTING D.5 Continued

```
/**
 * Not supported
 */
public void removePart(String[] parm1) throws java.io.IOException {
  throw new java.io.IOException("not supported.");
}

/**
 * Not supported
 */
public void removeResource(URL parm1, String parm2) throws
java.io.IOException {
  throw new java.io.IOException("not supported.");
}

}
```

FileOpenServiceImpl

This service has been implemented consistently with the JNLP implementation, in that it pops up a "File Open" dialog box for choosing one or more files. No security issues have been implemented. See Listing D.6 for details.

LISTING D.6 The `FileOpenServiceImpl` Class

```
package com.marinilli.b2.ad.util;
import javax.jnlp.FileOpenService;
import javax.jnlp.FileContents;
import javax.swing.JFileChooser;
/**
 * Appendix D - Implementation of the corresponding JNLP runtime service
 *
 * @author Mauro Marinilli
 * @version 1.0
 */

public class FileOpenServiceImpl implements FileOpenService {

  /**
   * construct
   */
  public FileOpenServiceImpl() {
  }
```

D

A JNLP UTILITY LIBRARY

LISTING D.6   Continued

```
/**
 * open up a single-file choice dialog returning the chosen FileContent file
 */
public FileContents openFileDialog(String param1, String[] notSupported)
throws java.io.IOException {
  JFileChooser jfc = new JFileChooser(param1);
  jfc.showOpenDialog(null);
  jfc.setMultiSelectionEnabled(false);
  return new FileContentsImpl(jfc.getSelectedFile());
}

/**
 * open up a multiple file choice dialog returning the chosen FileContent
files
 */
public FileContents[] openMultiFileDialog(String parm1, String[] parm2)
throws java.io.IOException {
  JFileChooser jfc = new JFileChooser();
  jfc.setMultiSelectionEnabled(true);
  jfc.showOpenDialog(null);
  int filesN = jfc.getSelectedFiles().length;
  FileContentsImpl[] result = new FileContentsImpl[filesN];
  for (int i = 0; i < filesN; i++) {
    result[i] = new FileContentsImpl(jfc.getSelectedFiles()[i]);
  }
  return result;
}

}
```

FileSaveServiceImpl

This service implementation (reported in Listing D.7) provides file save by means of user authorization. See the example (class Test later in Listing D.11) for a practical example of use.

LISTING D.7   The FileSaveServiceImpl Class

```
package com.marinilli.b2.ad.util;
import javax.jnlp.FileSaveService;
import javax.jnlp.FileContents;
import java.io.InputStream;
import java.io.FileOutputStream;
import java.io.File;
```

LISTING D.7 Continued

```java
import javax.swing.JFileChooser;

/**
 * Appendix D - Implementation of the corresponding JNLP runtime service
 *
 * @author Mauro Marinilli
 * @version 1.0
 */
public class FileSaveServiceImpl implements FileSaveService {

  /**
   * constructor
   */
  public FileSaveServiceImpl() {
  }

  /**
   * open up a save-as dialog
   */
  public FileContents saveAsFileDialog(String p1, String[] p2, FileContents fc)
throws java.io.IOException {
    JFileChooser jfc = new JFileChooser();
    jfc.showSaveDialog(null);
    return save(jfc.getSelectedFile(), fc.getInputStream());
  }

  /**
   * open up a save-as dialog
   */
  public FileContents saveFileDialog(String p, String[] ignoredParam,
InputStream in, String ignored) throws java.io.IOException {
    JFileChooser jfc = new JFileChooser();
    jfc.setMultiSelectionEnabled(true);
    jfc.showSaveDialog(null);
    jfc.setMultiSelectionEnabled(false);
    return save(jfc.getSelectedFile(), in);
  }

  /**
   * perform the actual file save
   */
  private FileContents save(File newFile, InputStream source) {
    byte buffer[] = new byte[1024];
    int i;
```

D

LISTING D.7   Continued

```
  try {
    FileOutputStream outputstream = new FileOutputStream(newFile);
    while((i = source.read(buffer)) != -1)
      outputstream.write(buffer, 0, i);
  } catch (Exception ex) {
      ex.printStackTrace();
  } finally {
      try {
        if(source != null)
          source.close();
      } catch (Exception exx) {
        System.out.println("closing InputStream "+exx);
      }
  }
  return new FileContentsImpl(newFile);
}

}
```

PrintServiceImpl

This service implementation supports basic printing via the JNLP runtime services API. Its implementation is shown in Listing D.8.

LISTING D.8   The `PrintServiceImpl` class.

```
package com.marinilli.b2.ad.util;
import javax.jnlp.PrintService;
import java.awt.print.*;

/**
 * Appendix D - Implementation of the corresponding JNLP runtime service
 *
 * @author Mauro Marinilli
 * @version 1.0
 */
public class PrintServiceImpl implements PrintService {
  private PrinterJob job;

  /**
   * constructor
   */
  public PrintServiceImpl() {
```

LISTING D.8 Continued

```
  job = PrinterJob.getPrinterJob();
}

/**
 * return default page
 */
public PageFormat getDefaultPage() {
  return job.defaultPage();
}

/**
 * print a pageable
 */
public boolean print(Pageable page) {
  job.setPageable(page);
  try {
    job.print();
  }
  catch (Exception ex) {
    System.out.println("PrintServiceImpl - print: "+ex);
    return false;
  }
  return true;
}

/**
 * print a Printable instance
 */
public boolean print(Printable prn) {
  job.setPrintable(prn);
  try {
    job.print();
  }
  catch (Exception ex) {
    System.out.println("PrintServiceImpl - print: "+ex);
    return false;
  }
  return true;
}

/**
 * show page format dialog
 */
```

LISTING D.8 Continued

```
public PageFormat showPageFormatDialog(PageFormat p) {
  return job.pageDialog(p);
}

}
```

PersistenceServiceImpl

The class detailed in Listing D.9 implements the JNLP 1.0 runtime persistence services by means of files saved on the local filesystem. All these files are rooted under the ".jnlpImpl" directory under the user home. On Windows machines such a directory is located in the Windows system directory and it is created on-the-fly.

> **CAUTION**
>
> The current implementation is not compatible with other JNLP Clients' implementations. This class cannot read data saved via the JNLP runtime API by another JNLP Client, because it relies on a different, file-based caching mechanism.

LISTING D.9 The PersistenceServiceImpl Class

```
package com.marinilli.b2.ad.util;
import java.net.URL;
import javax.jnlp.FileContents;
import javax.jnlp.PersistenceService;
import java.io.File;

/**
 * Appendix D
 *
 * @author Mauro Marinilli
 * @version 1.0
 */
public class PersistenceServiceImpl implements PersistenceService {
  public final static String SUPPORT_DIR = ".jnlpImpl";
  private static File sysDir = new File(System.getProperty("user.home") +
File.separatorChar + SUPPORT_DIR);

  /**
   * Constructor
```

LISTING D.9 Continued

```
      */
   public PersistenceServiceImpl() {
     try {
       if (!sysDir.exists())
         sysDir.mkdir();
     }  catch (Exception ex) {
       System.out.println("PersistenceServiceImpl() creating support directory:
"+ex);
     }
   }

   /**
    * Creates a new persistent storage entry on the client side named with the
given URL
    */
   public long create(URL urlKey, long param) throws
➥ java.net.MalformedURLException, java.io.IOException {
     File f = new File(sysDir, transformURL(urlKey));
     File parent = f.getParentFile();
     parent.mkdirs();
     f.createNewFile();
     //ignore param;
     return param;
   }

   /**
    * Removes the stream associated with the given
➥ URL from the client-side date persistence store.
    */
   public void delete(URL urlKey) throws java.net.MalformedURLException,
java.io.IOException {
     File f = new File(sysDir, transformURL(urlKey));
     f.delete();
   }

   /**
    * Returns a FileContents object representing the contents of this file.
    */
   public FileContents get(URL urlKey) throws java.net.MalformedURLException,
java.io.IOException, java.io.FileNotFoundException {
     return new FileContentsImpl(new File(sysDir, transformURL(urlKey)));
   }

   /**
```

LISTING D.9 Continued

```
     * Returns an array of Strings containing the names of all
➥ the entries for a given URL.
     */
    public String[] getNames(URL urlKey) throws java.net.MalformedURLException,
➥ java.io.IOException {
        File f = new File(sysDir, transformURL(urlKey));
        return f.list();
    }


    /**
     * Returns an int corresponding to the current value of the tag
     * for the persistent data store entry associated with the given URL.
     */
    public int getTag(URL parm1) throws java.net.MalformedURLException,
➥ java.io.IOException {
        System.out.println("Method getTag() not yet implemented.");
        return CACHED;
    }


    /**
     * Tags the persistent data store entry associated
➥ with the given URL with the given tag value.
     */
    public void setTag(URL parm1, int parm2) throws
➥java.net.MalformedURLException, java.io.IOException {
        System.out.println("Method setTag() not yet implemented.");
    }


    /**
     * transform an URl into a local file system path as a String
     */
    private String transformURL(URL url) {
        String s = url.toString().substring(url.toString().indexOf("://")+2);

        StringBuffer stringbuffer = new StringBuffer(url.getProtocol());
        for(int j = 0; j < s.length(); j++)
            if(s.charAt(j) == '/') {
                stringbuffer.append(File.separatorChar);
            } else
            if(s.charAt(j) == '&')
                stringbuffer.append("_");
            else
            if(s.charAt(j) == ':')
                stringbuffer.append("-");
```

LISTING D.9   Continued

```
      else
          stringbuffer.append(s.charAt(j));
    return stringbuffer.toString();
  }


}
```

FileContentsImpl

This class (reported in Listing D.10) implements the `FileContents` JNLP runtime service using a wrapped `File` instance.

LISTING D.10   The `FileContentsImpl` Class

```java
package com.marinilli.b2.ad.util;
import java.io.InputStream;
import java.io.OutputStream;
import java.io.FileOutputStream;
import java.io.File;
import javax.jnlp.JNLPRandomAccessFile;
import javax.jnlp.FileContents;

/**
 * Appendix D - a simple FileContents implementation
 *
 * @author Mauro Marinilli
 * @version 1.0
 */
public class FileContentsImpl implements FileContents {
  private File wrappedFile;

  /**
   * implementation constructor
   */
  protected FileContentsImpl(File f) {
    wrappedFile = f;
  }

  /**
   * return whether the file can be read
   */
  public boolean canRead() throws java.io.IOException {
    return wrappedFile.canRead();
  }
```

LISTING D.10 Continued

```java
/**
 * return whether the file can be written
 */
public boolean canWrite() throws java.io.IOException {
  return wrappedFile.canWrite();
}

/**
 * returns the inputStream
 */
public InputStream getInputStream() throws java.io.IOException {
  return wrappedFile.toURL().openStream();
}

/**
 * obtains the file length
 */
public long getLength() throws java.io.IOException {
  return wrappedFile.length();
}

/**
 * return the max length
 */
public long getMaxLength() throws java.io.IOException {
  System.out.println("Method getMaxLength() not supported.");
  return -1L;
}

/**
 * return file name
 */
public String getName() throws java.io.IOException {
  return wrappedFile.getName();
}

/**
 * Return an outputStream for the given file.
 * this method is aprtially supported
 */
public OutputStream getOutputStream(boolean boo) throws
➥ java.io.IOException {
  return new FileOutputStream(wrappedFile);
}
```

LISTING D.10 Continued

```
  /**
   * return a random access file
   */
  public JNLPRandomAccessFile getRandomAccessFile(String p)
➡ throws java.io.IOException {
    System.out.println("Method getRandomAccessFile not supported.");
    return null;
  }

  /**
   * set the max length
   * (Not supported)
   */
  public long setMaxLength(long p) throws java.io.IOException {
    System.out.println("Method setMaxLength not supported.");
    return -1L;
  }

}
```

An Example of Use

In this final section, we illustrate an example application that includes the utility package and makes use of the generalUtilites class. This, in turn, will take care of providing the needed JNLP runtime services to the application, even if this latter one is not launched via a JNLP file. The services provided in this test class are only illustrative.

The Test Class

As an example of use of this library in Listing D.11 is supplied an application that makes use of various JNLP runtime services. This class can be run seamlessly using a JNLP Client (the JNLP file is provided in Listing D.12) or launching it locally as a usual JAR file.

LISTING D.11 The Test Class

```
package com.marinilli.b2.ad;
import com.marinilli.b2.ad.util.*;
import javax.jnlp.*;
import java.net.URL;
import java.awt.print.*;
import java.awt.datatransfer.DataFlavor;
```

LISTING D.11   Continued

```
/**
 * Appendix D - A test class
 *
 * @author Mauro Marinilli
 * @version 1.0
 */
public class Test {

  /**
   * run the test
   */
  public Test() {
    GeneralUtilities.getInstance();

    System.out.println("title= "+System.getProperty("title"));
    System.out.println("hello= "+GeneralUtilities.getMsg("hello"));

    try {

      persExample();

      fileExample();

      printExample();

      clipboardExample();

      GeneralUtilities.getBasicService().showDocument
➥ (new URL("http://server"));

      System.exit(0);

    } catch (Exception ex) {
      System.out.println("test "+ex);
    }
  }

  private void persExample(){
    PersistenceService ps =
      (PersistenceService)GeneralUtilities.getService
➥ ("javax.jnlp.PersistenceService");

      try {
```

LISTING D.11   Continued

```
        URL u = new URL("http://server/ciao");
        ps.create(u,200L);
        FileContents fc = ps.get(u);
        java.io.OutputStream os = fc.getOutputStream(false);
        // just write something
        os.write(123);
        os.write(95);
        os.write(125);
        ps.delete(u);
    } catch (Exception ex) {
        System.out.println("test "+ex);
    }

}

/**
 * file example
 */
private void fileExample(){
    FileOpenService fos =
        (FileOpenService)GeneralUtilities.getService
➥("javax.jnlp.FileOpenService");
    FileSaveService fss =
        (FileSaveService)GeneralUtilities.getService
➥("javax.jnlp.FileSaveService");
    try {
        FileContents fc = fos.openFileDialog("ciao",null);
        fss.saveAsFileDialog("",null,fc);
    }
    catch (Exception ex) {
        System.out.println("FileExample: "+ex);
    }
}

/**
 * clipboard example
 */
private void clipboardExample() {
    ClipboardService cs =
        (ClipboardService) GeneralUtilities.getService
➥("javax.jnlp.ClipboardService");
    try {
        System.out.println("clipboard= " + cs.getContents()
➥.getTransferData(DataFlavor.stringFlavor));
```

LISTING D.11   Continued

```
    }
    catch (Exception ex) {
      System.out.println("clipboardExample: "+ex);
    }
  }

  /**
   * printing example
   */
  private void printExample(){
    PrintService prins = (PrintService)GeneralUtilities.getService
➥ ("javax.jnlp.PrintService");
    prins.showPageFormatDialog(new PageFormat());
  }

  /**
   * launch the test
   */
  public static void main(String[] args) {
    Test test1 = new Test();
  }

}
```

Depending on whether the Test program is launched as a standalone application or via a JNLP Client, the title property (line 22 of Listing D.12) will be provided by the JNLP file described as follows, or using the bundled jnlp.properties file. This latter mechanism is provided by the utility library, as mentioned before. The localization feature (see line 23 of Listing D.12, for instance) is always provided to applications launched in both modalities.

The JNLP File

Listing D.12 shows the JNLP file used for launching the test class in Listing D.11 previously presented.

LISTING D.12   The test JNLP File.

```
<?xml version="1.0" encoding="utf-8"?>
<jnlp spec="1.0+"
      codebase="http://server/b2/ad/"
      href="test.jnlp">
  <information>
    <title>A Utility Library Test</title>
```

LISTING D.12 Continued

```
    <vendor>Mauro Inc.</vendor>
    <homepage href="home.html"/>
    <description>Tests the utility library,
➡ running effectively in both modes!</description>
    <offline-allowed/>
  </information>
  <security><all-permissions/></security>

  <resources>
    <j2se version="1.3+"/>
    <jar href="test.jar"/>
    <jar href="utiljnlp1_0.jar"/>

    <property name="title" value="JNLP-Launched test" />

  </resources>
  <application-desc main-class="com.marinilli.b2.ad.Test"/>
</jnlp>
```

Such a JNLP file uses two JAR files, one for the test class itself and another one for the utility library. Note that both files need to be signed because the example class requests unrestricted access on the client computer. The test.jar file includes the application code plus the support properties files needed by the application, in this case two files only (jnlp.properties, which essentially supplies the property value as of line 19 in Listing D.12 to standalone applications; and messages.properties for locale-dependent strings).

The utiljnlp1_0 JAR file (provided in the example pack for this appendix with all other files) contains the utility library that needs not to be modified or repackaged any more, and could be organized in a component library for providing standard "standalone" support to already installed applications.

D

A JNLP UTILITY
LIBRARY

INDEX

SYMBOLS

A

Other Related Titles